GILES OF VITERBO ON CHURCH AND REFORM

STUDIES IN MEDIEVAL AND REFORMATION THOUGHT

EDITED BY

HEIKO A. OBERMAN, Tübingen

IN COOPERATION WITH

E. JANE DEMPSEY DOUGLASS, Claremont, California

LEIF GRANE, Copenhagen

GUILLAUME H. M. POSTHUMUS MEYJES, Leiden

ANTON G. WEILER, Nijmegen

VOLUME V

JOHN W. O'MALLEY, s. j.

GILES OF VITERBO ON CHURCH AND REFORM

LEIDEN
E. J. BRILL
1968

GILES OF VITERBO ON CHURCH AND REFORM

A STUDY IN RENAISSANCE THOUGHT

BY

JOHN W. O'MALLEY, s.j.

LEIDEN
E. J. BRILL
1968

PRINTED IN THE NETHERLANDS

For my Father

TABLE OF CONTENTS

PREFACE

The publication of this book in its present form would not have been possible without the interest taken in it especially by three institutions and by three individuals. The three institutions are: The American Academy in Rome, which awarded me a two-year fellowship from 1963-1965 enabling me to do the initial research upon which the book is based; The Harvard University Center for Italian Renaissance Studies (Villa I Tatti), Florence, which awarded me a fellowship for the academic years 1966-1968 enabling me to complete my research; and the University of Detroit, which granted me a leave of absence to accept the offer of the Harvard Renaissance Center. At the University of Detroit the Rev. Herman J. Muller, S. J., as chairman of the History Department in actual fact made the leave of absence possible. The University also provided a subventi on to aid in the publication of the book.

Of the three individuals to whom I feel especially indebted first place must certainly go to Professor Myron P. Gilmore, Director of the Harvard Renaissance Center in Florence. It was Professor Gilmore who first suggested Giles of Viterbo to me as a subject for research when I was still a doctoral candidate under his direction at Harvard University, and he has continued to offer encouragement and suggestions all through the long process of maturing the subject into a book. I am also very much indebted to the Rev. Francis X. Martin, O. S. A., Professor of Medieval History at University College, Dublin. Father Martin put the results of his own researches on Giles of Viterbo at my disposal, and he has allowed me to test my hypotheses against his detailed knowledge of Giles's life and activities. Finally, I must thank Professor Heiko A. Oberman of the University of Tübingen, Director of Tübingen's *Institut für Reformationsgeschichte* and co-editor of the Weimar *Ausgabe* of Luther's works. Professor Oberman manifested an active interest in my research on Giles of Viterbo from the moment I first undertook it. The interest culminated in the offer to publish my book in his series, "Studies in Medieval and Reformation Thought."

I also wish to thank those who, at one stage or another, read my text in its entirety: Professor Frank E. Brown, Director of the American Academy in Rome; Professor Jerrold E. Seigel, Princeton University; Rev. Pierre Blet, S. J., Pontificia Università Gregoriana, Rome; Rev. Edward L. Surtz, S.J., Loyola University, Chicago; and the Very Rev. Robert F. Harvanek, S.J., formerly of Loyola University, Chicago, and now Provincial Superior of the Jesuits of the Chicago area. I, moreover, want to acknowledge my gratitude to others who have read individual chapters of the book and have offered me their criticism and suggestions: Rev. R. Le Déaut and Rev. Pierre Proulx, S.J., Pontificio Istituto Biblico, Rome; Rev. William G. Thompson, S.J., Loyola University, Chicago, and Rev. John R. Keating, S.J., Fordham University. The Rev. Charles Burns of the Archivio Segreto Vaticano and the Rev. Balbino Rano, O.S.A., of the Augustinian General Archives, Rome, were helpful in guiding me through the proper archival material. For valuable assistance in the initial stages of the preparation of the text for publication I wish to thank my colleagues from the Society of Jesus: Rev. Edmund F. Miller, University of Detroit, and the Revs. Thomas H. O'Gorman and Francis J. Houdek.

To three other individuals who in indirect ways facilitated my research and made it more pleasant and profitable than it otherwise would have been I should like to express my gratitude: Mr. Richard A. Kimball, former Director of the American Academy in Rome; Princess Margherita Rospigliosi, Secretary of the American Academy in Rome; and the Rev. Francis P. Furlong, S.J., Rector of the Collegio Bellarmino, Rome. I am indebted to Miss Gloria Ramakus of the I Tatti staff for help with proofreading.

As regards the text of the book itself I might mention that in quoting from Latin sources, including Secret's edition of the *Scechina*, I have with few exceptions standardized the spelling and modernized the punctuation. I have made no attempt to reproduce the spelling, abbreviations, etc. of the manuscript sources, for I felt I would do the reader a better service if I presented him with the most readable text possible. In referring to letters I name one version, printed or manuscript, and do not mention others which I know to exist unless this is for some reason significant. For all persons, except those from antiquity, whose names appear in the book I have tried, whenever possible, to provide the dates, and to do this the first time the name appears. For figures in public life, such as kings, emperors, and popes, I have given dates for the years spent in the highest public office they held. For all others I give the year of birth and the year of death.

ABBREVIATIONS

The abbreviations used for books of the Bible are taken from *The Oxford Annotated Bible with the Apocrypha*, New York 1965, p. xvi. In accordance with the norm adopted by the series, "Studies in Medieval and Reformation Thought," sigla for journals and series are those employed by *Die Religion in Geschichte und Gegenwart*, 3rd edition, listed in every volume on pp. xv-xxvi. For the reader's convenience those sigla from *RGG* which were actually used in the course of this book are given below. Journals and series for which sigla are not found in *RGG* are written out in full in the notes and bibliography.

AFP	Archivum Fratrum Praedicatorum
AHDL	Archives d'Histoire Doctrinale et Littéraire du Moyen-Âge
AKultG	Archiv für Kulturgeschichte
ARG	Archiv für Reformationsgeschichte
ArtB	The Art Bulletin
CBQ	The Catholic Biblical Quarterly
ChH	Church History
CSEL	Corpus scriptorum ecclesiasticorum Latinorum
Denz.	H. Denzinger, Enchiridion symbolorum et definitionum, ed. Adolfus Schönmetzer, S. J., 33rd ed., 1965
HThR	The Harvard Theological Review
Mansi	J. D. Mansi, Sacrorum conciliorum nova et amplissima collectio
MIÖG	Mitteilungen des Instituts für österreichische Geschichtsforschung
MPL	J. P. Migne, Patrologiae cursus completus, series Latina
RechSR	Recherches de Science Religieuse
REJ	Revue des Études Juives
RThAM	Recherches de Théologie Ancienne et Médiévale
SAW	Sitzungsberichte der Akademie der Wissenschaften in Wien
Schol.	Scholastik. Vierteljahresschrift für Theologie und Philosophie
StT	Studi e Testi
ThQ	Theologische Quartalschrift
ThSt	Theological Studies
WA	M. Luther, Werke. Kritische Gesamtausgabe ("Weimar Ausgabe"), 1883ff.
WATR	M. Luther, Werke. Kritische Gesamtausgabe. Tischreden, 1912ff.
ZKG	Zeitschrift für Kirchengeschichte
ZSavRG	Zeitschrift der Savigny-Stiftung für Rechtsgeschichte

INTRODUCTION

THE PROBLEM, THE MAN, THE DOCUMENTS

Some recent studies on Church reform specifically differ from other investigations of this same topic by being more interested in examining reform thought than in describing practical reform programs.[1] These studies owe their origin to the keen awareness among scholars that the idea of reform takes its meaning at any given moment from concrete historical circumstances and from theories and presuppositions which are by no means constants in the history of thought. Under the same words and consecrated formulae can be masked dramatically different religious and intellectual orientations.

For a study of sixteenth-century reform ideology vague descriptions of reform thought as Catholic or Protestant, though not always without foundation, can be seriously misleading. They seem to denote the existence of two neatly distinct categories without any affinity for one another and without any disturbing overlapping, and they fail to suggest the almost infinite diversity which that century knew. Such descriptions, furthermore, tend to obscure the fact that there were certain ideas or assumptions common to both "Catholic" and "Protestant" reform thought in the sixteenth century which today very few educated persons—Catholic, Protestant or other—can really share. A case in point would be the widespread acceptance of decline-theories of history, which can be found, either as recurring theme or as significant detail, in a number of the religious thinkers of the century. The conviction that the world and the Church had for long been in a state or on a course of decline helped persuade many Christians that their age was the worst of all, more in need of reform than any other. What must

[1] The work of Gerhart B. Ladner deserves special mention: *The Idea of Reform: Its Impact on Christian Thought and Action in the Age of the Fathers*, Cambridge, Mass. 1959; "Die mittelalterliche Reform-Idee und ihr Verhältnis zur Idee der Renaissance," *MIÖG* 60(1952), pp. 31-59; "Two Gregorian Letters: On the Sources and Nature of Gregory VII's Reform Ideology," *Studi Gregoriani* 5(1956), pp. 221-242; "Vegetation Symbolism and the Concept of Renaissance," *De artibus opuscula XL: Essays in Honor of Erwin Panofsky*, ed. Millard Meiss, vol. I, New York 1961, pp. 303-322. See also Yves M.-J. Congar, O. P., *Vraie et fausse réforme dans l'église*, Paris 1950; Jeffrey Burton Russell, *Dissent and Reform in the Early Middle Ages*, Los Angeles 1965; Bernard J. F. Lonergan, S. J., "Existenz and Aggiornamento," *Focus* 2(1965), pp. 5-14.

be emphasized is that this conviction derived not from a dispassionate and methodologically sophisticated investigation of the pertinent historical data, nor even from an established sociological model of passage from some initial period of charism to succeeding periods of routine, but from other considerations which have little to do with the study of the past as we engage in it today. It often depended upon myths and schemes of history inherited from antiquity and the Middle Ages. It sometimes even related to metaphysics and would stratify the past in adaptation of the principle that all reality becomes increasingly weaker and more corrupt the farther it departs from its source. This approach to the method and meaning of history is illustrative of certain aspects of the thought of the sixteenth century and of how radically it is differentiated from our own.

A student of sixteenth-century problems can find no more striking indication of this differentiation as it touches the question of Church reform than the approval given today by churchmen and theologians to programs of reform which consist in an adaptation and adjustment of the Church to conditions of modern life. Such programs may imply nothing more than a desire to render forms and formulations of the past attractive to the contemporary world, or they may go so far as to postulate a review of the intrinsic meaningfulness of these same forms and formulations. In either case the desire to reform by a bringing up to date would, as such, have been greeted with profound shock by practically every exponent of reform in the sixteenth century. It would have implied novelty, "*res novae*," a designation which was generally interpreted as a devastatingly negative judgment on any person, doctrine or practice to which it was applied. What was needed was not to change the Church in the direction of making it more viable in the contemporary world, but to change the contemporary world by bringing it into conformity with the Church, i.e., with the authentic Church of the past. The age had at its disposal very few arguments which could be mustered to try to justify doing otherwise. It was an age which, for the most part and in theory, looked for its own renovation in a more or less static recovery of the artistic, literary and religious forms of the past. Before any different ideal of Church reform could be accepted a whole new intellectual frame of reference had to come into being in order to support it. This frame of reference tends to relativize the normative function of the achievements of the past, and it consists in assumptions and thought-forms which are operative today but which were not operative in the sixteenth century. Important among them would be our sense of historical perspective and historical differentiation, as well as a hermeneutics in which the cultural conditioning of patterns of thought and action plays a serious part.

Inseparably connected with any study of the concept of reform is a study of the concept of the Church. Like the concept of reform this concept, too, has varied from century to century and from thinker to thinker, and is always somehow dependent for its formulation on a fabric of thought and feeling of which it is only one particularization. To take an obvious example, in a world dominated by the myth of the Empire it would be practically impossible for the concept of the Church not to be elaborated in terms reminiscent of imperial ideology. Or if, as in the early Middle Ages, both clerical and lay society were dominated by monastic institutions it would be difficult for the Church not to think of itself as a monastery and not to transfigure Christ and the apostles into monks. In this latter case the reform of the Church would perforce be inspired by monastic ideals and the norm for Christian renewal would almost necessarily be a withdrawal from human society.

To understand any given instance of reform thought, therefore, we must first try to understand its ecclesiological setting. We must penetrate beyond an analysis of detached concepts and try to reconstruct a whole thought-world, in the hope that this will give some suggestion of the contingent historical influences which formed a particular concept of Church and reform. The scope of such an undertaking is immense and its procedure is difficult to control. This means that answers often will be only partial or halting, but it is to be hoped that they will not for that reason be deprived of all value.

The subject of this book is the thought on Church and reform of Giles of Viterbo. This subject is studied by an attempt to expose the most important elements of which Giles's style of thought was composed and then to relate these to his idea of Church reform. What we are trying to do, therefore, is to show how personal and historically circumscribed Giles's thought on reform was and how resonant with overtones from the world of religious and secular culture of the early sixteenth century. Because of the differences of opinion among scholars as to how the designation "humanist" is most properly applied, a certain circumspection is required in speaking of Giles's world as a world of humanism. Without misgiving, however, it can be described as a Renaissance world, for, no matter how many so-called medieval elements there may be in Giles's thought, his friends and his interests identify with central Italy in the late *Quattrocento* and early *Cinquecento*. The first three chapters of the book are dedicated in one way or another to a study of the Renaissance intellectual milieu which Giles knew and whose ideas he in part appropriated. In the course of these chapters the categories and assumptions which controlled his thinking will begin to emerge. Only then are we in a position to concentrate our efforts on his ideas about Church and reform, the subjects of the last two chapters.

Even an outline of the career of Giles of Viterbo is enough to whet the curiosity of anyone interested in the problem of reform in the early sixteenth century.[1] Giles combined a central and effective position in ecclesiastical administration with active participation in the leading academic and literary movements of the period. Moreover, from the first moment in which he exercised any jurisdiction within the Church he put his learning and culture at the service of reform, a cause which in one form or another then came to consume the major portion of his interest and energy.

In 1507, under the powerful patronage of Pope Julius II (1503-1513), Giles was elected prior general of the Augustinian order, an office which he held for over ten years.[2] The Augustinian friars or hermits, juridically distinct from the Augustinian canons, came into being as a religious order in the thirteenth century. In Giles's day they enjoyed a prestige and influence which they have never since equalled, number-

[1] Egidio da Viterbo, Aegidius Viterbiensis. His family name was Antonini, not Canisio as it sometimes appears. He was born in the late summer or fall of 1469 in Viterbo, and there in June of 1488 he entered the Augustinian order, of which he was appointed vicar general in 1506. He was elected prior general of the order at three successive general chapters, in 1507, 1511 and 1515. He formally laid down this office in February of 1518, some seven months after his nomination to the College of Cardinals, but he was named cardinal protector of the order by Leo X three years later. Besides the bishopric of Viterbo, Giles held several other benefices. He died on the night between November 11-12, 1532, in Rome, and he is buried there in the church of Sant' Agostino.

[2] Upon the death in 1506 of Agostino Faccioni, prior general of the Augustinian order, Julius II chose Giles to act as vicar general until a general chapter of the order could properly elect a successor to Faccioni. It seems clear from this move, as well as other attentions of the pope, that he wanted Giles to be elected. In a "*libellus*" containing an oration he delivered in Saint Peter's basilica on December 21, 1507, Giles, already prior general, addresses Julius II thus: "...in Augustiniensis reipublicae administratione, qua me fungi voluisti,..." Évora CXVI/1-30, fol. 5v. In a letter to Julius II dated August 18, 1508, Giles again reminds him that he wanted Giles as prior general, Giuseppe Signorelli, *Il Cardinale Egidio da Viterbo: Agostiniano, umanista e riformatore (1469-1532)*, Florence 1929, p. 235. In both of these instances Giles is possibly directly referring to Julius's formal approval, after the event, of his election as prior general.

ing an estimated fifteen thousand members, living in the thousand or so houses of the order. Under the prior general's jurisdiction there were, besides about twenty-six provinces of the conventuals, ten so-called observant congregations: six in Italy, two in Spain, one in Germany and another in Ireland.[1] As will be seen in the course of the book, Giles was a vigorous superior and made the weight of his authority felt throughout the order. It was during Giles's generalship, moreover, that the young Augustinian friar, Martin Luther (1483-1546), came to Rome, and it is more than likely that he met Giles during that fateful sojourn in the winter of 1510-1511.[2]

Giles's position in the Augustinian order, therefore, would alone be enough to establish him as a figure of no small importance for the story of the Church in the *Cinquecento*. His contact with the leading religious and political figures of the age, however, gives his career a further dimension. He always remained on close terms with Pope Julius II, who confided in him and employed him in various diplo-

[1] These figures are approximate and are conjectured on the basis of an official letter of Leo X to Giles's successor as prior general in 1518, some data which derives from the year 1505 which Father Martin utilized in his study of Giles, and Father Gutiérrez's insistence that the number of members must be put well under the conventional figure of thirty thousand. See Pietro Bembo, *Epistolarum Leonis decimi pontificis maximi nomine scriptarum libri sexdecim*, Venice 1535, lib. XVI, numero XVII; Francis X. Martin, O.S.A., "Egidio da Viterbo, 1469-1518: A Study in Renaissance and Reform History," unpublished doctoral dissertation, Cambridge University 1958, pp. 175-177, and David Gutiérrez, O.S.A., "Al margen de libros y artículos acerca de Lutero," *La ciudad de Dios* 169(1956), p. 621. On Giles's relationship to certain Augustinian canons, see L.-G. Pélissier, "Pour la biographie du Cardinal Gilles de Viterbe," *Miscellanea di studi critici edita in onore di Arturo Graf*, Bergamo 1903, pp. 813-815. On the rivalry between the canons and the friars, see Adolar Zumkeller, O.S.A., "Joachim von Fiore und sein angeblicher Einfluss auf den Augustiner-Eremitenorden," *Augustinianum* 3(1963), pp. 385-386, and Rudolph Arbesmann, O.S.A., "Henry of Freimar's 'Treatise on the Origin and Development of the Order of the Hermit Friars, and of its True and Real Title,'" *Augustiniana* 6(1956), pp. 37-145, esp. 58-61.

[2] Luther is mentioned by name only once by Giles, in his official register from 1513: "Fratrem Martinum Wittenberg. Lectorem facimus," as quoted in D. G. Kawerau, "Aus den Actis generalatus Aegidii Viterbiensis," *ZKG* 32(1911), p. 604. Luther speaks of Giles twice in the *Tischreden*, 1531 and 1536. He describes Giles as very learned, and in both instances depicts him as preaching against the abuses of the papacy, *WATR*, vol. II, pp. 347-348, and vol. III, p. 345. See also Hubert Jedin, "Die römischen Augustinerquellen zu Luthers Frühzeit," *ARG* 25 (1928), pp. 256-270; Reinhold Weijenborg, O.F.M., "Neuentdeckte Dokumente im Zusammenhang mit Luthers Romreise," *Antonianum* 32(1957), pp. 147-202, esp. 185-197; and Adolar Zumkeller, O.S.A., "Martin Luther und sein Orden," *Analecta Augustiniana* 25(1962), pp. 254-290.

Aside from what seem to be a few allusions to the Lutheran question in the *Scechina*, Giles's cabalistic treatise of 1530, we have no certainly authentic statement

matic and religious missions.[1] His relationship with Leo X (1513-1521) was equally cordial, and in the great consistory of 1517 he was created a cardinal by him. The next year Leo sent Giles as papal legate to the court of Charles of Spain, the future emperor (1519-1556).[2] This was

from Giles concerning it. He resigned as prior general just a short time after Luther's case came to the notice of Rome, and it seems that his duties as papal nuncio to Spain and Portugal (1518-1519), his duties as bishop of Viterbo (1523-1532), and his absorbing interest in Jewish literature kept him from taking active part in the controversy. This last reason was suggested by Andrea Alciato (1492-1550) in a letter to Francesco Calvo, April 5, 1521. See *Le lettere di Andrea Alciato giureconsulto*, ed. Gian Luigi Barni, Florence 1953, p. 26. Giles's failure to write for publication on any topic after his elevation to the cardinalate was noticed and regretted by his friends. See Naples II. F. 7, fols. 191v-195r.

Luigi Torelli (1609-1683) recounts, without revealing the source of his information, that Giles was taunted in consistory with the fact that Luther had been a member of his order. To which Giles supposedly replied: "Reverendissime Domine, si fuisset ex nostris mansisset nobiscum," *Secoli Agostiniani*, vol. VII, Bologna 1682, p. 503. Giles's retort is an application to Luther of 1 Jn. 2.19. Giles was a member of the commission of cardinals whose task was to suggest remedies for the Lutheran problem, and during the consistory of November 28, 1530, he was favorable to the calling of a council for handling the question. See P. Kalkoff, *Forschungen zu Luthers römischem Prozess*, Rome 1905, p. 86, and Ludwig Pastor, *The History of the Popes*, ed. Francis Ralph Kerr, vol. X, London 1923, p. 149. From the fact that Giles was enthusiastic about Henry VIII's (1509-1547) *Assertio septem sacramentorum* we can infer that he felt little sympathy for Luther's sacramental theology as he understood it from that work of controversy. See *Letters and Papers, Foreign and Domestic, of the Reign of Henry VIII*, ed. J. S. Brewer, vol. III.2, London 1867, under date of January 4, 1522, p. 829. A text of Johann Eck's (1486-1543) suggests that Giles felt Luther was being falsely accused of holding that Original Sin remains in the baptized until Eck showed him publicly, in the presence of Leo X and his fellow cardinals, that this was not the case. See François Secret, "Notes sur Egidio da Viterbo," *Augustiniana* 15(1965), pp. 414-415. Giles held the traditional view concerning indulgences, but insisted that the Augustinians preach them prudently and take care not to give offense to anybody, Siena G. X. 26, pp. 231-232, letter dated April 5, 1511, addressed to a certain Magister Ambrosius.

[1] Julius, for example, told Giles about his plans for driving the French out of Italy. See Giles's letter to Antonio Zocolo, July 29, 1510, Siena G. X. 26, p. 173, and the extracts from Giles's registers for July 15 and August 8, 1510, published by Pélissier, "Pour la biographie," p. 807. On Giles's missions for Julius, see Ang. Lat. 502, fols. 265r-268r, and Évora CXVI/1-30, fol. 79r. For letters from Giles to Julius, see Naples V. F. 14, fols. 1r-2v, as well as the letter previously referred to in Signorelli, *Egidio da Viterbo*, pp. 235-236. For four letters from the pope to Giles, see in the Biblioteca Laurenziana, Florence, Ashb. 287, fol. 57r-v. Giles describes the pope, Ang. Lat. 502, fol. 265r, as "[pontifex] spiritus acris vehementisque," and, *ibid.*, fol. 267v, as "ad iram propensus." See also *ibid.*, fol. 267r. On Giles and Julius II, see also Martin, "Egidio da Viterbo," pp. 151-173, 319-334.

[2] See Martin, "Egidio da Viterbo," pp. 334-344; Kawerau, "Aus den Actis," pp. 604-605; Pélissier, "Pour la biographie," p. 811. Charles V's esteem for Giles is clear from a letter of Girolamo Aleander (1480-1542) to Giles in March of 1521: "At Caesar jam confirmato animo in ea opinione quam initio de te conceperat, ita

by no means Giles's first or only association with the imperial or royal courts. In the winter of 1515-1516, for instance, he was dispatched by Leo to the court of the Emperor Maximilian (1493-1519) to try to persuade the emperor to make peace with the Venetians, and we have the texts of sermons Giles preached in Rome to honor Maximilian and King Manuel I of Portugal (1495-1521).[1] Pope Clement VII (1523-1534) named Giles bishop of Viterbo in 1523. It was Giles's personal friendship with Clement, as well as his reverence for the Holy See, which prompted him in 1527 to gather at his own expense a force of two thousand men to try to rescue the pope from the horrors of the sack of Rome.[2]

Giles of Viterbo moved with ease and familiarity in the most advanced intellectual circles of Padua, Naples, Florence and Rome. He was in Padua as a theological student at the Augustinian *studium generale* from 1490 to about 1493. His first publications, editions of three works of Giles of Rome (ca. 1247-1316), were made at Padua and reflect his interest in those problems of philosophy which were particularly critical there.[3] Giles of Viterbo eventually would take a strong stand against certain characteristically "Paduan" positions, and there is every reason to believe that he supported, or even promoted, the Fifth Lateran Council's condemnation of the theses which were attributed to this school, as we shall see in Chapter Two.

During the years Giles spent in and near Naples, probably from 1499 to 1501, he exercised a considerable and salutary influence on Giovanni Pontano (ca. 1422-1503), and was held in esteem by the members of the Neapolitan Academy, as Pontano's dialogue *Aegidius* indicates. What Pontano prized in Giles was his blending of piety with culture, and he looked to him as to the man who would restore

---

de tua excellenti doctrina et integritate vitae honorifice est locutus, talemque sui in te amoris notam edidit ut vere aliquod magnum commodum ex isto casu, Caesaris munificentia, in te profecturum," *Lettres familières de Jérome Aléandre (1510-1540)*, ed. Jules Paquier, Paris 1909, p. 75.

[1] "Oratio habita post tertiam sacri Lateranensis concilii sessionem," Rome 1512 (?). "De ecclesiae incremento," Évora CXVI/1-30. For a letter of Giles's to Maximilian, January 23, 1507, see Signorelli, *Egidio da Viterbo*, p. 225. On Giles's mission to Maximilian in 1515-1516, see *ibid.*, pp. 58-61, 247.

[2] Signorelli, *Egidio da Viterbo*, pp. 85-97.

[3] These three works were published in two volumes at Padua in 1493: (1) *Egidii Romani eremite de materia celi questio*, *Egidii Romani de intellectu possibili contra Averoim questio aurea*. See *Gesamtkatalog der Wiegendrucke*, vol. VI, Leipzig 1934, no. 7213. (2) *Egidii Romani comentaria in VIII libros physicorum Aristotelis*, no. 7197 in vol. VI of the *Gesamtkatalog*.

his order to high achievement in eloquence after the manner of Saint Augustine.[1]

Giles knew Marsilio Ficino (1433-1499) from a visit to Florence, probably in the winter of 1494-1495. This contact was to have a deep and lasting influence on Giles, and he became one of Ficino's most enthusiastic disciples. Giles was familiar with Giovanni Pico della Mirandola's (1463-1494) interpretations of the cabala, and he himself eventually surpassed Pico in the depth and accuracy of his understanding of it. Interest in the Talmud and cabala led Giles into correspondence with Johannes Reuchlin (1455-1522), and persuaded him to play a part in the settlement of the *cause célèbre* of which Reuchlin was the center. The effect which Ficino, Pico and Reuchlin had on Giles's thought will be discussed later. Their names are mentioned here merely to give some preliminary view of the breadth of Giles's interests and the immediacy of his communication with the great personages of his era.[2]

This is not the place to rehearse step by step the life of Giles of Viterbo, but perhaps enough has been said to suggest how two worlds encountered each other in his person. What is important is that we

---

[1] Giovanni Pontano, *I dialoghi*, ed. Carmelo Previtera, Florence 1943, pp. 243-284. See also F. Fiorentino, "Egidio da Viterbo e i Pontaniani di Napoli," *Archivio storico per le province napoletane* 9(1884), pp. 430-452; Giuseppe Toffanin, *Giovanni Pontano: Fra l'uomo e la natura*, 2nd ed., Bologna 1938, pp. 15-35, 129-180; Giovanni Pontano, *Lettere di Giovanni Pontano a principi ed amici*, ed. Erasmo Percopo, Naples 1907, pp. 60-62, 76-77, and the biography by Percopo, *Vita di Giovanni Pontano*, Naples 1938, pp. 239-243; Martin, "Egidio da Viterbo," pp. 47-62; Francesco Tateo, *Astrologia e moralità in Giovanni Pontano*, Bari 1960, pp. 20, 23, 28-29, 73, 130. See also Ang. Lat. 502, fol. 236r.

[2] Giles's interests were interwoven with those of other outstanding figures of the early *Cinquecento*. In 1526 he wrote a commendatory letter for Jacopo Sannazzaro's (ca. 1456-1530) "De partu Virginis." Erasmus (1466-1536) mentioned Giles's letter in a letter of his own in 1527 to Guillaume Budé (1467-1540), *Opus epistolarum Des. Erasmi Roterodami*, eds. P. S. Allen and H. M. Allen, vol. VII, Oxford 1928, pp. 94-95. Sannazzaro was present in 1507 at the general chapter which elected Giles prior general, Martin, "Egidio da Viterbo," pp. 170-171. On Sannazzaro, see Ang. Lat. 502, fols. 197v, 236r, and, for Giles's letter, E. Martène and U. Durand, *Veterum scriptorum et monumentorum historicorum, dogmaticorum, moralium amplissima collectio*, vol. III, Paris 1724, col. 1248. Erasmus met Giles in Rome in 1509, *Opus epistolarum*, vol. I, 1906, p. 62. For letters between Giles and Aleander, see, e.g., *Lettres de Aléandre*, pp. 37-38, 75-76; P. Balan, *Monumenta reformationis Lutheranae*, Ratisbon 1884, pp. 62-65, and Ang. Lat. 1001, fols. 262v-263r. The letter in Balan is mistakenly attributed to the papal vice-chancellor instead of to Giles. Giles knew and respected Gasparo Contarini (1483-1542). See L. Filalteo, *Philaltei libri tres epistolarum*, Pavia 1564, fols. 41r-42v. On Giles and Gian Matteo Giberti (1495-1543), see François Secret, "Un éloge oublié d'Egidio da Viterbo par Antonio Telesio," *Augustiniana* 13(1963), pp. 511-514, and for a letter of

find in him a humanist who had both the desire and the opportunity to reform. This makes Giles somewhat unique if compared with his contemporaries. For example, Jacopo Sadoleto (1477-1547) had a much less exciting intellectual background, arrived relatively late in life at a desire to promote reform, and even as papal secretary, bishop of Carpentras and cardinal never enjoyed such a central, almost autonomous, position in which to effect it.[1] The very uniqueness of Giles's position merits his reform thought an investigation.

For a person as centrally placed as Giles the question of his influence is bound to arise. There is some reason to believe that, through sermons and personal contact, he helped form the religious and theological thought of the papal court during the pontificates of Julius II and Leo X, and that this influence extended into the pontificate of Clement VII.[2] Girolamo Seripando (1492-1563), the great Augustinian theologian of the Council of Trent, was for a time Giles's protégé and, like Giles, became prior general of the order and cardinal. Seripando surely looked to Giles as to a master, and the respect he felt for him stayed with him to the end of his life.[3] In recent years traces of the

Giles's to Giberti, undated, see Martène, *Veterum scriptorum collectio*, vol. III, cols. 1260-1261. See also *ibid.*, cols. 1259-1260. Giles also corresponded with Jacques Lefèvre d'Étaples (ca. 1455-1536). See Martène, *Veterum scriptorum collectio*, vol. III, col. 1261. See also Ang. Lat. 502, fol. 195v, and Siena G. X. 26, p. 313. Six madrigals, attributed to Giles and addressed to Vittoria Colonna (1490-1547), were published in the last century by Francesco Trucchi, *Poesie italiane inedite di dugento autori*, vol. III, Prato 1847, pp. 124-129. For Giles's contact with Eck and for an undated letter to him from Willibald Pirckheimer (1470-1530), see Secret, "Notes sur Egidio da Viterbo," pp. 414-418. For some further indications of Giles's relationship with his contemporaries, e.g., with Pietro Bembo (1470-1535), see Francis X. Martin, O.S.A., "The Problem of Giles of Viterbo: A Historiographical Survey," *Augustiniana* 9(1959), esp. pp. 359-367. See also the biographies by Martin and Signorelli, and the article by François Secret, "Egidio da Viterbo et quelques-uns de ses contemporains," *Augustiniana* 16(1966), pp. 371-385.

[1] See Richard M. Douglas, *Jacopo Sadoleto (1477-1547): Humanist and Reformer*, Cambridge, Mass. 1959, pp. ix-x, 15, etc. On Giles and Sadoleto, see, e.g., Ang. Lat. 1001, fols. 31v-32v, and Jacopo Sadoleto, *Opera quae exstant omnia*, vol. IV, Verona 1738, pp. 304-305, 323, 324. Cajetan (Thomas de Vio, 1469-1534), as superior general of the Dominicans, was in a juridical position comparable to Giles's, but represented an entirely different intellectual tradition. See Étienne Gilson, "Cajetan et l'Humanisme théologique," *AHDL* 22(1955), pp. 113-136. On Cajetan and Giles, see, e.g., Martène, *Veterum scriptorum collectio*, vol. III, cols. 1264-1265, and Sadoleto, *Opera omnia*, vol. IV, pp. 323-324.

[2] The fact that Julius II chose Giles to preach for solemn and important occasions suggests that he esteemed his thought as well as his practical ability. It was at the request of Clement VII that Giles wrote his *Scechina*. Edgar Wind is convinced of Giles's influence for the period of Julius II, "Typology in the Sistine Ceiling: A Critical Statement," *ArtB* 33(1951), p. 44n.

[3] On Giles and Seripando, see Hubert Jedin, *Girolamo Seripando*, vol. I, Würz-

cabala have been discovered in traditions where it previously was not known to exist, and such discoveries suggest that the kind of learning Giles espoused had a greater impact than commonly has been recognized.[1] As always, the question of influence is a difficult and delicate one, and it is still too early to pronounce on just how intellectually effective Giles was even in central Italy in the early years of the sixteenth century. His influence in the great mainstream of European thought, of course, could not compare with that of someone of Ficino's stature.[2] He is important, in any case, for the insight he gives

---

burg 1937, pp. 24-33, 80-95. Jedin quotes Girolamo Borgia (1475-1550), p. 24, who addresses Seripando, "Tu enim a primis aetatis temporibus magni Aegidii concionantis divinam eloquentiam et artem dicendi admiratus totum te ejus auctoritati et virtutibus erudiendum addixisti." For a letter of Borgia to Giles, December 3, 1505, in which he requests that Giles send him a copy of his eclogue, "De Christi ortu," see Naples V. F. 20, fols. 296v-297r. The eclogue is to be found in Ang. Lat. 1001, fols. 39r-42v. In this same codex there are two other eclogues, fols. 36r-38v, 42v-44v, and a letter of Giles to Borgia, undated, fols. 246r-247r. See also Signorelli, *Egidio da Viterbo*, pp. 220-221. François Secret has emphasized Seripando's dependence upon Giles for his interest in the cabala, "Girolamo Seripando et la Kabbale," *Rinascimento*, seconda serie 3(1963), pp. 251-268. See also Secret's, "Notes sur Egidio da Viterbo," *Augustiniana* 15(1965), pp. 68-72. For a study of Giles's theology which takes its point of departure from Seripando's comment at Trent which seemed to link the concept of double justification with the theology of Giles, see Jules Paquier, "Un essai de théologie platonicienne à la Renaissance: le commentaire de Gilles de Viterbe sur le premier livre des Sentences," *RechSR* 13(1923), pp. 293-312, 419-436.

[1] See, e.g., François Secret, "Les Jésuites et le Kabbalisme chrétien à la Renaissance," *Bibliothèque d'Humanisme et Renaissance* 20(1958), pp. 542-555, and by the same author, "Les Dominicains et la Kabbale chrétienne à la Renaissance," *AFP* 27(1957), pp. 319-336. Secret's article, "L'interpretazione della Kabbala nel Rinascimento," *Convivium*, anno 24, nuova serie (1956), pp. 541-552, deals principally with the Christian cabala in Catholic authors after the Council of Trent (1545-1563) and especially in the writings of Saint Laurence of Brindisi (1559-1619). Secret's most extensive work on this topic, with ample bibliographical notes, is *Les kabbalistes chrétiens de la Renaissance*, Paris 1964. Other studies by Secret, especially as they concern Giles of Viterbo, will be cited in the appropriate places throughout the book. A fundamental article on the origins of the Christian cabala is by Gershom Scholem, "Zur Geschichte der Anfänge der christlichen Kabbala," in *Essays Presented to Leo Baeck*, London 1954, pp. 158-193. See also the article by Secret on this same topic, "Pico della Mirandola e gli inizi della Cabala cristiana," *Convivium*, anno 25, nuova serie (1957), pp. 31-47. The most comprehensive study in English on the Christian cabala is Joseph Blau, *The Christian Interpretation of the Cabala in the Renaissance*, New York 1944. Indications of the extent of the diffusion of the cabala in the Renaissance can be found in William J. Bouwsma's book on Guillaume Postel (1510-1581), *Concordia Mundi*, Cambridge, Mass. 1957. Ernst Benz's book deals principally with Friedrich Christoph Ötinger (1702-1782) and the German scene in the eighteenth century, *Die christliche Kabbala: Ein Stiefkind der Theologie*, Zurich 1958.

[2] Hubert Jedin judges that, although Ficino's influence in European intel-

us into a moment of history which he alone, by virtue of the unique jurisdictional and intellectual position he occupied, can offer us.

Only recently has scholarly interest in Giles of Viterbo effectively been aroused. Francis X. Martin has sketched the reasons for this neglect, which in general can be reduced to two: the Augustinians, who best controlled the sources, had little interest in investigating the man during whose generalate the Lutheran problem arose, a problem which in their eyes brought shame upon the order; Giles's articulate literary friends gave him such a reputation as a man of letters that every other aspect of his career tended to be forgotten.[1] Although the history of the historiography of Giles has already been very competently written, it will be useful here to bring it up to date and briefly to present the persons who today are actively engaged in research on him.[2]

Father Martin, building upon the helpful but eulogistic work of Giuseppe Signorelli, has written a meticulously detailed biography of Giles's early years and has devoted special attention to his activity as a reformer of the Augustinian order during this period.[3] Martin's work is, obviously, indispensable for anyone who hopes to understand Giles in the context of his life and times. In cataloguing Giles's manuscripts and in trying to reconstruct his library Martin is particularly useful for those who study Giles's thought.

---

lectual history was great, it was relatively unimportant, in the final analysis, on the specific issue of Catholic reform as this developed through the sixteenth century, *A History of the Council of Trent*, trans. Ernest Graf, O.S.B., vol. I, London 1957, pp. 155-156. It would be misleading, however, to slight the importance of the Florentine tradition in the religious and ethical thought of succeeding generations, especially in the "devout humanism" of Saint Francis of Sales (1567-1622) and Pierre de Bérulle (1575-1629), as Anthony Levi, S.J., recently has shown, *French Moralists: The Theory of the Passions (1585-1649)*, Oxford 1964, esp. pp. 40-51, 112-126, 136-141.

[1] See Martin, "Problem of Giles of Viterbo," 9(1959), pp. 357-379; 10(1960), pp. 43-60.

[2] Martin, "Problem of Giles of Viterbo."

[3] "Egidio da Viterbo." Besides this dissertation, which he is now preparing for publication, and the article mentioned in the previous note, there are three other articles on Giles by Father Martin: "Giles of Viterbo and the Monastery of Lecceto: The Making of a Reformer," *Analecta Augustiniana* 25(1962), pp. 225-253; "The Registers of Giles of Viterbo," *Augustiniana* 12(1962), pp. 142-160; "The Augustinian Order on the Eve of the Reformation," *Miscellanea historiae ecclesiasticae*, vol. II (Bibliothèque de la Revue d'histoire ecclésiastique, Fascicule 44), Louvain 1967, pp. 71-104. Signorelli's work was referred to above. For materials from Giles's library now in the Bibliothèque Nationale, Paris, see Charles Astruc and Jacques Monfrin, "Livres latins et hébreux du Cardinal Gilles de Viterbe," *Bibliothèque d'Humanisme et Renaissance* 23(1961), pp. 551-554.

Eugenio Massa over the course of the past fifteen or twenty years has written several articles dealing with Giles principally from a philosophical point of view.[1] Massa is now preparing editions of two of Giles's major works, the "Sententiae ad mentem Platonis" and the "Historia XX saeculorum." Needless to say, these editions will greatly facilitate all research on Giles.

As part of his study of the Christian cabala in the Renaissance, François Secret has made some important contributions to our understanding of Giles.[2] Secret's work is distinguished by the specialized background which he brings to bear upon the subject, thus opening up for the scholarly world an aspect of Giles's thought which otherwise could easily be neglected or misunderstood. In 1959 Secret transcribed and edited Giles's *Scechina*, the only major work of his as yet published.[3]

Other scholars, while treating of different topics, have come upon Giles and been able to throw some interesting light upon his career. Especially important is the book by Gérard E. Weil on the life and work of Elijah Levita (1469-1549), the Jewish grammarian and Masorete whom Giles took into his household in order to perfect his knowledge of Hebrew and Aramaic.[4] Giles has also attracted a certain amount of attention from art historians such as André Chastel and Edgar Wind.[5]

---

[1] "Egidio da Viterbo, Machiavelli, Lutero e il pessimismo cristiano," *Umanesimo e Machiavellismo: Archivio di Filosofia* (1949), pp. 75-123; "Egidio da Viterbo e la metodologia del sapere nel Cinquecento," *Pensée humaniste et tradition chrétienne aux XV et XVI siècles*, ed. H. Bédarida, Paris 1950, pp. 185-239; *I fondamenti metafisici della 'dignitas hominis' e testi inediti di Egidio da Viterbo*, Turin 1954, a booklet which is a revised version of an article which appeared in *Archivio di Filosofia* in 1951. In this booklet Massa has published, pp. 54-110, an excerpt from Giles's "Sententiae ad mentem Platonis," Vat. Lat. 6325, fols. 49v-79v, edited from four codices.

[2] Besides the works of Secret already mentioned, see "Le symbolisme de la Kabbale chrétienne dans la 'Scechina' de Egidio da Viterbo," *Umanesimo e Simbolismo: Archivio di Filosofia* (1958), pp. 131-154; *Le Zôhar chez les kabbalistes chrétiens de la Renaissance*, Paris 1958; "Aegidiana Hebraica," *REJ* 121(1962, 4 série, vol. I), pp. 409-416; "Notes sur les hébraïsants chrétiens de la Renaissance," *Sefarad* 22 (1962), pp. 107-127, esp. 109-117.

[3] Egidio da Viterbo, *Scechina e Libellus de litteris Hebraicis*, ed. François Secret, 2 vols., Rome 1959.

[4] Gérard E. Weil, *Élie Lévita: Humaniste et Massorète (1469-1549)*, Leiden 1963, esp. pp. 71-110, 203-211, and the bibliography. There are also a few pages on Giles in Giovanni di Napoli, *L'immortalità dell'anima nel Rinascimento*, Turin 1963, e.g., pp. 177-178, 181-182, 300-301.

[5] André Chastel, *Art et Humanisme à Florence au temps de Laurent le Magnifique*, Paris 1961, esp. pp. 70-71, 454-456. For Wind, besides the articles referred to elsewhere in this book, see *Pagan Mysteries in the Renaissance*, New Haven 1958,

Before moving on to Chapter One something should be said about the condition, content, location and authenticity of the writings attributed to Giles of Viterbo. On several occasions Giles spoke of his works as "tumultuous," a description unfortunately as accurate as it is disheartening for anyone who wishes to study them.[1] Giles was a busy man and was forced to write in haste during those moments which he could spare from his other duties, as he himself confessed.[2] Because of the frequent interruptions he had to suffer he easily digresses from the topic at hand.[3] Giles was propelled by an insatiable curiosity, and he sometimes gives the impression of hurrying through one piece in order to be able to begin another.[4] The problem is compounded by his cabalism and by the fact that most of his writings are still in manuscript.[5]

As mentioned earlier, the only one of Giles's major works which has been published is the *Scechina*. For anyone who has had the opportunity to examine the lengthy Paris autograph Secret's edition will long remain one of the most helpful contributions to scholarship on Giles of Viterbo.[6] Begun in 1530, just two years before his death, the *Scechina* is of the utmost importance for understanding the final development of his thought. The treatise is incomplete in its present

pp. 21, 26n, 44, 154. For Giles in another context, see Marjorie Reeves, "Joachimist Expectations in the Order of Augustinian Hermits," *RThAM* 25(1958), pp. 111-141, esp. 135-138. For a criticism of Reeves's article, see Zumkeller, "Joachim von Fiore," pp. 382-388. I have published three articles on Giles: "Giles of Viterbo: A Sixteenth-Century Text on Doctrinal Development," *Traditio* 22(1966), pp. 445-450; "Giles of Viterbo: A Reformer's Thought on Renaissance Rome," *Renaissance Quarterly* (formerly *Renaissance News*) 20(1967), pp. 1-11; "Historical Thought and the Reform Crisis of the Early Sixteenth Century," *ThSt* 28(1967), pp. 531-548.

[1] Martène, *Veterum scriptorum collectio*, vol. III, col. 1236, "scripta tumultuaria mea." See also Ang. Lat. 1001, fol. 205v; Siena G. X. 26, p. 129, and Évora CXVI/1-30, fol. 78r: "Sed haec hactenus inculto tumultuarioque stilo scripsisse satis fuerit." Giles perhaps never expected others to agree with his evaluation, which seems to have been something of a rhetorical form. Aleander, for instance, uses the same expression to describe his own style, *Lettres de Aléandre*, p. 38.

[2] Vat. Lat. 6325, fol. 109r, and "Libellus" (in *Scechina*, vol. I), p. 38.

[3] See, e.g., Vat. Lat. 6325, fols. 99v and 212v. See also Ang. Lat. 502, fol. 299v.

[4] See Vat. Lat. 6325, fols. 109r and 139r. He intended to write a treatise "De disciplinis Etruscis," Ang. Lat. 502, fol. 23r, and Évora CXVI/1-30, fols. 11v, 12v.

[5] Scholars have for a long time complained about Giles's style and the condition of his manuscripts. L.-G. Pélissier is the most bitter, *De opere historico Aegidii Cardinalis Viterbiensis*, Montpellier 1896, e.g., pp. 1-4. See also Massa, *Fondamenti metafisici e testi inediti*, p. 4.

[6] Paris Lat. 3363, fols. 157r-349v. The "Libellus" is to be found in Vat. Lat. 5808, a beautiful copy offered to the cardinal. See also Vat. Lat. 3146, fols. 1r-26v, and the comment by Secret, *Scechina*, vol. I, p. 23n.

form, but it seems it was not always so. Giles wrote it at the request of Pope Clement VII and addresses it to the Emperor Charles V.[1] The *Scechina*, along with the short "Libellus de litteris Hebraicis" of 1517, which was dedicated to the future Clement while he was still a cardinal and which accompanies the *Scechina* in Secret's edition, is the only surviving original treatise of Giles's which treats *ex professo* of the Christian cabala.[2] For the subject of Church reform the *Scechina* is of consequence in a number of particular details, as well as from its general purpose, which is to explain and justify Christian use of the cabala.

A few of Giles's shorter works, including some poetry, have been published over the course of the centuries. The most important of these on all counts is the oration with which he opened the Fifth Lateran Council in 1512 for Julius II.[3] This oration, with the justly famous norm it established for reform—"Men must be changed by religion, not religion by men"—is remarkable as a compendium of Giles's thought and concerns for the early years of his life.[4] True, it gives hardly a passing nod to his cabalistic interests, which were at that moment just beginning fully to develop, but practically all the other dominant themes are in some form to be found there, even if not in every case immediately recognizable.[5]

The only surviving text of the sermon Giles delivered in the church of Santa Maria del Popolo in Rome to celebrate the agreement by which on November 29, 1512, Julius II and Emperor Maximilian had settled their ecclesiastical and political differences is to be found in print in the Bibliothèque Nationale in Paris.[6] Giles sees in this rapproche-

---

[1] For Clement's letter, see J. F. Ossinger, *Bibliotheca Augustiniana*, Ingolstadt 1768, pp. 191-193. Giles's reply is printed in Secret's edition of the *Scechina*, vol. I, pp. 65-66.

[2] Secret, *Les kabbalistes chrétiens*, p. 110.

[3] Mansi, vol. XXXII, cols. 669-676. See Ang. Lat. 502, fol. 266v: "Jubet Julius me primum in concilio verba facere, populo senatuque flente, ..." On Giles's poetry, see Martin, "Problem of Giles of Viterbo," esp. 9(1959), pp. 359-360.

[4] Mansi, vol. XXXII, col. 669: "... homines per sacra immutari fas est, non sacra per homines: ...."

[5] But see Mansi, vol. XXXII, col. 675: "Et in arcanis Hebraeorum legimus,...."

[6] "Oratio habita post tertiam sacri Lateranensis concilii sessionem," Rome 1512(?). The Paris call number: Rés. B. 1930(27), pp. 517-530. The printed text is introduced with a letter of Sadoleto to Sannazzaro, to whom Sadoleto declares the piece dedicated. On the agreement between Julius II and Maximilian, see Pastor, *History of the Popes*, ed. F. I. Antrobus, vol. VI, pp. 421-428. See also Signorelli, *Egidio da Viterbo*, pp. 53-54.

ment an instance of God's providential care for the Church, which war and the schismatic Council of Pisa (1511-1512) had particularly threatened, and he takes advantage of the occasion to incite pope and emperor to new efforts against the enemies of Christendom, especially the Turks. Martin has recently edited "De Ilicetana familia," a short treatise on the religious life which Giles addressed to the monastery of Lecceto with which he became affiliated as an observant in 1503. This little sermon in the form of a letter, written probably between 1503 and 1506, helps us to understand the nature of Giles's religious idealism as a member of the Augustinian order.[1]

Besides some individual letters scattered in a number of different books, there are three short printed collections. The oldest of these is contained in volume III of Martène and Durand's *Veterum scriptorum collectio*, where eighteen letters from Giles appear along with a certain number to or about him.[2] An appendix to Signorelli's biography contains sixty-five letters and documents by or concerning Giles, including some from the Siena codex which Signorelli discovered and which is the only extant collection of his official correspondence as head of the Augustinian order.[3] In 1915 Fiovo Pazzaglia in a pamphlet containing eight letters promised a complete edition, but nothing beyond these solitary eight ever appeared.[4]

The vast bulk of Giles's writings, however, is still in manuscript and is to be found principally in Rome, Naples, Siena and Paris. His commentary on the first seventeen Distinctions of the first book of Peter Lombard's (ca. 1100-1160) *Sentences* done "according to Plato," is the most extensive of his early works and, except for a relatively short excerpt published by Massa, is still to be found only in manuscript.[5]

---

[1] Martin, "Giles and Lecceto," pp. 248-253. For his text Martin used the copy of this work which is in the Biblioteca Angelica, Rome, Lat. 1156, and which apparently was intended to be presented to Piero Soderini, "Florentinae reipublicae dictatori perpetuo illustri" (1502-1512), as the prefatory letter from a certain Fra Basilio of the Augustinian order indicates. The letter is not dated. It commends to Soderini the contents of the piece as well as the eloquence of the author. There are two other copies of the "De Ilicetana familia" of which Martin was not aware: Naples V. F. 20, fols. 123r-125v, 127v-131r, and Ang. Lat. 1001, fols. 105v-111v.

[2] Cols. 1233-1268.

[3] *Egidio da Viterbo*, pp. 217-256.

[4] "Lettere inedite del Card. Egidio Canisio [sic] Viterbese," ed. Fiovo Giuseppe Pazzaglia, Rome 1915.

[5] The manuscript copy of this commentary which will be used in this book is Vat. Lat. 6325. For critical comment on the different copies of this work, see Massa, *Fondamenti metafisici e testi inediti*, pp. 49-53. Giles describes his purpose as "nobis solis scripsimus," Vat. Lat. 6325, fol. 172r. For the Biblioteca Angelica,

Written over a period of years at least up into 1512, the "Sententiae ad mentem Platonis" reflects the enthusiasm for Ficino's Platonism, including the related interests from late antiquity, which was characteristic of Giles in this period.

For the problem under discussion in this book the most important single manuscript is the "Historia XX saeculorum," dedicated to Leo X and written during the early years of his pontificate after the Lombard commentary was laid aside.[1] This work, taking its cue from the medieval world chronicles, is for the most part a history of the papacy fashioned with the express purpose of indicating to the pope his duties and responsibilities at the present crucial moment of history. In reviewing the story of the papacy, as well as of the "first Church" of the ten ages of the Old Testament era, Giles conveys to us his ideas of reform and the ecclesiastical ideal in whose context these ideas are to be implemented. He drew heavily upon the *Liber pontificalis* and Bartolomeo Platina's (1421-1481) *Vitae pontificum*, using these sources with freedom and for his own purposes.[2] The only scholarly analysis of the "Historia" which has been made up to now misses the import of the most original element it contains, namely, themes and arguments taken from Talmudic and cabalistic literature, which help fashion the very structure of the work.[3]

Giles's correspondence, contained in various codices, falls into two groups: letters of friendship written to persons with literary and re-

---

Rome, see L.-G. Pélissier, "Manuscrits de Gilles de Viterbe à la Bibliothèque Angélique," *Revue des bibliothèques* 2(1892), pp. 228-240. In Naples Giles's manuscripts are to be found in the Biblioteca Nazionale; the Siena codex is in the Biblioteca Comunale; the Paris materials are all part of the so-called Ridolfi Collection in the Bibliothèque Nationale. For information on the Ridolfi Collection, see Astruc and Monfrin, "Livres du Cardinal Gilles," and Roberto Ridolfi, "La biblioteca del Cardinale Niccolò Ridolfi (1501-1550)," *La Bibliofilia* 31(1929), pp. 173-193. On some other manuscripts of Giles's, see Adolar Zumkeller, O.S.A., "Manuskripte von Werken der Autoren des Augustiner-Eremitenordens in mitteleuropäischen Bibliotheken," *Augustiniana* 11(1961), pp. 67-68.

[1] "Aegidii Viterbiensis Cardinalis historia XX saeculorum per totidem psalmos digesta." In this book I have used Ang. Lat. 502, collating it when necessary with Ang. Lat. 351 and with the Naples autograph, IX. B. 14. Signorelli, *Egidio da Viterbo*, p. 215, correctly argues for 1513-1518 for the dates of composition, as against Pélissier, *De opere historico*, pp. 41-43, who gives 1509-1516. See, e.g., Ang. Lat. 502, fol. 285r.

[2] These are the two sources Pélissier isolated, *De opere historico*, pp. 15-26. There are indications of other works Giles used or consulted, e.g., Ang. Lat. 502, fols. 83r, 149v, 151r-v, 168v.

[3] Pélissier, *De opere historico*, pp. 2-6. For the importance of the cabala in the "Historia," see Secret, *Les kabbalistes chrétiens*, p. 113.

ligious interests, and official letters written as prior general of the Augustinian order.[1] The first category provides us with a number of interesting insights, but the second, contained principally in the Siena codex, is of far greater importance. This Siena codex illumines an entirely new aspect of Giles's thought and personality; the theorist and theologian reveals himself as also a disciplinarian and practical reformer. These letters, though generally meager in speculative reflections, are rich in implication, so that we cannot speak of Giles's thought on reform without taking them into consideration. I have accounted for over six hundred letters written by Giles, many of which appear more than once in the various codices. These letters span his adult years up to about 1518, with a few letters from several years just before his death in 1532.

There are two short pieces still in manuscript which provide interesting data for our topic. One is the oration, "De ecclesiae incremento," preached before Pope Julius II on December 21, 1507, in Saint Peter's basilica, and sent the next year as a booklet to King Manuel I of Portugal. The occasion for this oration was the triumphal penetration of the Portuguese into the East, with all the commercial and religious possibilities this afforded. Giles describes the document as a discourse on the Golden Age.[2] The second piece, done in the form of a letter to his Augustinian brethren in Rome, is really a sermon revolving around love as central to Christianity and to the Church, and containing in brief many of the themes of his thought.[3] This letter is undated, but certainly was written before 1513, and probably even before Giles came to Rome as vicar general in 1506.

Mention must also be made of the official registers of Giles as prior

[1] The principal codices are Ang. Lat. 1001, 1170, 688; Naples V.F.20; Siena G.X.26. There are short collections of letters in Vat. Lat. 3146, fols. 27r-37v; Laurenz. Ashb. 287, fols. 37r-44v, 57r-58r; and Ang. Lat. 762, fols. 2r-7v. Individual letters are scattered elsewhere in libraries and archives. For official correspondence to Giles during his legateship in Spain, see Cesare Guasti, *I manoscritti Torrigiani donati al R. Archivio di Stato di Firenze*, Florence 1878.

[2] This manuscript, Évora CXVI/1-30, was discovered in the Biblioteca Pública of Évora, Portugal, by Martin, who kindly informed me about it. Although described as a "*libellus*" "de ecclesiae incremento" in Ang. Lat. 1118, fol. 143r, Giles on at least three occasions speaks of it as "de aurea aetate," Évora CXVI/1-30, fol. 5r-v; Ang. Lat. 1001, fol. 205v; and Pélissier, "Pour la biographie," p. 806. See also Ang. Lat. 502, fols. 191v-193r, and Siena G.X.26, p. 195. For a description of the occasion, see O. Raynaldi (Odorico Rinaldi), *Annales ecclesiastici*, vol. XI, Lucca 1754, p. 508. See also Signorelli, *Egidio da Viterbo*, pp. 41, 162-163, and Ang. Lat. 688, fol. 18v.

[3] It is found in two codices: Ang. Lat. 1001, fols. 11r-23v, and Naples V.F. 20, fols. 256r-281r.

general of the order. Incomplete though they now are, they complement the official correspondence and, like it, save us from the mistake of thinking of Giles as removed from hard daily realities.[1] From the time Giles laid down the office of prior general of the Augustinian order in 1518 until the *Scechina* of 1530 relatively little documentary evidence has been discovered concerning him, even as bishop of Viterbo, and there is practically nothing from his own hand in the way of original composition.[2]

---

[1] See Martin, "Registers," and Pélissier, "Pour la biographie," pp. 789-815. There are, moreover, five documents from the Ridolfi Collection in the Bibliothèque Nationale about which a word must be said: (1) Lat. 3461, fols. 20r-56r: contains sermon notes and jottings attributed to Giles. (2) Lat. 6589: contains a topical index to Aristotle followed by an "Index of the Errors of Aristotle." This is certainly a work of Giles's, as fol. 581r indicates. A cursory examination of the latter piece disclosed no textual relationship with Giles of Rome's *Errores philosophorum* and uncovered no material which would be of direct pertinence for our topic. (3) Lat. 3461, fols. 1r-19v: Massa, who once thought this was a work of Giles's, has conclusively shown it is an attack of Aleander on Erasmus, "Intorno ad Erasmo: Una polemica che si credeva perduta," *Classical, Medieval and Renaissance Studies in Honor of Berthold Louis Ullman*, ed. Charles Henderson, Jr., vol. II, Rome 1964, pp. 435-454. (4) Lat. 7863, fols. 1r-18r: an appeal for a campaign against the Turks preached before Emperor Charles V in 1523. There is as yet no convincing internal or external evidence to indicate Giles's authorship of this document, and the contents add nothing which is pertinent for us. (5) Lat. 3395, fols. 33r-78v (pp. 43-134): from internal evidence it is clear that this document is one of the memorials on the Lutheran problem which Pope Leo X called for in consistory on February 6, 1521. On this consistory, see Pastor, *History of the Popes*, vol. VIII, pp. 23-24. We have a letter from Rome of Giles's to Aleander, dated February 22, 1521, in Balan, *Monumenta*, pp. 62-65, which indicates Giles was in Rome at approximately the time of the consistory. Since Giles presumably was present at this consistory and since the document formed part of the Ridolfi Collection, the external evidence suggests Giles as the author. Such evidence, however, does not exclude other possibilities, and a careful examination of the internal evidence is needed before a safe attribution can be made. The document is polemically anti-Lutheran in tone and consists for the most part in a lengthy refutation of Luther's "Quare pontificis Romani et discipulorum ejus libri a D. Martino Luthero combusti sint," *WA*, vol. VII, pp. 161-182.

[2] See Signorelli, *Egidio da Viterbo*, for information and documents concerning this period of Giles's life.

CHAPTER ONE

PRINCIPLES OF CONCORD AND ORTHODOXY

Before undertaking a detailed examination of the specific intellectual traditions and the individual authors that seem most to have influenced the thought of Giles of Viterbo, it is imperative to make explicit two of his abiding concerns. They are of the utmost importance for understanding the spirit with which Giles approached every author he read, and they can, indeed, be considered two fundamental preoccupations which, in spite of a seemingly paradoxical opposition between them, give unity and intelligibility to his widely ranging intellectual interests. One is as significant as the other, and to slight either of them would be to distort the fundamental framework of his thought. Giles constantly endeavored, first of all, to bring into harmony with orthodox Christian dogma all that he felt was good in non-Christian thought, to the point of actually being able to discover Christian truth in authors and systems which fell outside the limits of institutional Christianity. At the same time he was passionately and sincerely devoted to Christian orthodoxy, and fidelity to it was the first norm against which every other doctrine had to be judged. Each of these two concerns must be examined with some care.

The effort to reconcile non-Christian authors with Christian teaching is certainly not original with Giles. On the contrary, it might be considered one of the fundamental strivings of Christian apologists from the day Christianity first confronted the pagan world, and it exists in explicit form at least from the time of Justin Martyr (ca. 100-165). Often viewed with suspicion and suffering many setbacks, it nevertheless struck such deep roots that it considerably affected the religious thought of the Fathers of the Church, the medieval scholastics and the humanists of Giles's day. The often quoted scriptural justification for this effort at reconciliation was Saint Paul's reminder to the Athenians, "...for 'In him we live and move and have our being;' as even some of your poets have said" (Acts 17.28). In the Middle Ages the effort resulted in the great syntheses of scholasticism, one of whose most significant working principles was "*Diversi, sed non adversi.*" This principle, though specifically applied to bring into accord apparently differing opinions of the Fathers, is not without relevance for illuminating the posture scholasticism adopted towards other sources, including non-Christian ones.[1]

The search for agreement, *concordia*, was particularly energetic in the fifteenth and early sixteenth centuries, partly as a reaction to the divisive tendencies resulting from the Great Western Schism (1378-1417). The desire to reconcile pagan and Christian authors, as well as warring scholastic schools, was to be found in late medieval Nominalists.[2] In certain humanist circles the search for *concordia* was at the center of interest. Saint Antoninus of Florence (1387-1449) had given explicit approval to the principle that all truth, no matter by whom uttered, comes from the Holy Spirit.[3] Ficino and especially Pico were to a large extent motivated by their belief in the possibility of reconciling different intellectual and religious traditions. The humanists had tired of what they felt were the useless and discordant complications of scholastic philosophy, and they sought a divine science which would reduce all differences to a simple unity and bring about a philosophical peace, "*pax philosophica*."[4] There was, moreover, a greater diffusion of the texts of the so-called *prisca theologia*, especially

[1] See Henri de Lubac, S.J., "À propos de la formule: Diversi, sed non adversi," *RechSR* 40(1951-1952), pp. 27-40, and also my article, "A Note on Gregory of Rimini: Church, Scripture, Tradition," *Augustinianum* 5(1965), pp. 365-378.

[2] See, e.g., Heiko A. Oberman, "'Facientibus Quod in Se est Deus non Denegat Gratiam,' Robert Holcot, O.P., and the Beginnings of Luther's Theology," *HThR* 55(1962), p. 320.

[3] Antoninus of Florence, *Chronicorum Opus*, ed. Petrus Maturus, S.J., vol. I, Lyons 1586, p. 1: "Veritas enim secundum Ambrosium a quocumque dicatur a Spiritu Sancto est." See also *ibid.*, p. 190. For the possible influence of Antoninus on Ficino, see Étienne Gilson, "Marsile Ficin et le *Contra Gentiles*," *AHDL* 24 (1957), pp. 101-113, and Paul Oskar Kristeller, *Le Thomisme et la pensée italienne de la Renaissance*, Montreal 1967, pp. 93-94. See Augustine, *De doctrina Christiana*, II. 28: "... immo vero quisquis bonus verusque Christianus est, domini sui esse intelligat ubicumque invenerit veritatem, ..." See Justin Martyr, I *Apol.* 46, and II *Apol.* 13.

[4] See A. Corsano, *Il pensiero religioso italiano dall'Umanesimo al Giurisdizionalismo*, Bari 1937, p. 31. Also: Ernst Cassirer, "Giovanni Pico della Mirandola: A Study in the History of Renaissance Ideas," *Journal of the History of Ideas* 3(1942), pp. 123-144, 319-346; Eugenio Garin, *Italian Humanism: Philosophy and Civic Life*, trans. Peter Munz, New York 1965, pp. 106-108; Michael Seidlmayer, "'Una religio in rituum varietate': Zur Religionsauffassung des Nicolaus von Cues," *AKultG* 36 (1954), pp. 145-207; Cesare Vasoli, "Temi e fonti della tradizione ermetica in uno scritto di Symphorien Champier," *Umanesimo e Esoterismo: Archivio di Filosofia* (1960), pp. 235-289, esp. 245; Delio Cantimori, "Anabattismo e Neoplatonismo nel XVI secolo in Italia," *Reale Accademia Nazionale dei Lincei*, *Rendiconti*, *Classe di scienze morali, storiche e filologiche*, serie VI, 12(1936), pp. 521-561, esp. 546, where he sees an essential difference between the scholastics' and the humanists' search for harmony between ancient philosophy and Christian dogma.

through Ficino's translations of the Hermetic literature and George of Trebizond's (1395-1484) Latin translation of Eusebius's *Praeparatio evangelica*, published in 1470. This gave added impulse to the idea of an ancient religious tradition which, while lying outside the direct line of Judeo-Christian transmission, was for one reason or another basically in accord with it.[1]

Giles of Viterbo was heir to these persuasions. His intellectual quest was, whenever possible, for those doctrines and ideas which united him with his fellow men rather than those which divided him from them. Giles's general attitude is illustrated by the norm he enunciated for the interpretation of ancient writers, especially the Fathers: their authority deserves respect and should be spared attack.[2] He insisted that an impartial consideration of the Greeks' doctrine on the procession of the Holy Spirit would show that it was not opposed to the Latins', but was actually "in agreement and accord" with it.[3] Besides counselling calm discussion of theological differences with the Greeks, he lays down the following norm for practical conduct: "It is my conviction that our brethren are not people whom we can feel free rashly to cast out from our company, but rather whom we must ever seek to embrace with warmth and understanding."[4]

The theme which Giles chose for the official public sermon he preached in the Piazza del Campo of Siena in celebration of the election and coronation of Pope Pius III in 1503 was the divine harmony in the universe.[5] Part of this harmony surely was the provi-

---

[1] See D. P. Walker, "Orpheus the Theologian and Renaissance Platonists," *Journal of the Warburg and Courtauld Institutes* 16(1953), esp. pp. 104-105, and by the same author in the same journal, 17(1954), "The *Prisca Theologia* in France," esp. pp. 204-208. See also Vasoli, "Temi e fonti," p. 244; Paul Oskar Kristeller, *Supplementum Ficinianum*, vol. I, Florence 1937, pp. cxxix ff.; Eugenio Garin, "Cusano e i Platonici italiani del Quattrocento," *Nicolò da Cusa: Convegno interuniversitario, 1960*, Florence 1962, esp. p. 93.

[2] Ang. Lat. 502, fol. 275v: "... veterum auctoritati parcendum." See also *ibid.*, fol. 103r.

[3] Vat. Lat. 6325, fol. 167v, "consentientem ac concordem." A comment in the *Scechina*, vol. I, p. 234, suggests that Giles later may not have been so convinced of the Greeks' orthodoxy, or at least of the admissibility of the formula "*per Filium*," as he was at the time of the "Sententiae." Peter Lombard held that the Greeks agreed in substance with the Latins, and Saint Thomas accepts this view, I *Sent.* d 11 divisio textus.

[4] Vat. Lat. 6325, fol. 167v: "... fratres siquidem nostros non temere ejiciendos, sed amice complectendos existimamus."

[5] Ang. Lat. 1001, fol. 65r, letter dated October 14, 1503, to Serafino Ferri: "Dixi de harmonia multa, quid Augustinus, quid Boetius, quid Ptolemaeus, quid in Timaeo Plato." See also Massa, *Fondamenti metafisici e testi inediti*, p. 7, and

dential diffusion of religious truth even in what otherwise might be considered profane sources.[1] Giles was convinced that in certain philosophical and poetic writings there was a hard core of such truth which somehow was identical with a number of fundamental Christian beliefs. This conviction allowed him to lift ideas and phrases out of their literary and historical context and to discover sometimes exotic parallels between them. He was, therefore, in possession of a hermeneutics which could filter out obvious and disturbing discrepancies between the authors and traditions he was discussing and which could retain and magnify a slight residue of superficial similarities. On the basis of this hermeneutics, for instance, he was able to relate triplets as diverse as: (1) efficient, exemplary and final causality; (2) the one, the true, the good; (3) Christ as the way, truth and life (Jn. 14.6); (4) the Father, Son and Holy Spirit; (5) the creation of all things in measure, number and weight (Wis. 11.21); (6) and, finally, the three Fates or *Parcae*—Clotho, Lachesis and Atropos.[2]

Among the motives which inclined Giles to his persistent search for *concordia* one must be singled out for special comment: his belief that God is not distant from any man and is eager to open up the "path of salvation" for all.[3] Giles finds empirical proof for this belief

---

Scechina, vol. I, p. 114, and vol. II, p. 44. On Ferri, see Signorelli, *Egidio da Viterbo*, pp. 11, 135.

[1] Vat. Lat. 6325, fol. 84v: "Omnia haec nostris in oraculis invenire est, quasi divina sit factum providentia, ut ne quis non crederet veritati, testes et sacros et prophanos veritas adinvenerit." See also "Libellus" (in *Scechina*, vol. I), p. 23: "Sane divinae res quae legi possunt secantur in partes treis [sic]: quaedam gentes, quaedam prophetae veteres, quaedam novae legis scriptores prodidere." For a similar opinion in Marsilio Ficino, see "In epist. ad Romanos, VI," *Opera omnia*, vol. I, Basel 1576, p. 436: "... communem notitiam divinorum Deus ipse sicut Judaeis revelaverat per prophetas, ita gentibus manifestam effecerat per philosophos."

[2] Vat. Lat. 6325, fols. 40r-41v. This style of argument was not used exclusively by Giles of Viterbo. His venerated predecessor, Giles of Rome, has a series of such triplets relating to the Trinity, I *Sent.* d.3 pars 1 princ. 2 q.2, Venice 1521, fol. 23v.

[3] Ang. Lat. 502, fol. 238r: "Movet enim omnes Deus ut salutis viam, formam veritatis, iter felicitatis intelligant." In this instance Giles clearly is speaking of the Romans before the coming of Christ. See also Vat. Lat. 6325, fol. 29r: "... neminem esse vult [Deus] qui eum esse non norit, ..." Also *ibid.*, fol. 84v, quoted above. He shows a certain reserve about the extent of the gentiles' opportunity before Christ's solemn commission to evangelize all nations, e.g., Ang. Lat. 502, fols. 32r, 176(a)r, and *Scechina*, vol. II, pp. 209-210, 274. As E. Monnerjahn has pointed out, Pico's thought is conditioned by the persuasion that God's Spirit is present in all men, *Giovanni Pico della Mirandola*, Wiesbaden 1960, p. 99: "Gottes Geist ist in allen Menschen gegenwärtig und lebendig, seien sie jung oder alt, Juden oder Heiden." Ficino expresses a similar idea, modifying it in a way which

in the fact that the voyages of discovery of the Spaniards and Portuguese have shown that people in every part of the world believe in God.[1] This conviction that God is near to each individual and has care for him must always be borne in mind for an adequate understanding of what spurred Giles to his efforts to find orthodox Christian doctrine outside the bounds of institutional Catholicism.

In what specific ways could a person not directly nourished by the Jewish and Christian traditions arrive at a knowledge of religious truth? The first answer Giles supplies to this question is "*natura*" and "*ratione*," by nature and by reason. At one point he seems to accept the idea of an innate knowledge of God's existence in all men.[2] He argues, at any rate, that God can be known from His effects in the natural world, and there is nothing that exists which is not a sign pointing to God as to its author and cause, whose wise decrees all nature humbly obeys.[3] For the Christian Giles readily grants reason the ancillary functions conceded it in scholastic theology, such as deducing new conclusions from the articles of faith,[4] and he heartily advocates that reason and faith work together to attain the fullest degree of religious wisdom.[5]

---

is reminiscent of Nicholas of Cusa, "De Christiana religione," *Opera*, vol. I, p. 4: "Idcirco divina providentia non permittit esse aliquo in tempore, ullam mundi regionem omnis prorsus religionis expertem, quamvis permittat variis locis et temporibus, ritus adorationis varios observari. Forsitan vero varietas huiusmodi, ordinante Deo, decorem quemdam parit in universo mirabilem." See Cusa, *De pace fidei*, eds. Raymond Klibansky and Hildebrand Bascour, O.S.B., *Opera omnia*, vol. VII (Heidelberg), Hamburg 1959, p. 15: "Una est igitur religio et cultus omnium intellectu vigentium, quae in omni diversitate rituum praesupponitur," and p. 62: "Augebitur etiam fortassis devotio ex quadam diversitate, quando quaelibet natio conabitur ritum suum studio et diligentia splendidiorem efficere, ..." See also Ralph V. Turner, "*Descendit ad inferos:* Medieval Views on Christ's Descent into Hell and the Salvation of the Ancient Just," *Journal of the History of Ideas* 27(1966), pp. 173-194.

[1] Vat. Lat. 6325, fol. 28r-v.

[2] Vat. Lat. 6325, fol. 31r: "... ait enim hic [Epicurus], teste Cicerone, cognosci esse Deum idque innatum esse omnibus, et [haec est sententia] etiam antiquorum theologorum, nam Damascenus ait, quod Deus existat unicuique natura insertum esse, quod quidem cum posteriores interpretari nituntur et corrumpunt et evertunt." See also *ibid.*, fol. 112r, and Massa, *Fondamenti metafisici e testi inediti*, pp. 77-78.

[3] Vat. Lat. 6325, fols. 29v, 31r-32v, and 193v: "Nam nihil plane rerum esse potest quod Dei signum non sit, veluti communis omnium et auctoris et causae." Also Ang. Lat. 502, fol. 141v.

[4] Vat. Lat. 6325, fols. 4v, 106r, and 83r, "astipulantem ancillam." See also Naples V.F. 20, fol. 74v.

[5] Vat. Lat. 6325, fols. 21r and 80r, and also Évora, CXVI/1-30, fol. 14r. See Giuseppe Toffanin, "Umanesimo e teologia," *Bibliothèque d'Humanisme et Renais-*

Giles, however, does not stop there. He has further things to say about the religious knowledge attainable by nature or by reason, and some of these seem hardy indeed. The most astonishing claim he makes is that man can come to a knowledge of the Persons of the Trinity by his natural power, "*natura*." Giles adduces the authority of Augustine, who affirmed that this was possible, and he himself is thoroughly convinced that in at least two passages Plato wrote so well on the Father and Son that nothing more explicit can be found even in the Gospels.[1]

Giles surely is not unaware of the scriptural and theological difficulties which such assertions must confront, nor that after Augustine "almost everyone" held that no philosopher could attain such knowledge or even suspect the existence of such truth.[2] More embarrassing still, to affirm nature's power to know the Trinity, even in an imperfect manner, seems to contradict a principle Giles never tires of

---

sance 11(1949), pp. 205-214, on Sadoleto and the harmony between creation and grace as presented, for example, in the liturgy.

[1] Vat. Lat. 6325, fols. 35v-36r: "...magnus Augustinus, parens meus, in eo libro, qui de divina civitate inscribitur, cum quaesisset unde nosse potuisset haec Plato, cum multa narrasset, illud etiam posuit, quod ex iis quae facta sunt haec nosse potuit, quod utique dici a tanto viro non debuit nisi et verum esse potuisset. Sed alio loco in confessionum libro longe id clarius ostendit, ubi non demonstrari posse ratione sed jam demonstratam fuisse ait divinam generationem, seque rationes vidisse illam manifestissime demonstrantes. Quamobrem et ratione et testimonio constat, recte sentire eos qui non fide tantum sed etiam ratione cognosci posse divinas personas." *Ibid.*, fol. 34r: "...duobus tamen in locis ita aperte rem pandit [Plato] ut evangelistam existimes, non philosophum," and fols. 34v-35r: "Rem [Patrem et Filium] postea ita disserit [Plato] manifeste clareque, ut nihil in evangelio legatur expressius...Quod nunc ad rem attinet jam liquido constat, non communia et idem tantum, sed diversum ac propria de trinitatis personis duabus a Platone esse tractata." Also *ibid.*, fol. 83r: "Habetur in Republica Platonis, ubi et gignentem Patrem et genitam Prolem aperte confitetur. Quare si quis in posterum de hac re haesitaverit, sciat se non solum sacrae eruditioni sed etiam philosophiae institutioni repugnare." See also Ang. Lat. 502, fol. 163r: "...trinitatis personas pandit duas [Plato], Parentem ac Filium." Giles does not limit Plato's knowledge to the first two Persons. See Vat. Lat. 6325, fol. 165v, quoted below.

[2] Vat. Lat. 6325, fol. 18v: "Dicunt hoc loco auctores fere omnes posteriores, qui sacra attigerunt, hanc rem nullis umquam philosophis notam fuisse, nullam philosophiam olfecisse, neminem naturae vestigatorem quidquam tanta de re umquam scripsisse." See also *ibid.*, fol. 36r. Peter Lombard allows only a vague and indistinct knowledge of the Trinity to the ancient philosophers, I *Sent.* d. 3 c.l. Giles of Rome denies that the real plurality of the divine Persons can be demonstrated, I *Sent.* d. 2 princ. 2 q. 2, and d. 3 pars 1 princ. 1 q. 4, Venice 1521, fols. 19v and 22r-v. As regards Plato and the Trinity, Ficino has a clear statement in a letter written in 1494 to the bishop of Rimini, "Epistolarum liber XII," *Opera*, vol. I, p. 956: "Ego igitur extra controversiam assero trinitatis Christianae secretum in ipsis Platonis libris numquam esse."

reiterating: man of himself is blind to divine truths, and without God's help he cannot find God.[1] True philosophy, according to Giles, confesses it needs the revelation of divine oracles.[2] At one point, in order to explain the sublime degree of Plato's knowledge of the Trinity, Giles reminds us that God reveals Himself to philosophers whose teaching is in accord with divine truth.[3]

How does Giles resolve his dilemma? How can he insist that man can attain to the mystery of the Trinity by his natural power and at the same time insist that such knowledge is impossible without God's help? We must recall that the assertions concerning Plato's attainments occur in the "Sententiae ad mentem Platonis," a work which professedly is an apology for the Christian values in Plato. There is, throughout, a deliberate attempt to exalt the merits of Plato and to minimize those of Aristotle.[4] Nature and reason, therefore, are to be interpreted with Platonic, not Aristotelian, overtones. What this means in the concrete is that reason is to be viewed not as acting entirely on its own, deriving all knowledge from the senses, but as illuminated by the interior light which descends from above. It is this inner illumination which enables man to have some grasp of the divine, and at the same time turns his mind to a consideration of the

---

[1] E.g., Vat. Lat. 6325, fols. 6r, 84r-v, 87v-88r, 112r-113r, 147r, etc.

[2] E.g., Vat. Lat. 6325, fols. 2r, 3v, 12r, etc.

[3] Vat. Lat. 6325, fol. 35r: "At dices, fides est substantia sperandarum rerum [Heb. 11.1], quomodo itaque per philosophiam? Sed alii articuli fidei nonnulli etiam a philosophis comprobantur, ut Deum esse unum,...Sed Patrem nemo novit nisi Filius et cui voluerit Filius revelare [Mt. 11.27]. Atqui id Paulus interpretatur et ait, de Graecis philosophis loquens, quod Deus illis revelaverit. Quare a vero non aberat, quod etiam philosophis revelaverit Deus, iis praecipue quorum philosophia oraculorum scientiae non repugnet." Ang. Lat. 502, fol. 105r: "...Patrem et rem divinam nosse neminem nisi Filium atque eos quibus Filius aperuerit." See also Vat. Lat. 6325, fols. 20r-21r, 24v-25r. The possibility of some sort of revelation to the philosophers was proposed, for instance, by Saint Thomas, I *Sent.* d. 3 q. 1 art. 4: "Respondeo dicendum, quod per naturalem rationem non potest perveniri in cognitionem trinitatis personarum; et ideo philosophi nihil de hoc sciverunt, nisi forte per revelationem vel auditum ab aliis." See also Giles of Rome, I *Sent.* d. 3 pars 1 princ. 1 q. 4 ad 3, Venice 1521, fol. 22v: "...hoc [trinitatem] non habuerunt ex naturali ratione [philosophi], sed per revelationem, vel ex his quae in scripturis legerunt, vel ab aliis audierunt,..."

[4] E.g., Vat. Lat. 6325, fol. 36r: "Non tamen mirum esse permultos fuisse quibus id [ratione cognosci divinas personas] verum visum non sit, nam cum post Augustinum alii ferme omnes qui divina aggressi sunt, cum solum Aristotelem inter philosophos viderint, facile adducti sunt ut quod ab Aristotele tractatum non est tractari id a nemine posse crederent." See also *ibid.*, fols 32v-33v, 35r, 83r, and 179r: "At virtus [divinae amicitiae] non ut Aristoteles existimat ex humana surgi origine sed,...ex Deo proficiscitur."

truths found in the oracles.[1] These are such constantly recurring themes in Giles's writings that they must be borne in mind when analyzing the statements concerning reason's power to know the Trinity. Giles clearly indicates, moreover, that Plato's knowledge of the Trinity was not equivalent in accuracy and certitude to that which the Gospels provide.[2]

In the present instance Giles implements his theory of illumination by means of a principle developed in scholastic theology: to the person who does what in him lies God does not deny His divine light.[3] The formula, "*Facientibus quod in se est Deus non denegat gratiam suam,*" has a long history.[4] It originally and principally was used to describe the

---

[1] See, e.g., Vat. Lat. 6325, fol. 21r: "...divinorum arcanorum intelligentia in humanas animas nonnisi ab illustrante proficisci Deo." See also *ibid.*, fols. 3r, 5r, 36v, 111v-112r, 132r, 198r, 212v, and Massa, *Fondamenti metafisici e testi inediti*, pp. 78-79, 104, etc. As we shall see further on, Giles maintains that Plato had some access to the genuine religious tradition which could be traced back to Noah, and he admits this could have acted as a catalyst to his "reason," Vat. Lat. 6325, fol. 36v.

[2] Vat. Lat. 6325, fol. 165v: "Quare tres illas enumerat [Plato] personas, quas sacra nostra oracula docuere, quamquam, ut saepe diximus protestatique sumus, citra omnem errorem sola evangelia eam sapientiam tradidisse intelligamus,..." See also *ibid.*, fol. 18v, and 20r: "Plato cum de diis et divinis dissereret [docet]... difficile esse res divinas demonstrare, quasi innuat probabiles quidem argumentationes haberi posse, necessarias haberi non posse." See also *ibid.*, fol. 35v.

[3] Vat. Lat. 6325, fol. 36v: "Quod etiam si sine Deo sciri divina non possunt, ut sine sole aut sine luce colores, ut Platoni placet, ideo tamen natura cognosci dicimus, quod ea homini a natura potestas data est, ut si ad divina investiganda nitatur agatque quidquid in se est, studio ac vitae cognatione, ut in epistola docuit Plato, divinum illi lumen deesse non potest, ut hominis generatio naturae tribuitur quamquam a Deo anima creatur." See also *ibid.*, fol. 21r.

[4] For the origin of the formula and its development up through the twelfth century, see Artur Michael Landgraf, *Dogmengeschichte der Frühscholastik*, vol. I.1, Regensburg 1952, pp. 249-264. In Saint Thomas there is a decided change in interpretation between his early commentary on Lombard and the *Summa theologica*, e.g., II *Sent.* d. 28 q. 1 art. 4: "Et ideo aliis consentiendo dicimus quod ad gratiam gratum facientem habendam ex solo libero arbitrio se homo potest praeparare, faciendo enim quod in se est gratiam a Deo consequitur. Hoc autem solum in nobis est quod in potestate liberi arbitrii constitutum est." *S.T.* I-II q. 109 art. 6 ad 2: "Ad secundum dicendum, quod nihil homo potest facere nisi a Deo moveatur, secundum illud Joan. 15.5, Sine me nihil potestis facere. Et ideo cum dicitur homo facere quod in se est dicitur hoc esse in potestate hominis secundum quod est motus a Deo." See also *ibid.*, I-II q. 112 arts. 2 and 3. Giles of Rome interprets the formula in a way similar to Thomas's mature opinion, "In epist. ad Romanos," *Primus tomus operum D. Aegidii Romani*, Rome 1555, fol. 76v: "Dicendum quod nos si nobis ipsi relinquamur semper declinamus ad illecebra et conformamur saecularibus rebus, propter quod adgeneratur in nobis forma et habitus saecularis concupiscentiae. Sed tamen per auxilium divinum possumus haec vitare. Verum quia Deus quantum est de se semper est paratus, ideo dicitur hoc esse in potestate nostra, quia utinam ita essemus parati facere quod in nobis est, sicut Deus paratus

movements of divine grace without special application to the problem of faith and belief, but by Giles's day it had long since explicitly been extended to that area and encapsulated an idea particularly operative among the Nominalist theologians.[1] It is significant that Giles of Viterbo, to help establish a harmony between the pagan past and Christian dogma, one of the characteristic aims of his Renaissance humanism, should call upon the "*Facientibus*" formula, one of the more characteristic principles adopted by the Nominalist school of scholasticism. Late scholasticism and humanism, so commonly thought of as without bond or affinity for one another, shared a desire to endow human nature with as great a dignity as they felt Christian faith allowed. The Scotist expression, "*dignificare naturam*," so aptly singled out by Paul Vignaux to describe the world of medieval scholasticism, applies equally well to certain aspects of Giles's Renaissance culture.[2]

Through the principle which the "*Facientibus*" formula enunciates some reconciliation is possible between the claims Giles makes for nature or reason and his insistence that knowledge of the divine is above man's powers. Man can do what in him lies, and God responds by illuminating the mind and by revealing Himself, either through the oracles or otherwise. Giles is thus able to save the transcendence of mystery, while making man's access to it somehow dependent upon human effort. At the same time he implicitly establishes a direct relationship between virtue and religious knowledge.

Even the principle "*Facientibus*" must be viewed in the total context of Giles's thought, lest we attribute to him a position which would give man an autonomous control over the flow of God's gifts. In this

---

est facere quod in se est." For the formula in Gabriel Biel (ca. 1410-1495), see Heiko A. Oberman, *The Harvest of Medieval Theology*, Cambridge, Mass. 1963, esp. pp. 129-145. During the Reformation it was a subject of polemic, e.g., *WA*, vol. I, p. 354.

[1] See, e.g., Saint Thomas, II *Sent.* d. 28 q. 1 art. 4 ad 4: "Ad quartum dicendum, quod etiam ad fidem habendam aliquis se praeparare potest per id quod in naturali ratione est; unde dicitur, quod si aliquis in barbaris natus nationibus quod in se est faciat Deus sibi revelabit illud quod est necessarium ad salutem, vel inspirando vel doctorem mittendo." Oberman quotes Holcot's (?-1349) formulation, "'Facientibus' and Holcot," p. 323n: "Nam si homo facit quod in se est satis informabitur de illis quae sunt necessaria ad salutem suam."

[2] Paul Vignaux, *Philosophy in the Middle Ages*, trans. E.C. Hall, New York 1959, p. 213: "If, not too bewildered, a modern man seeks to find something characteristic of the mental world of the Middle Ages, a stirring of living humanity, he finds at the center, as a function of this preoccupation with the transcendent and supernatural, a humanism embracing a naturalism that can be expressed by the Scotist formula *dignificare naturam*."

total context the first initiative in any good human action is always God's. Giles does not want to deny that man has a certain area of freedom in which he can refuse or accept the divine grace.[1] He repeatedly affirms, however, that God's action is always prior and prevenient, and he explicitly rejects Pelagianism.[2] It would seem, consequently, that even Plato the philosopher when he does what in him lies is not acting completely independently and that the nature in question is conceived as nature somehow under the influence of grace.[3] Unless this is the case the passages in the *Sentence* commentary on man's knowledge of the Trinity are curiously isolated from principles operative in the rest of the work and in Giles's other writings.

In spite of the claims Giles makes for reason, even for reason specially illuminated with divine light, he is not about to deny the necessity of revelation in the technical sense of a divine utterance received by man from without. He grants that some religious truths may be available to reason, but not all are, completely and correctly, and even those which are thus available require confirmation by the oracles. The fulness and perfection of truth is had only through revelation. Particularly in his later writings he for various reasons grows more insistent upon the necessity of the oracles, but even in the pages of the "Sententiae" the matter is unambiguous.[4]

---

[1] Massa, *Fondamenti metafisici e testi inediti*, p. 58: "...nec Deus divinis nos muneribus non afficiet nisi illis suscipiendis et annuamus et quantum in nobis est parati simus; licet enim omnia ab eo sint, sine nobis tamen omnino esse non possunt." See *ibid.*, p. 98, and Vat. Lat. 6325, fol. 201r: "...solis nostri lumine vel uti excolendo vel abuti negligendo possimus." See also *Scechina*, vol. II, pp. 91-92, 131, 189.

[2] See, e.g., Vat. Lat. 6325, fol. 181v: "...gratia in hominis potestate non est." *Ibid.*, fol. 174v: "...quidquid itaque spei, quidquid salutis, quidquid recti in hominibus esse potest, ex munere deorum esse voluit [Plato]." Also *ibid.*, fols. 177v-181v, 209r, and 210v: "...dilectus, inquit, meus mihi, et ego illi [S. of S. 2.16]. Incipit a sponso, qui causa est bonorum omnium, et amoris et gratiae." See also Massa, *Fondamenti metafisici e testi inediti*, p. 94, and Ang. Lat. 502, fol. 61r. On the prevenient nature of God's gifts see *Scechina*, vol. II, pp. 203-204, 219. For explicit anti-Pelagian statements, see Vat. Lat. 6325, fols. 200r and 202r: "...nec quidquam nobiscum Pelagius."

[3] See Vat. Lat. 6325, fol. 200r: "...quo loco Plato docet id quod postea Paulus, non esse volentis hominis sed Dei quidquid boni fit, idque omne non facultati humanae sed divinae dandum voluntati." Also *ibid.*, fols. 113r, and 147r: "Cognosci siquidem a mentibus ea natura possunt quae in rerum natura sita sunt. Divina, sicut ostendimus, intelligi omnino natura duce non possunt." See also Massa, *Fondamenti metafisici e testi inediti*, pp. 57-58: "Impuri itaque facti divinis inepti sumus...Purgatio vero duplex est, ignorationis et morbi,...prior in cognitione, posterior in affectu. Utraque Deum curatorem desiderat,..."

[4] Vat. Lat. 6325, fols. 2r, 12r, 18v, 20r-21r, 36v, and esp. 165v; Ang. Lat. 502,

What is to be said, then, about those men who fall outside the direct line of transmission of the Judeo-Christian revelation? Giles eagerly appropriates a common medieval belief that there was an ancient gentile tradition which had not been completely deprived of that revelation. It was the Platonic Academy of Florence which in the Renaissance particularly promoted the idea of such a tradition, believing that it was discoverable in writings supposedly as ancient as those of Hermes Trismegistus, Zoroaster and Orpheus—the "*prisci theologi*"—and that it could be found to a noteworthy degree in Pythagoras, upon whom Plato was especially dependent.[1] By adopting this idea Giles was able simultaneously to sustain the necessity of revelation and also to redeem for himself much that he found in pagan literature and philosophy.

The gentiles originally shared with the Hebrews a common primitive revelation which could be traced back to Noah, and after the Deluge there was enough intercourse between the peoples to account for a certain tapping by alert and pious gentile authors even of the patriarchal and prophetic tradition. Giles rejects the idea that Plato read Moses in Egypt on the grounds that the Pentateuch had not yet been translated into Greek.[2] But he does see Egypt as a center for the dif-

fols. 105r-v. 238r; *Scechina*, vol. II, p. 83, etc. See Delio Cantimori, *Eretici italiani del Cinquecento*, Florence 1939, pp. 5-7, for a discussion of the clash between a religious "rationalism" and "fideism" in the humanists between the time of Ficino and the Fifth Lateran Council.

[1] See, e.g., Paul Oskar Kristeller, "The Platonic Academy of Florence," *Renaissance News* 14(1961), pp. 147-159, esp. 156; Frances A. Yates, *Giordano Bruno and the Hermetic Tradition*, London 1964, pp. 1-19, and G. Anichini, *L'Umanesimo e il problema della salvezza in Marsilio Ficino*, Milano 1937, pp. 68-77; Karl H. Dannenfeldt, "The Pseudo-Zoroastrian Oracles in the Renaissance," *Studies in the Renaissance* 4(1957), pp. 7-30. It was Georgius Gemistus Pletho (1355-1450) who imparted to Ficino the conception of an old tradition of pagan theology which would reach back to Zoroaster, Trismegistus and Orpheus. See Paul Oskar Kristeller, "The Scholastic Background of Marsilio Ficino, *Traditio* 2(1944), p. 258. For Giles's interest in Pletho and Zoroaster, see Naples II. F. 7, fols. 191v-207r, a translation made for Giles in 1526 of a work of Pletho's entitled by the translator, "In oracula sive logia." The translator was the Augustinian friar Niccolò Scutelli, also known as Nicolaus Tridentinus (?-1542). For Ficino's order of transmission of this theology, see "Theologia Platonica, lib. XVII," *Opera*, vol. I, p. 386.

[2] Vat. Lat. 6325, fol. 36v. Giles's marginalia in his copy of Bessarion's *In calumniatorem Platonis*, Venice 1503, Biblioteca Casanatense, Rome, Incun. 1261, fols. 32r and 43v, show he was aware Bessarion accepted the idea of Plato borrowing from Moses, and he seems to admit at least the possibility in Ang. Lat. 502, fol. 253r. The idea that the Greeks borrowed from the sacred authors of the Old Testament goes back to Philo, according to V. F. Hopper, *Medieval Number Symbolism*, New York 1938, p. 47. See, e.g., Eusebius, *De evang. praep.*, lib. X. 2. Plato's borrowing from Moses was proposed by Justin Martyr, I *Apol.* 44, and was an

fusion of revealed truth,[1] and he on at least one occasion states that it was there that Pythagoras came into contact with the Hebrew religious tradition.[2]

More interesting is the role Giles assigns the Etruscans. Throughout the late fifteenth century there was a growing awareness in central Italy of Etruscan civilization, and Giles, along with his compatriot, Annio da Viterbo (Giovanni Nanni, 1432-1502), became one of the most enthusiastic exponents of their importance in history.[3] In the Middle Ages the euhemeristic tradition of regarding the gods of Greek and Roman mythology as mortal men who had falsely been worshipped as divinities combined with a curious bit of erroneous etymology to identify Janus with Noah or a son of Noah.[4] A link between the Etruscans and figures of the Old Testament had thus been early estab-

idea whose possibility was widely accepted during the Middle Ages, e.g., Eusebius, *De evang. praep.*, lib. IX. 3; Saint Thomas, I *Sent.* d.3 q.1 art.4 ad 1; Giles of Rome, I *Sent.* d.3 pars 1 princ.1 q.4 ad 3, Venice 1521, fol. 22v. Augustine substitutes Jeremiah for Moses, but like Giles of Viterbo eventually comes to the conclusion that the chronology does not fit, *De civ. Dei*, lib. VIII.11.

[1] Ang. Lat. 502, fols. 104r, 162r, 181r, 283r, and *Scechina*, e.g., vol. I, p. 113; vol. II, p. 130. See Joannes Reuchlin, *De arte cabalistica*, Hagenau 1517, p. 199. On Renaissance interest in things Egyptian, see Karl H. Dannenfeldt, "Egypt and Egyptian Antiquities in the Renaissance," *Studies in the Renaissance* 6(1959), pp. 7-27.

[2] Évora CXVI/1-30, fol. 27r, and also Ang. Lat. 502, fol. 291r. See also Hopper, *Medieval Number Symbolism*, p. 47, and Walker, "Orpheus the Theologian," pp. 104-105, 119-120.

[3] On the "Etruscan Revival," see Chastel, *Art et Humanisme*, pp. 63-71. On Annio da Viterbo, see E. N. Tigerstedt, "Ioannes Annius and *Graecia Mendax*," *Classical, Medieval and Renaissance Studies in Honor of Berthold Louis Ullman*, ed. Charles Henderson, Jr., vol. II, Rome 1964, pp. 293-310; R. Weiss, "Traccia per una biografia di Annio da Viterbo," *Italia medioevale e umanistica* 5(1962), pp. 425-441, and by the same author, "An Unknown Epigraphic Tract by Annius of Viterbo," *Italian Studies Presented to E. R. Vincent*, Cambridge 1962, pp. 101-120. See also Secret, "Egidio et quelques-uns de ses contemporains," pp. 371-377. As Weiss points out, "Traccia di Annio da Viterbo," p. 437, Giles of Viterbo owned a copy of the Rome, 1498, edition of Annio's *Antiquitates*. This incunabulum has extensive marginal notations by Giles and is now to be found in the Vatican Library, Vat. Inc. II. 274; it is listed under no. 2015 in vol. II of the *Gesamtkatalog der Wiegendrucke*, Leipzig 1926. A specific instance of Giles's dependence upon Annio would be his acceptance as genuine of Annio's forgery of the "Decretum Desiderii Regis Italiae." See Ang. Lat. 502, fols. 46v-47r, 149v. On the "Decretum," see Weiss, "Epigraphic Tract."

[4] See Arturo Graf, *Roma nella memoria e nelle immaginazioni del medio evo*, Turin 1915, pp. 63-70, and H. J. Erasmus, *The Origins of Rome in Historiography from Petrarch to Perizonius*, Assen 1962, pp. 40-44. See Vat. Lat. 6325, fol. 144v, and Ang. Lat. 502, fols. 131r-v, 277r. Annio da Viterbo identifies Janus and Noah, *Berosi sacerdotis Chaldaici antiquitatum libri quinque*, Wittenberg 1659, fols. 2r, 13v, 14v, 25r, etc.

lished, and the ground had been prepared for further elaborations of such a relationship.

Giles, influenced by the writings of Annio, tells us that after the Deluge Noah's religious teaching was carried into Etruria. This common origin explains the similarity in customs, language and religious doctrines between the Arameans and the Etruscans.[1] The Etruscans recognized the value of the message entrusted to them. They safeguarded it and incorporated it into every phase of their life and activity, surpassing in this endeavor even the Egyptians, to whom also Noah's teaching was transmitted. Divine providence had a special regard for the Etruscans, due to the exalted religious destiny of Rome, and Giles sees a close parallel between their history and that of the Hebrews.[2] Eventually the Etruscan religious tradition fed into Greek culture through Dardanus and Pythagoras, and thence to Plato.[3] Giles believed, moreover, that the Etruscans possessed knowledge of the cabala.[4]

It was in Virgil that the various gentile traditions of religious truth especially converged. Virgil put Plato's thought into Latin verse, and he was expertly informed about the religious learning of the Etruscans.[5] He was a student, moreover, of the message of the sibyls, whose teaching was drawn from the prophets.[6] For those who knew how to read him Virgil was a source of deep and genuine spiritual enlightenment, a prophet for the gentiles.

In spite of the distinguished ancestry Giles claims for much of pagan literature he was not an uncritical student of it, and he realized that many things in it could not be reconciled with Christianity. If this literature was the heir to authentic revelation, how explain the in-

---

[1] Évora CXVI/1-30, fol. 12v; Vat. Lat. 6325, fols. 144v-146r. See also, e.g., Ang. Lat. 502, fols. 2v, 4r, 5v-6v, 11r, 24r-v, 70v, 100r, 104r, 114v, and 91r: "Nos saepe Aramaeos Tuscos esse diximus, ..." *Ibid.*, fol. 283v: "Ea enim gente e Syria profecta est, ut lingua, litterae, monumenta confirmant." See also *Scechina*, vol. I, pp. 108, 185.

[2] Ang. Lat. 502, fols. 11r, 17r, 33v-34r, and Vat. Lat. 6325, fols. 89r, 144v-145r.

[3] Ang. Lat. 502, fols. 3r, 11r, 49r, 93r, 162r-v.

[4] Ang. Lat. 502, fols. 80v and 270v; and *Scechina*, vol. I, p. 185: "... prius in Italia nostra arcana apud Etruscos innotuisse constat." See Annio da Viterbo, *Berosi libri*, fol. 213v.

[5] E.g., Vat. Lat. 6325, fols. 145r, 163v, and Ang. Lat. 502, fol. 282v.

[6] Ang. Lat. 502, fols. 6v, 14v, 30r, 50r-v, 282v. For Postel's interest in Virgil and the sibyls, see Bouwsma, *Concordia Mundi*, pp. 62, 207-208. The sibylline tradition among Christians is ancient and widespread, e.g., Justin Martyr, I *Apol.* 44; Augustine, *De civ. Dei*, lib. XVIII. 23; Saint Thomas, *S.T.* II-II q.2 art.7 ad 3, and *De veritate* q.14 art.11 ad 5; Ficino, "De Christiana religione," *Opera*, vol. I, pp. 26-27; Savonarola, *Triumphus crucis*, ed. Mario Ferrara, Rome 1961, p. 101.

stances of marked deviation from it? Giles's answer is clear: the Greeks, as well as others, corrupted what they had received. First of all, they boldly translated into Greek the prayers and oracles given them in the sacred language of God. The seriousness of this charge will be seen in Chapter Three. Secondly, they applied prophecies meant for Christ and the Church to their own heroes and fatherland. Furthermore, God would no longer listen to them because they had translated the messages of the sacred language into their own. Thus revelation was distorted and religion turned into superstition, for the Greeks had not observed that most solemn religious obligation of preserving intact the divine traditions.[1] The ancients had, therefore, swerved from orthodoxy, and this was for Giles an intolerable perversion. The one unshakable norm for any philosophy or doctrine was always that it be conformed to the oracles, i.e., to the prophets and the Gospel.[2]

When an author from pagan antiquity is placed side by side with the canonical Scripture he is at times treated with surprising reserve. Even Virgil is not spared, and as something of a concession to human weakness Giles allows him to be read by those who prefer cultivated speech to the simple language of the prophets, but only on condition that with Virgil in one hand they hold the sacred writers, his authentic interpreters, in the other.[3] Although Giles does not hesitate to call the pagan poets "prophets," towards the end of his life he seems to suggest that he attributes something less than full meaning to this usage.[4] Giles is straightforward: it is not in Pythagoras or Plato or

---

[1] Évora CXVI/1-30, fols. 19v, 23r, 71r-v; Ang. Lat. 502, fols. 11v, 298v, 306r-v, and *Scechina*, vol. I, pp. 75, 108, 113; vol. II, p. 21. That the gentiles corrupted or misunderstood what they had received was a common theme, e.g., Eusebius, *De evang. praep.*, lib. XI. 14; Annio da Viterbo, *Berosi libri*, fols. 4v-5v; Ficino, "In epist. ad Romanos," *Opera*, vol. I, pp. 441-442, and "In Asclepium," *Opera*, vol. II, pp. 1859, 1867, 1870.

[2] Ang. Lat. 502, fols. 92v, 277v, and 164r: "Ex hoc itaque philosophiae praecepto veritatem e Dei manifestatione quaerendam statuente, illam dicendam esse philosophiam constat quae sacris prophetarum et evangeliorum, hoc est Dei oraculis, accedens, ..." See also *Scechina*, vol. I, p. 199. On a similar attitude in another humanist, see Paul Oskar Kristeller, "Sebastiano Salvini, a Florentine Humanist and Theologian, and a Member of Marsilio Ficino's Platonic Academy," *Didascaliae: Studies in Honor of Anselm M. Albareda*, ed. Sesto Prete, New York 1961, pp. 207-243. Giles rejects, for instance, the transmigration of souls, Ang. Lat. 502, fol. 75v. On this question in Ficino, see "Appendix in Timaeum," *Opera*, vol. II, p. 1484.

[3] Ang. Lat. 502, fols. 25r-v, 30r, and 170(a)r: "Testis est David vates, ... ubi sibyllarum et Maronis sententiae interpretatio est."

[4] *Scechina*, vol. I, p. 80. See also *ibid.*, p. 109. For Seripando's reservations, see Jedin, *Seripando*, vol. I, pp. 76, 81.

Socrates, nor even in Abraham or Moses, that he ultimately places his hope, but in Christ and Christ's revelation.[1]

Giles's zeal for the orthodoxy of this revelation is the second of his two presuppositions which, because of its fundamental importance, must be examined in some detail. In his "Historia XX saeculorum" he again and again defines for Leo X the pope's principal task as the preservation intact of the orthodox faith, especially in the face of the corruptions of the Peripatetics.[2] In his official capacity as prior general Giles does his best to insure that not the slightest suggestion of heterodoxy be attached to the Augustinian order.[3] For those who knowingly hold heretical doctrine he displays an intransigeance whose rigor is surprising, especially if they have tried to spread their false teaching. Of some interest is the graduated scale of culpability which Giles proposes, the most guilty being not those who believe and teach heresy but those who also spread it by committing it to writing.[4]

The practical norms Giles advances for deciding upon a doctrine's orthodoxy are as clear as they are unexceptional. The doctrine must agree with the faith of the "Roman or Vatican Church," a phrase to which Giles more than once recurs.[5] He is convinced that, in spite of corruptions of various sorts in the Church's long history, it never has been and never will be corrupt in its essential dogma, and he has no use for Berengar's 's proposition that the true doctrine of the Eucharist was lost in the course of centuries.[6] Pope and council have the duty in the face of heresy to declare the Church's faith, and their decision is authentic and final. As was often true among the scholastic authors, Giles does not consider the possibility that in its solemn teaching the

[1] Ang. Lat. 502, fol. 28v, Giles makes the sentiment his own: "... non in Pythagora, non in Platone, non in Socrate, non ullo aliorum philosophorum, quos minutos appellavit antiquitas, non denique in sanctorum ullo virorum, non in Abraham, non in Mose, sed in nato Deo spero." Also *ibid.*, fols. 27r, 103v, and Vat. Lat. 6325, fol. 20v: "... ideo tantum illi [Christo] credendum esse, ab illoque divinorum cognitionem requirendam." See also *Scechina*, vol. I, p. 109.

[2] Ang. Lat. 502, fols. 40v, 124v, 164v, 166r.

[3] Siena G.X.26, pp. 108-110, undated letter to the vicar of a Spanish observant congregation.

[4] Ang. Lat. 502, fols. 243r, and 162v, 183v-184v; "Oratio post 3am sessionem," p. 523.

[5] Vat. Lat. 6325, fol. 167v, and Ang. Lat. 502, fols. 25v, 40v, 156v, and esp. 273v.

[6] Ang. Lat. 502, fols. 93r, 156v, 273v, and, e.g., 51v: "... temeraria, avara, ambitiosa, sed quomodo sine ruga? Fides et decreta sine ruga, ..." In the total context of his thought the stain of error and heresy he attributes to the Church in the *Scechina*, vol. I, pp. 98-99, does not mean he believes it had lost its doctrinal prerogatives.

Church might not be in accord with the Gospels, whence comes its doctrine.[1] Though Giles has been described as a forerunner of Italian Evangelism, he surely did not share with that movement an indifference towards Church and dogma which is sometimes attributed to it.[2]

Judged against the objective norms which he himself enunciated, Giles's orthodoxy, in the technical sense of not pertinaciously holding a doctrine known to contradict the Church's solemn teaching, is beyond question.[3] His life and his writings testify to his deep desire to conform to the doctrines of the Roman or Vatican Church, and we have no evidence to suggest that he ever thought he had deviated from those doctrines. In particular we might point out that he was vigorous in his explicit denunciation of Arianism and never consciously sustained any sort of subordinationism, a doctrine which Neoplatonism was accused of fostering and which surely could be a danger with the cabala.[4]

Was Giles, nevertheless, at least an unconscious promoter of re-

---

[1] Vat. Lat. 6325, fols. 22v, 160r, 166v, and Ang. Lat. 502, fols. 40v, 105r-v, 185v, 273v.

[2] See Eva-Marie Jung, "On the Nature of Evangelism in Sixteenth-Century Italy," *Journal of the History of Ideas* 14(1953), pp. 511-527. For Giles as a precursor of Evangelism, see George H. Williams, *The Radical Reformation*, Philadelphia 1962, p. 18. Monnerjahn's final judgment on Pico, *Giovanni Pico della Mirandola*, p. 194, is that he was "ein a-kirchlicher Mensch," i.e., "a-dogmatisch und a-sakramental."

[3] See Ang. Lat. 502, fol. 200v, and Vat. Lat. 6325, fols. 86r, 153v. See also canon 1325 of the present code of canon law, as well as Clement VII's letter to Giles, Ossinger, *Bibliotheca Augustiniana*, pp. 191-193.

[4] E.g., Vat. Lat. 6325, fols. 9v-10r, 101r, 106r, 166v, and Ang. Lat. 502, fol. 117v. See *Scechina*, vol. I, p. 70: "... et quamquam illic in illa ineffabili unitate nihil sit posterius, nihil prius, inferius, superius, majus minusque omnino nihil, quod nunc in omni volumus hac sapientia ut immotum, inconcussum, inexpugnabile fundamentum esse jactum; plures tamen esse virtutes, perfectiones, vires, lumina atque potestates, ac veluti, sicut humana concipere potest mens, partem animarum comprendit praedestinatio, omnes praescientia, ..." On subordinationism and Renaissance Neoplatonism, see Cantimori, "Anabattesimo e Neoplatonismo," pp. 543-544, 553, and also Williams, *Radical Reformation*, p. 25. For Giles's attempt to reconcile the Second Person of the Trinity with cabalistic categories, see *Scechina*, vol. I, e.g., pp. 72, 96, 157, etc. Of interest in this regard, is the use he makes of the principle "omnia in omnibus," *Scechina*, vol. I, p. 213, and Ang. Lat. 502, fol. 202r-v. For Renaissance use and understanding of this principle, see Wind, *Pagan Mysteries*, pp. 42-44, 158-164. On general charges of heresy and religious error against the Renaissance Platonists, see Vasoli, "Temi e fonti," p. 239, and Paul Oskar Kristeller, "Francesco da Diacceto and Florentine Platonism in the Sixteenth Century," *Miscellanea Giovanni Mercati*, vol. IV, *StT* vol. CXXIV, Città del Vaticano 1946, esp. pp. 289-290. In Jedin's judgment Neoplatonism did not adversely affect Seripando's orthodoxy, *Seripando*, vol. I, p. 65.

ligious syncretism, tending to reduce all religious traditions to one indistinguishable mass in which Christian dogma might hold a primacy of honor but not in any sense be normative for the whole?[1] From what has already been said it should be clear that, although such a danger might lurk in his thought, it could hardly be fully actualized due to the regulating function he gave to Christian doctrine. Giles read Plato, the gentile theologians and even the cabala through the corrective lenses of that doctrine, and he always interpreted these authors in a manner to make them subserve his Christian beliefs. We cannot here enter into a discussion of whether or not his formulation of particular doctrines was always untainted by contact with these non-Christian sources. It would be misleading, however, to intimate that the effort at reconciliation produced no tension in Giles's thought. In most cases these sources represented a symbolic style of thinking radically opposed to the conceptual thinking which had produced the dogmatic formulations. The problem would be especially acute for the cabala, with its rich and varied symbolism. Even aside from the question of cabalistic metaphysics, Giles could not always have found it easy to assure doctrine's ultimate control while releasing it into the hands of metaphor and symbol, from which at an earlier stage of history it had so laboriously been extracted. The technical terminology of Christian theology had to be sturdy indeed to stand up under the pressure which would thus come to bear on it.[2] The very fact that the Godhead would be spoken of principally in terms of the number ten instead of three gives some indication of the magnitude of the task of reconciliation Giles had to undertake.

On various occasions Giles spells out for us what he considers to be the basic content of orthodoxy. In the opening oration for the Fifth Lateran Council he specifies the three mysteries of the divine unity, the Trinity and the Incarnation as fundamental beliefs of the Church, each attacked at one time or another by heretics and then defined by a council.[3] His longer enumerations of specific dogmas can be reduced roughly to the articles of the Apostles' Creed.[4] Throughout his writings, however, the doctrine which received particularly insistent attention was that of divine providence. Giles champions this doctrine with

[1] On this question in general, see Wind, *Pagan Mysteries*, pp. 26-28, 49, etc.

[2] For a treatment of this question, see Gershom G. Scholem, *On the Kabbalah and Its Symbolism*, trans. Ralph Manheim, London 1965, esp. pp. 96-97.

[3] Mansi, vol. XXXII, cols. 670-671. For a different listing of four fundamental beliefs, see Ang. Lat. 502, fol. 97r-v.

[4] Ang. Lat. 502, fol. 30r, and Évora CXVI/1-30, fols. 47r-51v.

unaccustomed vigor. His emphasis, explained in part by the fact that he thought the doctrine was being undermined by the false philosophers of his day, was due more basically to its supplying the indispensable assumption for the whole of his theological effort, as will become especially clear in Chapters Three and Four. Giles does not treat in any great detail the problems which were discussed by his scholastic and humanist contemporaries on the relationship of providence, fate and free will. He firmly believed that nothing happened by chance, that fate was best understood as simply another word for providence, and that man acted freely under God's decrees. He attempted no theoretical reconciliation of these three questions, devoting his energies instead to spelling out the practical implications of the doctrine of providence, especially in relation to his own scriptural hermeneutics and the divinely ordained course of Christian history.[1]

Before closing our discussion of the two controlling presuppositions of Giles's thought we must give some consideration to several related questions. The first of these has already been mentioned: a direct relationship between virtue and religious knowledge. Knowledge of religious truths is from above, from God's illumination of the souls of those who sincerely strive to know Him. From this framing of the problem it is easy to draw the conclusion that heterodoxy is the result of moral delinquency, of more or less culpable refusal to search for the truth or to accept it when presented. This is the conclusion Giles in effect does draw. He almost invariably links every deviation from orthodoxy with the desire for personal glory through the introduction of doctrinal novelty. He maintains at the same time that wealth also is often a factor in such downfalls, providing an atmosphere of laxity which of itself tends to foster bad doctrine.[2]

The most surprising aspect of Giles's thought on orthodox doctrine, however, is not the direct relationship he postulates between morality and orthodoxy, which long before his day was a tired commonplace in theological controversy, but rather his holding a

---

[1] Ang. Lat. 502, fols. 2r, 120r, 138v, 223v: "... et quamquam libere nos contingenterque agimus, principis tamen decreta constantia immotaque esse necesse est, ..." Vat. Lat. 6325, fols. 180r-181v, contains a brief explicit statement on the relationship of predestination and grace. See also "Oratio post 3am sessionem," p. 520, and *Scechina*, vol. I, pp. 73-74, and esp. 92. See also Kristeller, "Sebastiano Salvini," pp. 230-231, and "Francesco da Diacceto," p. 281.

[2] For personal glory, see Vat. Lat. 6325, fol. 22v; Ang. Lat. 502, fols. 92r, 95r, 138v, and Mansi, vol. XXXII, col. 671: "... qui gloriae cupiditate de rerum novarum studio illecti, ..." On wealth, see Ang. Lat. 502, fol. 142r.

progressive increase or expansion in doctrine after the death of Christ and the Apostles. His severe strictures against those who would introduce novelty or change hardly prepare us for what today would be called a statement on development of doctrine. The question was not entirely new and had been touched upon in a modest way by theologians and religious writers of the Middle Ages and Renaissance. Giles's text, nevertheless, has some features which make it especially interesting.[1]

The text occurs in the *Scechina*.[2] In the course of this lengthy apology for the cabalistic interpretation of Scripture Giles tries to ward off the objection that he is introducing something new or something that breaks with previous teaching. It is in this context that the development text must be understood. Building upon the scriptural basis of the Paraclete's teaching mission (Jn. 14.26), Giles makes the point that Christ's instruction was too rich and too concise to be grasped at once and in full, and that a gradual increase in understanding had to take place down through the ages. The cabala will be the great culmination of this process for his own age, in which Scripture will be opened to a depth never before dreamed possible.

What is noteworthy in the text is that Giles indicates three distinct moments of enlightenment: (1) the lifetime of Christ, (2) the Pentecostal experience of the Apostles, (3) the ecclesiastical councils or assemblies. By implication these three moments are put on a par, although from certain other passages we see that Giles assigns a fundamental importance to the first two and that the third moment is to be understood as some increase in knowledge acquired through pious searching of the text of Scripture.[3] In any case, the very paralleling of

---

[1] I take up this question in my article, "Giles and Development," and make specific comparisons of Giles's text with statements of Erasmus, Petrus Galatinus (ca. 1460-1540), Anselm of Havelberg (?-1158) and certain scholastics.

[2] *Scechina*, vol. I, p. 89: "*Ille vos docebit omnia quae dixero vobis*, quo dicere voluit [Christus], quae nunc ego brevi et per compendia, ille [Spiritus] abundantius cum apostolos afflabit, cum per decem post saecula per patrum senatus, per conventus, per concilia magis magisque in dies manifestabit. Comparant lucem Messiae surgenti ad orientem aurorae, quae non statim tenebras aut abigit aut fugat sed ex obscuris tenebris paulatim ascendit, ita non repente sed tempore, non statim sed per gradus, non subito sed morae spatio lucem terris affert. Haud secus Messiae lumen ante crucem dum cum mortalibus habitavit multa edocuit in Judaea, plura plenis apostolis in orbe universo, alia primorum decretis conciliorum, alia sequentium, atque ita nullum fuit saeculum quo non aliquid veritatis commonstraverit."

[3] *Scechina*, vol. I, p. 110: "Dices [Charles V], nonne in evangelio monstrata sunt omnia? Sunt quidem monstrata omnia quae ad summum assequendum bonum

Christ's teaching, Pentecost and post-apostolic development gives this last a dignity and importance which is considerable. The post-apostolic increase, moreover, is mediated through the institutional Church, viz. through the councils, and is not the function of charismatic teachers or visionaries. It is gradual, stretching across all the ages of Church history, and is accomplished without any sudden leap into a new age in which previous doctrines and institutions are transcended as merely provisional. We would have to search far to find a statement quite like this among the medieval theologians or even Giles's contemporaries.

One final question remains before we turn our attention to the individual authors and traditions which helped structure the thought of Giles of Viterbo. To what extent and in what way does his theology partake of the esoteric and aristocratic tendencies ascribed to Ficino, Pico and their disciples?[1] The fact is that from the early days of the "Sententiae" to the *Scechina* of his old age he espoused the principle that there was an inner core of religious wisdom not open to all, a sort of *disciplina arcani* which for one reason or another not everyone could avail himself of. As we move on we shall catch glimpses of the historical roots of such a belief in the authors Giles read. Right now we can briefly present the reasons he gives for the existence of such truth, hidden under the "poetic veil."

Truths are hidden lest they be exposed to ridicule by unbelievers.[2] Calling upon the metaphors and parables used in the Gospels, Giles justifies the concept of a higher truth not meant for all by the Gospel prohibition of giving holy things to dogs.[3] Underlying this prohibition, Giles maintains, is the danger of the ordinary simple believer being confused and actually being drawn away from more fundamental truths by the sophisticated knowledge open to the specially

pertinebant. At sacra docuerunt evangelia multa superesse quae haud quaquam illi ferre tunc possent, ac proinde scrutandas jubent scripturas." See also *ibid.*, vol. I, pp. 67, 89, and vol. II, p. 22.

[1] See Pico, "Commento alla canzone d'amore," in *De hominis dignitate, Heptaplus, De ente et uno*, ed. and trans. Eugenio Garin, Florence 1942, pp. 580-581; Ficino, "Comm. in Mysticam theologiam," *Opera*, vol. II, pp. 1015-1016, and Reuchlin, *De arte cabalistica*, p. 205. See also Paul Oskar Kristeller, *Il pensiero filosofico di Marsilio Ficino*, Florence 1953, pp. 16-19; Corsano, *Il pensiero religioso*, pp. 20, 29, and Jung, "Evangelism in Italy," p. 524. This is an aspect of Renaissance thought which Edgar Wind has especially insisted upon, e.g., *Pagan Mysteries*, pp. 18-21, 57-64, 166-167.

[2] Vat. Lat. 6325, fols. 4v, 145r.

[3] Ang. Lat. 502, fol. 95v: "... a Deo, Dei Filio, per parabolas, ... cum prohibuit sanctum dari canibus." Mt. 7.6.

initiated and of advantage to them.[1] Those who are already solidly established in the ordinary religious truths are in a position to be led to higher ones, as happens in every discipline when a person is gently led from the known to the unknown.[2] Moreover, the very sublimity of the divine message is such that it removes it from the more easily comprehensible patterns of ordinary speech.[3]

These explanations do not altogether satisfy. The more basic reason Giles held this core of knowledge reserved for the elite is that so many of the authors he read impelled him towards it, and he found in it a most convenient tool for enabling him to discover in non-Christian sources the Christian truths which, for one reason or another, he so earnestly wanted to find there. Furthermore, his intellectual activity reached its final stage with his adoption of the cabala as his preferred exegetical method. Belief in an ancient secret oral tradition limited to a select few was an explicit part of cabalistic teaching, and it was by making use of this that Giles could most easily explain how his interpretation of the sacred text, which might strike his readers as new and novel, actually enjoyed the sanction of a venerable antiquity.

---

[1] Ang. Lat. 502, fol. 231v: "... idcirco vetita [arcana sapientia] est in vulgus dari, ... ne ea quae sanctissima sunt et salutem afferunt sapientibus, male insipientibus cognita errori atque exitio cedant."

[2] *Scechina*, vol. I, p. 74: "... ut ex eis quae vulgo nota sunt passimque exposita, vulgata et trita, qui mos est omnium disciplinarum, a cognitis ad incognita transiremus, ac per communia manifestaque fundamenta ad occulta atque arcana aditum patefaceremus."

[3] *Scechina*, vol. II, p. 206: "... tum quia non possunt dici [sacrae res] ob sublimitatem. Quamobrem aperiam in parabolis os meum." Ps. 78(77). 2.

CHAPTER TWO

SEVERAL RENAISSANCE TRADITIONS

We are now in a position to begin our examination of the intellectual milieu in which Giles of Viterbo lived and worked. We shall try to single out the more important authors and personages with whom he had contact, endeavoring to locate them in a larger tradition and to assess in some approximate fashion the influence each seemed to have upon the structure of Giles's thought. The rabbinical and cabalistic works will be reserved for the next chapter because of their complexity and special importance, as well as because they were in point of time the last major tradition to influence Giles and incorporated into themselves much that went before them. The other three major divisions whose study we shall now undertake are pagan antiquity, the Fathers of the Church, and the scholastic theologians. To a certain extent the order of treatment is arbitrary, and to begin with the authors of antiquity—Aristotle, Plato and the ancient theologians, "*prisci theologi*"—is not meant to imply that Giles's preferences in these traditions were determinative of the others and in no way determined by them. There must have been, rather, a constant interplay of one upon the other, his esteem for Augustine, for example, reinforcing his appreciation of Plato, and both of them together tending to edge him ever farther away from scholastic patterns of thought.

The advantage of beginning with an examination of Giles's attitude towards Aristotle and Plato is that it fixes him clearly in time and place. To say that in the early sixteenth century Italian philosophy was dominated by the rivalry between Paduan Aristotelianism and Florentine Platonism would be a gross oversimplification. There is enough truth in it, however, to allow us to use it to set Giles in the intellectual context of his times, and to point out that the final philosophical option he made was not arrived at, as it were, in the abstracted atmosphere of a scholar's study, but amidst a burning contemporary controversy.

Fortunately we can begin our analysis with a very concrete fact: at the age of twenty-four, while a theological student at the Augustinian *studium generale* in Padua, Giles of Viterbo published the three tracts of Giles of Rome which already have been mentioned. Giles of Rome was the Augustinians' most renowned scholastic theologian and his doctrine was prescribed for all the order's *studia*. One of the three tracts published at Padua in 1493 was the *De intellectu possibili contra Averroim*. This publication was the occasion for Giles of Viterbo taking his first stand against the Averroistic Aristotelianism which he encountered at Padua. Loyalty to the anti-Averroist position of the order's master scholastic and the historical accident of being invited to complete these three editions in the absence of the original editor sparked Giles's interest and engaged his emotions in the problem. Giles's involvement in the vexing question of Paduan Aristotelianism can be dated from this moment. It will continue to the end of his life, involving him at the highest level of the controversy.[1]

Among the Paduan philosophers Giles knew Agostino Nifo (ca. 1469-ca. 1539) personally and attended his lectures at the university during the years Nifo still considered himself an Averroist. Nifo admitted Giles was a superior student, even though he sometimes challenged Nifo's views. Nifo always remained cordial towards Giles and was present at the general chapter in 1507 which elected Giles prior general, taking part on that occasion in a public philosophical disputation in Giles's honor.[2]

Giles's relationship to Pietro Pomponazzi (1462-1524) seems to have been altogether different. Giles speaks in harshly polemical terms of "impiety" moving in 1509 from Padua to Ferrara, and thence to Bologna. He does not mention Pomponazzi by name, but this itinerary corresponds precisely with the facts of Pomponazzi's career and would seem to be a clear allusion to him. As Martin has shown, moreover,

---

[1] Giles very briefly described his intellectual experience at Padua: "Sequenti anno Patavium perrexi, insudavi uti si possem cognoscere quid Aristoteles, quid sapienter alii de vita mortalium, quid de divinis rebus, quid de ipsa tandem anima sentirent," undated letter to Niccolò Mannio di Canepina in Martène, *Veterum scriptorum collectio*, vol. III, col. 1249. On Giles of Rome and Averroes, see G. Bruni, "Egidio Romano antiaverroista," *Sophia* 1(1933), pp. 208-219. On Mannio, see Signorelli, *Egidio da Viterbo*, pp. 19, 144.

[2] On Giles and Nifo, see Martin, "Egidio da Viterbo," pp. 9-20, 170-171, and Massa, *Fondamenti metafisici e testi inediti*, pp. 42-48. On the development of Nifo's philosophical position, see di Napoli, *L'immortalità dell'anima*, pp. 203-214. See also Étienne Gilson, "Autour de Pomponazzi," *AHDL* 28(1961), esp. pp. 236-253, and *passim* in the two volumes by Bruno Nardi, *Saggi sull'Aristotelismo padovano dal secolo XIV al XVI*, Florence 1958, and *Studi su Pietro Pomponazzi*, Florence 1965. For a collection of studies on Paduan Aristotelianism, see *Aristotelismo padovano e filosofia aristotelica*, Atti del XII congresso internazionale di filosofia, vol. IX, Florence 1960. See also John Herman Randall, Jr., *The School of Padua and the Emergence of Modern Science*, Padua 1961, esp. pp. 69-114 on Pomponazzi.

Ambrogio Flandino (ca. 1460-1531), an Augustinian bishop who was an admirer of Giles, identified Giles as the object of the philippic which Pomponazzi delivered in the final paragraphs of his *Apologia* of 1518.[1] It can be inferred from Flandino that Giles provoked Pomponazzi's anger by his opposition to Pomponazzi's view that the immortality of the human soul could not be proved by reason. From Flandino, therefore, we have some reason for believing that Giles was instrumental in procuring the Fifth Lateran Council's condemnation of the thesis that at least according to philosophy the human soul is mortal.[2] What is absolutely certain is that Giles approved of the council's proscribing the Peripatetic philosophy of which this thesis was an expression and he called upon Leo X to work with the council for its extirpation.[3] Giles's opposition to the Paduan Peripatetics had

[1] See Ang. Lat. 502, fol. 191r, as well as *ibid.*, fol. 29v and Vat. Lat. 6325, fol. 195v. See also Martin, "Egidio da Viterbo," pp. 142-146, and François Secret, "Notes sur Paulus Ricius et la Kabbale chrétienne en Italie," *Rinascimento* 11(1960), esp. pp. 183-189. On Flandino's part in the Pomponazzi controversy, see Gilson, "Autour de Pomponazzi," pp. 230-236. On Pomponazzi, besides the studies referred to in the previous note, see Garin, *Italian Humanism*, pp. 136-145, and Paul Oskar Kristeller, "Two Unpublished Questions on the Soul of Pietro Pomponazzi," *Medievalia et Humanistica* 8(1955), pp. 76-101.

[2] For the text of the condemnation, see *Conciliorum oecumenicorum decreta*, eds. Joseph Alberigo et al., Rome 1962, pp. 581-582. See also Siro Offelli, "Il pensiero del concilio Lateranense V sulla dimostrabilità razionale dell'immortalità della anima umana," *Studia patavina* 2(1955), pp. 3-17; A. Deneffe, "Die Absicht des V. Laterankonzils," *Schol.* 8(1933), pp. 359-379. On the sources for information about the council, see E. Guglia, "Studien zur Geschichte des 5. Lateranconcils," *SAW* phil-hist. Cl., no. 10, 140(1899), and no. 3, 152(1906). Giles calls Leo X's attention to his labors in opposing the false doctrines of the Peripatetics, Ang. Lat. 502, fol. 162v. See also *ibid.*, fol. 164v.

[3] For Giles's association of Leo with the council against the Peripatetics, see Ang. Lat. 502, fols. 21r, 28r. In his formulation of certain of the offensive Peripatetic doctrines, Giles almost paraphrases the council's condemnation, e.g., Ang. Lat. 502, fol. 160v: "... animam deinde humanam aut unam omnium esse aut emori," and *Scechina*, vol. II, pp. 182, and 205: "... statuens aut neminem suam habere animam, aut certe mortalem, ..." He does not further qualify, as the council does, that this doctrine at least is true for philosophy, which was the part of the condemnation which comes closest to what Pomponazzi taught. See *Conciliorum decreta*, p. 581, for the pertinent part of the council's text: "... quod videlicet [anima rationalis] mortalis sit, aut unica in cunctis hominibus; et nonnulli temere philosophantes, secundum saltem philosophiam verum id esse asseverant; ...." Giles specifically subscribes to the idea of ecclesiastical surveillance of philosophers, Ang. Lat. 502, fol. 5v. On December 15, 1503 he wrote a non-polemical letter to Serafino Ferri on the soul's origin and destiny, Naples V. F. 20, fols. 78r-79v. Cajetan, the prior general of the Dominicans and Giles's colleague in the defense of the mendicants in the council, did not give unqualified approval to the text of the condemnation, Mansi, vol. XXXII, col. 843. He did not believe that the philosophers should be obliged to teach the immortality of the soul and

a broader base than any one doctrine, and a full year before the condemnation he insisted upon drastic action in the council against those enemies within Christendom who were trying to seduce men from the truth.[1]

What were the errors of the Peripatetics? Giles is not at all hesitant to list them for us and one of the recurring themes of his "Historia," written during the Fifth Lateran Council when the crisis was at its peak, is the danger to the Church stemming from Paduan philosophy. In this work Giles's many admonitions to Leo X to safeguard pure doctrine are directed very specifically against the Peripatetics. He ingenuously takes occasion, for instance, to enumerate the pernicious doctrines which no one would have dared utter before such a good and wise king as Robert II of France (970-1031): a previous motion is required for every other motion; heaven and the stars are eternal; from nothing nothing can come; there is one soul for all men; our souls and senses end with death; God does not know human affairs, or else He does everything from necessity; the Son does not proceed from the Father, nor does the Holy Spirit proceed from the Father and Son; the Son did not become man or redeem mankind.[2] As is obvious, these are, with a few exceptions, classic Christian objections to Aristotelian philosophy which in some form or other had been in circulation in the West since the thirteenth century and even before.

Giles dedicates several lengthy pages to a description of the heretical doctrine which he gratuitously attributes to Abelard: eternity of matter; unicity or mortality of the human soul; denial of reward and punishment in the afterlife, with the consequent necessity of seeking happiness here and now; denial of revelation and insistence that all

---

other truths of faith. Giles surely would have disagreed with Cajetan's position, Ang. Lat. 502, fol. 29v. On Cajetan and this question, see di Napoli, *L'immortalità dell'anima*, pp. 214-226, and see also the two articles by Gilson, "Autour de Pomponazzi," pp. 173-183, and "Cajetan et l'Humanisme théologique," pp. 113-136.

[1] "Oratio post 3am sessionem," p. 529: "... intra viscera reipublicae scelera et flagitia audet omnia, et falsa serit dogmata, ... animos nostrorum et cupiditate incendit et mendacibus disciplinis a veritate seducit."

[2] Ang. Lat. 502, fol. 87r-v: "Nemo cum eo dicere ausus esset motum omnem anteisse motum, caelum et sidera luxisse semper, fieri de nihilo nihil, mentem hominibus inesse unicam, aut animos sensusque morte extingui; quod vero ad divinam rem pertinet, res humanas aut latere Deum aut necessitate agere illum omnia, de Parente Prolem aut de utroque amorem non proficisci, Prolem praeterea aut homini non junctam fuisse aut homines morte non liberasse, ..." On the denial of the "Incarnation and other mysteries of Christ" as an error condemned by the Fifth Lateran Council, see *Conciliorum decreta*, p. 581.

knowledge comes through the senses; denial of God's knowledge of concrete singular beings or human actions, which entails a consequent denial of providence; belief in the world's eternity; denial of the existence of angels and demons, etc.[1] Sprinkled throughout the "Historia" are other shorter passages wherein Giles attacks one or the other of the aforementioned doctrines, some of which he already opposed in the "Sententiae" and which he would continue to combat up to the time of the *Scechina*.[2]

As might be expected from what has been said earlier, among the errors which Giles most vigorously opposes is the denial of divine providence. Time and time again he charges the Peripatetics with this false teaching. By denying God's knowledge of individual created realities and His concern for them, and by constructing a divinity who acts and creates out of necessity, they destroy God's providential government of the world and His ability to intervene in history. Giles finds these doctrines in the twelfth book of the *Metaphysics* of Aristotle. If they are true, Giles concludes, then Moses, the prophets and even the Gospels are false. God is stripped of those very attributes which make Him God—His supreme power, wisdom, providence and eternity.[3]

---

[1] Ang. Lat. 502, fols. 160r-161r.

[2] E.g., Ang. Lat. 502, fols. 103r-v, 129r, 235v, and 95v-96r: "... ea vero quonam pacto philosophia dicenda est quae Deum non solem sed caecum facit, ... nihil nisi necessitate molientem ... animas praeterea humanas aut morti obnoxias esse, aut praeter unam esse nullas, ..." *Ibid.*, fol. 229r: "... cum homines de anima, de providentia, de initio fineque rerum, de praemiis bonorum, de suppliciis malorum, de inferis, daemonibus, partim dubitare, partim nihil recipere didicere, ut omittam quae ad Deum hominem factum pertinent." See also Vat. Lat. 6325, fols. 41r-v, 101r, 184r and, e.g., 99r: "Deinceps sententia, qua Peripateticus utitur aliosque usos esse ait, ad creationem tollendam, ea est ex nihilo nihil fit." See *Scechina*, for attacks on various Peripatetic doctrines, vol. I, pp. 99-100, 231; vol. II, pp. 181-182. See Kristeller, "Francesco da Diacceto," p. 290, for the errors of Aristotle as listed by that humanist.

[3] Ang. Lat. 502, fol. 103r: "... [in the twelfth book of the *Metaphysics*] eruuntur namque Deo oculi cum latere illum mortalia dicuntur, eripitur providentia cum res humanas efficiunt neglegentem, truncantur brachia cum agere praecipuunt omnia et semper et necessario, quae si vera essent nec Moses, nec prophetae, nec sacratissima evangelia vera essent. Carere enim oporteret Deum quattuor illis muneribus quae illum praecipue faciunt esse Deum, ... summa potentia, ... sapientia, ... providentia, ... aeternitate." See also *ibid.*, fols. 21r, 95v-96r, 229r, 288v-289r, and 22v: "... et Deum fugere ac latere mortalia, quae si vera sint, ut enarrare videtur interpres Arabs, nihil est sacerdotio quo fungeris [Leo X] ridiculum magis, nihil ecclesiae studiis inanius." See also "Oratio post 3am sessionem," pp. 520, 522; Vat. Lat. 6325, fols. 41r-v, 101r, 184r; *Scechina*, vol. I, pp. 92, 99-100, and vol. II, pp. 16, 182, etc.

Another charge which Giles repeated leveled against the Peripatetics was that they deny the oracles their proper place. This denial made their philosophy impious and proudly self-sufficient, setting it in marked contrast with the pious philosophy, "*pia philosophia*," which recognized that its true function was to lead to the oracles and to bring itself into conformity with them. What is at stake here is the attempt made by philosophy at Padua to win for itself greater autonomy from theology. This attempt often provoked, justly or unjustly, the accusation of an espousal of the so-called Averroist doctrine of the double truth, as the condemnation of the Fifth Lateran Council more than suggests. Giles does not take up in so many words this formulation of the question. He contents himself with the generalization that the Peripatetics, maintaining that all truth comes through the senses, deny revelation its proper place and teach doctrines which make the truths of faith look ridiculous.[1] True and pious philosophy, on the other hand, is so intimately connected with the oracles that philosophy's function for Giles seems to be simply that of handmaid to theology. There is perfect harmony, perfect concord between the oracles and philosophy. This is true to such an extent that lines of demarcation between philosophy and theology finally tend to blur, and philosophy finds itself with scarcely any other purpose than to lead to revealed truths and to confirm them. "*Pia philosophia*" and "*sapientia*" become in practice other names for theology.[2]

---

[1] Ang. Lat. 502, fol. 164r: "... illam dicendam esse philosophiam constat quae sacris prophetarum et evangeliorum, hoc est, Dei oraculis, accedens non contraria invenitur sed veritati cognata vera exposuisse deprehenditur. ... At Peripateticorum scriptorum et Academicorum illud discrimen quod illa ea decernunt quae supra narravimus, unde omnes fidei partes irridentur, Academia ea docet ... unde fides commendatur, probatur, defenditur." See also Vat. Lat. 6325, fols. 1v-2r, 32v, and *Scechina*, vol. I, pp. 80, 139, 191. On Pomponazzi's idea of the relationship between philosophy and theology, see Kristeller, "Two Unpublished Questions of Pomponazzi," esp. pp. 83-84.

[2] Naples V.F. 20, fol. 74v, letter dated December 28, 1503, to Serafino Ferri: "Quas ob res hujus quoque viri [Platonis] philosophia non modo legislatoris mei veritati non repugnat, verum etiam quasi reginae e coelo profectae ... consentit, paret, servit, ancillat." See Vat. Lat. 6325, fol. 12r, and Ang. Lat. 502, fol. 62r: "Quod si nihil boni nomen mereri vult [Plato] nisi sapientiam eamque non humanam, ut dixit, sed divinam, divina vero sapientia nulla est, ut ipse idem sexto Reipublicae libro scripsit, nisi vel sol ille boni Dei filius, vel ea lux quae ab eo sole proficiscitur." See Marie-Thérèse d'Alverny, "Quelques aspects du symbolisme de la 'Sapientia' chez les humanistes," *Umanesimo e Esoterismo: Archivio di Filosofia* (1960), p. 325: "La philosophie légitime n'est donc autre que la vraie religion, et la religion légitime n'est peut être que la vraie philosophie." Giles, in theory at least, sometimes implied the distinction which in fact he tended to deny, e.g., Ang.

Convinced as Giles was that the Peripatetics were enemies of Christian dogma and, what was worse, that by their denial of providence and the necessity of revelation they overturned the very basis of that dogma, he launched a campaign against them in his writings of bitter and sweeping accusations, especially in the "Historia." He sought opportunities to blacken the name of Aristotle and to designate his philosophy as the cause of innumerable heresies and calamities which afflicted the Church in the past and in the present. On account of the Peripatetics, for example, God punished the Church with the failure of the crusades, the fall of Constantinople and the contemporary threat of a Turkish conquest.[1] The Peripatetics not only believed and spread false doctrine but dared with the aid of wicked secular princes to have it printed, thus being able to lead astray an immense multitude and transmit their errors to posterity.[2] For Giles Aristotle was separated from the Gospel by an unbridgeable gap. His was the fallacious philosophy condemned by Saint Paul as captivating men's souls and leading them to their eternal loss.[3]

Who was the Aristotle whom Giles found to be so pernicious? There is evidence from Giles's writings and library that he had first-hand knowledge of Aristotle himself. The manuscript index of the errors of Aristotle in Paris follows closely the topics and chapter divisions of the *Physics*. Paquier has shown that Giles used the *De anima* and the *Metaphysics* in the "Sententiae." In at least one passage in the "Historia" Giles indicates familiarity with the structure of the *Metaphysics* and suggests he knows the rest of the Aristotelian corpus.[4] Giles was, moreover, generally aware of the part Averroes played in

Lat. 502, fols. 162r-163r, 234v-235r. For the practical identification of Aristotle with philosophy in this period, see Gilson, "Cajetan et l'Humanisme théologique," pp. 113-136.

[1] Ang. Lat. 502, fols. 170r-171r, 229r-v, 285r, etc.

[2] Ang. Lat. 502, fol. 162v: "... cum viderim eius [Aristotelis] philosophiae quae nunc in ore omnium est sententiis fidem everti, fidei contraria ab incunabulis disci, per omnem aetatem disputari, et principibus conniventibus, immo etiam arridentibus, utinam non praemiis adhortantibus, cartis credi, libris defendi, posteritati mandari." See also *Scechina*, vol. II, p. 183.

[3] *Scechina*, vol. I, p. 191: "... ac denique per fallacem philosophiam, ut Apostoli verbis utar, quae est per elementa mundi, quae ab omni divinitate, ut remotissima distant, ita captos animos arcent, deturbant atque abalienant." See Col. 2.8.

[4] Giles's own summary of the work contained in the Paris manuscript is: "Cum supra philosophiae partes litteris collegimus, hic notavimus Aristotelis errores," Lat. 6589, fol. 581r. See also Martin, "Egidio da Viterbo," p. 16. For Giles's comments on the *Metaphysics*, see Ang. Lat. 502, fol. 103r-v. He once owned a Greek text of the *Nicomachean Ethics* which is now in the Vatican Library, Ross. 412.

the history of the interpretation of Aristotle, and he was able to distinguish what was proper to the Philosopher from what was due to the Commentator. He saw Averroes, in general, as a corrupting influence on the already worldly philosophy of Aristotle, and came to describe him as "bold," "impious" and "monstrous."[1] In the "Sententiae," his earliest major work, Giles sometimes used arguments from Averroes to support his own position and to give an authentic interpretation of Aristotle.[2] He even excuses mistakes in Averroes on the grounds that he had never seen Aristotle's Greek text.[3] But Giles's hostility towards Averroes increased as the years went on. This growing antipathy towards him can be explained at least in part by the fact that the "Arab interpreter" in effect denied providence by teaching that God did not know the affairs of men.[4]

Giles, however, was not really interested in the history of the interpretation of Aristotle. He confronted the very live problem of "Padua," and under that general denomination he assembled the doctrinal errors of his day. Padua was in a worse condition than the Greeks ever were because for the Greeks the Peripatetics were but one among many sects, whereas at Padua there was no choice. Furthermore, Padua, not content with Aristotle himself, took unto itself the contaminating interpretation of Averroes. This, then, was the "affrontery and boldness of Padua," and the source of the "Paduan dogmas, enemies to piety." Giles saw the Averroist Nicoletto Vernia (ca. 1420-1499) as the teacher under whose influence Padua began to infect the rest of the world.[5] The fact that the Augustinian *studium* at

[1] Vat. Lat. 6325, fol. 23v, "audacissimus," and Ang. Lat. 502, fol. 190v, "impiissimus, immanissimus," and fol. 175(a)r: "Nam quem umquam hostem acerbiorem Averroe pietas invenit?" Aristotle was the "contemptor irrisorque divinorum omnium," Naples V.F. 20, fol. 64r, letter dated January 6, 1503, to Serafino Ferri. For another humanist's more indulgent attitude towards Aristotle himself coupled with antipathy for the moderns who wrongly called themselves Peripatetics, see Kristeller, "Francesco da Diacceto," p. 289.

[2] E.g., Vat. Lat. 6325, fols. 7r, 11v, 43r, and Massa, *Fondamenti metafisici e testi inediti*, p. 67.

[3] Vat. Lat. 6325, fol. 81v. This same idea is to be found in Ficino, "Theologia Platonica, lib. XV," *Opera*, vol. I, p. 327.

[4] Ang. Lat. 502, fol. 22v, quoted above. Giles of Rome accuses Averroes, but not Aristotle, of denying providence, *Giles of Rome: Errores philosophorum*, ed. Josef Koch, trans. John O. Riedl, Milwaukee 1944, pp. 10-12, 24. The first printed edition of this work was Vienna, 1482. Giles of Viterbo presumably possessed a Hebrew translation of some of Averroes's commentaries, Paris Hébreu 927.

[5] Ang. Lat. 502, fols. 190v, "Patavina audacia," and 29v, "Patavii inimica pietatis dogmata." See also Vat. Lat. 6325, fol. 195v. On Vernia, see Ang. Lat.

Padua was a source of concern for Giles because of its indiscipline during his first years in office as prior general surely did not tend to mitigate his harsh judgments on the evil effects of the impious atmosphere created by Padua's bad doctrine.[1] In the "Sententiae" Giles frequently makes explicit effort to reconcile Plato and Aristotle and to show that the differences between them are verbal rather than real.[2] These generous early attempts to point out a certain agreement between the two great philosophers, however, were no match for Giles's steadily deepening conviction that the Paduan Aristotle, the Aristotle who was most meaningful to him, was the enemy of all that he stood for.

The fact that Giles left us no detailed commentary on any Paduan work or author makes it difficult to ascertain upon just what basis in actual fact his damning judgments were made. He singles out Averroes so often by name that the importance of Alexander of Aphrodisias in the Paduan controversies tends to slip out of sight.[3] His rejection of the Averroist doctrine of the unicity of the intellect was a rejection of a position held by few, if any, of his contemporaries.[4] Aside from the question of providence and some rather standardized listings of Aristotle's errors in the "Historia," Giles's attacks tend to repeat the substance of the condemnation by the Fifth Lateran Council, with special emphasis on the submission of philosophy to faith. He leaves us, therefore, with the decided impression that his zeal for orthodoxy, frightened as it was by the dangerous religious consequences it saw lurking under the label of Averroist Aristotelianism, was a more

502, fol. 96v. On his doctrine and career, see di Napoli, "*L'immortalità dell'anima*, pp. 179-193, and Nardi, *Saggi sull'Aristotelismo padovano*, pp. 95-126. Di Napoli repeatedly states that Giles was a pupil of Vernia's, *op. cit.*, pp. 177, 182, 214, 239. The Parisian Peripatetics are also attacked by Giles, Ang. Lat. 502, fol. 159v.

[1] See, e.g., Siena G. X. 26, pp. 42, 54-57, 146-151, 269, and Ang. Lat. 688, fols. 30r-33r. For a more positive attitude towards Padua, see Siena G. X. 26, p. 31.

[2] For attempts to reconcile Plato and Aristotle, see Vat. Lat. 6325, fols. 40r, 92r, 126v-127r, and Massa, *Fondamenti metafisici e testi inediti*, pp. 65, 67, 77-78. See also Giles's marginalia in his copy of Bessarion's *In calumniatorem Platonis*, fol. 118v, where Bessarion attempts to reconcile Plato and Aristotle.

[3] We miss in Giles a distinction as clear as Ficino's, "Epistolarum, liber VIII," *Opera*, vol. I, p. 872: "Totus enim terrarum orbis a Peripateticis occupatus in duas plurimum divisus est sectas, Alexandrinam et Averroicam. Illi quidem intellectum nostrum esse mortalem existimant, hi vero unicum esse contendunt. Utrique religionem omnem funditus aeque tollunt." Possibly belonging to Giles was a manuscript copy of Alexander's commentary on the *Metphysics* of Aristotle, now in the Biblioteca Angelica, Rome, Grec. 102; see Marin, "Egidio da Viterbo," p. 36.

[4] See Paul Oskar Kristeller, "Paduan Averroism and Alexandrism in the Light of Recent Studies," in *Aristotelismo padovano*, pp. 147-155, esp. 150-151.

significant factor impelling him to his attack on Padua than was a dispassionate study of the contemporary evidence available to him.[1]

Ficino's Platonism, far from rejecting the oracles, welcomed them and saw in them the proper completion of philosophy's task. The religious attraction which such a viewpoint could exercise upon Giles is clear. After the rigorous arguments of Padua, seeking a differentiation between philosophy and dogma, the line of harmonious continuity between the two which Ficino proposed must have been almost irresistible.

From his veneration for Saint Augustine, for instance, Giles probably was favorably predisposed towards Plato before he had any contact with Ficino. His visit to Florence in 1494-1495 was, nevertheless, decisive for the rest of his career. Soon after the Florence sojourn he spent two years at Capo d'Istria lecturing on theology and devoting every free hour to the study of Plato, after which he was called to Rome to take the examination for the *magisterium* in theology. In this examination, as he later proudly related to Ficino, he expounded theology according to the doctrine of Plato against the criticism of the Peripatetics. The examination signaled his public adherence to the style of theology Ficino taught and promulgated.[2]

Giles's letters and his library testify to his desire to read and possess the original Greek texts of Plato. Repeatedly he requests his correspondent to buy for him the latest printed editions, and he urges Aldo Manuzio (1449-1515) himself to an early publication of the Platonic corpus.[3] Giles read Plato, nevertheless, through the filters of Ficino and the Neoplatonic tradition. His own statements leave no doubt as to the indebtedness he felt towards Ficino and the veneration in which he held him. When Giles tells Ficino that his revival of Platonic

[1] Gilson, speaking of Flandino's opposition to Pomponazzi, makes an observation which is suggestive for Giles's role in the Paduan controversy: "Du côté des théologiens ses adversaires, l'intérêt prédominant était religieux," "Autour de Pomponazzi," p. 233.

[2] See Martin, "Egidio da Viterbo," pp. 24-40. We have no specific information about Giles's contacts with Ficino in Florence either in 1494-1495 or when he returned to teach theology there in 1497.

[3] Ang. Lat. 688, fol. 36v, letter dated February 24, 1508: "Aldo dicas [Gabriele della Volta, also known as Gabriel Venetus, 1468-1537] universam Italiam post Plutarchum Platonem expectare." See *ibid.*, fols. 46v, 56r, and also Martène, *Veterum scriptorum collectio*, vol. III, cols. 1251-1252. On Giles and Aldo, see Martin, "Problem of Giles of Viterbo," 9(1959), p. 365. The works of Plato contained in the Vatican manuscript Ross. 558 probably belonged to Giles. See also Astruc and Monfrin, "Livres du Cardinal Gilles," pp. 553-554, on Timaeus texts from Giles's library.

theology heralds the return of the Golden Age, he is not altogether allowing rhetoric to carry him beyond his sober convictions.[1] In keeping with his acceptance of Ficino's Plato is his recognition of Plotinus as an interpreter of Plato's true mind, and his use of the doctrine and interpretation of Proclus, Porphyry, Iamblichus and other authors from late antiquity.[2]

What especially commended Plato's philosophy to Giles was the fact that it was in accord with the oracles and with piety, as Augustine assured him.[3] With enthusiasm Giles takes up Ficino's theme of the "*pia philosophia*" and identifies it by implication with the "*Christiana philosophia*," i.e., the Gospel message.[4] Plato is the greatest of the

---

[1] Kristeller, *Supplementum Ficinianum*, vol. II, p. 316: "Quo factum est, ut divina providentia missum Marsilium Ficinum arbitremur, qui misticam Platonis theologiam nostris sacris institutis in primis consentaneam atque illorum previam declararet. Hec sunt, mi Marsili, Saturnia regna, hec toties a Sibylla et vatibus aetas aurea decantata, hec Platonis illa tempora, quibus fore praecinuit ut sua quam optime studia nota fierent." See also Ang. Lat. 502, fol. 187r. Jedin shows that Seripando's Platonism derived ultimately from Ficino, *Seripando*, vol. I, p. 66.

[2] On Plotinus, see *Scechina*, vol. I, p. 139; "Libellus" (in *Scechina*, vol. I), p. 42, and also Vat. Lat. 6325, fol. 13r: "Plotinus denique Platonis mentem ostendit, ..." For Proclus, consult Secret's index in *Scechina*, vol. II, p. 336, for many references. Giles had two manuscript copies of Proclus which are now in the Vatican Library, Vat. Grec. 237 and, possibly, Ross. 962, and there is another in Naples, II. F. 7, fols. 74r-184r. See also Paul Oskar Kristeller, *Iter italicum*, vol. I, London 1963, p. 188. On Proclus in the Renaissance, see Proclus, *The Elements of Theology*, ed. and trans. E. R. Dodds, 2nd ed., Oxford 1963, p. xxxii, and Wind, *Pagan Mysteries*, pp. 42-44, 158-174. On Porphyry, see *Scechina*, vol. I, p. 74. There is a Porphyry manuscript of Giles's in the Vatican Library, Barb. Lat. 322, and another in Naples, II. F. 7, fols. 210r-227r. In a letter written between 1517 and 1521 Celio Calcagnini (1479-1541) describes Giles thus: "Accedit Aegidius Cardinalis, vir singulari integritate ac nominis celebritate, qui Porphyrii mysteria et Procli theologiam Latinam fecit," *Opera aliquot*, Basel 1544, p. 101. On Iamblichus, see *Scechina*, vol. I, pp. 113, 139; "Libellus" (in *Scechina*, vol. I), pp. 25, 30; Ang. Lat. 502, fol. 11r, and the Vatican manuscripts Barb. Grec. 62, and Ottob. Lat. 1786, as well as Kristeller, *Iter italicum*, vol. I, p. 188. For Ficino's attitude towards these figures, see "Epistolarum liber XII," *Opera*, vol. I, p. 956, and "De Christiana religione," *Opera*, vol. I, p. 25, and also see Kristeller's index of authors cited by Ficino, *Il pensiero Ficino*, pp. 451-463. For the attitude of a Christian cabalist, see Reuchlin, *De arte cabalistica*, pp. 192, 195, 199, 208, etc. Giles, we must assume, was not untouched by the Stoic elements in the thought of Ficino and other figures of the Italian Renaissance, which has recently been emphasized by Levi, *French Moralists*, pp. 40-51. See, e.g., Ang. Lat. 502, fol. 80r, for a mention of Epictetus.

[3] Ang. Lat. 502, fol. 187r: "Educavere illi [Medici] quidem Ficinum Marsilium, qui arcanam et pietati longe consentaneam, si Augustino meo creditur, Platonis philosophiam Latinam fecit." See Vat. Lat. 6325, fol. 34r: "... ita aperte rem [trinitatem] pandit [Plato] ut evangelistam existimes non philosophum." For Ficino, see "Comm. in De div. nominibus," *Opera*, vol. II, p. 1025.

[4] E.g., Vat. Lat. 6325, fols. 83r, 96v; Ang. Lat. 502, fol. 161v, and Naples V. F.

philosophers because he is the most pious and the only one of them whose philosophy leads to a knowledge of divine things.[1] He preached about the Son of God long before the Gospels were written and, as we have seen, he had some knowledge of the mystery of the Trinity.[2]

The clear correlation which Giles discovered between the theory of knowledge insinuated in John's Gospel and that developed by Plato, especially in the *Republic* and the seventh epistle, was perhaps the most important single proof Giles adduced for Plato's Christian sense.[3] From this theory of knowledge followed all sorts of corollaries, significant for Giles's asceticism as well as for his speculative theology. Giles found an astounding parallel between the "Sun of Justice" who "enlightens every man who comes into the world" (Jn. 1.9) and the myth of the sun and the cave of Plato. The world is the cave, Christ is the sun, and the soul is somehow midway between the two. The soul's choice, then, is to turn from one to the other, from the darkness to the sun, and this turning constitutes the soul's conversion. The Augustinian overtones are unmistakable.

The world is the world of sense, enveloped in the darkness of the cave. Created by God, it is not altogether devoid of the vestiges left by His creative activity. These vestiges lie hidden, however, under darkness and shadows, i.e., under appearances, and can be discovered by a "*via negationis*," for the appearances tend to hide the true divine imprint. Thus it is that we proceed through enigmas from the world of sense to a higher level of intelligibility, from the cave to the Sun. As is obvious, this aspect of Giles's Platonism is the epistemological root for the esoterism we have already noted.[4]

20, fols. 88r and 64r, letter dated January 6, 1503, to Serafino Ferri: "...Plato tamen philosophiae verioris [than that of Aristotle] quam postea Christus aperuit opinatissimus auctor, ..." On Ficino's "*pia philosophia*," see Kristeller, *Il pensiero Ficino*, p. 18, and Garin, *Italian Humanism*, pp. 90-94.

[1] Ang. Lat. 502, fols. 105r, 160v. Giles takes up the idea which derives from Numenius of Plato as the "Attic Moses," *Scechina*, vol. I, p. 79. For other instances of this theme, see Eusebius, *De evang. praep.*, lib. XI. 6; Reuchlin, *De arte cabalistica*, p. 180, and Ficino, "Epistolarum liber VIII," *Opera*, vol. I, p. 866.

[2] Ang. Lat. 502, fol. 163v: "Ecce Dei Filius a Platone praedicatus."

[3] Ang. Lat. 502, fols. 57r-v, 62r, 161v-162r; Vat. Lat. 6325, fols. 3r, 198r, 207v; Massa, *Fondamenti metafisici e testi inediti*, pp. 78, 79, 104; *Scechina*, vol. I, pp. 107-108; "Libellus" (in *Scechina*, vol. I), pp. 41-42, and "Oratio post 3am sessionem," p. 520.

[4] Vat. Lat. 6325, fols. 15v, 37v, 38r, 112r-v, 122r; Évora CXVI/1-30, fols. 14v-15r; Ang. Lat. 502, fol. 3v; Paris Lat. 527, fol. 298r. See also *Scechina*, vol. I, p. 154, and "Libellus" (in *Scechina*, vol. I), pp. 41-42. See Ladner, *Idea of Reform*, p. 49, on conversion and Plato's myth.

The body is of the world of sense. By turning from it inwards to the soul, which bears not a mere vestige of God but His image and likeness and is the place wherein He dwells, we can contemplate Him more directly. Giles's religious anthropology is explicit: the soul *is* man; the body is the soul's prison and sepulchre from whose contact the soul takes contagion. Man's exalted dignity derives from the fact that his soul through creation and grace is like unto God.[1] By withdrawing from the body and by contemplating one's own soul one is able, therefore, to come to a more perfect knowledge of God.[2] Contemplation and the knowledge of God lead further to an even greater good, divine charity. Whereas in heaven our beatitude will consist in the perfect satisfaction of both intellect and will, here below our effort is to excite charity in ourselves, for charity is the one thing necessary to attain the supreme good of heaven. We engage in contemplation precisely in order that we might grow in charity, i.e., in the "*voluntatis opera*."[3]

Fundamental though the above described epistemology and anthropology are for Giles's thought, they hardly can be said to avoid in their broad outline Platonic and Augustinian commonplaces. More detailed analyses of them, done from a different point of view, have appeared elsewhere.[4] What is of greater interest to us are some of their implications which relate to the general subject matter we are treating.

---

[1] *Scechina*, vol. I, pp. 186, 232, and vol. II, p. 144: "Factor aliarum rerum Elohim; animae, qui homo verus est, Adonai." See also Vat. Lat. 6325, fols. 17v, 96r, 179r-v, etc.; Massa, *Fondamenti metafisici e testi inediti*, pp. 54ff, and Évora CXVI/1-30, fols. 14r and 7r: "Sed animus quamquam prope divinus, corporea tamen moli permixtus, ..." See Paquier, "Un essai de théologie platonicienne," p. 430. For the identification of man with his soul in Ficino, see "Epistolarum liber I," *Opera*, vol. I, p. 626, and "Comm. in Convivium Platonis," *Opera*, vol. II, pp. 1331-1332. On the link between Platonic philosophical dualism and reform, see Russell, *Reform and Dissent*, pp. 188-229.

[2] Massa, *Fondamenti metafisici e testi inediti*, pp. 58-59, 66. On this question, see Kristeller, "Platonic Academy," pp. 152-153, and Ladner, *Idea of Reform*, pp. vii, 3, 83-107.

[3] Naples V.F. 20, fols. 244v-245r, letter to Serafino Ferri, April 8, 1508. See also *ibid.*, fols. 256r-264v, and Siena G.X. 26, p. 140, letter entitled "Pro baccha-lariatu," undated: "Amor vero qui ex divina cognitione proficiscitur caritas nuncupatur, quae una ad beatam vitam et praeparat et producit. Ad hanc itaque excitandam sacra divinarum rerum contemplatio instituta est." See also Vat. Lat. 6325, fol. 6v, and Massa, *Fondamenti metafisici e testi inediti*, p. 106. For Ficino, see Kristeller, *Il pensiero Ficino*, pp. 291-296, esp. 296: "...il primato della volontà e dell'amore sull'intelletto come opinione più matura e definitiva del Ficino."

[4] Massa, *Fondamenti metafisici e testi inediti*, pp. 1-48, and Paquier, "Un essai de théologie platonicienne."

The rational justification in Platonic epistemology for much of Giles's esoterism has already been pointed out. Equally important is the basis which this epistemology provides for a strong emphasis on ethics and morality. As a matter of fact, morality in the broad sense of the term plays an important part in the beginning and end of the knowing process: one must discipline oneself to withdraw from the body and the things of sense to come to contemplation, and contemplation itself is to lead one to charity in the "*voluntatis opera.*" Moreover, as we have seen, it is virtuous striving to find God which prompts Him to give His light so that one indeed will be successful in the quest, according to the doctrine of Plato's seventh epistle.[1] The explicit effort in all this is to withdraw from the lower world of sense and, by implication, to some extent from the world of human society.

Although Giles in the opening folios of the "Sententiae" is careful to define theology as the science of revealed truths, "*revelationum scientia,*" and to classify it as speculative rather than practical, there persists throughout his writings a tendency to shift the emphasis from the intellect to the will. The ultimate purpose of the speculation or contemplation of theology is to set the soul afire with love, and what is most proper to theology is to move to virtue and charity.[2] Without identifying virtue with knowledge, Giles does insist that philosophy accord with piety, and he often explicitly delineates it in terms of good and holy living, "*bene beateque vivendum.*"[3] Just as he looked with disfavor on Padua's attempt to establish hard lines of demarcation between philosophy and theology, in his own efforts to define theology he almost imperceptibly moves towards confounding it with piety, describing it in terms of its ability to promote virtue. His fondness for the meditations of "*pia philosophia*" on death and the afterlife

---

[1] See the discussion in Chapter One of the formula "*Facientibus quod in se est.*" See also Vat. Lat. 6325, fols. 3r and 29v: "...[pro Platone] divina cognitio non studio sed consuetudine fit in anima." See also Massa, *Fondamenti metafisici e testi inediti*, p. 55: "Nam si beata hic vita esse homini potest, quemadmodum et Platonis Symposium et nos supra disseruimus, et contemplatione, ut Symposium, et vitae cognatione, ut epistola docet."

[2] Vat. Lat. 6325, fols. 1r, 4v-6r, 189r-v.

[3] Ang. Lat. 502, fols. 225r, 232v; Vat. Lat. 6325, fol. 202r; Siena G. X. 26, pp. 117, 319; Naples V. F. 20, fol. 265r. For the same idea in Reuchlin, see *De arte cabalistica*, p. 270: "Tota namque philosophia nostra haec est, ut bene vivendo, bene moriamur,...."

indicates this same trend.[1] He sustained an abiding interest in the ethical and religious implications of doctrine.[2]

Giles never denied the intellect its place. In his letters as prior general concerning the *studia* of the order, he makes a clear distinction between the intellectual function Giles of Rome plays in the order's academic training and the religious or moral function of Augustine.[3] Even so, underlying Giles's search for knowledge and understanding there is the vaguely formulated conviction that the test and purpose of truth is its ability to produce a spiritually and morally better person. Without judging the ultimate validity or invalidity of such an assumption, we can assert that it tends to make one impatient with academic efforts undertaken simply as pure research, for the intellectual satisfaction involved, and distrustful of any system wherein a contribution to personal piety is not immediately evident. Surely here we have another clue to Giles's antipathy to Padua.

In a later chapter we shall see what great stress Giles lays upon a reform of studies as part of his general program for the reformation of the Augustinian order and, by extension, for the reformation of the Church as a whole. The direct relationship he postulates between theology and piety, like the direct relationship between orthodoxy and virtue, must be kept in mind if we are to understand his insistence that learning and reform march hand in hand. It is not a case of theology providing merely a deeper and fuller insight into the Christian mysteries which in itself is satisfying for the soul and leads to a helpful up-

---

[1] Naples V. F. 20, fols. 88r, 295v, and esp. 287v, letter dated simply the ides of August, to Antonio Zocolo: "Nos mortis et eorum quae post mortem sunt meditatio tenet; id enim divus Plato piam philosophiam esse arbitratur." See also Vat. Lat. 6325, fol. 216v; Massa, *Fondamenti metafisici e testi inediti*, pp. 60-61; "Libellus" (in *Scechina*, vol. I), p. 42. For the "*meditatio mortis*" in Ficino, see Kristeller, *Il pensiero Ficino*, pp. 363-364. Ficino felt his Platonic theology would do for the reform of the clergy what scholasticism had failed to do, Jedin, *Trent*, vol. I, p. 155. On Zocolo, see Signorelli, *Egidio da Viterbo*, p. 19.

[2] Naples V. F. 20, fol. 238r-v, letter dated September 20, 1507, to Hieronymus Genazanensis: "Cupimus, amantissime fili, ut non minus ea in parte philosophiae quae ad mores pertinet quam in naturae cognitione excellas; hujus vera intelligere, illius temperate, prudenter, juste, constanter agere finis est; illa ad intelligentiam ducit etiam scelestissimo cuique communem, haec solos vere sapientes ad vitam beatissimam traducit." See also Siena G. X. 26, pp. 129 and esp. 117, letter entitled "De instituendo regente," undated: "Quare si, ut Apostolo placet, summa virtus est caritas quae Deo nos jungit, summae virtuti proxima esse debet doctrina quae nos erudiendo jungit caritati." See also *Scechina*, vol. I, p. 159. On Pontano and Giles concerning ethics and rhetoric, see the texts adduced by Massa, "La metodologia," pp. 192-194.

[3] Siena G.X.26, p. 118, "De instituendo regente," undated letter.

dating for the Church of theological knowledge. For Giles theology must somehow more directly foster piety and more directly relate to moral reform.

The origin of the religious knowledge possessed by the ancient theologians, "*prisci theologi*," has already been discussed. We can now very briefly try to evaluate their importance for Giles's thought. The writings attributed to Hermes Trismegistus, Zoroaster and Orpheus we now know to be apocryphal products of late antiquity, strongly influenced by Neoplatonism and Neo-Pythagoreanism. Virgil is not, strictly speaking, to be listed among the "*prisci*," and he falls into a class by himself. As we have seen, his access to religious truth was partly through the Platonic tradition, and for Giles he was one of the authentic Latin interpreters of Plato, "*Platonicus Maro*." Through the sibyls, furthermore, he was a prophet, "*vates*," and his verses from the "Fourth Eclogue" and the *Aeneid* recur again and again in Giles's writings as predictions of the coming of Christ and of the meaning of the world-wide mission of the Roman Church.[1]

Giles sees Hermes Trismegistus, Zoroaster, Orpheus and Pythagoras as bearers of the ancient theology, along the general lines established by Ficino and Pico.[2] Pico intended to develop a "poetic theology" based upon what he supposed were the authentic writings of these authors and in the course of which he would be able to interpret pagan myths in their proper philosophical and theological sense, showing that under different names and different fables a single religious truth was to be found.[3] Giles actually carries out the intention Pico expressed, devoting a great part of the "Sententiae" to explaining the Christian meaning of the myths. He identifies Venus, for instance,

---

[1] E.g., Vat. Lat. 6325, fols. 5r, 96r; Ang. Lat. 502, fols. 36v, 210r; Évora CXVI/1-30, fols. 16r, 25v; *Scechina*, vol. I, pp. 141, 173, etc. For Homer, e.g., Ang. Lat. 502, fols. 102r, 131r, 175(a)r, 295r, and *Scechina*, vol. I, p. 109; Vat. Lat. 6325, fols. 5r, 108r.

[2] Évora CXVI/1-30, fols. 13v, 23r; Vat. Lat. 6325, fols. 34r, 36r, 40v, 114r, 175r; *Scechina*, vol. I, p. 138. In Naples there is Giles's manuscript copy of "Orphei et aliorum laniamenta," II.F.7.

[3] For Pico's intention to treat at length of this theology, see *De hominis dignitate, etc.*, pp. 150, 581. See also Garin, *Italian Humanism*, pp. 83-84; Wind, *Pagan Mysteries*, pp. 24-30, and Jean Seznec, *The Survival of the Pagan Gods*, trans. Barbara F. Sessions, New York 1953, esp. pp. 95-99. The historical roots for the concept of such a poetic theology are long, and reach back far beyond Pico and his generation. See, e.g., Eusebius, *De evang. praep.* lib. IV, proemium; Augustine, *De civ. Dei*, lib. VI. 5 and 6; Lactantius, *De ira Dei*, lib. XI. For Pico's final rejection of the "*prisca theologia*," see Giovanni di Napoli, *Giovanni Pico della Mirandola e la problematica dottrinale del suo tempo*, Rome 1965, pp. 277-282.

with the Holy Spirit, Apollo with Christ, and discovers in Saturn's devouring of his children the mystery of the divine unity.[1]

Convinced as Giles was that these authors and myths somehow possessed certain truths of revelation, he tried to disclose them under the "poetic veil."[2] The poets received special divine illumination and their science was God-given. Orpheus is described as "both poet and theologian," and Dionysius the Pseudo-Areopagite advises us that divine truth is not able to reach us except under poetic veils.[3] The message which Moses conveyed to the Hebrews by his own leadership to the promised land Homer conveyed to the Greeks in the person of Ulysses, and Virgil to the Romans in Aeneas. Eloquence thus was joined to religious wisdom, and children learned divine truths while they suckled their nurse's milk. Teachers who use these poets only to

---

[1] Vat. Lat. 6325, e.g., fols. 13v, 22v, 215v. See also *ibid.*, fols. 144v-146r. The excerpt from the "Sententiae" edited by Massa is replete with examples, *Fondamenti metafisici e testi inediti*, pp. 54-110. See also, e.g., Ang. Lat. 502, fol. 14v. Massa takes up the question of Giles's poetic theology, "La metodologia," pp. 188-194. The ultimate explanation for the remarkable agreement in religious truths rests upon providence's care to inspire and protect them, esp. among the Hebrews and the Etruscans, Ang. Lat. 502, fol. 8r: "Et quoniam uterque locus atque utraque gens, quae veterem legem expectabat Judaea at quae novam Tyrrhena, suo utraque ab angelo secundum eandem divini luminis perceptionem regebatur." Though the symbols and fables might differ from people to people, the underlying truth was the same: "In dispari tamen fabula par consilium fuit," Massa, *Fondamenti metafisici e testi inediti*, p. 99. See also Vat. Lat. 6325, fol. 136r-v, 210r.

[2] The idea of poetry being used to disguise a higher wisdom is ancient, and Plato spoke of Homer's doing it, Hugo Rahner, S. J., *Greek Myths and Christian Mystery*, trans. Brian Battershaw, London 1963, p. 282. For Augustine's fascination with the allegorical and secret meaning of poetry and Scripture, see H.-I. Marrou, *Saint Augustin et la fin de la culture antique*, 4th ed., Paris 1958, pp. 484-498. The great propagator of the idea of divine truth hidden under a veil, however, was Dionysius the Pseudo-Areopagite, and it is to his proposition that both Giles and Saint Thomas allude, Vat. Lat. 6325, fol. 5r, and *S.T.* I q 1 art. 9. Great impetus was given to the idea in the Renaissance with the publication of Giovanni Boccaccio's *Genealogie deorum gentilium libri*, which had the express purpose of discovering what the ancients had hidden "sub ridiculo cortice fabularum." See the edition by Vincenzo Romano, vol. I, Bari 1951, pp. 1, 4, 8 and 19, as well as Seznec, *The Survival of the Pagan Gods*, pp. 220-224. Pletho gave added impulse to the idea in Florence, and Giles's contemporaries were captivated by its possibilities, e.g., Ficino, "De Christiana religione," *Opera*, vol. I, p. 29; "Theologia Platonica," *Opera*, vol. I, p. 386; "Epistolarum libri VII, VIII," *Opera*, vol. I, pp. 855, 871. Also Pico, *De hominis dignitate, etc.*, p. 162, and Reuchlin, *De arte cabalistica*, p. 186. The idea was taken up with great vigor by Giles's admirer and fellow cabalist, the Franciscan, Petrus Galatinus, e.g., in his commentary on the Apocalypse, Vat. Lat. 5567, fols. 19r-v, 27r, 128r. Giles finds scriptural justification for the enigmatic nature of the utterances of the oracles, *Scechina*, vol. II, p. 270. See also Ang. Lat. 502, fol. 95v.

[3] Vat. Lat. 6325, fols. 5r, 114r.

teach eloquence and who maintain silence on the revelation contained in them are like people who are so captivated by the beauty of a tree's foliage that they forget all about its fruit.[1]

Giles was not unaware of Plato's strictures against the poets. He has no use for Catullus, or even for Homer when he relates the adulteries of the gods, and he severely reprehends the poets who spurned Plato's fables and corrupted the divine message entrusted to them. Certain other authors from antiquity such as Livy, Pliny and some of the orators do not contain religious knowledge and lead to a neglect of sacred literature.[2] Giles's enthusiasm, however, for the religious poets of the past extends to the humanists of his own day. He has high praise for Pontano, Sannazzaro and Angiolo Poliziano (1454-1494), feeling that with them, after many years of literary barbarism, eloquence had once again come to life from the ashes. Whereas for centuries sacred truths were written in uncultivated style and the good stylists devoted their talents to less worthy, even obscene, subjects, now finally piety and eloquence have once again joined company.[3]

Giles approached the ancient poets with the awe justly reserved for those who by their antiquity were closest to the original sources of revelation, and his enthusiasm for them was far indeed from any self-conscious paganizing tendency. Their theology was Christianity in disguise, hidden under the poetic veils of the myths, and their philosophical assumptions, so marvellously in accord with Plato, added

---

[1] Ang. Lat. 502, fols. 52v, 288r-v.

[2] Vat.Lat. 6325, fol. 5r; *Scechina*, vol. I, p. 108; "Libellus" (in *Scechina*, vol. I), p. 30; Ang. Lat. 502, fols. 57v, 129r; Naples V. F. 20, fol. 258v. Ficino also attacked the poets, Garin, *Italian Humanism*, pp. 91-92.

[3] Ang. Lat. 502, fol. 230r: "...post tot annos et barbariem evadere et eloquentiam redivivam e cineribus excitare,...." *Ibid.*, fol. 197v: "Quae enim sancte prius minus eleganter, quae eleganter non sancte scribebantur. Nunc eadem simul sancte eleganterque scripta sunt." See also *ibid.*, fols. 207v, 236r, and Pélissier, "Pour la biographie," p. 797. For the idea of rebirth and revival in the Renaissance, see Wallace K. Ferguson, *The Renaissance in Historical Thought*, Cambridge, Mass. 1948, pp. 18-28; B. L. Ullman, "Renaissance—The Word and the Underlying Concept," *Studies in Philology* 49(1952), esp. pp. 106-107, and H. Weisinger, "Renaissance Accounts of the Revival of Learning," *Studies in Philology* 45(1948), pp. 105-118. On the Renaissance and historical perspective, see the "Translator's Introduction" in Garin's *Italian Humanism*, pp. xxi-xxii. For a clear instance of Giles's sense of distance from antiquity, see Ang. Lat. 502, fol. 267v. Towards the end of Giles's life his interest in the poetic theology of the myths was overshadowed by his enthusiasm for the cabala, *Scechina*, vol. I, p. 109: "Altissima hic quaestio exoritur: cur duo apud Graios nomina sortita sint. Dicunt enim nunc Pallada, nunc Minervam....Sed quid illi sibi voluerint, ipsi viderint. Sed quod ad nos attinet, Caesar [CharlesV], est prophana non curare, si quid faciant ad nostra non spernere."

dignity and authority to that author's "*pia philosophia*," helping to substantiate its authentically religious character.

Giles's attitude towards the Fathers of the Church and other non-scholastic Christian writers is of a piece with his attitude towards the authors of antiquity. He favors those whose Platonism brings them most into harmony with his own religious ideas, especially if he can find reasons for believing that they were recipients of a secret oral tradition. This last prescription is most obviously met by Dionysius the Pseudo-Areopagite, to whom Saint Paul confided his secret theology. Origen and Augustine, though they themselves did not receive a message directly from the Apostle, confirmed by their doctrine what Dionysius related, and thus they too win a privileged place among the theologians of the past.[1]

Dionysius had other qualities to recommend him besides the fact of his intimate association with Saint Paul. He transmitted a theology of divine names, which became increasingly important for Giles as his interest in the cabala grew more intensive. Dionysius, moreover, had evolved epistemological principles governing man's knowledge of the divine which Giles found extremely useful, the *via affirmationis* and the *via negationis*. These principles had been known, of course, by the great scholastics and were used by Saint Thomas himself. As might be expected, Giles develops especially the implications of the *via negationis*, which in his poetic theology helps him discover truths in otherwise unpromising sources. For all these reasons, then, Giles had the highest praise for the Pseudo-Areopagite and, like Ficino, he is either unaware of Lorenzo Valla's (1407-1457) doubts about his authenticity or unconvinced by them. He realizes that Dionysius does not exhaust the possibilities of the name-theology but, even so, he justly deserves to be considered the very apogee of Greek theology, "*Graecae theologiae unicum lumen.*"[2]

---

[1] Ang. Lat. 502, fol. 175(a)r: "...altam arcanamque theologiam deprehendimus, a Deo patribus datam per Homerum primum atque Orpheum,...in nostris uni Dionysio significandam, susceptam Origeni, Augustinoque imprimis probatam, ..." Ficino associates the three names of Dionysius, Origen and Augustine as "Platonicos excellentissimos," "Theologia Platonica, lib. V," *Opera*, vol. I, p. 147.

[2] Ang. Lat. 502, fol. 27v. See also, e.g., Vat. Lat. 6325, fols. 5r, 32r, 122r, 153v, and *Scechina*, vol. I, pp. 73, 90, 219-220. Ficino speaks of Dionysius as "Platonicorum facile princeps," "Comm. in De div. nominibus," *Opera*, vol. II, p. 1024. M.-D. Chenu's reminder is salutary and can with profit be recalled even when treating of the sixteenth century: "Malgré la crue de l'aristotélisme, l'Aréopagite commande la théologie du XIII siècle," *La théologie au douzième siècle*, Paris 1957, p. 278. See also Wind, *Pagan Mysteries*, pp. 20-21, 57-58, 64. For Giles's reserves

The orthodoxy of Origen, a subject of seemingly perennial fascination for theologians, once again came up for sharp debate during Giles's lifetime.[1] Giles's partiality towards Origen was unambiguous: in 1503 Aldo Manuzio dedicated to him his edition of Origen's Homilies, and in 1512 Giles had a Latin translation of the *Peri Archon* and Pamphilius Martyr's defence of Origen copied for himself. Origen's Platonism and the elements of esoterism he inherited from Clement of Alexandria surely would appeal to Giles. More important, possibly, would be Origen's theories of exegesis, most particularly the "third sense" reserved for the "perfect" which was enunciated in the *Peri Archon.* Giles often refers to Origen and, without excusing whatever doctrinal indiscretions he may have been guilty of, feels that he was as important for Greek theology as Augustine for Latin.[2]

Trying to assess the influence of Augustine upon Giles is in a microcosmic way like trying to assess his influence upon the West as a whole. Augustine's thought impinged upon Giles from every conceivable angle—as a member of the Augustinian hermits, as a Christian Platonist, and as an exponent of the literary and ethical humanism which since Petrarch had invoked Augustine as its particular patron. Augustine is Giles's guide, "*dux meus*," through the Distinctions of the "Sententiae," and in the *Scechina*, in spite of the fact that he did not know the sacred language, he can still be described as most wise.[3]

---

on Dionysius, see Vat. Lat. 6325, fol. 167r. Ang. Lat. 502, fol. 270v, must be read in such a way as to be understood in the light of *Scechina*, vol. I, p. 90.

[1] See H. Crouzel, "Pic de la Mirandole et Origène," *Bulletin de littérature ecclésiastique* 66(1965), pp. 81-106, 272-288; D. P. Walker, "Origène en France au début du XVI siècle," *Courants religieux et Humanisme à la fin du XV et au début du XVI siècle: Colloque de Strasbourg, 1957*, Paris 1959, pp. 101-120, and Edgar Wind, "The Revival of Origen," *Studies in Art and Literature for Belle da Costa Greene*, ed. D. Miner, Princeton 1954, pp. 412-424, esp. 416-418 on Giles.

[2] Vat. Lat. 6325, fols. 137v, 176r; Évora CXVI/1-30, fol. 57r; Ang. Lat. 502, fols. 135v, 161r, 194v, 276r; Martène, *Veterum scriptorum collectio*, vol. III, col. 1249; *Scechina*, vol. I, p. 107; vol. II, pp. 34, 244; "Libellus" (in *Scechina*, vol. I), pp. 36, 48. Giles's copy of the *Peri Archon*, etc., is in the Biblioteca Angelica, Rome, Lat. 1244. For the Alexandrian origins of Christian esoterism, see Jean Daniélou, S. J., "Aux sources de l'ésotérisme judéo-chrétien," *Umanesimo e Esoterismo: Archivio di Filosofia* (1960), pp. 39-46. On the importance for medieval exegesis of the *Peri Archon* and for the fascinating story of Origen's career in the Middle Ages, see Henri de Lubac, S. J., *Exégèse médiévale*, vol. I.1, Paris 1959, pp. 198-207, 221-304. Ficino considered Origen "vir doctrina vitaque apprime mirabilis," "De Christiana religione," *Opera*, vol. I, p. 72.

[3] Massa, *Fondamenti metafisici e testi inediti*, p. 84, and *Scechina*, vol. II, p. 143. See also *Scechina*, vol. I, pp. 122, 222, etc.; Siena G. X. 26, pp. 107-108; Ang. Lat. 502, fol. 243r; Vat. Lat. 6325, fol. 167r. Giles's enthusiasm for Plato was recogniz-

We have already presented a resumé of the Augustinian epistemology which Giles adopted, and we could list any number of Augustinian themes which recur in his writings. Congar has pointed out that, historically speaking, reform movements in the West have almost always related to Augustinian theology, with its emphasis on conversion and the soul's movement from the image to the true, and the degree of such influence upon Giles the reformer should not be underestimated.[1]

There are, however, two specific roles assigned by Giles to Augustine which deserve our special attention. The first of these is Augustine as interpreter and teacher of the cabala, that is, of the more secret theology, "*secretioris theologiae*." H.-I. Marrou has called attention to Augustine's taste for allegory and numerology as part of the general influence of late antique culture upon him. In actual fact Giles's use of Augustine in the *Scechina* is rather modest, and he is hard pressed to find specific points of cabalistic doctrine for which he can adduce the authority of Augustine. He contents himself with referring to Augustine's exhortations to learn the sacred language and with showing how Augustine's trinitarian theology, for instance, agrees with the cabala.[2]

Giles accepted Augustine without question as the founder of the Augustinian order, and he was convinced of the truth of the legend that Augustine lived in retirement in Tuscany for a few years after his conversion, founding there the first monastery of Augustinian hermits. According to this legend Augustine visited the hermitage of Lecceto, a few miles west of Siena. It is in the light of these beliefs that we must understand the "Augustinian" nature of Giles's reform program. He insisted, first of all, upon a strict observance of the rule of Saint Augustine and he encouraged the printing of it in 1508, along with the constitutions of the order. In his work of reform he felt himself to be the mere executor of the master-plan left by Augustine. Giles's task was not to question it or adapt it, but to put it into execution. Furthermore, the living example of how the Rule could be

ed as early as 1503 in the dedication to him of the Venice edition of Gregory of Rimini's commentary on the first two books of Peter Lombard, fol. 1v.

[1] Congar, *Vraie et fausse réforme*, pp. 223-226.

[2] Ang. Lat. 502, fol. 292v. Also *ibid.*, fols. 23r, 181r, and *Scechina*, vol. II, p. 143: "Sapientissimus enim Augustinus, cui ego arcana quae Johannes recenset, ut potui homini a mea lingua alieno, explicavi." Marrou, *Saint Augustin*, pp. 259-262, 478-498. See also Hopper, *Medieval Number Symbolism*, pp. 78-88, and de Lubac, *Exégèse*, vol. I,2, Paris 1959, pp. 396-400.

reduced to action was the observant monastery of Lecceto, where Augustine's spirit presumably still lived on. This helps explain why Giles himself joined Lecceto in 1503 and why he tended to pattern his reform along the general lines of the way of life of the Observant Congregation of Lecceto.[1]

We can only mention in passing that Giles was familiar with Eusebius's *Praeparatio evangelica*, with its providential plan of history,[2] and that his knowledge of the *Koran* was first-hand.[3] Reserving Saint Jerome for the next chapter, we shall skip over a number of centuries to one of Giles's most curious interests, Joachim of Flora. Quite firmly in the "Sententiae" Giles opposes Joachim's speculations on the divine essence in the Trinity, and in the *Scechina* he rejects quaternity theories. He also implies in the "Sententiae" that, although Joachim was more successful in his popular prophetic preaching than in his trinitarian theology, he in neither case was free from a desire for personal fame.[4] In 1527, however, Silvestro Meucci (?-1535) dedicated to Giles his edition of Joachim's commentary on the Apocalypse. As part of the upsurge of enthusiasm for Joachim in the late fifteenth and early sixteenth centuries there was a group of Augustinians in the neighborhood of Venice who under the leadership of Silvestro Meucci published between 1515 and 1527 a number of Joachimite works. In Silvester's dedication of the Apocalypse commentary he recalls the interest Giles showed in the works of Joachim when he spent some time in Venice after the Spanish legateship was ended, therefore in 1519, and relates how at that time Giles urged him to continue the publication project, especially wanting to see the present work in print. That Giles's interest was not simply a polite courtesy is further indicated by the fact that his library presumably possessed a Pseudo-

---

[1] Martin, "Giles and Lecceto," esp. pp. 235-237, 249-250, and Arbesmann, "Henry of Freimar's 'Treatise.'" See also Siena G.X.26, p. 121, undated letter to Antonius Astensis: "Augustino illa [complaints about the difficulty of the rule] dicenda erant, non nobis. Ille vitae nostrae instituta posuit, non ipsi." See also *ibid.*, pp. 117-118, 138-139, 220; Ang. Lat. 502, fol. 39r; Aug. Gen. Archives, Rome, Cc. 37, fol. 112r. The Rule is contained in *Regula beati Augustini*, Venice 1508.

[2] See, e.g., Ang. Lat. 502, fols. 17v, 20v, and *Scechina*, vol. I, p. 117.

[3] See Secret's note, *Scechina*, vol. I, p. 18, along with Astruc and Monfrin, "Livres du Cardinal Gilles," pp. 553-554. See also ms. D.100 inf. in the Ambrosian Library, Milan, which contains a Latin translation of the Koran facing the Arabic text. On fol. 2v of this manuscript it is stated that the translation was done for Giles while he was legate in Spain, i.e., 1518-1519.

[4] Vat. Lat. 6325, fols. 91v and 93r, and *Scechina*, vol. I, pp. 85, 132-133; vol. II, p. 254.

Joachimite manuscript, now in the Bibliothèque Nationale, Paris. Giles's "Historia" was completed before his 1519 visit to Venice, and specific dependences upon Joachim in Giles's works have yet to be established. It is true, however, that some of Giles's ideas are compatible with those which, broadly speaking, can be classed as Joachimite, such as a real development or increase of doctrine beyond that found in the apostolic tradition. It was the Joachimite tradition, moreover, which heightened expectation in the later Middle Ages for an eschatological purification and renovation of the Church.[1]

Giles's relationship to the scholastics is extremely interesting. From what has already been said about his intellectual commitments we might expect that, after a youthful burst of enthusiasm for Giles of Rome, he would altogether reject the scholastics as too tainted with Aristotle and too rigorously systematized for him to be able to tolerate. This turns out not to be the case. Although it is true that as his interest in the cabala grew his esteem for the whole Latin tradition diminished, even in the pages of the *Scechina* scholastic categories recur and are often explicitly correlated with those of the cabala.[2] In his commentary on the *Sentences* he follows in a general way the topics treated by the great scholastics and, although his manner of argument is different from theirs, his conclusions are not so distinctive as we might have anticipated. Giles employs the basic concepts of hylomorphism, and he gives evidence he is aware of certain of the classic scholastic disputes.[3] Giles was interested in Gregory of Rimini (ca. 1300-1358), James of Viterbo (ca. 1250-ca. 1307), and Hugolino of Orvieto (ca. 1300-1373), three important Augustinian scholastics, and within the order he promoted study of the theology of Giles of Rome

[1] *Expositio magni prophete Abbatis Ioachim in Apocalipsim*, Venice 1527. Paris Lat. 3363, fols. 79r-149r, "In Isaiam." On this Paris manuscript, see Secret, *Les kabbalistes chrétiens*, p. 115. For a comprehensive study on Joachim, see M. W. Bloomfield, "Joachim of Flora: A Critical Survey of His Canon, Teachings, Sources, Biography and Influence," *Traditio* 13(1957), pp. 249-311, esp. 260-271 on his doctrinal themes. See also Ernst Benz, *Ecclesia spiritualis*, Stuttgart 1964 (photo-reprint of the original 1934 edition), as well as the studies mentioned earlier: Reeves, "Joachimist Expectations," and Zumkeller, "Joachim von Fiore."

[2] *Scechina*, e.g., vol. I, pp. 70, 85, 132-133; vol. II, pp. 14-15, 89, and, e.g., 26, "...educi e potentia aliquid in actum."

[3] God is "pure act," and "prime matter" is "pure potency," Vat. Lat. 6325, e.g., fols. 44r, 116r, 123v, 127v. God is ubiquitous by reason of His "presence, essence and power," *ibid.*, fols. 175r, 193v. Theology is a subalternate science, *ibid.*, fol. 2v, and Ang. Lat. 502, fol. 164r. For an indication of Giles's awareness of scholastic disputes, see Vat. Lat. 6325, fols. 199v-202v.

with an insistence truly remarkable for somebody convinced that the properly Christian philosophy was that of the Ficinian Plato.[1] How can we explain this strange anomaly?

Perhaps the first fact to be recalled is the scholastic element in Ficino's own work. Even though the precise extent of Ficino's dependence upon the scholastics has yet to be determined, there is no doubt that there was such a dependence, especially in the case of Saint Thomas.[2] The scholasticism to which Giles would have been exposed during his studies as a member of the Augustinian order would have found sympathetic response in much of Ficino's thought.

Due to the absence of printed texts the exact degree of Giles's indebtedness to the scholastics is even more problematic than Ficino's. The fact that Giles only rarely names a scholastic as an authority for his argument makes it difficult to identify whatever scholastic sources he might be using. In the commentary on Lombard, for instance, it is hard to find an obvious and consistent correlation between Giles's work and the corresponding ones of Saint Thomas and Giles of Rome. In this area, as in so many others, Massa's edition of Giles's commentary will facilitate detailed textual comparisons.

There is, however, some indication that Giles did not have a profound first-hand knowledge of the scholastic authors. On no occasion, for instance in discussing the accomplishments of the great scholastics of the thirteenth century, does Giles give any suggestion that he is clearly aware of what intrinsically differentiated one scholastic from another. His attempt to draw a parallel between Platonic and Thomistic epistemology, though not without foundation for the specific point he is making, is misleading and arouses doubts about his understanding of Thomas's theory.[3] He is never quite able to

---

[1] The Venice, 1503, edition of Gregory of Rimini was dedicated to Giles, and he mentions Gregory by name, *Scechina*, vol. I, p. 72. For James of Viterbo, see Massa, *Fondamenti metafisici e testi inediti*, p. 77, and Ang. Lat. 688, fol. 39r. For Hugolino of Orvieto, see Ang. Lat. 688, fol. 39r. To give some idea of his interest in Giles of Rome: Vat. Lat. 6325, fols. 27r, 46v; Siena G. X. 26, pp. 117-118, 131, 319; Ang. Lat. 502, fols. 101r, 122v, 163v-164r, 175r, 178v-179r; Massa, *Fondamenti metafisici e testi inediti*, pp. 16, 22.

[2] See Gilson, "Ficin et le *Contra Gentiles*;" Kristeller, "Scholastic Background of Ficino," and by the same author, *Le Thomisme de la Renaissance*, pp. 93-104.

[3] Ang. Lat. 502, fols. 101r, 122v, 178v-179r, and esp. 163v-164r: "Quod si credimus theologis, lux illa divina verior est, et longe quam corporea prior. Quam ob rem efficitur ut si illa lux vera, ita sol etiam ille verior, hic secundus imaginarius et umbratilis nominari velit. Immo, sicuti prius exposuimus, utramque illic Plato significat: intelligendi rationem illam a sensu, quam tenebras, hanc a

explain precisely what the scholastics were about, and he describes Thomas's achievement in vague terms as monuments of correct doctrine.[1] Albert the Great's theology is analyzed as an attempt to join philosophy with sacred subjects and to confirm religion with the aid of philosophy.[2] Such a description, especially if it be extended to the scholastic enterprise as a whole, is commonplace and inadequate. Tending to see philosophy, i.e., Aristotle, as something extrinsic to scholastic theology and at most only an external confirmatory support for doctrinal truths, he could accept a form of that theology which excluded those Aristotelian arguments which were erroneous.

We are almost forced to conclude, finally, that the praise Giles generously metes out to Albert, Scotus and especially to Thomas can best be explained by the fact that their work had been accepted as orthodox by the Church, and Giles, for reasons already discussed, was willing to accept this judgment, particularly since it was confirmed in the case of Saint Thomas by resplendent holiness of life, "*incredibilem sanctitatem*."[3] On one point Giles would not give way: whatever excellence the scholastics attained was due to their God-given intelligence, their probity and their sanctity, and not to the "sect," i.e., the Peripatetics.[4]

Giles of Viterbo insisted while prior general of the Augustinians that the preeminent place accorded Giles of Rome in the order's legislation and traditions be kept unchanged. One reason for this insistence is certainly that he saw Giles of Rome as one of the glories of the order, and he knew that it was his duty to promote whatever redounded to the order's good name.[5] Moreover, as we have already pointed out,

---

divini solis radiis quam lucem diemque cognominat. Quid quod tamquam divi Thomae aut Aegidii mei scripta legisset, scientiam nostram divinae prolem scientiae esse vult, ac proinde illi obnoxiam ac subjectam esse et, ut nostrorum verbo utar, subalternam." See also Naples V. F. 20, fols. 244v-245r. Giles mentions, in general terms, that the scholastics differ from one another, Ang. Lat. 502, fol. 122v.

[1] Ang. Lat. 502, fol. 172r, "monumenta doctrinae exactissimae absolutissimaeque."

[2] Ang. Lat. 502, fol. 172r.

[3] Ang. Lat. 502, fol. 172r. Ficino calls Thomas "Christianae splendor theologiae," "Theologia Platonica, lib. XVIII," *Opera*, vol. I, p. 410.

[4] Ang. Lat. 502, fol. 159v: "Non eo inficias clarissima Christianorum lumina ex ea palaestra [Paris] nata esse, viros summo ingenio, summa eruditione praeditos.... At id, quidquid fuit, ingeniorum probitati, integerrimorum hominum sanctitati, non sectae et disciplinae laudi dandum est. Non enim aliunde quam ex eo fonte natum est quod parum jam fides recipitur, parum sacris creditur,...."

[5] Siena G. X. 26, pp. 131, 319, and Ang. Lat. 502, fol. 175r.

Giles of Viterbo in his efforts to reform the order did not question its solemn legislation or traditions, and therefore he never questioned the wisdom of the order's decree of 1287, many times renewed, prescribing the teachings of Giles of Rome. Giles of Viterbo's desire to continue this prescription is more understandable when we recall that the purpose of the Augustinians' *studia* was not so much a scientific theological education as a spiritual formation in the ideals of the order. In the *studium* the Augustinian friar continued a training begun in the novitiate which made him different from the friars of the other mendicant orders, thus helping to justify the distinct existence of his order alongside the others. This fact partly explains why Giles can urge as a program for the Paduan *studium generale* that it make use of "*our*" teachers, viz., Saint Augustine and Giles of Rome.[1]

We have already mentioned the relationship between the scholastic principle, "*Facientibus quod in se est*," and Giles of Viterbo's solution to the problem of knowledge of the Trinity. Without indicating other arguments which were specifically scholastic in his writings, we can point out one definite tendency which seems at least partially derived from the famous scholastic theologians of his order: the strong emphasis upon the monarchical, almost absolute, position of the pope in the Church. Giles of Rome gave the so-called curial concept of the Church its scholastic formulation, and his successors in the order, notably James of Viterbo and Augustine of Ancona (Augustinus Triumphus, ca. 1250-1328), further developed it. As is well known, it was from Giles of Rome's *De ecclesiastica sive de summi pontificis potestate* of 1302 that Boniface VIII (1294-1303) drew the doctrine of "*Unam sanctam*" of that same year. Giles of Viterbo shows little sympathy for the personality and peremptory procedures of Boniface VIII, and he does not adduce scholastic authors by name as support for his own views on the nature of the Church. Nevertheless, his "Historia XX saeculorum," without enunciating an extreme or exclusive position, does propose a very papal concept of the Church, and certain statements in it practically paraphrase the doctrine found in Giles of Rome and "*Unam sanctam*." The papal doctrine of the Augustinian scholastics

[1] Siena G. X. 26, p. 118, letter entitled "De instituendo regente," undated: "...utramque animae partem instituas, litteris doctoris nostri Aegidii intellectum, praeceptis parentis nostri Augustini voluntatem." On the purpose of the *studium*, see R. Kuiters, O.S.A., "The Development of the Theological School of Aegidius Romanus in the Order of Saint Augustine," *Augustiniana* 4(1954), pp. 157-177, esp. 173-174.

is rooted, of course, in an earlier tradition. One can assume, however, that they imparted to their order an emphasis upon the role of the papacy in the Church which was still very much alive in the time of Giles of Viterbo.[1]

---

[1] For instances of Giles of Viterbo's interpretation of the pope's position, see Ang. Lat. 502, fol. 268v: "... ita pontificia vel vis vel auctoritas, imperare omnibus, nulli mortalium parere agnoscitur," and *ibid.*, fol. 45r: "... pontificem ad homines non pertinere; a Deo uno creari, cognosci judicarique oportere." See also *Scechina*, vol. II, p. 133. For Giles of Rome, see his *De ecclesiastica potestate*, ed. Richard Scholz, Weimar 1929, esp. pp. 6-9. For pertinent passages from "Unam sanctam," see Denz. nos. 870-875(468-469). See also canon 1556 of the present code of canon law. On the papal theories of Giles of Rome, James of Viterbo, Augustine of Ancona, see F. Merzbacher, "Wandlungen des Kirchenbegriffs im Spätmittelalter," *ZSavRG*, kan. Abt. 39(1953), pp. 274-361, esp. 295-305, and Michael Wilks, *The Problem of Sovereignty in the Later Middle Ages: The Papal Monarchy with Augustinus Triumphus and the Publicists*, Cambridge 1964, esp. pp. 455-478 on the question of "papa a nemine judicatur." Giles of Viterbo is careful in the "Historia" to make Giles of Rome an intimate of the gentle Celestine V (pope 1294) and not of Boniface VIII, for whom Platina, presumably, had taught him an aversion, Ang. Lat. 502, fols. 175r, 198r-v. For evidence that the strong emphasis on the papacy and on the Roman Church's plenitude of power, as a tradition in the Augustinian order deriving from Giles of Rome and Augustine of Ancona, was still operative in 1520, see T. Kolde, "Luther und sein Ordensgeneral in Rom in den Jahren 1518 und 1520," *ZKG* 2(1878), p. 479.

CHAPTER THREE

SCRIPTURE AND THE CABALA

Giles of Viterbo was a Christian theologian, and of all the sources upon which he drew Scripture held the primacy. It was the "oracle" *par excellence*. In the "Historia XX saeculorum" Giles attempts an interpretation of the history of the world by drawing upon the text of the first twenty psalms, and he wrote the *Scechina* as an apology for his new scriptural exegesis and as an exposition of its method and doctrine. The "Sententiae" is less obviously dependent upon the Bible, but traditionally the commentators on Peter Lombard felt that Scripture was the ultimate source from which their conclusions were drawn.

There is no better indication of the esteem Giles had for the sacred text from his earliest days than the place of honor which he accorded it in his preaching. As early as 1503 he confided to an Augustinian confrere that his apostolic activity consisted in "preaching the Gospel of the Kingdom through the countryside," and that the fabric of his sermons was the message of Scripture. His opening oration at the Fifth Lateran Council in 1512 with justice described his ministry throughout Italy in terms of "interpreting the Gospels to the people."[1] The sermon jottings preserved in the Bibliothèque Nationale and the suggestive sermon texts which he noted in his registers as prior general confirm the fact that the sermons took Scripture as their point of departure.[2] In 1530, looking back over the forty years of his priestly life, Giles once again saw his active ministry principally as an elucidation of the meaning of Scripture through the office of preaching.[3]

Giles's preaching career has been judged harshly. Heinrich Böhmer saw in him a man who, sincere and pious though he may have been,

---

[1] Naples V. F. 20, fol. 73v, letter dated December 28, 1503, to Serafino Ferri: "Discurro praedicans evangelium regni per castella. Secundet Dominus Deus retia nostra ut boni simus piscatores hominum." *Ibid.*, fol. 75r: "Nos vero, monstrante Deo, retibus uti sacrarum scripturarum, ..." Mansi, vol. XXXII, col. 669.

[2] On Paris Lat. 3461, see Martin, "Egidio da Viterbo," p. 137. See also Aug. Gen. Archives, Rome, e.g., Dd. 12, fols. 16r, 17v, 19r, 39r. For further instances of Giles's preaching noted in his registers, see Pélissier, "Pour la biographie," pp. 796-815.

[3] *Scechina*, vol. I, p. 66.

was more intent upon cultivating a Ciceronian style, displaying his humanist learning and pleasing his high-placed listeners than with delivering a sermon which could effect a real religious conversion after the manner of Savonarola; Giles's preaching was well received, especially in the Roman Curia, but it produced no lasting effect, not least of all because Giles was a humanist and a rhetorician.[1] We can question the presuppositions upon which Böhmer founds his judgment and conclusions. This is not to say, however, that there may not be some basis in fact for his assessment. Giles freely admits using Plato and other authors from pagan antiquity in his sermons and such use of the classics, no matter what one's understanding of their meaning, is certainly not without danger of eclipsing Scripture's importance.[2] Furthermore, the praise for the Medici and other contemporaries which sometimes occurred in these sermons can offend our sense of religious propriety.[3] An illuminating insight into Giles the preacher comes from his outline of a series of five sermons preached in 1502: the first four days correspond *ex professo* to the matter of the four books of Peter Lombard and are outlined in philosophic, not biblical, categories; only on the last day, when treating of the beatitude of heaven, does he abandon the *Sentences* of Lombard for Scripture.[4] Ambrogio Flandino defended Giles against what he tells us was Pomponazzi's accusation that Giles used his sermons as occasions for parading his erudition.[5]

In the face of this evidence we must not lose sight of the fact that Giles himself was sincerely convinced that his sermons were based upon the prophets and the Gospels and that they were directed towards promoting true piety. Whatever elements the sermons may have contained which might seem extraneous to these sources and to this

[1] Heinrich Böhmer, *Luthers Romfahrt*, Leipzig 1914, p. 41, "... und zwar nicht zuletzt weil er zu sehr Redekunstler und Humanist war."

[2] Ang. Lat. 1001, fol. 65r-v, letter dated October 14, 1503, to Serafino Ferri.

[3] See, e.g., Marino Sanuto, *I diarii*, vol. XXIII, Venice 1888, cols. 486-488, and Signorelli, *Egidio da Viterbo*, pp. 24, 146.

[4] Naples V. F. 20, fol. 60r-v, letter dated September 20, 1502, to Serafino Ferri: "Praedicavimus huic populo quinquies: [1] est siquidem in natura causa; [2] est id quod fit; [3] est aliquid quod et causa et effectum est; [4] est quarto dispositio qua causam effecta assequuntur; [5] est denique finis cujus gratia et agit omnia agens et fiunt quaecumque fiunt. Ita primo die de Deo qui causa est rerum, ... ac denique ut Parens naturali intelligentia gignat, ... atque haec quidem ex universo sententiarum volumine primo. Die altero ...." Thus he continues through the five days.

[5] See Martin, "Egidio da Viterbo," pp. 142-146, and Secret, "Notes sur Paulus Ricius," p. 184.

purpose, whether they came from pagan antiquity, the Fathers of the Church or the scholastics, he would justify as aiding in the understanding and meaningfulness of the sacred message or in making it acceptable to those who for some reason or other were disaffected towards it. On this latter point Giles is eloquently explicit.[1] A more ringing call to scriptural primacy can hardly be imagined than the one Giles himself gives: "The Gospels alone are our books. They alone are to be heard and read, and their prescriptions alone are to be observed. Only the man who regulates his life on them can with certain hope say, 'It is in God that I trust.'"[2]

Böhmer's contention that Giles's preaching did not have a lasting spiritual effect is extremely difficult, if not impossible, to substantiate, especially when he takes Savonarola as a norm against which to judge Giles. What can be asserted without misgiving is that for Giles preaching often had a moral purpose and he associated proclamation of the Gospel with a certain measure of threat and fulmination.[3] Giles's boast was that he preached Christ crucified after the example of the Apostle.[4]

Though Giles was always devoted to Scripture, he seems to have experienced a significant deepening of interest in it just about the time he assumed office as prior general. In that very year, 1507, in a letter

---

[1] Ang. Lat. 502, fols. 162v-163r: "...is [Christus] solus omnia solusque sat esse tam possit quam debeat bonis animis, sunt tamen sicut in cibis nonnulli stomacho ita vel delicato vel laeso ut vesci nisi aceto famem excitante non possint. Haud secus sane quidam sacra aut fastidiunt aut minus excipiunt, nisi philosophorum et veterum scriptorum testimonio comprobentur."

[2] Ang. Lat. 502, fol. 29r-v: "... sola suscipienda evangelia, sola audienda, lectitanda, servanda. Quod qui facit solus certa spe plenus ait, in Deo confido." See also Vat. Lat. 6325, fols. 20v and 165v: "Quare tres illas enumerat [Plato] personas quas sacra nostra oracula docuere, quamquam, ut saepe diximus protestatique sumus, citra omnem errorem sola evangelia eam sapientiam tradidisse intelligamus, ..."

[3] Martène, *Veterum scriptorum collectio*, vol. III, col. 1250, undated letter to Niccolò Mannio di Canepina: "... enarro evangelium; ... multo terrore moneo hortorque, ut par est." Also Naples V. F. 20, fol. 88r, letter dated January 15, 1505, to Serafino Ferri: "... in vitia moresque fulminarem ...." See also Martin, "Egidio da Viterbo," pp. 107, 133, 140, for other instances of Giles railing against immorality.

[4] Ang. Lat. 502, fol. 162v: "... fateor nihil scire me, sicut Apostolus ait, nisi Christum et hunc crucifixum [1 Cor. 2.2], quem in cunctis Italiae urbibus multos jam annos, et si minima doctrina, maximo tamen publicae salutis Christianaeque libertatis studio praedicavi." On the power and dynamism of the sacred word, see *Scechina*, vol. I, p. 159. It is interesting to compare Giles's description of his work with Pico's desire, expressed shortly before his death, to take up the life of an itinerant preacher, as quoted in Corsano, *Il pensiero religioso*, p. 46: "... et crucifixo munitus, exsertis nudatisque pedibus, orbem peragrans, per castella, per urbes Christum praedicabo."

to the convent at Padua there occurs a mention of a Gospel text which eventually would become one of the dominant themes of his intellectual activity, "*scrutamini scripturas*" (Jn. 5.39).[1] Giles probably had learned the elements of Hebrew during his Florence sojourn, 1494-1495, but he does not seem to have had the opportunity extensively to develop this interest until after the lapse of some years. By the time he began the "Historia," 1513 or shortly thereafter, he already had made a great deal of progress in Hebrew and Aramaic, as well as in Talmudic and cabalistic literature, and we catch some urgency in his insistence that "in the Gospel we are commanded to search the Scriptures."[2] In 1515 Elijah Levita arrived in Rome, where he was befriended by Giles. Giles soon took him and his family into his household, asking in return only that Elijah act as his teacher. Elijah stayed with Giles for some ten years, until the sack of 1527.[3] By the time of the *Scechina*, 1530, Giles has so completely dedicated himself to the task of investigating the meaning of Scripture, in obedience to the Gospel text, that all his other intellectual interests were consciously absorbed into it and had meaning only in relationship to it.[4] His knowledge of Jewish literature was now extensive and reached, for instance, even to the work of medieval grammarians such as David Kimhi (1160-1235).[5]

The index of Scripture references in Secret's edition of the *Scechina* shows clearly that Giles had a wide ranging familiarity with the whole of the Old and New Testaments. He easily used the Song of Solomon, for instance, as a sermon text, giving it an allegorical interpretation and favorably discriminating it from the obscene verses of Catullus.[6]

---

[1] Siena G. X. 26, p. 54, letter dated February 24, 1507.

[2] Ang. Lat. 502, fol. 194v: "... praeceptum [est] in evangelio, scrutamini scripturas." Giles wrote to Gabriele della Volta, Ang. Lat. 688, fol. 49r-v, letter dated January 9 (V Idus), 1514: "Nos quidem in studiis sanctae linguae Hebraeae libentissime conquiescimus, ut optamus optimos quosque in eo genere sortiri libros."

[3] See Weil, *Élie Lévita*, pp. 53-90.

[4] *Scechina*, vol. I, p. 85: "Audi commune in hoc praeceptum sapientiae meae, liminibus pernecessarium et portae bibliothecae grandioribus eisdemque aureis litteris insculpendum, scrutamini scripturas." The phrase, "*scrutamini scripturas*," is quoted or alluded to, e.g. *Scechina*, vol. I, pp. 69, 74, 85, 86, 99, 106, 109, 110, 111, 145, 152, 153, 155, 159, 166, 179, 191, 192, etc.; vol. II, pp. 25, 27, 42, 43, etc.

[5] See *Scechina*, vol. I, p. 147, as well as Ang. Lat. 3, Giles's Latin translation of Kimhi's Hebrew dictionary. For further indications of the extent of Giles's familiarity with this literature, see Secret's "Introduction," *Scechina*, vol. I, pp. 9-20, and his index, *ibid.*, vol. II, p. 323. See also his article, "Le symbolisme de la Kabbale chrétienne," pp. 135-136.

[6] Naples V. F. 20, fol. 258v, letter undated, to Antonio Zocolo and the Augustinians in Rome: "Hic cantica cecinit divinum undique et arcanum opus, ubi

There can be no doubt that among the authors of the New Testament Saint John was his favorite. In the "Sententiae" Giles already is convinced that divine wisdom was transmitted to John in greater abundance than to other sacred writers, and that it is his doctrine which is found in the writings of Plato.[1] The *Scechina* demonstrates that Giles's study of the cabala confirmed his earlier esteem for John, whom he now sees as the glory of all theologians.[2] Unlike his contemporaries, Erasmus and Luther, he gives no indication that he felt any particular reserve was required in using John's Apocalypse.[3]

Giles was convinced that his own age was on the threshold of a great revival of scriptural studies and he was proud to be playing a part in a movement which would open up to the Christian world biblical treasures of which it had long been deprived. We have already called attention to Giles's gratification at the rebirth of eloquence in the poets of his day. He saw the same kind of a renaissance in biblical studies, and he tells Leo X that, just as his father Lorenzo was responsible for the restoration to mankind of lost and forgotten works written in Greek, so he, Leo, by his patronizing of arts and letters would bring back to life a proper understanding of Scripture.[4] In the *Scechina* Giles dates the beginning of the revival roughly at the time of the birth of Charles V, whom he is addressing, and identifies it with the fact that scholars in different parts of Europe began to study the sacred language of the Bible.[5] An understanding of language, however, was insufficient to penetrate to the inner meaning of the text. For this was needed the works of the "Hebrews and Arameans" which, marvellous to say, were now finally available to Christians. In these works Christians discovered truths which by right were theirs since

---

multo suavior visus in sacris castisque amoribus Salomon quam in obscenis ac perditis Catullus." See also Aug. Gen. Archives, Rome, Dd. 12, fols. 16r, 17v, and Vat. Lat. 6325, fol. 176r.

[1] Vat. Lat. 6325, fols. 34v-35r, 165v, 171v.

[2] *Scechina*, vol. II, pp. 86, 263. See also Ang. Lat. 502, fols. 48v, 61v, 76r.

[3] Mansi, vol. XXXII, cols. 669, 673; Évora CXVI/1-30, fols. 28v, 39r-v; Ang. Lat. 502, fols. 55v, 86v, 90r, 176(a)v. On the reserves of Erasmus and Luther, see M. Bataillon, "Évangélisme et millénarisme au Nouveau Monde," *Courants religieux et Humanisme à la fin du XV et au début du XVI siècle: Colloque de Strasbourg, 1957*, Paris 1959, p. 27. Annio da Viterbo's commentary on the Apocalypse was first published at Genoa in 1480, and Petrus Galatinus also wrote a commentary on it, Vat. Lat. 5567, fols. 1-417.

[4] Ang. Lat. 502, fol. 8r: "...ita te pontifice...et utraque lex et universa sacra tamquam ab interitu et ab ipsis velut cineribus reviviscant."

[5] *Scechina*, vol. I, p. 156.

they had accepted the Messiah, for whose sake and in view of whom the Law was given.[1]

How did Giles fit the present revival into the total history of biblical studies? To his way of viewing the question the first practical step in the West had to be the establishment of a translation which represented as accurately as possible the original, i.e., the "*Hebraica veritas*," for which were needed, of course, scholars who had a profound knowledge of Hebrew and Aramaic. It is for this reason that in his eyes Jerome could claim the special gratitude of all theologians, for it had been Jerome's aim to emend the Latin text in accordance with the original and he never ceased to advocate a return to it. Jerome's fidelity to the Hebrew text imparted to his interpretation and translation a real and lasting value.[2] Unfortunately, Jerome never had the opportunity to read the "*arcana*," the cabalistic works in which Giles found the inner meaning of the sacred text. This deficiency resulted in the strange paradox of Jerome's thinking he was attaining the "*Hebraica veritas*," whereas in actual fact he was unable to get into the deep meaning of it.[3]

Giles had honest respect for Jerome's translation. This does not mean, however, that he felt it was definitive. In the *Scechina*, for example, he sometimes makes use of the translation of his contemporary, the Dominican exegete and Hebraist, Santi Pagnini (1470-1536).[4] Giles explains that Jerome was prevented from making certain corrections in the received translation by the fact that the errors had been consecrated by long acceptance and usage, but he also agrees with Jerome

---

[1] Ang. Lat. 502, fol. 196v: "Apparuit hoc tempore mira res, libris innumerabilibus Hebraeorum Aramaeorumque disputata, nulli hactenus, ..., Christianorum cognita, nullis Christianorum libris aperte tradita, tametsi constat finem legis esse Messiam, eorumque gratia datam fuisse qui Messiam essent recepturi." See also *ibid.*, fol. 195v: "...ex ipsa Turcarum impietate quotidie naves libris novis onustae trajiciunt in Italiam, et ad divina vaticinia et pietatis amplexanda studia incitamenta ad nos movendos ex ora impiorum hostium convehuntur."

[2] Ang. Lat. 502, fol. 110v: "...secundum veritatem Hebraicam atque Hieronymi interpretationem." See also *ibid.*, fols. 14r, 38v, 113v, 125v, 194v-195r, 198r, 275r, 279r; "Libellus" (in *Scechina*, vol. I), p. 37. In the Middle Ages for Rupert of Deutz (ca. 1070-1129), for instance, the "*Hebraica veritas*" was practically identical with the Latin text of Jerome: "Secundum nostram translationem, Hebraicam scilicet veritatem," as quoted in de Lubac, *Exégèse*, vol. II.1, Paris 1961, p. 244.

[3] *Scechina*, vol. I, p. 196: "Divus Hieronymus, quem praeceptorum culpa haec secreta latuere, cum Hebraicam se veritatem sequi arbitraretur ab arcana Hebraeorum veritate recessit." See also Ang. Lat. 502, fol. 205v.

[4] For Giles's use of Santi Pagnini, see *Scechina*, vol. I, p. 81n, and vol. II, p. 317. See also Ang. Lat. 502, fol. 195v. For a study on Pagnini, see T. M. Centi, O.P., "L'attività letteraria di Santi Pagnini (1470-1536) nel campo delle scienze bibliche," *AFP* 15(1945), pp. 5-51.

that these errors should frankly be recognized as such.[1] One of Jerome's great insights was that for the true understanding of the text every minutest detail of it, e.g., the word order, was of the utmost importance.[2] In spite of some reservations, then, Giles saw in Jerome a landmark in the history of biblical scholarship, and he was convinced that the publication of Jerome's works which was being undertaken in his own day was one of the signs that a real scriptural renaissance was under way.[3]

In the centuries which intervened between Jerome's age and the revival of learning not only did Christians not read what Jerome had written but they even allowed his writings to be lost. How could such a tragedy happen? Giles's answer is clear: it was due to the barbarians from the north who invaded Italy and destroyed its culture.[4] Thus the dark night of ignorance engulfed learning, and it was not until a relatively short while ago that Nicholas of Lyra (ca. 1270-1340), moved by the writings and example of Jerome, turned to the study of the language of the prophets and began to dispel the ignorance of centuries.[5]

By focusing attention on the sacred language Nicholas of Lyra initiated a new era in Scripture studies. He was succeeded by Paul of Burgos (ca. 1353-1435) and Jacobus Perez de Valencia (ca. 1408-1490). The work of these men was so contagiously successful that, according to Giles, there now are scholars in all nations and in all religious orders who know the sacred language.[6] It is only Rome that lags behind. The French and the Spaniards drove out the Jews, but tried to imbibe some of their learning. The Italians, completely absorbed with conjectural knowledge deriving from the senses, welcome the exiled Jews

---

[1] Ang. Lat. 502, fols. 37v-38r, 53r, 79r-v, 194v, 196r-v, 307v.

[2] Ang. Lat. 502, fol. 294v; *Scechina*, vol. I, pp. 20n and 36n.

[3] Ang. Lat. 502, fol. 195v: "...nunc ut pia a pietatis studiosioribus sedulo excoluntur, curatumque est uti Hieronymi scripta publicarentur."

[4] Ang. Lat. 502, fol. 195r: "...in causa fuit barbarorum illuvies, toties Alpium vallum transgredientium, toties Italiam diripientium, ..." The same reason was given in 1518 by G. Francesco Pico della Mirandola in a letter to Santi Pagnini, as quoted in Centi, "Santi Pagnini," p. 11.

[5] Ang. Lat. 502, fol. 195r: "...veritatis lucem ab errorum tenebris vindicavit." See also *ibid.*, fol. 2v. According to Zumkeller, "Manuskripte," p. 67, Giles's marginalia appear on the manuscript entitled, "Nicolaus de Lira, de differentia translationis nostrae ab Hebraica in toto Veteri Testimento," Staatsbibliothek, Munich, Lat. 307.

[6] Ang. Lat. 502, fol. 195r-v. For Erasmus's very different evaluation of Nicholas of Lyra and Paul of Burgos, see de Lubac, *Exégèse*, vol. II.2, Paris 1964, pp. 434-435. For Ficino on the same two figures, see "De Christiana religione," *Opera*, vol. I, p. 39.

into Italy but, as a general rule, pay no attention to their learning. The greatest disgrace of all is that Rome, the capital city of the world and of the Church, now must be instructed by others in the very fundamentals of religious learning.[1]

In spite of the praise Giles has for Nicholas of Lyra, he recognized in him the same deficiency he saw in Jerome. Because of Nicholas's knowledge of the sacred language he was able to arrive at the literal sense of Scripture, but he could not penetrate to its inner mystical meaning.[2] Something further was needed to bring the scriptural revival to its full fruition. This something was the cabala, i.e., the "tradition of the ancients." Pico was the first to open the cabala to Christians, and he was followed by Paolo Riccio (?-1541) and Reuchlin.[3] For Giles the discovery of the cabala by the Christians of his own day marked the great turning point in the history of exegesis. The importance of this discovery, moreover, was not limited to the field of exegesis and theology. It had repercussions which affected all humanity and the total life of the Church. It was a cause and a symptom of the spiritual unity of mankind which Giles hoped soon to see accomplished. This dimension of the cabala's meaning was proposed by Giles to Gian Matteo Giberti (1495-1543) in a letter written during the pontificate of Leo X, and it would become a dominant theme of the *Scechina* of 1530.[4]

Giles saw Pico as the initiator of the Christian cabala, and his judg-

---

[1] Ang. Lat. 502, fols. 195v-196r: "Patiturque urbs Roma, orbis terrarum princeps, extrema in divinis studiis tenere, et quamquam religionis est caput ad religionis fundamenta cognoscenda ab universo orbe patitur invitari, ..." See also *ibid.*, fol. 182r.

[2] Ang. Lat. 502, fol. 2v. De Lubac shows that Nicholas's reputation for promoting the literal sense of Scripture needs qualification, and he points out the strongly Joachimist traditions which insinuated themselves into his exegesis, *Exégèse*, vol. II.2, pp. 344-367. In this same chapter de Lubac comments on Paul of Burgos and Jacobus Perez de Valencia.

[3] "Libellus" (in *Scechina*, vol. I), p. 24: "Soli qui per cabala, hoc est patrum traditionem quasi per manus accepere, magna vi librorum aggressi id sunt, sicut Picus nobis primus innuit, deinde Paulus Israelita [Riccio] silvam adiit, denique Joannes Capnio [Reuchlin] non parum sacrae materiae in sacra aedificia comportavit." See also Ang. Lat. 502, fol. 195r-v.

[4] Martène, *Veterum scriptorum collectio*, vol. III, col. 1261, letter undated: "Millia jam annorum Aramaeorum decreto latuere [secreta]. Nunc simul et Aramaea religio quae a Romana sede sejuncta est legatos mittit, et Aramaea secreta se aperiunt, ut pastorem Leonem agnoscant ac salutent, dicatque mecum non Italia, non Europa modo, sed orbis universus pastori suo, ut jumenta facti sumus apud te." Ps. 73(72). 22. For no other single gift, after that of salvation itself, was greater gratitude owed to God than for the fact that in the present age the "*arcana*" had been made available, Ang. Lat. 502, fol. 104r.

ment has been confirmed by modern scholarship.[1] Pico was by no means the first Christian to use the cabala for a Christian purpose, i.e., to interpret cabalistic themes in a Christian sense or to interpret Christian doctrines by means of cabalistic categories, in the belief that the cabala was in essence identical with Christian teaching. He was, however, the first Christian of non-Jewish extraction to do this, and to do it not with an apologetic or missionary purpose, but simply for the benefit of Christians themselves and of speculative Christian theology as such. Moreover, the previous attempts at a "Christian cabala" were made by persons who were at best on the periphery of the intellectual life of their day, whereas Pico was at its center. Giles saw that Pico sometimes missed rather obvious cabalistic truths, but this fact did not obscure for Giles the pivotal role Pico played in the history of the Christian cabala.[2]

Giles was also quite correct in assigning an important role to Paolo Riccio, a Jewish convert to Christianity. Riccio translated into Latin the *Porta lucis*, a cabalistic work on the divine names, and he wrote several treatises of his own. He was a former student of Pomponazzi and knew some of the more renowned personages of his age, especially from the north of Europe—Johannes Eck, Albrecht Dürer (1471-1528), Willibald Pirckheimer, and others. Significantly enough, he vigorously took up the defence of the Pseudo-Areopagite against those who cast doubt on his authenticity.[3]

Of the three initiators of the Christian cabala whom Giles mentions his personal involvement was certainly greatest in the case of Reuchlin. Giles had high praise for him for his accurate knowledge of Hebrew, and he owned a copy of Reuchlin's *De arte cabalistica* which was a gift of the author himself.[4] He took an active interest in the controversy

[1] Secret, *Les kabbalistes chrétiens*, pp. 1-2, and 40: "En conclusion, si Pic de la Mirandole ne fut qu'un chaînon dans le développement de la kabbale chrétienne à la Renaissance, la légende qui a souvent raison contre l'histoire en a justement fait le père de la kabbale chrétienne." See also Scholem, "Anfänge der christlichen Kabbala," esp. pp. 158-159, 170. For the interest in Jewish religion and literature of Ficino, Poliziano and Pico, see U. Cassuto, *Gli ebrei a Firenze*, Florence 1918, pp. 277-323, and Cecil Roth, *The Jews in the Renaissance*, New York 1965, esp. pp. 111-136.

[2] See "Libellus" (in *Scechina*, vol. I), p. 40. See also *ibid.*, p. 25n; *Scechina*, vol. I, p. 152; and di Napoli, *Giovanni Pico della Mirandola*, esp. pp. 77, 282-287.

[3] See Secret, *Les kabbalistes chrétiens*, pp. 87-97, and "Notes sur Paulus Ricius," pp. 169-192.

[4] Ang. Lat. 502, fol. 79r: "...omnium ut in Hebraicis litteris cognoscendis accuratissimus, ita quidem in tradendis commodissimus." See also *ibid.*, fol. 274v, and Johannes Reuchlin, *Reuchlins Briefwechsel*, ed. Ludwig Geiger, Tübingen 1875,

which raged around the writings of Reuchlin, as is clear from a letter to Jacques Lefèvre d'Étaples in which he speaks of his activity "in defending the truth of Reuchlin's cause."[1] Three of Giles's letters to Reuchlin were published in the second edition, 1519, of the *Illustrium virorum epistolae*, and in one of these, in his official capacity as prior general, he made Reuchlin an affiliated member of the Augustinian order.[2] His correspondence with Reuchlin reveals the high regard in which he held him, as well as his conviction that Talmudic and cabalistic wisdom was essential for the well-being of the Church. It was not Reuchlin whom he was defending, but the Church and the Church's interests.[3]

Giles was in communication with other students of rabbinic or cabalistic literature. The Franciscan, Petrus Galatinus, and the Dominican, Agostino Giustiniani (1470-1536), were perhaps the most outstanding.[4]

---

p. 276. Reuchlin gives credit to his predecessors—Pico and Riccio—for their study of the cabala, *De arte cabalistica*, p. 213, and to Pico alone, pp. 216, 226-227, 239, 240, etc.

[1] Martène, *Veterum scriptorum collectio*, vol. III, col. 1261: "Ecce recitantur litterae tuae in conventu praesulum et theologorum qui defendendae veritatis Reuchlin gratia conveneramus." This letter is dated July 11 (V Idus), 1511, by Martène and Durand, which is certainly too early. To be preferred would be the date given in Vat. Lat. 3461, fol. 27r, July 11 (V Idus), 1516, or that given in Ang. Lat. 1001, fol. 255v, June 27 (V Kalendas Julii), 1516. From external evidence Augustin Renaudet suggested 1515 as the date, *Préréforme et Humanisme à Paris pendant les premières guerres d'Italie (1494-1517)*, Paris 1916, pp. 654-655. Dom Anselm Hufstader, O.S.B., called my attention to Renaudet's dating. Another copy of this letter, undated, is to be found in Siena G. X. 26, pp. 310-311. Professor L. Bieler of University College, Dublin, confirmed for me the fact that the letter in Vat. Lat. 3461 is not an autograph. As late as May 11, 1520, Reuchlin was counting on Giles's help in his defence. See Ludwig Geiger, *Johann Reuchlin: Sein Leben und seine Werke*, Leipzig 1871, p. 450.

[2] See *Reuchlins Briefwechsel*, pp. 260-261, 276, and Vat. Lat. 3146, fols. 31v-32r, as well as Martin, "Problem of Giles of Viterbo," 9(1959), pp. 363-364. For an entry in Giles's registers, see Aug. Gen. Archives, Rome, Dd. 12, fol. 82v: "Dedimus litteras familiares ad D. Reuchlin."

[3] See *Reuchlins Briefwechsel*, p. 261, and Vat. Lat. 3146, fol. 32r, letter dated October 25, 1516: "...non te [Reuchlin] sed legem, non Thalmud sed ecclesiam, non Reuchlin per nos sed nos per Reuchlin servatos et defensos intelligimus." Giles regrets not having met Reuchlin when he was in Germany and congratulates him on his work, especially with the *Zohar*. He then tells him: "...per te denique servati thesauri sunt scientiae et sapientiae Dei in Thalmud libris....quae insanientium et imperitorum vitio interiissent, tuo unius supersunt beneficio, in opes et ornamentum ecclesiae Romanae," *ibid.*, fol. 31v. See also Ang. Lat. 502, fol. 297r.

[4] On Galatinus, see Arduinus Kleinhans, O.F.M., "De vita et operibus P. Galatini, O.F.M., scientiarum biblicarum cultoris," *Antonianum* 1(1926), pp. 145-179, 327-356. On Galatinus and A. Giustiniani, see Secret, *Les kabbalistes chrétiens*, pp. 99-106, and *Scechina*, vol. I, p. 19. Giles refers to Giustiniani, Ang. Lat. 502, fols. 195v, 279r, and Ang. Lat. 1170, fol. 40r.

Giles knew Felice da Prato (ca. 1450-ca. 1550), the Jewish convert who entered the Augustinian order, and he was to some extent influenced by him.[1] His recognition of the accomplishments of these men only served to point up for him, however, the deplorable condition in which most Christian theologians found themselves. They were ignorant of the sacred language and of the cabala. Giles was extremely sensitive to these deficiencies and considered them a terrible scandal. The mistakes which Christian exegetes made were so stupid and elementary as to provoke even Jewish children to laughter, an observation to which Giles so often recurs as to suggest that he himself at times must have witnessed such laughter.[2] Giles saw the remedy to this situation in the spread of sacred learning among the Christians of his day.

Only in the light of what has already been said can we understand the full import of what Giles meant by the term "*Hebraica veritas*." Correction of the errors in the translation by recurring to the Hebrew original was certainly the first thing he had in mind, and in this his usage of the phrase comes closest to what it meant to Jerome and the medieval commentators.[3] Erasmus's usage shows that humanist circles contemporary with Giles, especially those strongly influenced by Lorenzo Valla, meant practically the same thing and that they spoke in a context of textual clarification and emendation.[4] Giles himself practiced

---

[1] See Secret's comments, *Scechina*, vol. I, pp. 11-12, and *Les kabbalistes chrétiens*, pp. 106-123, esp. 107. See also Paul Kahle, "Zwei durch Humanisten besorgte dem Papst gewidmete Ausgaben der hebräischen Bibel," *Essays Presented to Leo Baeck*, London 1954, pp. 50-74, esp. 53-58. For reservations on Felice da Prato's work, see Weil, *Élie Lévita*, p. 306. But see also Paul Kahle, *The Cairo Geniza*, 2nd ed., Oxford 1959, pp. 120-124, and Pélissier, "Pour la biographie," p. 812. For a list of Jews who were at one time or other in Giles's service, see Secret, *Les kabbalistes chrétiens*, p. 109.

[2] E.g., Ang. Lat. 502, fols. 2v, 7v, 14r; "Libellus" (in *Scechina*, vol. I), p. 25. See also Ang. Lat. 502, fols. 115v, 116r. Giles's contemporaries—Savonarola and Santi Pagnini—were preoccupied with the concern not to excite the contempt or derision of unbelievers by their exegesis, Centi, "Santi Pagnini," p. 7. Saint Thomas felt this same concern, *S.T.* I q 68 art. 1.

[3] Ang. Lat. 502, fols. 21v, 38r, 196r-v; *Scechina*, vol. I, p. 94: "...et patimini tu [Charles V] et pontifex [Clement VII] hos errores legi?" Also *ibid.*, vol. I, p. 179; vol. II, pp. 10, 114-115. For medieval understanding of the term, see de Lubac, *Exégèse*, vol. II.1, pp. 238-250.

[4] Werner L. Gundersheimer, "Erasmus, Humanism, and the Christian Cabala," *Journal of the Warburg and Courtauld Institutes* 26(1963), esp. pp. 42-43. Erasmus was aware that in order to understand the text of the New Testament it was necessary to know the institutions and customs of the times in which it was written. See Myron P. Gilmore, *Humanists and Jurists*, Cambridge, Mass. 1963, pp. 105-114. For the urgency of the term "*Hebraica veritas*" among Giles's contemporaries, especially Ficino, Pico and Poliziano, see Humfredus Hodius (Hody), *De bibliorum*

what he preached and through dint of hard effort mastered Hebrew and Aramaic, and was one of the relatively few men of his age who knew Arabic.[1]

For Giles Hebrew was the language in which God spoke to man. This made it a language set apart from the others and transcendently different from them. In this he differed from Augustine and from the trilingual theories of some of the medievals who, though seeing Hebrew as a language created to express divine truths, did not as a rule consider it essentially different from Latin and Greek. Giles, however, is in earnest when he asserts that Hebrew is the only language which has been transmitted to men by the Holy Spirit.[2]

We do not realize what an extreme position Giles takes on this question until some specific instance is examined, e.g., the inner meaning of the letter Aleph. This letter in its actual written form expresses the mystery of the Trinity, and God means to communicate the mystery to men through this letter. From the fact that it is made up, according to Giles's analysis, of a Vau and two Yods he draws the conclusion that it symbolizes the divine Trinity.[3] Obviously enough, once an alphabet and a language no longer are believed to be a set of arbitrary symbols but a divinely ordained code for transmitting sacred doctrines, they are endowed with a nobility and transcendence which put them into a simply different category of reality from other alphabets and languages. Only when we are aware of this theory can we fully appreciate the depth of meaning with which Giles endowed the

---

textibus originalibus libri IV, Oxford 1705, pp. 438-488. Pico, for instance, would emend the Septuagint in the light of the Hebrew text, "Diputationes adversus astrologos," *Opera omnia*, Venice 1557, p. 115r: "...sicubi vero in sacris voluminibus editio Graeca in hac annorum permensione ab Hebraica veritate discordat, non potest quisquam recto judicio auctori ipsi praeponere fidem translatoris, ..."

[1] Secret, *Les kabbalistes chrétiens*, pp. 107-109; Karl H. Dannenfeldt, "The Renaissance Humanists and the Knowledge of Arabic," *Studies in the Renaissance* 2(1955), pp. 96-117. Martin discovered in the Biblioteca Angelica some notes on Arabic grammar which were compiled in 1519 at Giles's order, SS. 11. 11(4), fols. 26r-41r, and in which he is described as "Arabicae linguae scientissimus," fol. 26r.

[2] "Libellus" (in *Scechina*, vol. I), p. 26: "At cum haec sola lingua a divino sit Spiritu tradita, cum Latina Graecaque convenit in litteris aliis, triplici aspirandi forma dissentit, ut facile almi Spiritus divinum munus cognoscas." The Greeks corrupted the sacred alphabet, *ibid.* See also *ibid.*, pp. 31-32, 36, 54; *Scechina*, vol. II, p. 27; Ang. Lat. 502, fol. 113v. See de Lubac, *Exégèse*, vol. II.1, pp. 244-252, esp. 247.

[3] "Libellus" (in *Scechina*, vol. I), p. 36: "Occurrit prima littera Aleph quae una simplexque cum sit ex tribus constat, Vau media et duobus Iodim. Volunt Aramaei hanc significare primam trinitatem."

phrase *"Hebraica veritas."* The sacred text in every conceivable way down to the minutest detail—word order, structure and position of the letters, etc.—was the bearer of divine truth to men.[1] All that was needed was the key to unlock the treasures of wisdom and instruction contained in the *"Hebraica veritas."*

Giles very explicitly spells out for us the meaning of the divine command to search the Scriptures, and he tells us that it comprises the two elements which we have just been discussing in relation to his understanding of the term *"Hebraica veritas."* First of all the Christian exegete must be equipped with a sound knowledge of Hebrew grammar, syntax and vocabulary in order to understand the language itself, and secondly, in order to grasp the inner meaning of the sacred text, he must make use of the doctrine and exegetical techniques of the cabala.[2]

In Chapter One we saw how convinced Giles was that he could find Christian truths in the authors of pagan antiquity. He was even more firmly convinced that he found them in his Hebrew and Aramaic sources as part of the secret oral tradition which had been theirs from of old. He often cites evidence for knowledge of the Trinity in these sources, and in the *Scechina*, which is shot through with trinitarian speculation, he gives the "Arameans" credit for greater orthodoxy in the *"Filioque"* controversy than he does the Greeks.[3] In the *Zohar* he found many truths about the Messiah, and he thought the Arameans

---

[1] "Libellus" (in *Scechina*, vol. I), p. 51: "Scrutari enim is [Christus] jubet scripturas, quod est non corticem a limine salutare, sed penitus arcana quae latent intus aspicere, quod praecipue nosse est in situ, partibus, usu litterarum. Quae res etsi ridicula est in linguis aliis quae humanis ingeniis inventae, ut cuique visum est, receptae sunt, in litteris quas a Deo optimo maximo traditas mortalibus constat, ut ex Mosis et prophetarum testimoniis visitur, est non modo inter seria et gravia verum etiam inter maxime sacra longe sacratissima." Also *Scechina*, vol. I, p. 159: "Voces enim litteraeque mortalium idcirco nullam vim habent, quod nuda signa sint, atque idcirco Latinae Graecaeque ac gentium multarum, quod inventa hominum et curta imitamenta primarum, jure contemnere potestis." Also *ibid.*, p. 180: "Sed ut videas, eos qui vestris traductionibus fidunt non evangelia audire, non scrutare scripturas, sed aquas potare turbidas." See Gershom G. Scholem, *Major Trends in Jewish Mysticism*, 3rd ed., New York 1961, pp. 17, 133-135, on the mystical meaning of the divine language.

[2] See Giles's marginal notation in the codex entitled "Dictionarium sive liber radicum," Ang. Lat. 3, fol. 2r: "Id non omiserim, praecepto Domini obtemperari non posse sine his, cum scripturas scrutandas esse mandavit, quibus duo esse apud Hebraeos constat admodum necessaria, et has grammaticales institutiones ad linguam et arcanas commentationes ad intellectum."

[3] Ang. Lat. 502, fols. 18r, 117r, 196v, 288v-300v; *Scechina*, vol. I, p. 234. See Pico, *De hominis dignitate, etc.*, p. 160.

knew why the rites of the New Law were unbloody.[1] Perhaps the most curious of all the truths Giles felt were fully comprehensible only "*ex arcanis*" was the meaning of the triple crown of the papal tiara.[2]

As was true for the works of pagan antiquity, Giles did not accept uncritically the widely diversified corpus of Jewish literature with which he was familiar. He realized that some of the ideas contained in these works were incompatible with Christian teaching and even inimical to it. He distinguished three kinds of doctrines and described the use Christian theologians could make of each of them: the false ideas were to be refuted, the ideas which were neutral were to be made to function in the Gospel's favor, and the ideas which agreed with the Gospel were to be accepted.[3] As in the case of the pagan classics Giles insisted that Christian orthodoxy was the ultimate norm against which these writings must be judged. He realized that in making use of them he was traveling through somewhat alien territory, but he did so only in order that he might arrive at Christian truth.[4]

Once the full implication of what was meant by the "*Hebraica veritas*" dawned upon Giles it caused him to adopt a very severe attitude towards those who tried to attain divine truth without using the proper means.[5] He saw that the result of such an approach to revelation was that there were divine truths whose existence these Christian theologians did not even suspect.[6] Needless to say, Aristotle figures among the improper means specifically rejected, and his sophistries are not the way to arrive at an understanding, for instance, of the meaning of the divine names.[7] Giles's attack in this case, however, is not directed principally against the Paduan Aristotelians, but against all Christian theologians who are ignorant of the sacred language and the "*arcana*" and who think they can find divine truths outside them.

Giles does not mean to imply that the Church and the Christian faithful have been deprived of the essentials of belief because they

[1] Paris Lat. 527[1], fol. 298r, and see also, e.g., *Scechina*, vol. I, pp. 228-229; Ang. Lat. 502, fol. 49v.

[2] Ang. Lat. 502, fols. 236v-238v.

[3] Paris Lat. 527[1], fol. 460v: "...aliquae adversus nos, quaedam nobis favent, aliae mediae; illae uti refellantur, aliae uti nostrum in usum redigantur, postremae, ne quae rem sacram augent ignorentur, quaerendae intelligendaeque sunt... ." See also *Scechina*, vol. I, p. 66. Some of the Talmudists are enemies to Christian truth, *ibid.*, p. 147.

[4] *Scechina*, vol. I, pp. 66, 147.

[5] *Scechina*, vol. I, p. 86.

[6] *Scechina*, vol. I, p. 135: "...quod ipsi ne olfecerunt quidem."

[7] *Scechina*, vol. I, p. 224.

have not known the sacred language and the "*arcana*." This would be contrary to his belief in the Church's unfailing orthodoxy through the centuries. He makes an explicit distinction between the articles of belief which have always been the secure possession of the Church and those truths which pertain to a full and deep understanding of Scripture's meaning.[1] What disturbs and embarrasses him, therefore, is that those who profess the Christian faith do not grasp it in a more profound and satisfying way.[2] His use of classic theological categories in explaining the meaning of the cabala indicates that he is not about to reject out of hand the whole of the theological tradition of the West.[3] By the time of the *Scechina*, however, he was fully convinced that the truly proper theological method was the direct study of the text of Scripture, interpreted by means of the cabala.

His reflections on the nature and transcendent dignity of the Hebrew language swung him to a new definition of the term "barbarian." Early in his life he seems to have understood by it that which fell outside the Greco-Latin culture of the Mediterranean area, which was in a generic way the accepted meaning of the term in Italian humanist circles.[4] Once Giles was initiated into rabbinic and cabalistic writings he saw that for the expression of religious truths every language was inept, and therefore barbarian, in comparison with Hebrew, the language of the Holy Spirit.[5] The Egyptians, realizing how unique the sacred character of Hebrew was, resorted to hieroglyphs to protect its truths from corruption.[6] The Greeks, inordinately attached to elegant

[1] Ang. Lat. 502, fols. 134v, 197r, 277r; *Scechina*, vol. I, p. 110.

[2] "Libellus" (in *Scechina*, vol. I), p. 30: "...qui fidei veritatem profitetur, fidei fundamenta non novit."

[3] E.g., Ang. Lat. 502, fols. 117v, 290r; *Scechina*, vol. I, p. 85; vol. II, p. 89.

[4] See Giles's marginalia in his copy of Bessarion's *Correctio librorum Platonis de legibus, Georgio Trapezuntio interprete*, printed as the fifth book of the *In calumniatorem Platonis*, fol. 113v. See also Ang. Lat. 502, fols. 195r, 199r. See Denys Hay, "Italy and Barbarian Europe," *Italian Renaissance Studies: A Tribute to the Late Cecilia M. Ady*, ed. E. F. Jacob, London 1960, esp. pp. 57-60.

[5] "Libellus" (in *Scechina*, vol. I), pp. 30-32.

[6] *Scechina*, vol. I, p. 113: "Aegyptus, si alii comparetur sapientissima clarissimaque, si meae linguae et manca et barbara, quod cum sentiret a scribendo abstinuit, ne divina in barbariem obrueret, et integris alimonium plantarum aliarum rerum formis agendum decrevit. Agnovit illa barbariem omnium linguarum, atque ideo ad hieroglypha confugit. Id quod non duxit esse scribendum reliquit sapientibus cogitandum." On the hieroglyphs, see further *ibid.*, pp. 119-120; Vat. Lat. 6325, fols. 89r, 146r; Paris Lat. 527[1], fol. 404v; Ang. Lat. 502, fol. 181r, etc. For the importance in Ficino's circle of the *Hieroglyphica* of Horapollo Niliacus (2nd or 4th century, A.D.), first published by Aldo Manuzio in 1505 but in circulation in manuscript form in Italy since 1419, see Seznec, *Survival of the Pagan Gods*, pp. 99-103.

expression, contemned the sacred languages as barbarian and tampered with what should have been left untouched.[1]

Giles insists again and again that all languages are barbarian in comparison with Hebrew, but he takes particular pain to point out that Latin and Greek, which preen themselves on their polished eloquence, are no better than the rest. A more striking contrast with the exaltation of Latin which was to be found in some circles of Italian humanists is hard to imagine. Lorenzo Valla's suggestive paralleling of the Christian religion with Latin literature fits ill with Giles's description of Latin as barbarian and inadequate to divine truth.[2]

Giles was convinced that the key to a full understanding of Christian doctrine lay in Hebrew and in Jewish literature, treasures possessed in his day almost exclusively by the Jewish community. What was his attitude towards the Jews and how did he explain their refusal to embrace Christianity? For Giles the Jews' situation was precisely the reverse of the Christians'. The Christians believed the truths of faith, but did not know how to arrive at a deeper understanding of them through Scripture. The Jews did not adhere to the truths of faith, but they did have the tools to discover these truths and their deeper ramifications.[3] What is curious, of course, is the fact that with this key to unlock the Christian mysteries the Jews are not converted to Christianity. Giles is once again thrown back to postulating some direct relationship between virtue and understanding. The Jews are not converted because they deliberately close their eyes to the truth, being a hard-necked and obstinate people whose treachery keeps them from understanding.[4] Giles is under no illusions: by studying the cabala he

---

[1] "Libellus" (in *Scechina*, vol. I), pp. 30-31: "Audiant Iamblichum mysteria scribentem, qui Graecos ait religionem aut sustulisse aut certe per multum imminuisse, quod novitatis et suae elegantiae nimium cupidi sacras linguas ut barbaras inverterint, a Deo ipso tradita corruperint, quae tangenda non fuerint immutaverint. Audiant denique Sanctum Spiritum, qui arcana quaedam verba in linguam extraneam et adeo alienam ac tamquam barbaram transferre non passus sit, ..."

[2] See, e.g., "Libellus" (in *Scechina*, vol. I), pp. 26, 30-32, 46; *Scechina*, vol. I, pp. 113, 193, 222; Ang. Lat. 502, fols. 27v, 129v, 195v. Lorenzo Valla, "Laurentii Vallae opuscula tria," ed. M. J. Vahlen, *SAW* phil-hist. Cl. 62(1869), pp. 97-98: "...et quia religio nostra aeterna etiam Latina litteratura aeterna fore:...."

[3] Ang. Lat. 502, fol. 277r: "...Hebraeos in tenebris et nocte caligare quod ad ea quae credenda sunt pertinet; quod vero ad scripturarum enarrationem facit nostros innumerabilia mysteria latere, ..." See also *ibid.*, fol. 134v.

[4] Naples V. F. 20, fol. 276r-v, and Évora CXVI/1-30, fol. 25v: "...qua in re detestanda venit perfidia Hebraeorum, qui quod gentes [Trismegistus, Plato, et al., about Christ] procul a Deo assecutae sunt, ipsi Deo junctissimi assequi noluerunt."

is taking the sacred "*arcana*" out of the hands of the impious enemy and delivering them into the hands of the Christians, "to the praise and honor of Christ and the Catholic Church."[1]

At one point Giles treats of this problem more at length and gives a more satisfying answer. The Jews are not converted because of weaknesses in Christian apologetics and the fact that very few persons have the leisure and desire to study divine things. There is, also, a veil cast over the eyes of the Jews because of the sins of their fathers. Conversion, moreover, calls for too many changes in their habitual way of thinking and acting, i.e., there are too many traditions and prejudices to overcome.[2]

What must be kept in mind is that Giles's aversion for the Jews was something almost forced upon him by cant pseudo-theological phrases and by his own epistemological presuppositions. The aversion, we might almost say, was theoretical, and did not relate to individuals whom he knew personally. Giles's close association with Elijah Levita, for instance, seems to have been marvellously cordial and free from bigotry, and we have no reason to suspect that his contacts with other members of the Jewish community were any different.[3] He never sug-

[1] Paris Lat. 527[2], fol. 170v: "...ab impiorum eripui manibus, medioque ex hoste recepi ad Christi et ecclesiae Catholicae laudem et honorem." See also Paris Lat. 598, fol. 65r.

[2] Ang. Lat. 502, fols. 98v-99r. See Selma Stern-Taeubler, "Die Vorstellung vom Juden und vom Judentum un der Ideologie der Reformationszeit," *Essays Presented to Leo Baeck*, London 1954, esp. on Reuchlin's attitude, which seems friendlier than Giles's, pp. 199-201.

[3] See Secret, *Les kabbalistes chrétiens*, pp. 106-126; Weil, *Élie Lévita*, pp. 81-90, and Elijah Levita, *Massoreth Ha-Massoreth*, ed. and trans. C. D. Ginsburg, London 1867, pp. 96-97: "Now I swear, by my Creator, that a certain Christian [Giles] encouraged it and brought me thus far. He was my pupil ten years uninterruptedly, I resided at his house and instructed him, for which there was a great outcry against me [on the part of some Jews], and it was not considered right of me. And several of the Rabbins would not countenance me, and pronounced woe to my soul because I taught the law to a Christian, ...When the prince [Giles] heard my statement, he came to me and kissed me with the kisses of his mouth, saying, ... Blessed be the God of the Universe, who brought thee hither, and bade thee come to meet me. Now abide with me and be my teacher, and I shall be to thee as a father, and shall support thee and thy house, and give thee thy corn, thy wine, and thy olives, and fill thy purse, and bear all thy wants. Thus we took sweet counsel together, iron sharpening iron. I imparted my spirit to him, and learned from him excellent and valuable things, which are in accordance with truth." Giles taught Elijah Greek, *ibid.*, pp. 19, 71. Elijah describes Giles, *ibid.*, p. 96, as "a very distinguished nobleman, a prince of great dignity, and wise as Solomon, ..." Elijah gives us a good insight into the friendly relationship which obtained between himself and other Christians in Rome, *ibid.*, p. 100: "Furthermore, I must inform you, that much good has resulted therefrom; for I solemnly declare that

gests any politically restrictive or vindictive measures against the Jews, and as part of his general indictment of the person and policies of Pope Clement V (1305-1314) he lists Clement's expulsion of the Jews from France. On the other hand, he seemingly approved of the drastic anti-Jewish policies of the Spanish monarchs, and he did not want converted Spanish Jews admitted into the Augustinian order.[1]

We are now in a position to take a closer look at the Jewish "*arcana*" which Giles so highly esteemed and which came to play so determinative a role in structuring his thought. He made extensive use of Talmudic sources, especially the Babylonian Talmud, and clearly distinguished this literature from the cabala.[2] He held the books of the Talmud in high regard, but he believed they were dependent upon the cabala for their knowledge of the "*arcana*."[3]

The cabala was of the utmost importance in patterning Giles's thought. Only recently have we arrived at a scientific understanding of what the cabala is and how it was formed.[4] The word itself (*Kabbalah*) means tradition. The *Zohar*, the greatest of all cabalistic works, was produced in Castile sometime after 1275. The cabala, at least in the form it took in the *Zohar*, is perhaps best described as a form of gnosis or theosophy, restricted to an elite of the chosen, and is "mystical" more in the sense that its speculations are based on intuition and couched in symbolic language than in the sense of describing or trying to lead to experiential knowledge of God. This is not to say, of

all the Christians whom I know, and whom I or others have instructed, are all of them good and upright men, and with all their power have acted kindly towards Israel, ..." Giles alludes to Elijah as his teacher, Ang. Lat. 502, fol. 195v.

[1] On Clement V, see Ang. Lat. 502, fol. 200r. For Giles's strong letter on the problem of Spanish Jewry, see Siena G. X. 26, pp. 107-112, letter undated, to the vicar of a Spanish observant congregation. See also Ang. Lat. 502, fol. 321r. See also *Scechina*, vol. I, pp. 180, 189, and 195-196, where Giles implies the inevitability of exile until the Jews recognize the Messiah.

[2] *Scechina*, e.g., vol. I, pp. 147, 151, 217; vol. II, p. 27. See also Secret's comments, *ibid.*, vol. I, p. 15. On the Talmud, see Isidore Epstein, *Judaism*, Baltimore 1964, esp. pp. 121-131.

[3] *Scechina*, vol. I, p. 151, and vol. II, p. 27.

[4] Of fundamental importance is the work of Gershom G. Scholem, especially the three books entitled: *Major Trends in Jewish Mysticism*, *On the Kabbalah and its Symbolism*, and *Ursprung und Anfänge der Kabbala*, Berlin 1962. The studies of Georges Vajda are also important: *Introduction à la pensée juive du moyen âge*, Paris 1947, and *Recherches sur la philosophie et la Kabbale dans la pensée juive du moyen âge*, Paris 1962. Scholem would maintain that the gnosticism of the cabala has only tenuous historical threads connecting it with Gnostic traditions of antiquity, and that for the most part it developed independently from within the cabala itself, *Kabbalah Symbolism*, pp. 97-98. On Gnosticism, see R. M. Grant, *Gnosticism and Early Christianity*, New York 1959.

course, that such knowledge was foreign to the cabalists. As is clear, the cabalists must be sharply distinguished from their medieval Jewish contemporaries who in the tradition of Moses Maimonides (1135-1204) were attempting to reconcile Judaism with Greek philosophy, and they to some extent came to represent an opposition to this attempt.[1]

Generally speaking, the cabala can be said to interest itself in three basic problems: (1) doctrines concerning the inner life of the Godhead and its relationship to creatures; (2) messianic and apocalyptic speculations; (3) a theory and technique of scriptural exegesis. The first of these elaborates the stages of the pulsating divine life, the ten Sefiroth, i.e., the ten numbers or numerical spheres. These Sefiroth manifest the hidden world of God, the *En-Sof*, i.e., the Infinite, which is unperceivable and unintelligible except by God. The ten Sefiroth are emanations strictly within the Godhead itself, and taken together they constitute a dynamic organism of divine vitality and power. The created world is a development outside God of forces which are active and pulsating within God, and all created reality reflects the world of the ten Sefiroth. The last of the Sefiroth, for instance, is the Shekinah, the majestic presence or manifestation of God among men, which eventually came to be considered a feminine and personalized reality, in some way correlated with Sion, the synagogue and the community of Israel.[2]

Messianic and apocalyptic speculations, though not central to the cabala, were always part of its doctrine, and these strains were intensified by the catastrophe of the expulsion of the Jews from Spain in 1492.[3] They contained ideas of cyclic return to a state of perfection such as that of the Garden of Eden, and they became bound up in some instances with theories of human history not altogether devoid of resemblance to those of Joachim of Flora, though probably not influenced by them.[4]

---

[1] See Vajda, *Introduction à la pensée juive*, p. 198, and Scholem, *Major Trends*, pp. 1-39, 205-207.

[2] See Scholem, *Major Trends*, pp. 205-243, and by the same author, "Zur Entwicklungsgeschichte der kabbalistischen Konzeption der Schechinah," *Eranos Jahrbuch* 21(1952), esp. pp. 46, 51, 90-96. For something of a parallel of the Shekinah with the humanists' "wisdom," see d'Alverny, "'Sapientia' chez les humanistes," p. 333.

[3] See Scholem, *Major Trends*, pp. 244-251; Secret, *Les kabbalistes chrétiens*, pp. 117-118, and A. H. Silver, *A History of Messianic Speculation in Israel from the First through the Seventeenth Centuries*, New York 1927, pp. 90-93.

[4] See Gershom G. Scholem, "La signification de la Loi dans la mystique juive," *Diogène* no. 15(1956), pp. 102-108, 111-112; *Ursprung der Kabbala*, pp. 410-411, and

The metaphysical speculations on the divine nature and the ten Sefiroth had repercussions on the theory of exegesis. The cabalistic conception of God was dynamic and postulated that the divine nature, especially in its relation to creatures, was one of movement and development. It was the mystics' affirmation that the Lord was a *living* God, and was relatively much less concerned than were the theologians and philosophers to assure the divine transcendence.[1] God spoke and things were made: the creative energy of God manifests itself in word, in the divine language, which is the medium in which the divine energy expresses itself. The cabalists thus found in Scripture, the word of God, not a formulation of philosophic ideas, but a symbolic representation of the process of development by which the divine life expands through the emanations of the Sefiroth. This theory combined with the midrashic and rabbinic assumption that every word and every letter of Scripture was a source of endless meaning, to be made more fully explicit for each generation. Thus for the cabalist each word, each letter, each number in the text of Scripture represented a concentration of energy and was capable of expressing almost an infinitude of meaning. Every word, every letter, every combination or separation of letters revealed profound mysteries to the cabalist, and this is why he was so eager to pass from the literal meaning of the surface of the text to the spiritual meaning of its inner core.[2]

There is, therefore, no single meaning for any given verse or passage of Scripture. Every slightest element in the sacred text is capable of bearing unlimited variety of interpretation, provided only that the broad lines of orthodoxy be observed and that the intuition somehow relate to cabalistic doctrine. The scope thus given to free and untethered imagination is almost infinite, and is surely incapable of excluding the Christian interpretation which the cabalists of the Renaissance would profer.

It is not hard to see why the cabala would appeal to Giles of Viterbo. The cabala supposedly was sanctioned by the most venerable antiquity. It was far removed from Aristotelian categories and systems, and relatively easily linked to certain elements in the late antique authors

Kabbalah Symbolism, pp. 54, 83-84. See also William J. Bouwsma, "Postel and the Significance of Renaissance Cabalism," *Journal of the History of Ideas* 15(1954), p. 231.

[1] Scholem, *Kabbalah Symbolism*, pp. 87-117. See *Scechina*, vol. I, p. 92.

[2] Scholem, "Entwicklungsgeschichte der Schechinah," pp. 88-89, and *Major Trends*, pp. 17, 133-135. See also de Lubac, *Exégèse*, vol. II.2, pp. 399, 407.

with whom Giles already was familiar. The loose reins of cabalistic hermeneutics, moreover, allowed Giles to integrate all phases of knowledge around the text of Scripture and in this way bring them into the harmony he had long ago postulated and been seeking.[1]

Giles's knowledge of the cabala was, for his day, extensive and profound, and was, according to Secret, the most noteworthy of all the efforts of the Christian humanists to assimilate its doctrine. Giles far outstripped the accomplishments of Pico and Reuchlin.[2] Pico had relied mainly on a mediocre commentary on the *Zohar* for his knowledge, and Reuchlin used sources which were for the most part pre-Zoharic. Through one of his teachers, Baruch of Benevento, Giles had first-hand knowledge of the *Zohar*. In 1514 he wrote to his friend and subject in the Augustinian order, Gabriele della Volta, to have a copy of it bought for him in Damascus, and he himself later translated excerpts from it.[3] Giles's correspondence with della Volta from the year 1512 onwards is often taken up with requests for Jewish books of exegesis. The remains of his library which are preserved in the Bibliothèque Nationale and elsewhere, and which includes translations of such important cabalistic works as the *Sefer Ha-Temunah* and the *Sefer Ha-Bahir*, testify to the success of his searchings.[4] Giles himself describes the immense enterprise of buying and copying these works as done "with great zeal, greater labor and at exceedingly great expense."[5] The *Scechina* shows that, far from letting these texts lie idly

[1] Some suggestion of Giles's search for *concordia* is conveyed by the following, "Libellus" (in *Scechina*, vol. I), p. 35: "Litteras volunt veteres Hebraeorum Mosen accepisse de ora Geura, qui ignis est. Quattuor primae litterae sanctae quibus se ostendit, et alia nomina, cognomina nominavit quibus virtutem operum suorum annuntiavit populo suo [Ps. 111 (110). 6]. Sed disci haec non possunt nisi Dei formae intelligantur qui decem numeri sunt, ab Aramaeis et Hebraeis numerationes et mensurae nuncupatae. Alterum nomen Pythagoras, alterum Plato cepit et ideas vocavit, hoc est rerum et formas et mensuras. Decem membra numerantur in canticis, ubi ille arcanus numerus intelligitur. Tria eminentissima in Deo ipso mundum supremum faciunt. Septem deinde sequuntur quae constituunt mundum medium, per quem ultimus hic sensibilis procreatur."

[2] Secret, *Les kabbalistes chrétiens*, p. 120.

[3] Ang. Lat. 688, fol. 51r, May 8, 1514, and the corresponding entry in Giles's register, Aug. Gen. Archives, Rome, Dd. 12, fol. 2r.

[4] E.g., Ang. Lat. 688, fols. 46r, 49v, 53r; Aug. Gen. Archives, Rome, Dd. 12, fol. 92r. For some indications on the remains of Giles's library, see Secret's "Introduction," *Scechina*, vol. I, pp. 9-20, and Pélissier, "Manuscrits de Gilles de Viterbe."

[5] Ang. Lat. 502, fol. 162r: "Latuere hactenus haec arcana. Numquam Pythagorae, Philolai, Archytae, numquam Aegyptiorum, Caldaeorum, Etruscorum disciplinae apparuere. Nos illas ex Aegypti Damascique penetralibus eruimus magno studio, majore labore, maximo sumptu, aut ementes veteres et situ exesos libros,

on his shelves, he incorporated themes from them into his own Christian synthesis.

What was Giles's understanding of the origin of the cabala? The definition which he gives the term sets up the basic structure which he later fills in with historical details. Cabala means the reception or acceptance of a tradition, and Giles defines it as the reception of a divine revelation which originally had been received from God and then was passed on from hand to hand, as it were, through the centuries.[1] Giles's description of the cabala as an unwritten tradition is not altogether without resemblance to the description the Council of Trent later used to delineate an unwritten Christian tradition distinct from that found in the canonical books of Scripture.[2]

God opened to Adam, Moses and others hidden treasures of divine wisdom, which He ordered put into writing only after generations of oral transmission.[3] This early, mythical origin of the cabala fits well with the explanation of the diffusion of orthodox religious truths among the gentiles which Giles had adopted long before he wrote his cabalistic treatises and which we described in Chapter One. The Etruscans, for instance, have as part or whole of their patrimony of

---

aut accurate transcribi procurantes. Juvere ad hanc nos rem Veneti, qui quidquid terrarum mercaturae gratia adeunt nostra causa diligenter exploravere." On Giles and Vatican codex Neofiti 1, a Palestinian Targum to the Pentateuch, see Alejandro Diez-Macho, "Una copia completa del Targum Palestinense al Pentateuco en la Biblioteca Vaticana," *Sefarad* 17(1957), pp. 119-121; Martin McNamara, M.S.C., "Targumic Studies," *CBQ* 28(1966), pp. 1-19, esp. 4-6; M. FitzMaurice Martin, "The Palaeographical Character of Codex Neofiti 1," *Textus* 3(1963), pp. 1-35, and the critical comments by Gérard E. Weil, "Le Codex Neofiti I: A propos de l'article de M. FitzMaurice Martin," *Textus* 4(1964), pp. 225-229. I am indebted to the Rev. F. X. Martin, O.S.A., for several of these references. See also *Scechina*, vol. I, p. 88.

[1] Ang. Lat. 502, fol. 294v: "Cabala enim receptionem per auditum significat rerum latentium atque divinarum, quae a Deo sacris tradita viris, deinde per manus aliis per saecula traducta sunt." See also "Libellus" (in *Scechina*, vol. I), p. 24; *Scechina*, vol. I, p. 167, and vol. II, pp. 149, 176. See Reuchlin, *De arte cabalistica*, p. 123: "Unde cabala dicitur ab auditu acceptio." Also *ibid.*, p. 124: "Est enim cabala divinae revelationis, ad salutiferam Dei et formarum separatarum contemplationem traditae, symbolica receptio, ..."

[2] *Conciliorum decreta*, p. 639: "... perspiciensque [Tridentina synodus] hanc veritatem et disciplinam contineri in libris scriptis et sine scripto traditionibus, quae ab ipsius Christi ore ab apostolis acceptae, aut ab ipsis apostolis Spiritu Sancto dictante quasi per manus traditae ad nos usque pervenerunt, ..." For a corresponding concept in Judaism earlier than the cabalistic tradition, see Renée Bloch, "Écriture et tradition dans le Judaïsme," *Cahiers Sioniens* 8(1954), esp. pp. 12, 19-20, and see also Scholem, *Kabbalah Symbolism*, p. 47.

[3] *Scechina*, vol. I, pp. 68, 157, 220; vol. II, p. 149. See Scholem, *Major Trends*, p. 21.

primitive revelation knowledge of the secrets of the cabala, as we have seen.[1] Paul and the apostles were, of course, recipients of this special revelation, and the divine Son of God was, in actual fact, "the blessed author of the cabala."[2]

The cabala provided Giles with both a method of exegesis and a doctrine. This is not the place to give a detailed exposition of his adaptation of it for Christian purposes. It is important, however, to outline the broad structure of this adaptation and to try to see some of its dominant ideas and assumptions. Giles subscribed to the whole elaborate metaphysics of the ten Sefiroth as explanations of the inner nature of the divinity. For him the first three Sefiroth corresponded to the Persons of the Trinity and constituted the "*mundus supremus*," which was sublimely self-contained. The remaining seven Sefiroth made up the "*mundus medius*," and their function was to administer the "*ultimus mundus*," i.e., the sensible world in which we live.[3] This tidy schematization was subject to unlimited and radical diversification and complication from the fact, for example, that the Sefiroth could be numbered from top to bottom or vice versa, that they were in every way absolutely equal to one another but had their own characteristics, and that above them there was another supereminent reality, the *En-Sof*.[4] The plasticity of cabalistic doctrine was nowhere more evident than in the names and functions Giles attributes to the Shekinah, the tenth Sefirah. As the abiding presence or glory of God it was, to call attention only to its more important designations, the Temple, the Kingdom, the heavenly Jerusalem and even the Holy Spirit.[5]

This seemingly arbitrary flow of concepts and images is understandable only when attention is called to what Georges Vajda considers "*le sentiment absolument dominant*" of the cabala: God is utterly unknowable. Giles, without adopting this principle in all its rigor, was quite willing to agree that the divinity is above our grasp and,

---

[1] Ang. Lat. 502, fols. 100r, 104r; *Scechina*, vol. I, pp. 97, 185. See Annio da Viterbo, *Berosi libri*, fol. 213v, and François Secret, "L'astrologie et les kabbalistes chrétiens à la Renaissance," *La Tour Saint-Jacques* no. 4(1956), p. 47.

[2] Ang. Lat. 502, fol. 292v, "sanctae cabalae et theologiae auctor beatissimus." See also *ibid.*, fol. 99v, and *Scechina*, vol. I, p. 161.

[3] "Libellus" (in *Scechina*, vol. I), pp. 35, 54. For a different division of three "worlds," see Ang. Lat. 502, fol. 292r.

[4] "Libellus" (in *Scechina*, vol. I), p. 35; *Scechina*, vol. I, pp. 84, 121-123.

[5] *Scechina*, vol. I, pp. 96, 195, 207; vol. II, p. 273; Ang. Lat. 502, fol. 301r. See Reuchlin, *De arte cabalistica*, p. 237. Vajda's description of the cabala is to the point, *Introduction à la pensée juive*, p. 208: "... une souplesse et une plasticité qui laissera un champ pratiquement illimité à la dextérité interpretative...."

therefore, ineffable.[1] It was this conviction of the absolute impossibility of knowing God as He is in Himself and of being unable to express the divine reality adequately in human concepts which led him as a cabalist to an almost unrestrained abundance of metaphor, as he tried to catch some dark glimpse of the "real world" of God and then to articulate it. In the cabala God had done what He could to communicate some knowledge of Himself, but this meant using figures of speech which distort in the very moment of trying to clarify.[2] Man must realize that this distortion was inevitable, even in the sacred books, and must do his best "piously to interpret" what is meant when the divinity is spoken of in sensible and anthropomorphic image. This pious interpretation is not unrelated to the "*via negativa*" of the Pseudo-Areopagite.[3] The sense world, from which the images were taken, is the false world, the world of darkness and shadow, incapable of representing the real world of God but adapted to the exigencies of human weakness.[4] The modicum of true understanding which we have comes from the activity of the Sefiroth themselves within us, illuminating our minds from above so that we become capable of heavenly wisdom.[5] A touching insight into Giles's purpose in pursuing the cabala is given by a prayer found with one of his cabala translations: "And because no man can see You face to face and live, we

---

[1] *Scechina*, vol. II, p. 20: "Nam cum omnia ibi ineffabilia sunt, ..." See Vajda, *Introduction à la pensée juive*, p. 203.

[2] *Scechina*, vol. II, p. 45: "Quod multifarie multisque modis, ut Pauli verbis utar, in prophetis loqui consuevi [Heb. 1.1]. Nam cum humanae mentis tenuitas atque angustiae tantum a celsitudine divinitatis abscedat, ut rudem sicut possum instruam et rem illi longe abjunctissimam, ut fas est, notam faciam, statui omnia tentare, nihil omittere, omnem, ut aiunt, lapidem movere."

[3] *Scechina*, vol. I, p. 83: "... et quando integrum non potestis, ut porrigam quae potestis, insectile seco, non scissile scindo [ego, Shekinah]...." Also *ibid.*, vol. I, p. 85; vol. II, pp. 92 and 20: "Sed cum illa audis pie interpretare. Quaecumque enim de Deo aut in sacris libris aut extra illos referuntur, ut descendere, ascendere, dormire,.... "Very explicitly, *ibid.*, vol. I, p. 83: "Quamobrem vestrae conditionis hominis rationem [sic], in omnibus oraculis figuris, proverbiis, similitudinibus, metaphoris usa sum [ego, Shekinah], ut immortalia per mortalia, unita per partes, ... quibus de rebus me prophetasque meos vobis vestraeque debilitati consuluisse, ..." On Dionysius, see *ibid.*, vol. I, p. 90.

[4] *Scechina*, vol. I, p. 154; vol. II, pp. 8, 9; Paris Lat. 527[1], fol. 5r.

[5] *Scechina*, vol. I, pp. 107-108: "Nam sicut a luce dicitis illustrare et illucescere, sic a sephirot, quae sunt divina lumina a quis homines et fiunt et facti illuminantur. Liceat mihi vocabula necessitate imperante novare, a sephirot dicetur sephirare, quod est ut lucem menti illucescere, lucem infundi, sic sephirot sephirare est sephirot suam lucem influere, quod faciunt beando mentes et animas in caelo, quibus enarrant gloriam, quod est dant sephirando et infundendo gloriam, qua fruuntur beatique fiunt. Faciunt item non in caelo tantum beando, sed etiam in terris illustrando."

would contemplate You through these formulas, as befits our mortal condition. Grant that we who have here sought Your interests, from behind, as it were, may be filled with the joy of seeing Your countenance."[1]

Giles made ample use of all the metaphors the cabala put at his disposal. He described the Sefiroth and their activities by comparing them to a tree and to different species of trees, to rivers, mountains, hills and the ten members of the human body. This last is interesting because he felt there must be some correspondence between the members of the body and God since God said, "Let us make man in our image, after our likeness" (Gen. 1.26).[2] Giles tried to render this multiplicity of metaphor and symbol more acceptable to his readers by calling attention to the fact that Christ, who insisted upon the simplicity and unity in God, still spoke of the "many mansions" in His heavenly home (Jn. 14.2), and that the more conventional theology had to describe the activities of the divine intellect in terms of predestination, foreknowledge, providence, etc., as if these were somehow distinct.[3] Thus it was that to describe the Shekinah Giles tumbled forth one metaphor after another in trying to capture in them the richness of the Shekinah's reality. It was the spouse, the moon, the fountain, the dove, the eagle, besides the more exalted titles we have already mentioned.

Giles accepted the cabalistic belief that God revealed Himself when He revealed the alphabet, His name and the meaning of numbers. We have already seen an example of how he was able to find the mystery of the Trinity in the letters of the Hebrew alphabet. The only further point which might now be insisted upon as regards these letters is that they participated in the divine energy in a way that made them not merely symbols of divine reality but also gave them the power to penetrate into the minds of the pious and humble and to make themselves understood there.[4]

---

[1] Paris Lat. 527[1], fol. 404v: "Ut quia homo te de facie non videt et vivit, per has te formulas, sicut fas est mortali, te docente contemplaremur. Fac ut qui tua hic a tergo quaesivimus a fronte impleamur laetitia cum vulto tuo."

[2] Ang. Lat. 502, fol. 292r: "... ut dixerit membris illis suis, faciamus hominem ad imaginem nostram." Giles tends to abstain from describing the ninth Sefirah in explicitly phallic terms, and in one passage he seems to indicate that this is unbecoming a Christian, Paris Lat. 527[1], fol. 217r. See, however, Ang. Lat. 502, fols. 300v-302r. On this question in the Jewish cabala, see Scholem, *Major Trends*, pp. 225-229.

[3] *Scechina*, vol. I, p. 70.

[4] *Scechina*, vol. I, pp. 107-108, 217, and esp. 159: "Quamobrem humanae [voces

Giles believed that the Tetragrammaton literally contained the entire narration of the Pentateuch, and that it had locked up within itself, indeed, the whole of theology.[1] This belief rested upon the theory which Giles found in Plato, Dionysius, the prophets and the cabala that names, when properly bestowed, express a thing's essence.[2] God, therefore, surely gave Himself a name which expressed the full richness of His infinity. The reason Giles provides to indicate why God made the Hebrews His chosen people was the fact that He had revealed to them His name.[3]

Numbers also are vehicles for conveying divine truth. An important scriptural foundation for Giles's numerology was the statement in the Book of Wisdom (11.21) that God created the universe in measure, number and weight.[4] Giles's principal attention is focused on the numbers from one to ten, even though the meaning of those from eleven onwards is also rich and complicated.[5] As early as the "Sententiae" Giles was convinced from his knowledge of Plato and Pythagoras that number was constitutive of the essence of things, but it was not until he was inducted into the cabala that this conviction received full confirmation from divine revelation: "Receive now the revelation of My sacred numbers, with which I created, incised and established all things."[6]

Although Pico extolled Moses Maimonides as a cabalist, Giles correctly excludes him from this company, basing his judgment very largely upon the fact that Maimonides rejected the hidden meaning of numbers. For Giles, therefore, he becomes a "destroyer of sacred truth," equivalently denying providence by implying that the numbers

et litterae] ut cadavera et hominum mutae imagines, divinae ut viventes vires et spirituum ardentium inflamandi vim habentium intrant animos, permovent, cient, excitant et incendunt .... quod vivus sit sermo divinus [Heb. 4.12]." See Ficino, "Comm. in Philebum Platonis," *Opera*, vol. II, p. 1217.

[1] *Scechina*, vol. II, pp. 120-121, and Ang. Lat. 502, fol. 98r: "In eo [nomine] namque universa theologia picta est."

[2] "Libellus" (in *Scechina*, vol. I), pp. 23-24; Ang. Lat. 502, fol. 28r, and Vat. Lat. 6325, fols. 34r, 108r. See also Naples V. F. 20, fol. 272r.

[3] "Libellus" (in *Scechina*, vol. I), pp. 38-39; *Scechina*, vol. I, p. 102, and Ang. Lat. 502, fol. 278r.

[4] See Vat. Lat. 6325, fols. 40r, 41r, 205r; Ang. Lat. 502, fol. 277r; *Scechina*, vol. II, p. 36, etc.

[5] *Scechina*, vol. I, p. 131.

[6] *Scechina*, vol. I, p. 79: "Accipe nunc sacratissimos meos numeros, quibus omnia condidi, impressi, constitui." See also Vat. Lat. 6325, fols. 49v, 125v, 202v; Massa, *Fondamenti metafisici e testi inediti*, pp. 107-108; Ang. Lat. 502, fols. 92v, 100r, 103v-110r, 177(a)v-178(a)r, 277r. See also Ficino, "In octavum librum de Republica Platonis," *Opera*, vol. II, p. 1418.

in Scripture have no particular significance. In Maimonides we have a clear instance of the writings of a Jew which are inimical to Christianity and whose errors must be refuted.[1]

Each number has its own character. The number two, for example, is imbued with some suggestion of imperfection, for it is the first to depart from the unity which is the essence of the number one.[2] With seven and eight Giles can call upon the long Christian tradition of speculation on the seven days of creation and the eighth day of the Resurrection: seven symbolizes human happiness, and eight indicates redemption.[3] Ten is the number of perfection and of consummation, the most sacred of all. It contains in itself all the numbers which precede it, and marks the end of the digits. By multiplication of itself it goes into infinity. It is a combination, furthermore, of three, the number of the Trinity, and seven, the number of human happiness. Its significance and holiness is confirmed by its use in Scripture—ten commandments, ten virgins, ten drachmas, etc.[4]

The point which must be insisted upon in all this, however, is that these numbers are such because they correspond to a similar but supereminent numerical reality in God in which they somehow participate and by virtue of which they are what they are. All reality, including historical reality, participates with metaphysical necessity in number, and is essentially constituted and regulated by it. It is the numerical reality in the Godhead, for example, which perforce divides human history into ten ages for the old dispensation and ten for the new.[5]

In keeping with cabalistic theories Giles worked out a hermeneutics which postulated different levels of meaning in Scripture. It is probable that the Jewish creators of the cabala in the Middle Ages were influenced by the fourfold meaning of Scripture elaborated by their Christian contemporaries.[6] For Giles, at any rate, there was a neat

[1] *Scechina*, vol. I, p. 79; vol. II, pp. 255-256. For another rejection of Maimonides, see Vat. Lat. 6325, fols. 14v-15v.

[2] Ang. Lat. 502, fol. 35v. See also *ibid.*, fols. 23r, 167r. Saint Thomas, for instance, speaks of the "perfection of the number three," *S.T.* I q 32 art. 1 ad 1, and III q 53 art. 2.

[3] Ang. Lat. 502, fols. 1r-v, 12r, 105v, 107r; *Scechina*, vol. I, pp. 124, 141.

[4] Ang. Lat. 502, fols. 1r-v, 4r, 51r-52r, 77r, 106r, 239r; *Scechina*, vol. I, pp. 104, 123, etc. On the antique origins of medieval numerology and in particular on the Neo-Pythagorean symbolism of the number ten, see Hopper, *Medieval Number Symbolism*, esp. pp. ix-x, 10-11, 34-38, 61-63, 85.

[5] Ang. Lat. 502, fols. 1r-v, 100r, 105v, 107r, 148r, 178r-179r; *Scechina*, vol. I, pp. 130, 202, 203.

[6] Scholem, *Kabbalah Symbolism*, pp. 50-65.

convergence of cabalistic and Christian views, both of which looked for a meaning in Scripture beyond the literal sense of the text.

Giles differentiated two basic levels of meaning: the obvious and literal, which was merely the cortex of the scriptural message, and the hidden spiritual sense, which was the inner substance, available only through the cabala. The literal sense is none other than the straightforward narrative, "*nuda historia*," of the biblical text.[1] One arrives at it by use of "grammar," and it is at times useful and enlightening. On the other hand, God has not become the author of Scripture merely to tell us stories, and the historical facts in the Bible are sometimes distorted just in order to reveal a more sublime spiritual truth.[2] Beyond this historical sense there lies another, that of Scripture's allegorical meaning.[3]

The literal, and to some extent even the so-called allegorical, sense of Scripture must be carefully distinguished from the spiritual or theological sense, which centered around the Sefiroth and interpreted them so as to make them accord with Christian doctrine. This sense was attained by means of the "divine dialectic" of cabalistic method, e.g., by transposing letters, by substituting one letter for another according to some arbitrary equivalence, by attributing to each letter a numerical value, etc. In other words, the interpreter had to employ the standard cabalistic exegetical methods such as gematria and notarikon. Giles very aptly compares Scripture to a wartime code which surrenders its real meaning only to those who know the key, i.e., the "*sapientiae methodus*."[4] The most marvellous characteristic of this spiritual sense is that it is inexhaustibly multiple, reflecting the inexhaustible and unfathomable richness of the divinity itself.[5] Giles reveals the frame of mind with which he approached the interpretation of Scrip-

---

[1] *Scechina*, vol. I, pp. 104, 106, 112; vol. II, p. 28; Ang. Lat. 502, fol. 277r. See also Évora CXVI/1-30, fol. 66r.

[2] *Scechina*, vol. I, pp. 91-92, 112, 119-120, 193; vol. II, pp. 8, 42-43, 96, 113, 121, 263, 282; Ang. Lat. 502, fol. 110v. For the emphasis on the non-literal sense of Scripture by Erasmus and Lefèvre d'Étaples, see Henri de Lubac, S.J., "Les humanistes chrétiens du XV-XVI siècle et l'herméneutique traditionelle," *Ermeneutica e Tradizione: Archivio di Filosofia* (1963), pp. 173-182.

[3] *Scechina*, vol. II, p. 43.

[4] *Scechina*, vol. I, pp. 113, 120, 146, 153, 155; vol. II, pp. 14-16. See Vajda, *Introduction à la pensée juive*, p. 207, and Weil, *Élie Lévita*, p. 7. Little trace is left of the interpretative norm Giles enunciated in the "Sententiae," Vat. Lat. 6325, fol. 92r: "Quid autem quisque sentiat non ex verbis sed ex sententia dijudicandus [sic] est."

[5] *Scechina*, vol. II, p. 86. See Hopper, *Medieval Number Symbolism*, pp. 100-103, and esp. Scholem, *Kabbalah Symbolism*, p. 12.

ture when he tells why he preferred John to the Synoptics: "John is the only one of the evangelists who undertook to write not only about the deeds of the Messiah, but also about the secret theology and divine wisdom."[1]

To whom is this spiritual sense of Scripture open? Giles does not disappoint us: it is open to the "wise," i.e., to the humble and pious. Spiritual wisdom is a gift of God, who interiorly enlightens the mind, and He does not grant it to the proud, the rich or the powerful, much less to those who ridicule His truth. Once again we see how for Giles truth is dependent upon moral values, and how he looks for a reformation of life as the fruit of studies.[2]

It is only at this point, after an examination of Giles's hermeneutics, that we can see how crucial to him was the problem of divine providence and why he took such an impassioned stand against Padua on it. To question providence was to allow that some letter of Scripture might be arbitrary, and such a possibility would destroy Giles's exegesis in its entirety.[3] Giles shared the traditional Jewish and Christian belief in the inerrancy of Scripture, and he saw in it the most important instance of control of reality by providence.[4] He pressed this belief to its ultimate limits by wringing the most extreme meaning out of the Gospel verse which promised that not one jot or tittle of the sacred text would ever perish.[5] Giles recurs to the jot-and-tittle argument with unashamed repetition. For him this text articulated one of his most profound convictions, and anyone who should endanger the truth it stood for was an enemy of God and the Church.

In the same way Giles never tires of insisting upon the "safe and accepted norm" for understanding Scripture, and indeed for under-

[1] *Scechina*, vol. I, p. 191: "Joannes evangelistarum unus qui Messiae non actiones humanas tantum, ut alii, sed arcanam theologiam et divinam sapientiam conscribendam suscepit, ..."

[2] Ang. Lat. 502, fol. 100r: "Usui quidem nobis sunt prophetarum enarrationes, quae emendant mores." See also *ibid.*, fols. 22v, 98v, 142r, 175(a)r; *Scechina*, vol. I, pp. 133, 188, 193; vol. II, pp. 28, 270.

[3] Ang. Lat. 502, fol. 2r: "Duo praeterea fundamenta capit Hebraeus theologus: ... alterum a Deo optimo maximo nihil agi incassum, nihil frustra; alterum id non modo rebus, dictionibus, sensibus datae legis, sed in ipsis quoque sacris litteris, et litterarum punctis intelligi."

[4] Ang. Lat. 502, fols. 98v, 294v, 307r; *Scechina*, vol. I, p. 153.

[5] E.g., *Scechina*, vol. I, pp. 149, 189, and esp. "Libellus" (in *Scechina*, vol. I), p. 29: "Iota unum aut unus apex non praeteribit a lege [Mt. 5.18]. Ubi commonitos nos non dubitamus non modo orationes et verba sed ipsa quoque tum elementa, tum puncta esse piis contemplatoribus observanda. ... Adde quod haec a Deo homini tributa, a quo nihil incassum, nihil non exactum, nihil non absolutum proficisci potest." Also Paris Lat. 598, fol. 163v.

standing all reality, i.e., the verse from the Lord's prayer, "on earth as it is is in heaven," "*sicut in caelo et in terra.*" Everything on earth, and most especially the text of the Bible down to the minutest detail, corresponds to something in the divine nature and reveals some reality within it. Therefore, not the least jot or tittle is without importance for understanding God and the world of the Sefiroth.[1]

The minutest details of the sacred text reveal not only God's nature and activity, but also predict the future. Scripture for Giles is a tissue of predictions whose meaning is opened by means of the divine dialectic, i.e., the combination and manipulation of numbers, letters, etc.[2] Giles's attitude towards dreams, auguries, and astrology was reserved, if not altogether incredulous, but he firmly believed that one of the most important functions of Scripture was to foretell and to foreshadow the future.[3] Without denying free will he saw the course of history as determined by God's decrees and by the nature of the divinity, "*sicut in caelo et in terra.*"[4] From his study of Scripture and history he induced the rule that God never did anything important without somehow beforehand intimating it to His people or to their leaders.[5]

To suggest, therefore, any philosophical doctrine which might weaken belief in providence was to strike Giles a doubly heavy blow. It was the equivalent of saying that God could not know, determine and reveal the future in Scripture, and also that the least detail of the sacred text was not necessarily a prefabricated conveyor to the initiate of information about the divine nature and coming events. Only in the light of these considerations can Giles's attack on Paduan philosophy be fully understood.

---

[1] *Scechina*, vol. I, p. 119; vol. II, p. 37; Ang. Lat. 502, fols. 256v, and 276v: "... omnium quae in scripturis divinis continetur receptissima regula, quod ut infra ita supra est, quemadmodum in terris humana apparent ita in caelo eorum causae quae divinae sunt."

[2] *Scechina*, vol. I, p. 158: "Sicut saepe repetimus, iota unum aut unus apex non praeteribit a lege donec omnia fiant, ubi luce clarius vides litteras apicesque fata continere, futura praetendere, saeculorum ordinem texere, nulla non eventa significare."

[3] Ang. Lat. 502, fols. 255r-v, 308v; Siena G. X. 26, pp. 109-110; Évora CXVI/1-30, fols. 22v-23r, 67r. Extraordinary phenomena in nature are signs of nature's sensitivity to the divine will, and can be interpreted as portents of it, Ang. Lat. 502, fols. 141r-142r, 265v; *Scechina*, vol. I, pp. 212-213; vol. II, pp. 79, 145.

[4] Ang. Lat. 502, fol. 223v: "... et quamquam libere nos contingenterque agimus, principis tamen decreta constantia immotaque esse necesse est, utpote qui ait, per me reges regnant." Prov. 8.15.

[5] Évora CXVI/1-30, fols. 53v-54r, 67r; Ang. Lat. 502, fol. 129r-v.

The relationship which Giles postulated between the Old Testament and the New Testament can best be understood in the context of Scripture's predicting function. The Old Testament, taken in its literal sense, contrasted unfavorably with the New: it was the dispensation of darkness, severity, revenge and justice, in contrast with the dispensation of light, gentleness, forgiveness and mercy; it was "*scientia*," promising only human rewards, in contrast with Christian "*sapientia*" which imparted divine and heavenly treasures.[1] However, the events, institutions and course of the old dispensation foreshadowed and prefigured those of the new.[2]

The spiritual sense of the Old Testament which the cabala unlocked leads the truly pious interpreter to discover hidden in the Old Testament truths which Christ preached in the Gospels. Occasionally in the *Scechina* Giles indicates that all supernatural truth, without exception, can be found in the Old Testament.[3] He does seem to believe, nevertheless, that such full knowledge was not available, even to the initiates of the Old Law such as Moses, until after Christ's revelation.[4] For the Christian cabalist, at any rate, the spiritual sense of Scripture fathomed unsuspected depths in all the doctrines revealed by Christ and removed the veil from history's mystery.

The very particular application which Giles makes of this theory is in his understanding of the psalms, and this in turn determines the structure of his "Historia XX saeculorum." The psalms are about Christ. The Epistle to the Hebrews attributes to Christ the words, "In the head of the book it is written of me" (10.7), and Giles, without excluding the possibility that the "book" might also refer to the whole of the Old Testament beginning with Genesis, interprets it to be the book of the psalms.[5] In keeping with a long tradition of Christian interpretation of the psalms Giles extends the meaning of "Christ" to include His "Mystical Body," i.e., the Church.[6] Thus it is that the

[1] *Scechina*, vol. I, p. 208; vol. II, p. 81; Ang. Lat. 502, fols. 58r, 173(a)r, 180v, 274r; Évora CXVI/1-30, fol. 20r.

[2] *Scechina*, vol. I, p. 124; Ang. Lat. 502, fols. 70r, 245v, 304r-v, and 25v: "Illud imprimis animadverti opus est, quod saepe diximus, in veteribus saeculis nova significari, ... ut primus psalmus Hebraeorum primo respondeat psalmo Christianorum, ..." See also Naples V. F. 20, fols. 274v-275r.

[3] *Scechina*, vol. I, pp. 161-162.

[4] *Scechina*, vol. I, pp. 129, 205, 230-231; Ang. Lat. 502, fols. 108v, 109r.

[5] Ang. Lat. 502, fols. 1r, 1v, 6r.

[6] Ang. Lat. 502, fol. 1r: "Mos vero sacris oraculis usitatissimus est ut cum Christum dicimus quandoque Verbum hominem factum cogitemus, quandoque non ipsum illum sed quod vocant corpus Christi mysticum ac credentium eccle-

psalms become a history of the Church in capsule form, the first ten corresponding to the "Church" of the Old Testament, and the second ten to the Church of the New. Giles finds in the psalms, then, a cryptic narrative of all that has transpired in the Church up to his own day. More important still, he knows that they contain the story of what is in store for the Church in the future until the day it reaches its final consummation.

Before bringing our discussion of the cabala to a close we might call attention to the fact that, although Giles published neither of his two cabalistic tracts, he was enough convinced of the merits of the cabala to make profession of believing in it at a time and place when this would not have been altogether easy. Reuchlin finally had been censured by Pope Leo X, and men as different as Erasmus and Johannes Cochlaeus (1479-1552), the Catholic controversialist, were making known their contempt for the cabala.[1] Giles was by no means insensitive to the criticism, and even ridicule, to which his esteem for the cabala exposed him, but he did not allow this to deter him from continuing to study it.[2] He realized that the seeming novelty of his approach was bound to arouse questions and make some people uneasy, and by 1530 the religious upheaval in Germany had reached such proportions that its tensions were felt even in Italy.[3]

---

siam intelligamus, ut rex pro regno, pro membris caput, princeps pro populo subinde nominetur." See also *ibid.*, fols. 25v, 129v, 136r, 325v. As regards this tradition of psalm interpretation, see, e.g.: (1) Augustine, "Ennarationes in psalmos," *MPL*, vol. XXXVI, col. 443: "14. In capite libri scriptum est de me, ut faciam voluntatem tuam: ... Ecce ad membra respexit, ecce et ipse fecit voluntatem Patris. Sed in quo capite libri scriptum est de illo? Fortasse in capite libri hujus psalmorum." (2) Nicholas of Lyra, *Biblia sacra cum glossa interlineari ordinaria, et Nicolai Lyrani postilla*, vol. III, Venice 1588, fol. 83v: "Quamvis liber psalmorum apud Hebraeos inter hagiographa computetur, tamen apud Latinos inter libros propheticos reputatur, nec immerito: ... Et hoc modo prophetia in hoc libro contenta dicitur magna, quia quodammodo se extendit ad omnia, quae in sacra scriptura continentur. Secundum autem Cassiodorum super librum istum, totus Christus (quantum ad caput et membra) est subjectum in tota sacra scriptura, ..." (3) Luther, *WA*, vol. III, p. 218. (4) For similar ideas in Erasmus, see de Lubac, "Les humanistes chrétiens," p. 177. (5) Felice da Prato, *Psalterium*, Venice 1515, fol. 9r. (6) Jacobus Perez de Valencia, *Centum ac quinquaginta psalmi Davidici*, Lyons 1517, fol. 12r-v.

[1] See *Scechina*, vol. I, p. 14, and Gundersheimer, "Erasmus, Humanism, Cabala."

[2] Paris Lat. 596, fol. 216v: "... me rident ut barbara sectantem." It was suggested by Antonio Magliabecchi (1633-1714) that Giles did not publish for fear of hurting his reputation, Signorelli, *Egidio da Viterbo*, p. 198. See also Naples II. F. 7, fols. 191v-195r.

[3] *Scechina*, vol. I, p. 66: "... homines usitata complectuntur et amant, nova ut respuunt, ita damnant."

In requesting Giles to write the *Scechina* Pope Clement VII did as much as he could to put him at his ease, and emphasized that his researches should be made available to others for their profit. The pope went on to assure Giles that the scholar was always free to discuss and write about the results of his investigations, so long as he did not contumaciously reject the judgment and tradition of the Church.[1] Giles responded to Clement's encouragement and at the pope's request agreed to put his Christian cabala in writing.[2] As he points out to the pontiff, he had often spoken of the cabala in public, even in sermons, and there is indeed a mention of the "*arcana Hebraeorum*" in his solemn opening oration for the Fifth Lateran Council.[3] Leo X was surely aware of Giles's interest in Hebrew and in the "*arcana*," as is clear from Giles's letter to him upon his election as pope, even if he possibly never saw the text of the "Historia" in which Giles tried to disclose to him the mysteries of the cabala which were most pertinent for his pontificate.[4] In any case, there was never any question of Giles's not adhering to the ultimate norm which Clement VII laid down, of his not being convinced that the judgment and tradition of the Roman or Vatican Church was of peremptory and final authority. It is to Giles's concept of that Church that we now turn our attention.

---

[1] Ossinger, *Bibliotheca Augustiniana*, p. 193, letter dated July 22, 1530: "... cum tamen multa liceat vel disputare vel scribere, quae non alii sentiant, dummodo aliena a veritate, et sanctae ecclesiae universali traditione prave non sentiantur, ... Quia quod quis studiose indagavit, pie ac sincere proferat, dum prolatum non contumaciter asserat, sed ecclesiae judicio semper subjiciat."

[2] *Scechina*, vol. I, p. 66, letter undated: "At quando tu [Clement VII], qui navi praees, pericula non extimescenda, hanc tibi curam committendam mandas, jam pareo atque oram solvo."

[3] Mansi, vol. XXXII, col. 675.

[4] Martène, *Veterum scriptorum collectio*, vol. III, col. 1258, letter undated. See, e.g., Ang. Lat. 502, fols. 3r, 205v. See also Ang. Lat. 688, fol. 53r, letter to Gabriele della Volta, January 6 (VIII Idus), 1515, in which Giles relates that Leo made him a gift of a Targum and some other books. For identification of these manuscripts as including a Hebrew Bible and a cabalistic miscellany, now in the Biblioteca Angelica, see Martin, "Egidio da Viterbo," pp. 100* and 109*, and Weil, "Le codex Neofiti I," p. 228.

CHAPTER FOUR

THE CHURCH IN TIME AND PLACE

Giles of Viterbo's thought on the nature of the Church must be set into the framework of time and place he gives Church history if it is adequately to be understood. The Church was for him, first and foremost, an historical reality. Giles accepted the consequences of this point of view, and he tried to locate the Church of his day in its proper moment of time and to discover if it had a special relationship to any given place. The "Historia XX saeculorum" is devoted, in its substance, to these questions, and even in the *Scechina* we see that they are underlying preoccupations. Giles was convinced that the Church of his day was entering a dramatically new and different era. He was also convinced that by its very essence the Church was localized in place, that it was by divine decree Roman, and he intimates that this fact perhaps gives us our best indication of the kind of reality the Church truly is. In this chapter we shall investigate these two aspects of Giles's thought on the nature of the Church, employing them to bring into focus the whole of his ecclesiology and, eventually, to throw light on his concept of reform.[1]

How did Giles envision history's movement? There are two important considerations which must be underscored at the outset. First of all, as was mentioned in the last chapter, Giles pictured history as a shadowy reflection of the divinity, as a more or less inadequate terrestrial image of the dynamic energies of God, i.e., of the Sefiroth. He tells us straightforwardly that sacred history is nothing else than a likeness of the ten Sefiroth, a mirror to the dispositions of providence, and an imitation of the divine realities.[2] The psalms, as well as

[1] Suggestive for the topics discussed in this chapter is the study of the concepts of sacred time and sacred place by Mircea Eliade, *The Sacred and the Profane: The Nature of Religion*, New York 1961, pp. 20-113. On the relationship between the concept of time and "cosmological renewal ideas," see Ladner, *Idea of Reform*, pp. 10-16.

[2] *Scechina*, vol. I, p. 130: "... nihil esse aliud historiam sacram quam sephirot figurae, providentiae imago, exemplarium processio, rerum imitamenta divinarum." Also *ibid.*: "... idque quod in caelo erat mundoque divino historiae veritas imitatur in terris, factum sicut in caelo et in terra." See also *ibid.*, vol. I, pp. 89, 140; vol. II, pp. 13-14. Ang. Lat. 502, fol. 60r: "Addo Aramaeorum arcanum, cum in universa lege tum vero in Daniele scriptum: saecula Deum imitari. In Deo

the course of history, reflect the ten-structure of the Sefiroth. There is, therefore, a direct correspondence between the psalms and history, and the one can be used to interpret the other.[1] The determinism latent in such a view laid out for history an inexorable path, and led Giles to force the facts of history into a rigid, prefabricated schematization. For many of Giles's humanist contemporaries a correct study of history supposedly yielded a rich harvest of political lessons from the past or principles and living examples for a moral philosophy. For Giles it yielded, instead, an understanding of the nature of the Godhead and a glimpse of what the future held in store for the Church. History's secrets, those of the past and present and future, were disclosed to view, and God's providential plan was exposed in its entirety. Just as it was necessary in the myths of the gentiles and in the text of Holy Scripture to penetrate beyond the surface of literal and conventional meaning to an inner core of spiritual truth, it was necessary also in the study of history to uncover the hidden and divine meaning of otherwise secular, and perhaps even commonplace, events. The same heuristic principle pervaded all his thinking: beneath the obvious lies the secret and the sublime.[2]

The second consideration to which we must advert is that as a Christian Giles believed in a form of the linear view of history. The strongly eschatological nature of his thought overrode whatever cyclic tendencies were contained in it, and he was convinced that one day there would be an end to human history as we know it. He himself was living in the tenth age, an age of amplification and fulfillment, and he could speculate on what would happen "once the story of this world is ended."[3]

Pythagoreum denarium ponunt, quem numerum rerum et mundi initium faciunt." Also *ibid.*, fol. 256v: "Est enim in mysteriis passim vulgata sententia, quae in superiori mundo fiant in imo quoque fieri oportere." See also *ibid.*, fols. 258v, 276v. See Robert Gillet, O.S.B., "Temps et exemplarisme chez Saint Augustin," in *Augustinus magister*, vol. II, Paris 1955, pp. 933-941, esp. 937.

[1] *Scechina*, vol. II, p. 89: "Divisi enim psalmi sunt sicut et saecula, ..." See also *ibid.*, vol. I, p. 89.

[2] *Scechina*, vol. II, p. 113: "Historia sacra speculum est ubi umbram suspicitis divinorum; eadem, si interiora penetres, aenigma est sub quo recondita mysteria contemplamini." On humanists' views of history, see Gilmore, *Humanists and Jurists*, esp. pp. 1-37. Mention might also be made of the article by W. von Leyden, "Antiquity and Authority: A Paradox in the Renaissance Theory of History," *Journal of the History of Ideas* 19(1958), pp. 473-492.

[3] *Scechina*, vol. I, pp. 101, 180, 199; vol. II, p. 103; Ang. Lat. 502, fols. 34r-v, 51v, 161r. On Christian rejection of pagan cyclic history in Augustine, see J. Guitton, *Le temps et l'éternité chez Plotin et Saint Augustin*, Paris 1933, pp. 358-363.

There is, however, a strongly cyclical, or at least repetitive, element in Giles's concept of historical time, in spite of its fundamentally eschatological character. For Giles the events of the Old Testament prefigure those of the New. More significant is the fact that their prefiguring function is further extended to the whole of Christian history, just as the decline-consummation pattern of the old dispensation is applied to the entire Christian era. There is, besides, a more literal correspondence between events of the Old Testament and those of the history of the Christian Church than mere prefiguration and typology provide. What was done under the old dispensation must now be repeated under the new.[1] Basing his argument on this principle, Giles argues to the necessity, for instance, of recapturing Jerusalem; this event was related in the Old Testament and therefore must be repeated or re-enacted in the history of the Christian Church.[2]

At times the cyclic undercurrent comes even more explicitly to the fore. Giles suggests that the teaching of Pythagoras, Plato and Virgil on the "*magnus annus*" is a partially corrupted version of a doctrine which they derived from the Arameans, viz., that the events of Old Testament times are to be repeated in the history of the Church.[3] More than once he quotes or alludes to the verse from Virgil's Fourth Eclogue, "*Magnus ab integro saeclorum nascitur ordo*," and insists on the necessity all creation has to return to its origin and the fount of its being.[4] Giles means to point up by these reflections either the new beginning of history ushered in by Christ or simply the creature's ultimate need for the Creator, and he is not trying to establish the foundation for ceaselessly recurring historical cycles. It must be noted,

---

Calo Calonymos dedicated to Giles his *Liber de mundi creatione*, and in it he advocates a linear over a cyclical time-concept as more in accord with orthodox Judaism; see P. Duhem, *Le système du monde*, vol. V, Paris 1917, pp. 223-228.

[1] Ang. Lat. 502, fol. 306r: "... quae in veteri lege acta, in nova esse, suo tamen ordine, iteranda. Unde Pythagoras, Plato, Maro annum magnum introduxere, in quo sint quae antecesserint iteranda, ... Ab ortu itaque Messiae magnus ab integro saeclorum nascitur ordo. Iteranda voluere ferme omnia, ut quae a veteribus in umbra agerentur, ut futurarum flores atque indicia rerum, postea gerenda in luce essent." See also *ibid.*, fols. 25v, 179v, 245v.

[2] Ang. Lat. 502, fols. 304r-v, 306r, 308r. See de Lubac, *Exégèse*, vol. II.2, pp. 327-330.

[3] Ang. Lat. 502, fol. 306r. On the "world year," see Ladner, *Idea of Reform*, pp. 10-12. For a defence of the "world year" concept against the Peripatetics by a Florentine Platonist of Giles's day, see Kristeller, "Francesco da Diacceto," pp. 281, 291.

[4] Ang. Lat. 502, fols. 14v, 30r, 306r; *Scechina*, vol. II, pp. 279-280. He speaks of "temporis rota," Siena G. X. 26, p. 263. Eclogue 4.5.

however, that, although Giles proposes the present tenth age as in some sense the "last," he is altogether too prudent to exclude the possibility of further ages or cycles of ten.[1]

This cyclic or repetitive element in Giles's concept of time had its origins in antiquity and in the cabala, and perhaps was not altogether unrelated to the historical views of some of his humanist contemporaries.[2] The Church itself fostered cyclic thinking through the annual repetition of the liturgical festivals and a case can be made for the hypothesis that in any age religious man can be discriminated from his profane counterpart simply by his desire to live in some form of circular time.[3] But whatever the origin and ultimate significance of cyclic concepts of time, they easily correlate with the concept of reform, which almost by definition postulates a new beginning or a return to a previous state of presumably greater perfection.

Giles was heir to many of the commonplaces used to describe history's course. He tried to apply to history the Hesiodic scheme of decline from a Golden Age to ages of ever baser metals.[4] Although

---

[1] Ang. Lat. 502, fol. 268v: "Erit itaque saeculorum hoc [decimum] nostrum, si numeri mysticam spectes rationem, ultimum, nisi alia ab integro sint sua in vestigia recursura; inaccessa plane, atque invia humanis ausibus, quippe quae, sicut testantur oracula, in sua pater posuit potestate." Also *ibid.*, fol. 321v; *Scechina*, vol. I, p. 124. See esp. Ang. Lat. 502, fol. 25v.

[2] On cyclic recurrence in the cabala, connected with the number seven and multiples thereof, see Scholem, *Ursprung der Kabbala*, pp. 407-419. See in this regard Ang. Lat. 502, fols. 14v, 23r, 108v, and *Scechina*, vol. I, p. 124; vol. II, pp. 280-281. On the suggestion of cycle in Niccolò Machiavelli (1469-1527), see Ladner, *Idea of Reform*, p. 22. See also Gilmore, *Humanists and Jurists*, pp. 101, 108-109. On recurrence ideology in Origen, see Ladner, *Idea of Reform*, p. 16. On Augustine's refusal to accept cycle, see Guitton, *Temps et l'éternité*, pp. 358-363, and T. Mommsen, "Saint Augustine and the Christian Idea of Progress," *Journal of the History of Ideas* 12(1951), p. 354. For cycles in antiquity, see Arthur O. Lovejoy and George Boas, *Primitivism and Related Ideas in Antiquity*, Baltimore 1935, pp. 79-92, 156-166, etc. See also Arnaldo Momigliano, "Time in Ancient Historiography," *History and Theory* 5(1966, Beiheft 6), pp. 1-23.

[3] Eliade, *Sacred and Profane*, p. 70.

[4] Ang. Lat. 502, fol. 321v: "Porro octo saecula per metalla distinximus Hesiodum Danielemque, et in eo Sancti Spiritus ordinem secuti." See also *ibid.*, e.g., fols. 36v, 42v-43r, etc., and Évora CXVI/1-30, fol. 24r. Interesting in this regard is another use of the metal metaphor, Vat. Lat. 6325, fols. 180r-181v. The Hesiodic decline is the earliest Greek version of the progressive degradation of mortals, and it offers no explanation as to why this should be the, apparently inevitable, pattern. See Lovejoy and Boas, *Primitivism*, pp. 23-53. Giles's pessimism shows itself also in his description of the Church as old and moribund, e.g., Ang. Lat. 502, fols. 21v, 52r, 56r, etc. For instances of historical pessimism in Philo, Augustine and Prudentius, see George Boas, *Essays on Primitivism and Related Ideas in the Middle Ages*, Baltimore 1948, pp. 5-6, 52-53, 184-185.

for the pre-Christian era all suggestion of decline had to compete with a metaphor of organic growth from twaddling infancy through various stages of increasing maturity, the pessimistic view definitely tended to dominate for the Christian era, at least up into the ninth age of the cabalistic tenfold division.[1] Giles's pessimism was qualified with the hope of a return of the Golden Age. For Giles the archetype of this Golden Age was the lifetime of Christ and the primitive Church of the first centuries, and it is for the return of something resembling that idealized state that he awaits in the reform of the Church. He at times spoke of a new Golden Age heralded for his own lifetime by such unmistakable signs as Ficino's philosophy and the accomplishments of Pope Julius II.[2]

Giles incorporated into his cosmic view of history the theory of the four kingdoms which had been developed especially by Christian writers from the book of Daniel (2. 39-41; 7. 1-28). The fourth of the kingdoms was Rome. A great deal of the history of the Church must perforce be devoted to explaining the "mystery of the city of Rome," i.e., the part the city plays in the history of salvation.[3] Giles uses the four-kingdom schematization of history to support his concept of the Roman nature of the Church, as will become clear later in the chapter.

Underlying Giles's stratification of the historical past into distinct periods was his numerology, especially as this related to the cabalistic Sefiroth: ten ages for Old Testament times and ten for the period of the Church. Into this basic framework he fitted all other historical divisions. He tried to incorporate into it, for instance, the traditional Christian speculation on the numbers seven and eight: seven is the number of the Old Law and is applied, therefore, in an over-all way to the first ten ages; eight is the number of redemption, corresponding

[1] Ang. Lat. 502, fols. 1r-17r, esp. 4r, 13v. See also Vat. Lat. 6325, fol. 194v.

[2] Kristeller, *Supplementum Ficinianum*, vol. II, p. 316; Évora CXVI/1-30, fol. 23v; Ang. Lat. 502, fol. 36v. The Golden Age and its return is a theme of the Évora manuscript. On Golden Age expectations in Erasmus, see Gilmore, *Humanists and Jurists*, pp. 108-109, and for the Renaissance in general, Ladner, "Vegetation Symbolism," pp. 308, 317. Giles himself by no means always describes the tenth age in terms of gold, e.g., Ang. Lat. 502, fol. 322r.

[3] *Scechina*, vol. I, p. 201. See also *ibid.*, vol. I, pp. 189-190, 224; vol. II, pp. 167-168, 178; "Libellus" (in *Scechina*, vol. I), p. 49, and Ang. Lat. 502, fol. 20r-v. For the origin and developments of this four-kingdom theory, see Mommsen, "Augustine and Progress," pp. 348-349; John M. Headley, *Luther's View of Church History*, New Haven 1963, pp. 240-241, and the observations of Guitton, *Temps et l'éternité*, pp. 290-291. Giles also divides the Christian era into four ages, *Scechina*, vol. I, pp. 209-213, and the Évora manuscript, by speaking of several distinct Golden Ages, indicates still other divisions of history.

to the day of Christ's resurrection, and hence applies to the ten ages of Christian history.[1] Nevertheless, in spite of a certain amount of somewhat confusing overlapping of number symbolism, it is the tenfold division of the Old Testament and Christian eras which constitutes his fundamental historical periods.[2]

For the history of the Church how are the ten ages divided? The first age, which stretches from the time of Christ to Pope Sylvester (314-335), is the true Golden Age, normative for all that follows it. It was the age made golden by the presence of Christ upon earth and the sending forth of the Holy Spirit.[3] It was, furthermore, the age in which the apostles preached throughout the world the necessity of spurning human things in order to attain the divine. Their success was great, for in no other age has the Church been so rich in divine grace and so poor in worldly possessions. The popes, knowing that it was their duty to preside over the Church by reason of good example and holiness of life as well as by their authority, lived in the mountains or in hiding places within the city of Rome. The first age was, in a word, the age of the perfect Church, poor and spiritual. Giles's analysis is ethical in tone and often identifies apostolic evangelization with exhortations to poverty and asceticism. The ideal of the first age is the ideal of hard primitivism.[4]

Adapting to religion and history a principle he knew from metaphysics, Giles proposed that the farther the Church departed from its origins the spiritually weaker and more corrupt it became.[5] Like

---

[1] Ang. Lat. 502, fol. 26v. On the origins of Christian symbolism for seven and eight, see Daniélou, "L'ésotérisme judéo-chrétien," pp. 45-46. See also Roderich Schmidt, "Aetates mundi: Die Weltalter als Gliederungsprinzip der Geschichte," *ZKG* 67(1955-1956), pp. 288-317. On Francesco da Meleto, a contemporary of Giles's who expounded a scheme of history based on numerology, the four kingdoms, etc., see Cantimori, *Eretici italiani*, pp. 14-16, and Eugenio Garin, "Paolo Orlandini e il profeta Francesco da Meleto," *La cultura filosofica del Rinascimento italiano*, Florence 1961, pp. 213-223.

[2] For the tenfold division of history in antiquity, esp. in the fourth of the Sibylline Books, and for its diffusion in the Latin tradition, e.g., through Servius and Juvenal, see Ernst Sackur, *Sibyllinische Texte und Forschungen*, Halle 1898, pp. 150-151.

[3] Évora CXVI/1-30, fols. 27v-28v, 41v-43v.

[4] Ang. Lat. 502, fols. 33r-v, 35r-v, 37r; Vat. Lat. 6325, fol. 130r; *Scechina*, vol. I, pp. 165-166. For the concept of "hard primitivism," i.e., the glorification of the initial era of history because of the trials and hardships it imposes, see Lovejoy and Boas, *Primitivism*, pp. 9-11.

[5] In the context of the fact that the religious doctrine originally entrusted to the Etruscans was bit by bit adulterated, Giles observes, Évora CXVI/1-30, fol. 23r: "Omnia namque bonis e fontibus emanavere, sed facile tandem adulterantur om-

Hesiod's scheme for man's progressive degradation in history this principle meant that the Church was of necessity condemned to a course of constant decline as it gradually receded from the age of Christ and the apostles. Giles at times mitigated his pessimism about the Church's ongoing spiritual degeneration with the reflection that it was able to attain certain desirable objectives, for instance in its organization, due to its established position in political and social life.[1] In the long run, however, this was small compensation for the loss of its pristine virtue and poverty. As a matter of fact, the invariable law of human conduct is that the more men seek after the things of this world the more they neglect the divine. God then punishes them, as for example with the present Turkish scourge, and then they lose even their worldly gains.[2]

The first notable change for the worse in the history of the Church came in the time of Pope Sylvester and Constantine, and this marked the beginning of the second age of Church history, corresponding to

---

nia, nihilque adeo initio praestans est quod exiguo deinde tempore non labefactetur. Ita in pejus prona est natura rerum." Also Ang. Lat. 502, fol. 52r: "... et quoniam a fonte sanctitatis et lucis, justitiae ac sapientiae sole, inter dexteras aetates abest [aetas quinta] quam longissime, idcirco septentrionis et Ripheorum more, dieculam habet exiguam, divorum numerum et temporis spatium haud utique magnum. Nam divinarum rerum amor, qui primo aureo saeculo sole fulgente incendia excitavit, duodecim illos principes tamquam ardentes montes incendit, in animos eas flammas injecit, ut res humanas vitamque contemnerent, in ignes, in tela, in enses sponte ruerent, nullum genus supplicii formidarent, ille inquam amor ire per haec saecula desiit imminutusque est, ut rivus solet qui primum in arva corrivatur, bibente enim solo, quo procedit longius fit minor, quo usque, vincente terrae siti, esse desit, ita in hanc aetatem tamquam in canitiem senescentis ecclesiae descendens, ut habuit parum virium, ita parum assequi potuit vel hominum vel annorum." See also *ibid.*, fol. 23r. Also Vat. Lat. 6325, fol. 194v: "Cum praecipue fides, quo a suis initiis magis magisque procedit, aquarum a fonte recedentium more, ac per caenum limumque transeuntium, eo degenerat a prima et praestantia et claritate magis." For this principle used in metaphysics, see *ibid.*, fol. 44r: "... altera [materia] praestantior erit, jam illa non maxime [a Deo] distabit. Longior enim abest quae deterior." This is posed as an objection to the opinion Giles is defending, but on fol. 46r he answers the objection without denying the principle. For Giles's acceptance of Plato's idea that the ancients were nearer the gods and had, therefore, a pure truth, see the text edited by Massa, *Fondamenti metafisici e testi inediti*, p. 64. On this idea in Plato, see Josef Pieper, "The Concept of Tradition," *The Review of Politics* 20(1958), pp. 465-491, esp. 476-480. For a somewhat similar idea in Jacques Lefèvre d'Étaples, see Eugene F. Rice, Jr., "The Humanist Idea of Christian Antiquity: Lefèvre d'Étaples and his Circle," *Studies in the Renaissance* 9(1962), esp. pp. 134-136. For a similar idea in Pontano, see Massa, "La metodologia," p. 191.

[1] The metals get stronger, for instance, even if less precious, as time goes on, Ang. Lat. 502, fols. 47r-48r.

[2] "Libellus" (in *Scechina*, vol. I), pp. 29-30.

the twelfth psalm. Under "pious Constantine" the Church left the mountain caves, abandoned the eremitical life, and began to adorn itself with the riches of this world. The popes and the clergy throughout this age, Giles assures us, still led blameless lives, but the worldly spirit already infected great numbers of the laity. In adopting this interpretation of the meaning of Constantine's recognition of Christianity Giles joins himself to a long, but not unanimously accepted, historical tradition. This tradition, much influenced by Joachimite thought, yearned for a return especially to the poverty, or even to the destitution, of the primitive Church. The primitive Church was idealized into a state of primordial innocence and perfect virtue, contrasting dramatically with the sordid realities of the all too human Church known from daily experience.[1]

Each of the following ages constituted a further weakening of the Christian fiber. The third age, for instance, was the age which included the pontificate of Gregory the Great (590-604). Up to that time the faithful, though now rich, had at least known how to use their wealth in keeping with their Christian profession, namely, in helping the poor and in building churches. But bit by bit, especially after the fifth age, greed and selfishness took over. The early fervor was lost.[2] It was thus that the Church was to move through history, ineluctably going from bad to worse.

When Giles arrives at the eighth age, which corresponds roughly to the high Middle Ages, he has to face a difficulty, for eight is the number of redemption. He also must take into account the accomplishments of Saint Francis (ca. 1181-1226), Saint Dominic (1170-1221) and the Parisian scholastics. Giles does his best to give due credit to the great medievals, but in principle he does not abandon the decline-theory of Church history. The loss of Jerusalem to the infidel, as well as other evils, tends to balance whatever good the age could boast.[3]

The ninth age from Pope Celestine V to Pope Julius II was even

---

[1] Ang. Lat. 502, fol. 37r-v; "Libellus" (in *Scechina*, vol. I), p. 29; *Scechina*, vol. I, pp. 165-166; vol. II, pp. 170, 173-175; Mansi, vol. XXXII, col. 670. For Eusebius's more generous view of the Constantinian era, see Ladner, *Idea of Reform*, pp. 119-120, and for the same sense in Nicholas of Lyra, see de Lubac, *Exégèse*, vol. II.2, pp. 349-350. For the opposing view, see Dante, *Inferno*, 19. 115-118. In 1415 one of the errors of John Wycliffe (ca. 1320-1384) which was condemned by the Council of Constance was: "Silvester papa et Constantinus imperator errarunt ecclesiam dotando." See *Denz.*, no. 1183(613). For the Joachimite tradition of ecclesiastical decline, see Benz, *Ecclesia spiritualis*.

[2] Ang. Lat. 502, fols. 38v, 47v; *Scechina*, vol. II, p. 174.

[3] Ang. Lat. 502, fols. 110r, 119v, 167v, 169r, 175v-176v, 178v.

more of a problem. Giles divides it into three parts, each relating to the three great tragedies the Church suffered during it: (1) the Avignon exile, (2) the Great Western Schism, (3) the fall of Constantinople. Perhaps even more serious than any of these tragedies was the fact that during this age the Peripatetic philosophy became truly insolent with its success and began to threaten the very foundation of Christianity. In spite of all these heavy blows which the Church had to bear, Giles's final judgment on the ninth age was a favorable one, for he saw in it the signs of the consummation which the tenth age would bring. The discovery of the New World, the decision to build the new Saint Peter's basilica, the renaissance of Scripture studies and the joining of elegance with piety—these were the earnests of what Giles hoped the tenth age would bring to fulfillment.[1]

Before turning our attention to the tenth age we must take note of two facts: (1) Giles finds it impossible to adhere strictly to the decline-theory. It neither takes care of all the data as he knows it, nor does it, in its consistent form, provide for the culmination of history which he expects. By the time of the *Scechina* this culmination is not conceived of with as much optimism as in his earlier writings, but the hopeful note is never completely lost. (2) Although Giles insists upon the Church's ever greater degradation in the course of history, he does not abandon his belief that the Church is indefectible. The Church's doctrine is never essentially corrupted, and God never deserts it to the point of leaving it without saints, even when the majority of the faithful are bent on leading evil and worldly lives. The Church's pastors do not lose their authority nor are their sacramental functions deprived of their efficacy because of the minister's unworthiness. In spite of sin "Peter's bark," Giles believes, cannot be altogether submerged.[2]

---

[1] Ang. Lat. 502, fols. 185r-186r, 191r, 228v-229v, 234v, and esp. 198r: "... ut rursus arridere incipiente fortuna, ut laeta ambitum universi orbis agnoverit, ut de Africae littoribus per Ferdinandum, de Indiae per Emanuelem triumphaverit; ut admirabilem templi molem per Julium incohaverit; ut legem perperam translatam emendaverit ad arcanaque de se scripta penetraverit; ut denique summae pietati summam elegantiam copulaverit [ecclesia]." Also *ibid.*, there is a different threefold division of the ninth age from that given on fol. 228v.

[2] Ang. Lat. 502, fol. 58v-59r: "Abstulitque [divinus ille Filius] pastoribus nostris non claves, non auctoritatem, non potestatem, non inquam caeli occludendi ac recludendi manus. Nam juravit Dominus et non paenitebit eum. Sed perpetuam illam, ac tamdiu perseverantem, familiarem consuetudinem interrupit, ..." Also *ibid.*, fol. 61r: "... qua tempestate, quibus fluctibus, qua scelerum procella, non demersam Petri naviculam quis non miretur,...." Also *ibid.*, fols. 51v, 63v, 85r-v; *Scechina*, vol. I, p. 203: "At ecclesia per tot saecula esset decepta. Decepta

The consummation which Giles foresaw for the tenth age was a reflection of the sense of tension, expectation and religious crisis of the times in which he lived. There was a preoccupation with the apocalyptic and eschatological. This preoccupation was expressed in literature and the arts, as well as in popular sermons, and the number of more or less bizarre figures professing to be the bearers of special messages of consolation or of impending doom was indeed remarkable. Savonarola is perhaps the name we most spontaneously associate with this mood, but even Ficino was not untouched by it. Lorenzo de' Medici's own device, "*Le temps revient*," suggests a consciousness of renewal and rebirth, implying the close of one era and the beginning of another. The conversion of the infidel, the scandals in the Church, the beginning of a new age of peace or a new age of calamity—these were frequent themes.[1]

Giles of Viterbo's thought was colored with eschatological expectations. He himself stated clearly in his oration opening the Fifth Lateran Council that his sermons for the previous twenty years, his active preaching career up to that time, had often consisted of themes taken from the book of Revelation, the Apocalypse.[2] The cabalistic and Joachimite interests he cultivated probably contributed most heavily to this feeling of tense expectation for reform and renovation in his later years.[3]

---

ipsa non est, quae fontem aquae vivae non abjecit sed integrum servat, immixtum possidet, intactum amplectitur."

[1] For an interesting summary of this question, see André Chastel, "L'Antéchrist à la Renaissance," *Cristianesimo e Ragion di Stato; L'Umanesimo e il Demoniaco nell'arte*, Atti del II congresso internazionale di studi umanistici, ed. Enrico Castelli, Rome 1953, pp. 177-186, and by the same author, *Art et Humanisme*, pp. 341-351. See also, e.g., Giuseppe Ermini, ed., *L'attesa dell'età nuova nella spiritualità della fine del medioevo*, Todi 1962, esp. pp. 11-35; Norman Cohn, *The Pursuit of the Millennium*, London 1962; Donald Weinstein, "Savonarola, Florence, and the Millenarian Tradition," *ChH* 27(1958), pp. 291-305, along with the comments of Marvin B. Becker, *ibid.*, pp. 306-311; E. H. Gombrich, "Renaissance and Golden Age," *Journal of the Warburg and Courtauld Institutes* 24(1961), pp. 306-309; Garin, "Paolo Orlandini e Francesco da Meleto" and "Il 'nuovo secolo' e i suoi annunciatori," in *La cultura filosofica*, pp. 213-223, 224-228; Cesare Vasoli, "La profezia di Francesco da Meleto," in *Umanesimo e Ermeneutica: Archivio di Filosofia* (1963), pp. 27-80; Hans Preuss, *Die Vorstellungen vom Antichrist im späteren Mittelalter, bei Luther und in der konfessionellen Polemik*, Leipzig 1906.

[2] Mansi, vol. XXXII, col. 669: "Nam cum annis abhinc circiter viginti, quantum in me fuit, et perexiguae vires tulere, evangelia populis interpretatus sim, prophetarum vaticinia aperuerim, Joannis Apocalypsim de successu ecclesiae, universae ferme Italiae enarraverim,...." Significantly enough, this very council tried to put restrictions on popular prophetic preaching, Session XI, December 19, 1516, *Conciliorum decreta*, pp. 610-614.

[3] See Secret, *Les kabbalistes chrétiens*, pp. 114-118.

With Giles, as with a number of his contemporaries throughout Europe, eschatological speculation was intimately related to the question of the reform of the Church.[1] For Giles the tenth age was, quite simply, the age of ecclesiastical renovation. His whole scheme of history leads up to the tenth age, in which, one way or another, a halt will be called to the Church's decline and it will recover its pristine purity.[2] The ancient prophecies had foretold that in the last ages there would be a great upsurge of spiritual energy precisely "in order to restore the Church."[3] The Lord promised through the prophets to save His Christ, i.e., the Mystical Body of Christ, and, therefore, the Church was sure in the tenth age to receive its renewal and healing.[4]

Giles nourished his concern for reform with all his vast erudition and with the ideas and assumptions of the several intellectual traditions upon which he drew. The consummation of the tenth age was in part identified with the returning Golden Age of Platonic theology, with the revival of eloquence and the arts, with the purgation of the Church from the errors of the Peripatetics, with the rebirth of biblical studies, and with the renewed hope for the religious unity of the world springing from the discovery of the New World and from a firmer determination to conquer the Turks. The sack of Rome and the other disturbances of the second decade of the sixteenth century somewhat changed the tone of this great expectation, made more explicit the fact that the goal would not be achieved except through a certain measure of suffering and purgation, and put one or other factor just mentioned into greater relief. They did not, however, destroy the basic structure of the scheme.

There is a sense in which it is quite true to say that Giles passed from an optimistic to a rather pessimistic view of how the Church's reform in the tenth age was to be accomplished. He thought that that age began with Leo X's accession to the papal throne. At the time of the "Historia," written during Leo's pontificate, he gives the impression that he felt the regeneration might be completed, at least for the most part, during Leo's lifetime. Leo, of course, died young and unexpectedly, and by the time Giles wrote the *Scechina* Rome had been

[1] See, for instance, M. Bataillon, *Érasme et l'Espagne*, Paris 1937, pp. 61-62.

[2] From the closing paragraph of the "Historia," Ang. Lat. 502, fol. 325v: "...incipiatque ecclesia, sponsa tua [Leo X], a lapsu religionis diu misera, ...suae felicitati restitui, ..."

[3] Évora CXVI/1-30, fol. 1r: "...ad rem sacram instaurandam."

[4] Ang. Lat. 502, fol. 325v.

struck with several major disasters and others were threatening. This surely accounts for the change in tone and emphasis. But we must not exaggerate the degree of this change. Even though Giles could see a turn for the better in the latter part of the ninth age, he was still extremely severe on the Church and society of his own day long before the sack made clear that the Church was in need of even greater purgation before its renewal could take place. He saw in the pontificate of Sixtus IV (1471-1487), for instance, a worsening of morals in the Church, and he had bitter words for the evils of the Rome of Alexander VI, Roderigo Borgia (1492-1503). In a letter to a fellow Augustinian written in 1505 he describes the condition of the Church in the most depressing terms: the Church has lost the gift of divine charity, and is so near extinction that he actually can hear the death rattle.[1] On the other hand, even after the sack Giles does not entirely surrender hope for a happier issue of the Church's travail than events would seem to warrant. The *Scechina* tells Charles V that the times are ambiguous, and can resolve themselves either to the Church's utter ruin or to its great gain.[2]

Although on several occasions Giles suggests that the hope for the renewal of the Church owed a great deal to the pontificate of Julius II, he placed his true expectations in Leo X, who was the "first pontiff of the tenth age." Leo would undertake the many tasks Giles conceived as proper to the reforming pope of the era, among which a reformation of morals held a specially high place.[3] Closely associated in Giles's mind with this ethical reform was the study of Scripture,

[1] Naples V. F. 20, fols. 94v-95r, letter dated August 15, 1505, to Serafino Ferri: "Mater ecclesia jam prope extincta est....Refrixit multis jam annis haec regina; obriguit nostra luna, quoniam refrixit caritas multorum....Ecce jam media propinquat nox. Audio mortis strepitus." The general tone of this letter, however, is one of hope and consolation. In another letter, probably written about the same time, but certainly before 1513, to Antonio Zocolo and the Augustinians in Rome, *ibid.*, fol. 264r: "At demum apud Matthaeum [Mt. 24.12] nostrae tempestatis miseriam praesagiens: Heu, heu, tempora, inquit, quibus refrigescet caritas multorum." The Church is old and dying, Ang. Lat. 502, fols. 21v, 52r, 56r, etc. The world is moribund, *ibid.*, fols. 51v, 57v. On the question of "human and cosmic senescence" in antiquity, see Lovejoy and Boas, *Primitivism*, pp. 98-102. On the pontificate of Sixtus IV, see Ang. Lat. 502, fol. 248r-v, and on that of Alexander VI, see *ibid.*, esp. fol. 260v. For further observations on the collapsed condition of Christianity, see Ang. Lat. 502, fol. 26r; Vat. Lat. 6325, fols. 86r-v and 195r-v; *Scechina*, vol. I, p. 104; Mansi, vol. XXXII, col. 675.

[2] *Scechina*, vol. II, p. 186: "...tempore extremi periculi, temporeque extremae aut ruinae aut felicitatis instituendum coepi." See also *ibid.*, vol. II, pp. 146-147, 150, for the final optimism of Giles's vision.

[3] Ang. Lat. 502, fol. 316v.

from which he hoped to see emerge a more perfect observance of the Christian moral code.[1] Amidst the spiritual degradation which he saw on all sides Leo X stood out as the hope for a new era of ecclesiastical regeneration.

How did Giles come to see in Leo the felicitous initiator of the tenth age? In the first place, Leo ascended the papal throne at a time when a number of promising movements in Rome were seemingly reaching a climax, as we have already seen. Giles was aware, moreover, of the great hope which Leo's election stirred in Rome itself and throughout Europe, especially in humanist circles, and this surely inclined him to see in Leo the great restorer.[2] Giles's faithful devotion to the Medici family, which may not in every instance have been free from a certain amount of unconscious preferment seeking, also tended to enhance the person and character of Leo with qualities he may not in actual fact have possessed in the eminent degree attributed to him. In any case, among the reasons which predisposed Giles to view the pontificate of Leo as the beginning of the tenth era, an era whose duration he does not specify, were those derived from intuitions into the mystic significance of the name Leo and the number ten, as well as certain other considerations of the same general nature, such as Leo's supposed Etruscan origin.[3] These reasons were strong enough to keep Giles convinced of the pivotal role of Leo's pontificate in the course of Church history even after Leo's death and the dashing of Giles's easy hopes by the horrors of the sack and the other disasters of the decade after Leo's death in 1521.[4]

We can now review the various events and movements which Giles saw as earnests of the arrival of the tenth age. For reasons which will become clear a little later in the chapter these signs for the most part

[1] Ang. Lat. 502, fol. 196r-v: "...tam in servanda [scriptura] accurati simus, quam fuimus in scrutanda diligentes." Also *ibid.*, fols. 3v, 8r.

[2] Ang. Lat. 502, fol. 4v: "...et hominibus magna, sancta, divina omnia ab uno te [Leo] sperantibus, ..." Also *ibid.*, fols. 251r, 323r, and 319v: "...ut altius [in splendorem] res procedere vix credi posthac posse videatur." See his letter to the whole order upon Leo's election, Siena G. X. 26, p. 288, letter undated: "Misit [Deus] novum et sanctum sponsum ecclesiae, spem magnam Italiae et orbis, ac tutelam doctrinarum, cujus consilio ecclesia sponsa juvenescet, ... renovabitur." For the generally enthusiastic reaction to Leo's elevation to the papacy, see Pastor, *History of the Popes*, ed. Francis Ralph Kerr, vol. VII, pp. 25-28, 42-43.

[3] Ang. Lat. 502, fols. 3v, 4v, 34r-v, 51r-v, 254v-256r. Even in the "Historia" Giles by no means rules out the possibility that not Leo but his successors will reap the full fruit of the last age, *ibid.*, fol. 307r. It is Pélissier who insists upon Giles's unworthy motives in his praise of the Medici, *De opere historico*, p. 44.

[4] *Scechina*, vol. I, pp. 89, 143.

concerned Rome, or at least the Roman Church. First place, therefore, should perhaps be given to the new civic peace and stability which Giles observed in Rome as a result of the energetic measures taken by Julius II and continued by Leo X. Giles saw such peace and stability as necessary preconditions for the flourishing of religion and the arts.[1]

Giles never identified poverty with ignorance or with artistic insensitivity. The return to the ideal of the poor, simple, and eremitical primitive Church did not in his mind exclude a rebirth of art and learning. He never quite seems to have been aware of any difficulty, or even practical impossibility, in simultaneously striving for these two goals. Pope Nicholas V (1447-1455) brought new hope to the Church by fostering culture and learning, hoping to revive them from the ashes of barbarism.[2] Plato taught that sight and hearing are the senses which are most spiritual and most easily lead to the divine, and Giles, consequently, sees in the eloquence of Pope Pius II (1458-1464) and in the adornment of liturgical vestments and furnishings begun by Pope Paul II (1464-1471) signs that the Church was rising towards the promise of the tenth age.[3] For Italy as a whole the promotion of art and learning for which Lorenzo de' Medici was responsible was of overwhelming importance.[4]

In Giles's opinion the most significant artistic endeavor of his day was the decision to glorify anew the basilica dedicated to the Prince of the Apostles. For Julius II's ambitions for the new Saint Peter's Giles has unremitting praise, and he eloquently extols the idea of raising the new church "up to the very heavens."[5] Seemingly forgetful of his wistful yearning after the mountain caves of the primitive Church, Giles wants to see the new basilica rise to be a "most mag-

[1] Ang. Lat. 502, fol. 315r: "Nunc vero te [Leo] principe id pacis apparuit genus, ea lux quam, ut diximus, nullis umquam saeculis vidit urbs Roma." Also "Libellus" (in *Scechina*, vol. I), p. 29. On Julius, see Évora CXVI/1-30, fols. 57r-60r.

[2] Ang. Lat. 502, fol. 230r: "... eloquentiam redivivam e cineribus excitare posse speraret [ecclesia]."

[3] Ang. Lat. 502, fol. 236r: "Fuit itaque opus hoc saeculo non modo Pontanos, Sannazzarios, Hermolaos [Ermolao Barbaro, 1453-1493], Picos eloquio florere, sed pontificem quoque facundiae laude pollentem audiri, ut omne laudis et splendoris decus in sacro religionis apice conspiceretur. Enituit itaque prius Musa in Pio, opum, auri et gemmarum splendor in Paulo. Alter ut auribus eloquio, alter ut oculis sacris ornamentis satisfaceret." See *ibid.*, fols. 74v, 197r-198r, 207r-v, 235v-240r; Massa, *Fondamenti metafisici e testi inediti*, pp. 87, 105; Vat. Lat. 6325, fol. 36v.

[4] "Libellus" (in *Scechina*, vol. I), p. 29

[5] Évora CXVI/1-30, fol. 59v.

nificent edifice, that God might be more magnificently adored."[1]

Still more pregnant with theological meaning were two other phenomena, which Giles often linked to each other: (1) the territorial expansion of Christianity through conquest of the Turk and the voyages of discovery, and (2) the acquisition of the full inner meaning of Scripture through the cabala. Giles's enthusiasm for the voyages and conquests of the Spaniards and Portuguese can be traced back to the early years of the "Sententiae" and continues to the time of the *Scechina* as the religious significance of these events became more evident to him.[2]

At times when Giles speaks of the meaning of the discoveries and conquests he seems to consider that it consists simply in an entirely unexpected opportunity to spread the Gospel and "apostolic piety" among new peoples, much along the line of the nineteenth-century missionary concept, even to the point of suggesting a certain measure of that century's so-called missionary imperialism.[3] Giles saw, however, deeper theological subtleties beneath these events. As regards the conquest of the East he understood that this was another striking instance of the general law of sacred history's circular pattern: just as the nascent Church came out of the East, so in the last age must it return there, to its source.[4]

The relationship which Giles postulates between the new discoveries and the adoption of the cabala by Christians is curious. He sees in

---

[1] Ang. Lat. 502, fol. 193v: "... magnificentissimus esset locus, ... ut magnificentius adoretur, ..."

[2] See, e.g., Vat. Lat. 6325, fols. 28r, 88r, 143v; Évora CXVI/1-30, fols. 11v-11(a)r, 23v,43v, 54(a)v; Ang. Lat. 502, fols. 176v-177v, 191v-193v, 266r-v; *Scechina*, vol. I, pp. 77, 142; vol. II, pp. 95, 156, etc. Jacques Lefèvre d'Étaples also felt that knowledge of the ancient languages and the spreading of the Gospel in the New World were signs of the approaching end of the world. See J. Dagens, "Humanisme et évangélisme chez Lefèvre d'Étaples," *Courants religieux et Humanisme à la fin du XV et au début du XVI siècle: Colloque de Strasbourg, 1957*, Paris 1959, esp. p. 132. Johann Albrecht Widmanstetter (1506-1557), who knew Giles and had occasion to consult his library, with a suggestion of millenarism links the ideas of the discovery of the new lands and the recovery of the ancient languages, *Liber sacrosancti evangelii de Jesu Christo*, Vienna 1562, fols. 3r, 8v-10r. For a similar idea in Luther, see Headley, *Luther's View*, pp. 234-235. For the expectations raised among the Jews by the discovery of America, see Silver, *Messianic Speculation*, pp. 114-116.

[3] Évora CXVI/1-30, fols. 11v-11(a)r, 43v, 51v-52r, 54(a)v; Ang. Lat. 502, fol. 192v: "... et gentes victas Christianorum subire jugum cogit [Manuel I of Portugal], ..." See also *Scechina*, vol. I, pp. 83, 160: "... armis intrare compelleres [Charles V]." Lk. 14.23.

[4] Ang. Lat. 502, fol. 177r-v. A similar idea is expressed in a letter to Julius II, August 18, 1508, Siena G. X. 26, p. 205.

these two phenomena but one great divine act, proper to the tenth age: the opening up to mankind of secrets long withheld. For the tenth age all secrets are to be revealed, those of the divine and eternal world through the implementation of the method of the cabala, and those of the created and transitory world by means of the voyages of discovery.[1]

As these considerations have already made clear, Giles viewed the discovery of the New World and the conquest of the Turk very much as religious and eschatological realities. Underlying his thought on these events, besides the ideas already mentioned, was the assumption that they were paving the way for the sign *par excellence* of the last age, the spiritual unity of mankind. The persuasion in western Christendom that the "*plenitudo gentium*" corresponded to the "*plenitudo temporis*" was ancient. It picked up tremendous impetus through the eschatological motivation commonly preached during the Crusades, found echo and support in the Joachimite speculation of the late Middle Ages, and took on new urgency with the discovery of America and the seriousness of the Turkish threat in the late fifteenth century. Expectations were high for the final accomplishment of the Johannine prophecy, "So there shall be one flock, one shepherd" (Jn. 10.16).[2]

Giles believed that the tenth age should effect the conversion of the world and that that age had already begun.[3] He thought he saw hopeful signs among the Jews, especially because of the friendly treatment accorded them by Leo X.[4] The war against the Turks was assumed

[1] *Scechina*, vol. I, p. 156: "Ego [the Shekinah] tuo saeculo tibique [Charles V] utrumque duxi mundum demonstrandum, ..."

[2] See P. Alphandéry and A. Dupront, *La chrétienté et l'idée de croisade*, vol. I, Paris 1954, p. 41; vol. II, Paris 1959, pp. 278-280, and also A. Dupront, "Croisades et eschatologie," *Umanesimo e Esoterismo: Archivio di Filosofia* (1960), pp. 175-198. See also Bataillon, *Érasme et l'Espagne*, pp. 56-62, 243-244, and by the same author, "Évangélisme et millénarisme au Nouveau Monde," *Courants religieux et Humanisme*, pp. 25-36; Chastel, *Art et Humanisme*, pp. 453-454. On the importance of the preaching of Saint Vincent Ferrer (ca. 1350-1419) in the early fifteenth century, see Marjorie Reeves, "The Abbot Joachim and the Society of Jesus," *Medieval and Renaissance Studies* 5(1961), esp. pp. 167-170. On the "one flock and one shepherd" theme in Florence in the late fifteenth century, see Garin, *La cultura filosofica*, pp. 167, 180-181, 225. On that same theme, see Annio da Viterbo, *Glosa* [*sic*] *sive expositio super Apocalypsim*, Cologne 1531, proemium; Galatinus, "Comm. in Apocalypsim," Vat. Lat. 5567, fols. 1v, 165v-169v; Ficino, "Epistolarum liber VI," *Opera*, vol. I, p. 814. Giles consistently associates the idea of plenitude with the Messiah, e.g., *Scechina*, vol. II, pp. 134, 262-263.

[3] Ang. Lat. 502, fol. 25v. See also Évora CXVI/1-30, fols. 61v-62r, 73r-74r; Martène, *Veterum scriptorum collectio*, vol. III, cols. 1260-1261; *Scechina*, vol. I, pp. 142-143.

[4] Ang. Lat. 502, fols. 23v-24r. See also *Scechina*, vol. I, pp. 195-198. On the

into this eschatological complex. The military defeat of the Turks would help accomplish the grouping of all peoples around the one shepherd, but it had eschatological overtones of even greater significance. It meant that Jerusalem would be recovered, which for Giles was part of the divine plan for the end of the ages, and also that the Antichrist, whom the Turk embodied, would receive his final crushing blow. Even the full revelation of the cabalistic "*arcana*" was dependent upon the emperor's undertaking the campaign against the Turk.[1]

The force of the problem raised by the discovery of the New World and of the war against the Turk was so great that over the course of the years it led Giles to shift his attention from the papacy to the emperor. Although Clement VII requested the writing of the *Scechina*, Giles dedicated it to the emperor, Charles V. It was the emperor's ships which were sailing to the new lands and it must be the emperor's armies which would conquer the Turk. Whereas Leo X had been the charismatic figure of the "Historia," it is Charles V who plays this role in the *Scechina*. Giles does not by any means intend to exclude the papacy from its proper function.[2] On the other hand, the emperor is the shepherd of the flock who is to gather all into the one sheepfold.[3] The *Scechina* is pervaded with hints of this imperial messianism, as Charles V becomes the "prince sent from heaven" and the true king of Jerusalem.[4]

The emperor's investiture with a messianic role comes clearly to the fore in Giles's many descriptions of the sack of Rome in 1527. Here Charles is the "new Cyrus," the instrument of divine wrath and the divinely appointed purger of the evils of the Roman Church. Giles maintains the view that the sack was an act of God and that Charles was simply the divinely appointed minister of it. This was, after all, the official interpretation put on the deed by Charles himself in the

---

expression "convertentur ad vesperam" which Giles uses in association with the Jews' conversion, see Bataillon, "Évangélisme et millénarisme," p. 30. Ps. 59 (58). 6.

[1] Évora CXVI/1-30, fols. 46v, 62r, 80r; Ang. Lat. 502, fols. 25v-26r, 43r, 304v, 305v; *Scechina*, vol. I, p. 110: "... sed ne tibi [Charles V] quidem prius quam ad hostes religionis accederes debellandos." See Dupront, "Croisades et eschatologie," pp. 177-178, on the mystic significance of Jerusalem.

[2] *Scechina*, vol. I, p. 233: "Tuum est opus, Caesar, cum Clemente septimo, pontifice maximo, ..." Also *ibid.*, vol. I, p. 76.

[3] *Scechina*, vol. I, pp. 160-161, and vol. II, pp. 148-149. See Bataillon, *Érasme et l'Espagne*, pp. 243-244, for a similar description of Charles V by Alfonso de Valdés (ca. 1500-1532).

[4] *Scechina*, vol. I, pp. 69, 116. See also *ibid.*, vol. II, p. 13.

message composed in his chancery by Alfonso de Valdés and sent to the Christian princes in July, 1527.[1]

The long and graphic descriptions Giles gives of the horrors of the sack indicate the tremendous impression it made upon him, even though he did not personally witness it. This event signaled for him, as for so many of his contemporaries, the beginning of a period of special distress and upheaval.[2] What he seems to have felt most bitterly, however, was that the catastrophe did not provoke real repentance. Giles has forebodings that even worse disasters are in store, and he views the restoration of the Church in terms of painful, even bloody, purgation.[3] Once again he calls upon his theory of the repetitive pattern of sacred history, and concludes that just as the Church was founded on the shedding of blood it is only by the shedding of blood that it can be renewed.[4]

This further purgation he sees as the possible victory of the Turks, and even the capture and overthrow of the city of Rome. In this sense Charles and Suleiman (1520-1566) are put on equal terms, and thus some of the messianic aura which surrounded the emperor is dispersed.[5] In any case, what is most important for our purposes is that by the time of the *Scechina* we clearly see that, without denying the validity of the very hopeful signs which he saw in the "Historia" and some of which he insisted upon even more energetically in the *Scechina*, Giles now feels that the tenth age possibly will have to endure even greater tribulations than those already suffered before the renewal of the Church is accomplished.[6] It is with this rather frightening possibility that he ends his speculation on the meaning of the precise moment of time at which the Church now finds itself and on what the future holds in store for it. We can, therefore, turn our attention to a discussion of the Church itself, especially as it relates to the city of Rome.

---

[1] Bataillon, *Érasme et l'Espagne*, pp. 397-398. See also Graf, *Roma nella memoria del medio evo*, p. 752. On Joachim's expectations from "Cyrus," see de Lubac, *Exégèse*, vol. II.2, p. 325. On Charles and the sack, see *Scechina*, vol. I, pp. 105, 156-159, and vol. II, p. 144.

[2] Ang. Lat. 762, fol. 3r, letter dated July 30, 1528, to Gio. Francesco Libertà.

[3] *Scechina*, vol. I, pp. 104-106, 217-218.

[4] *Scechina*, vol. II, p. 146: "... ecclesiam sanguine institutam, ... non sine multo sanguine renovatam ...." There is a similar sentiment in a letter as early as August 15, 1505, to Serafino Ferri, Naples V. F. 20, fol. 94r: "Sanguine jam fundata fides, nunc sanguine rursus ad purum instauranda ...."

[5] *Scechina*, vol. I, p. 161: "... tibi [Charles V] Sulimanoque." See also *ibid.*, pp. 104-105, 217-218.

[6] *Scechina*, vol. I, p. 104: "Erit tribulatio qualis numquam fuit." Mt. 24.21. See also *ibid.*, vol. I, p. 213; vol. II, pp. 144-150.

As we have seen, Giles often describes the Church as the Mystical Body of Christ. This metaphor, taken from Saint Paul and developed by the theologians and writers of the Middle Ages, flowed easily from Giles's pen and summed up many of his beliefs about the Church. Without Giles perhaps even being aware of a conflict, Christian tradition in this instance won out over what certain of his Neoplatonic assumptions might logically have demanded. The Church was a body, i.e., no matter how spiritual it might become it could never shake off certain necessary consequences of that fact. It had members; it had a head; it played a part in real history and it related to real time and real places.

The source of life for this body was Christ. He possessed the "fulness of grace" and He communicated this to the Church, channeling it for the most part through the apostles and their successors. He thus imbued the organism with inner dynamism and brought it into vital contact with Himself.[1] Using another metaphor of the Church as the spouse of Christ, Giles insisted on the intimate union between the two to the point of their being two in one flesh.[2] A certain identity of function, power and authority in this way was effected between them, so that Giles could conceive an injury to the Church as an injury to Christ Himself.[3] In somewhat the same fashion the Church had certain doctrinal prerogatives stemming from its close union with the Savior, who promised that the Church's faith would not fail.[4] The Church as a whole, as well as the individual Christian, was imagined as being animated by the spirit and grace of Christ, and this gave to the Church its authority and sacramental efficacy.[5]

Giles expressed in a very succinct manner why the Church was endowed with transcendent functions and powers, becoming a sort of

[1] Naples V. F. 20, fols. 275v-276r, letter undated, to Antonio Zocolo and the Augustinians in Rome: "Nam unctus [Petrus] a Domino in sacerdotem maximum, quia unxerat Jacob petram Petrus vocari jussus a Domino est, quasi novae ecclesiae constans atque immotum fundamentum; unguentum primo in capite, gratiae plenitudo in Christo, inde descendit in barbam, barbam Aaron, in Petrum summum sacerdotem; denique in ora vestimentorum veluti in ultima vasa gratiae ...." Ps. 133(132).2.

[2] See *Scechina*, vol. I, p. 95; vol. II, p. 32. Eph. 6.31-32.

[3] Siena G. X. 26, p. 176, letter dated October 21, 1510, to the French Augustinians: "Censuras enim ecclesiae contemnere nihil est aliud nisi ecclesiam sponsam et Christum sponsum contemnere."

[4] Ang. Lat. 502, fols. 40v, 156v, 273v; Évora CXVI/1-30, fol. 40r; Vat. Lat. 6325, fol. 197r-v.

[5] Naples V. F. 20, fols. 201v, 257v, etc.; Vat. Lat. 6325, fols. 189r, 190r, 197v. The earthly Church has a heavenly counterpart, e.g., *Scechina*, vol. I, p. 95.

intermediary between God and man. Although God could save men without using the ministrations of the Church, He did not ordinarily do so because He wanted man to be saved through the help of his fellow man.[1] God therefore delivered to the Church control over certain spiritual realities which would enable it to carry out this sanctifying mission.

Principal among the Church's means for sanctification were the sacraments, especially the Eucharist. It was by means of them that grace was conveyed to the Christian. The Eucharist was the symbol of the "new Israel," uniting all peoples, races and nations around its table, and bringing them into true communion and spiritual unity. The Eucharistic sacrifice, however, was to be celebrated with proper love and inner devotion, for otherwise it would be a useless formality, "*vanum opus*."[2] The Church fosters contemplation, which in turn fosters this love and devotion. Giles was convinced of the need for retirement and private contemplation, as well as of the value of the sacraments and public liturgical prayer, and he insisted upon the necessity of "flight from the things of this world" with such single-minded conviction that he found even his duties as prior general of the Augustinian order conflicted with this almost eremitical ideal.[3] The Christian, as a result of the divine love which flows into him through prayer and the sacraments, becomes divinized. In lines more reminiscent of patristic theology than of what is commonly thought of as Renaissance deification of man through a rejection of his dependence upon God, Giles exhorts the Augustinian community at Rome with the bold thought that through the love of God men come to participate in the divine.[4]

---

[1] Ang. Lat. 502, fol. 85v: "Non quia solus servare Deus non possit homines, sed voluit ut auxilio esset homo homini." Also *ibid.*, fols. 122r, 280r-v.

[2] Naples V. F. 20, fol. 264v, undated letter to Antonio Zocolo and the Augustinians in Rome. See also Ang. Lat. 502, fols. 9v-10r, 49v-50v, 92v-93r, 101r-v, 134r, 178(a)v, 302v. See also Vat. Lat. 6325, fol. 198r.

[3] *Scechina*, vol. I, p. 214; Naples V. F. 20, fol. 181r-v, which should be contrasted with Ang. Lat. 502, fol. 308r; Siena G. X. 26, p. 140.

[4] Naples V. F. 20, fol. 256v, letter undated, to Antonio Zocolo and the Augustinians in Rome: "... hoc est [Deus] hominem fecit unde homines dii facti sunt, amore plane eodem et filii excelsi omnes, quotquot receperunt eum." Also *ibid.*, fol. 257r: "Sed quid id mireris quod homo fiat deus, nam Deus effectus est homo et Verbum caro factum? ... ex Deo nati sunt amore, non natura." The same idea is repeated in the *Scechina*, vol. I, p. 206: "Homines deos fecit." See also *ibid.*, vol. II, pp. 12, 197, and also Ang. Lat. 502, fol. 121v. On the patristic roots of the concept of the dignity of man up to the time of Ficino and Pico, see Eugenio Garin, "La 'dignitas hominis' e la letteratura patristica," *La Rinascita* no. 4, 1 (1938), pp. 102-146.

Besides its teaching and sanctifying functions the Church also has the duty of the spiritual governance of the Christian faithful. Giles never questioned the validity of the hierarchical structure of the Church, and he clearly affirmed that the Church exercised its authority as an unbroken continuation of the authority of its Founder.[1] Giles had a broad view of the agents through whom this authority was exercised, and he cannot without qualification be relegated to any of the standard classifications of curialist, conciliarist or spiritualist.[2] On the other hand, there is no doubt that, while avoiding Giles of Rome's identification of the Church with the pope, he did take a strikingly strong papal or curial view of ecclesiastical authority.

Christ gave to Peter and to his successors His own authority, and the pope exercises his office in the name of Christ. The popes are the true heirs of Christ, and, as such, they have supreme authority in the Church, enjoying the unique prerogative of being able to command all and of being obliged to obey none[3]. While holding a forceful position on this primacy of jurisdiction which the pope has in the Church, Giles does not necessarily consider the pope's actual administration of the Church his principal task. The pope's first duty is a strictly spiritual one. He must teach, pray for the Church, and offer sacrifice for it. Like all other pastors in the Church, he must lead his people and instruct them primarily by his good example.[4]

[1] Ang. Lat. 502, fol. 131v: "... [per] Petrum et sacerdotii heredes imperat Christus, ..." *Scechina*, vol. II, p. 168: "... per Messiam et ejus legatum successoremque Petrum ...." Évora CXVI/1-30, fol. 40r: "Quid est enim Romanae sedis auctoritas nisi divina, quam a Jesu nostro delecti heroes [apostoli] olim acceperunt?"

[2] For a discussion of these schools of ecclesiology in the late Middle Ages, see Merzbacher, "Wandlungen des Kirchenbegriffs."

[3] Ang. Lat. 502, fol. 308v: "... nec habere se [Christum] tantum regni divini claves et auctoritatem, sed etiam Petro tuisque [Leo X] pontificibus tradere." See also *ibid.*, fols. 5v, 6v, 7r, 16r, 21r, 86r, 167r-v, 268v, 317v, etc. On the meaning of the two keys, see Vat. Lat. 6325, fol. 197r: "Habet autem sponsa claves geminas, alteram doctrinae et sapientiae, ut indicet et erudiat, alteram facultatis ac potestatis, ut et purget et Deo purgatos adjungat, ..." See also *ibid.*, fol. 161v. Giles would have felt little sympathy for Luther's anti-papal attack of 1519, "Resolutio Lutheriana super propositione sua XIII de potestate papae," *WA*, vol. II, pp. 183-240. Giles had opportunity to know this work as quoted in its entirety by Johann Faber (1478-1541) in his *Opus adversus nova quaedam et a Christiana religione prorsus aliena dogmata Martini Lutheri*, Rome 1522. Faber gave a copy of his book to Giles, which is now in the Biblioteca Angelica, Rome. See Martin, "Egidio da Viterbo," p. 396. Luther's same "Resolutio" exists in manuscript form among the documents of the Ridolfi Collection in the Bibliothèque Nationale, Paris, Lat. 3395, pp. 1-40.

[4] Ang. Lat. 502, fols. 273v-274r; Mansi, vol. XXXII, col. 672. On the qualities required in the pope, see Ang. Lat. 502, fol. 48r.

Giles's opening oration at the Fifth Lateran Council could give grounds for suspecting that he supported some form of conciliarism and that he thought the frequent convocation of councils was the healthiest possible procedure in the Church. Councils are the font of moral probity and doctrinal orthodoxy, and Giles gives little hint that he entertains any misgivings concerning them. In the *Scechina*, furthermore, he urges the emperor to do his best to have a council convoked.[1] The actual fact is, however, that Giles saw councils as ambiguous realities in the life of the Church, and as assemblies which very easily became tools in the hands of unscrupulous secular princes. The bitter memories of the Council of Pisa assembled in 1511 by Louis XII (1498-1514) of France were still vivid when he wrote that councils were the instruments princes used when they wanted to cause trouble for the Church, and he correctly observed that the popes of his day feared and suspected the very word "council".[2] Although he does not directly confront the issue of pope over council, there is no reason to infer that he thought a council legitimately could under ordinary circumstances challenge the papal authority.[3]

An important consequence of the Church's being a body was that it related to a particular place. Spiritual though Giles would like to make the Church he realized he could not disembody it. As a matter of fact, there is in his thinking a rather paradoxical contrast between

[1] *Scechina*, vol. I, p. 69; Ang. Lat. 502, fols. 187r and 321r: "... [concilium] quod unicum remedium esse solet, ..." See also Signorelli, *Egidio da Viterbo*, pp. 52-53, 100, 169, 199.

[2] Ang. Lat. 502, fol. 225v: "... [concilium] unicam, ut diximus, principibus turbandarum rerum viam, ..." *Ibid.*, fols. 222r, and 240r: "... semper suspectum pontificibus fuerit et reformidatum concilii nomen, ..." See also "Oratio post 3am sessionem," pp. 522-523. At the time of the Council of Pisa, 1511, Giles demanded of his subjects forthright loyalty to Julius II, Siena G. X. 26, pp. 266-269, undated letter to an unnamed provincial. He was also employed by Julius to win back from Pisa four schismatic cardinals. See Martin, "Egidio da Viterbo," p. 331. See also Augustin Renaudet, ed., *Le concile gallican de Pise-Milan*, Paris 1922, pp. 583-584, 659. On October 25 (VIII Kalendas Nov.), 1510, Giles addressed a letter to Julius II in which he tried to dissuade him from his anti-Ferrara policy on the grounds that it was seriously injurious to the cause of Church unity and had already caused schism in the College of Cardinals, Naples V. F. 14, fol. 1v. On April 5 of the next year, however, Giles expressed his wish for a victory of Julius over the Duke of Ferrara and his ally, the King of France, Siena G. X. 26, p. 230, letter to Seraphinus Florentinus.

[3] Ang. Lat. 502, fol. 222r: "... utque nihil concilio sanctius si jure absolvatur, ita nihil ridiculosius si ignaviter, nihil periculosius si temere habeatur." Also see *ibid.*, fol. 244r on consistories. For the settlement of the Great Western Schism Giles seems to recognize the council's authority to depose contending popes, *ibid.*, fol. 218r.

the Church conceived as a withdrawn, eremitical and spiritual reality, and the Church conceived as "Roman," i.e., as divinely committed to a particular city, as a providential continuation of the empire, and as a society totally involved in the actual problems of the times. It is not that Giles reluctantly concedes this latter aspect to the Church as a temporary condition which it must strive to overcome and to transcend, and far less does he consider it an abuse. On the contrary, he exults in the Roman character of the Church, and he finds that this aspect of the Church's reality demonstrates it to be the continuation of Israel and the converging point of all religious history.[1]

Giles delights in contrasting Rome and the Vatican with Jerusalem and Sion. Without compromising the authentic character of the "old Church of the Hebrews," he regards the Roman Church as the transcendent fulfillment of all that was imperfect and incomplete in the "Synagogue." In like manner Rome surpasses Jerusalem in spiritual excellence, and the hill of the Vatican becomes the true Mount Sion.[2] What was essential to the "first Church" was its transitoriness, but what is most proper to the Roman or Vatican Church is that it will endure to the end of time. This could not be more graphically proved than by the fact that Solomon's Temple did not last even to the end of the eighth age of the old dispensation, whereas the eternal Temple of the New Law on the hill of the Vatican is even now rising to new magnificence.[3] Rome is the holy city *par excellence* and the final focal point of history. It is, in a word, the holy Latin Jerusalem, "*sancta Latina Jerusalem*."[4]

Reminiscent of the theory of the translation of the empire is the idea that the Church migrated out of Asia into Europe, from Jerusalem to Rome.[5] There was nothing casual about this event. By etymologically relating the name of the city of Rome to Edom, the land where

[1] See Chastel, *Art et Humanisme*, pp. 451-457, on the upsurge of interest in the mystique of the city of Rome in the High Renaissance. See also my article, "Giles and Renaissance Rome."

[2] Ang. Lat. 502, fols. 5v, 9v, 12r, 12v. Also *ibid.*, fol. 70v: "... in Vaticano Italiae, vero non umbratili monte Sion." See also *ibid.*, fols. 16r, 109v, 220v, and esp. 129r-136v; *Scechina*, vol. I, p. 116.

[3] Ang. Lat. 502, fols. 10r, 15v-17v; *Scechina*, vol. I, p. 151. See Kenneth J. Pratt, "Rome as Eternal," *Journal of the History of Ideas* 26(1965), pp. 25-44, esp. 35-38, on the renewed vigor given the idea of Rome's eternity in the sixteenth century.

[4] Siena G. X. 26, p. 60, undated letter to unspecified Augustinian convent in Rome. *Scechina*, vol. I, p. 155: "... Jerusalem humanam, urbem Romam."

[5] Ang. Lat. 502, fol. 24r. For the theme in medieval historiography of the

Esau settled, Giles is able to link Rome's origins with the biblical narrative, and thence to draw a series of illuminating contrasts between Esau and Jacob, i.e., between Rome and Israel.[1] In the providential course of history God used the Romans for the sacred task of world conquest by their arms, thus paradoxically preparing the way for a reconquest of the Romans by "Hebrew piety," i.e. by the religion of the early Christians.[2] Peter and Paul came to Rome, according to the prophecy of Virgil, and by their piety they gradually won the city for Christianity. Whereas the Romans destroyed Jerusalem, the Jews preserved and cared for Rome, for it was to be the eternal center of the true religion.[3]

The transfer of the seat of religion from Jerusalem to Rome was absolutely necessary because of the universal character of the new religion. The Church could not rest satisfied within the narrow confines of "Asia," but had to insert itself into the empire, the great universal institution of antiquity. Giles thus placed in the first generation of Christianity the seed for the eschatological hope for the religious unity of the human race, and he joined this hope indissolubly with the destiny of the city of Rome.[4]

Rome was prepared from the very beginning to be the center of Christianity. On this point Giles brings to bear his Etruscan lore as well as much of the patristic and medieval tradition concerning the city of Rome. His interest in the Vatican, as such, is explained by his eager desire to promote the cause of the Etruscans, and not only by the project for the new Saint Peter's. Janus, the founder of the Etruscan religion, bore to the Vatican and Janiculum the true religious

movement of power, wisdom and religion from East to West, see Headley, *Luther's View*, pp. 241-242.

[1] See "Libellus" (in *Scechina*, vol. I), p. 43; *Scechina*, vol. I, pp. 108-109, 118-119, 120, 142, 158, 160, 224; vol. II, p. 79; Ang. Lat. 502, fols. 12r, 90v. See also Felice da Prato, *Psalterium*, fol. 29v; Josephus, *Jewish Antiquities*, trans. H. Thackeray, Loeb vol. IV, London 1930, pp. 169-171.

[2] "Libellus" (in *Scechina*, vol. I), p. 41: "Vincunt Hebraeos Romani, sed armis; Romanos Hebraei superant pietate." See also Ang. Lat. 502, fol. 282r.

[3] "Libellus" (in *Scechina*, vol. I), p. 41; *Scechina*, vol. I, pp. 118, 134, 190, 200; vol. II, p. 79. *Aeneid*, 8.503: "externos optate duces."

[4] "Libellus" (in *Scechina*, vol. I), p. 41: "Non sum unius tantum populi Deus, sed gentibus omnibus idem. Idcirco orbem aequemus, gentes una religione jungamus. Horum locum, illorum imperium copulemus. Romanus orbis felicitate, Hebraeus pontificis sit auctoritate contentus, uterque rerum et imperii aeternitate laetus. Atque ita junctis animis, juncto hinc loco hinc principe, aeternam statuamus pietatis sedem et ex utraque gente urbem faciamus eandem .... una urbs Roma." See also *Scechina*, vol. I, pp. 118, 120; Ang. Lat. 502, fols. 16v-17r, 20r-v.

tradition, which later was obscured.[1] Thus the Etruscan bank of the Tiber, expecially the Vatican, was sanctified from the earliest times, and, as we have seen, the Etruscans were under the same divine providential care as were the Hebrews.[2] The parallel between Janus and Peter as keybearers was too obvious for Giles to miss, and he finds in this fact a confirmation that the Vatican was from the most ancient times consecrated for Christianity.[3]

Giles is clear, however, on what the single historical fact was which articulated Rome's claim to be the center of the religious world. Rome was the site to which Peter and Paul came, and it was hallowed by their preaching and martyrdoms. The Vatican, as the tomb of Peter, was particularly sanctified, becoming the incorruptible custodian of Trinitarian orthodoxy and enjoying a privileged relationship with sacramental grace.[4] By reason of the sepulchre of the Prince of the Apostles energies of grace and sanctification were concentrated in the Vatican, and these constituted it the seat of the new religion.[5] It was for this reason that Rome became the center of Christianity and the legitimate successor to Jerusalem.[6] The city of Rome and the supreme

---

[1] Ang. Lat. 502, fols. 24v, 70v.

[2] Ang. Lat. 502, fols. 8r-v, 17r, 39r, 78v, 84v. For contrasts with the Roman bank of the river, see *ibid.*, fols. 6v, 131r. See also Naples V. F. 20, fols. 277v-278r; Évora CXVI/1-30, fols. 11r-23v, 28v.

[3] Ang. Lat. 502, fol. 7r.

[4] Ang. Lat. 502, fol. 158r: "Monuimus persaepe hoc saeculum [octavum] peculiari conjunctione Petri sepulchro Vaticano, ... esse consecratum, ubi sapientia, hoc est, alta trinitatis cognitio, numquam divariaverit, totius orbis errores castigaverit emendaveritque." *Ibid.*, fol. 134r: "Sacramenta quibus a Samaritano sanamur et gratiam inimus ... pertinent ... ad Vaticanum, cumque vera sanctificatio sacramentis fiat, solus Vaticanus, aeterna sedes Petri, mons sanctificationis vocandus est, ubi sanctificationis est caput."

[5] Ang. Lat. 502, fol. 225v: "... ecclesiarum omnium caput esse urbem Romam sedemque Vaticanam, ubi sortitum sit tumulum apostolorum caput [sic]." *Ibid.*, fol. 5r-v: "... super montem sanctum Dei. Non Asiae et Judaeae in quo filius extrema passus est, non imperavit; sed is est mons sanctus Dei in quo, ubi revixit filius et in sidera se recepit, aeterni sedem erexit sacerdotii sanguine et cruce Petri, ad dexteram Tiberis ripam, ..." See also *ibid.*, fols. 6v, 91r, 172(a)r-v, and Vat. Lat. 6325, fol. 166r.

[6] Ang. Lat. 502, fol. 5v: "... primus heres est Petrus praedicans praeceptum ejus [Christi], et praedicando in monte sancto deficiens, in monte sancto [Vaticano] sepultus est, ubi aeterna imperandi auctoritas jusque in perpetuum orbis administrandi." Siena G. X. 26, p. 60, letter undated, to unspecified Augustinian convent in Rome: "Civitas haec, sancta Latina Jerusalem ... sanctorum apostolorum Petri et Pauli morte instaurata, sanctorum martyrum sanguine adauctata sedis, et sancto Petro heredi dedicata." See also Ang. Lat. 502, fols. 36v, 65v, 78v, 91r, 116v, 132r-v, 170(a)v, 184v, 190r, 193v, 194r, 225v, 257r, 278v; *Scechina*, vol. I, pp. 156, 227.

pontiff were joined by a divine and eternal bond, and what God had thus joined no man should dare separate.[1]

Giles's fascination with Julius II's project to rebuild Saint Peter's basilica was a reflection of his fascination with the importance for Christianity of the precious tomb which the new church would house. The repetitive pattern in sacred history was deeply etched in his consciousness by the parallel between the stories of Saul, David and Solomon in the building of the old Temple and the popes of the Renaissance in the building of the new basilica.[2] Giles informs us of the dispute between Bramante and Julius II over Bramante's plan to move the tomb of Saint Peter to another part of the new church and to change the direction the church would face. With relish Giles relates Julius's refusal to approve this plan on the grounds that the sacred must be kept unchanged and never can be modified for the sake of some profane purpose. Julius cannot, therefore, permit the tomb of the apostle to be touched.[3]

Giles seems to have pictured a series of concentric circles of divine predilection radiating out from Saint Peter's tomb: from the tomb to the Vatican, from the Vatican to the city of Rome, from the city of Rome to Etruria and the rest of Italy, and from Italy to the whole world. The result of Rome's election was that she became the head of the Church, having a primacy over other churches such as those of Alexandria, Antioch and Constantinople. This primacy was similar to Peter's primacy over the rest of the apostles.[4] Rome had the weighty

[1] Ang. Lat. 502, fol. 35r-v.

[2] Ang. Lat. 502, fols. 245v-249r, esp. 245v: "...omnia veterum enim acta formulam figuramque fuisse futurorum, imprimisque ea quae de regno et templo lectitantur." For the theme of Solomon's Temple in the Vatican of the Renaissance, see Eugenio Battisti, "Il significato simbolico della Cappella Sistina," *Commentari* 8(1957), pp. 96-104.

[3] Ang. Lat. 502, fol. 194r: "Conatus Bramantes, architectus hujus temporis princeps, quo usus est Julius cum ad alia aedificia, quae extruxit quam plurima, tum praecipue ad templum maximum divo Petro exaedificandum, conatus, inquam, est ille persuadere Julio apostoli sepulchrum ut commodiorem in templi partem transferretur, templi frons non ad orientem solem ut nunc vergit, sed uti in meridiem notumque converteretur, ut obeliscus magna in templi area templum ascensuris occurreret. Negare id Julius; immota oportere esse sacra dictitare; movere non movenda prohibere. Contra instare Bramantes; rem omnium accommodissimam futuram polliceri, ... Nihilosecius Julius in sententia perstat. Nihil e vetere templi situ inverti, nihil e primi pontificis tumulo attrectari se passurum dicit. Quid Caesaris obeliscum deceat, ipse viderit. Se sacra prophanis, religionem splendori, pietatem ornamentis esse praepositurum, cum scriptum non sit, tumulum in templo, sed templum in tumulo esse aedificandum."

[4] Ang. Lat. 502, fols. 16r, 147r-v, 172(a)r-v, 225v, 229r; Naples V. F. 20, fol. 278v.

duty of teaching the Gospel to the other churches and of preserving intact Christian doctrine, but an even weightier obligation to excel all others in holiness. Giles was quite willing to speak of the holy places in Rome, but he cautioned that they were such only by an extension of the term. It was holy lives, especially of priests, which must make Rome holy in the proper sense of the word.[1]

As Giles's presentation of the role of the Vatican is more significantly related to the Rome of the restored papacy than to the medieval city, his *Italianità* is also related to the general awakening of national consciousness in Italy at the beginning of the sixteenth century. Giles speaks of Italy in traditional biblical terms as the true Promised Land, but it seems rather clear that his consciousness of Italy as a totality was sparked by the recent incursions into Italy of Charles VIII (1483-1498) and Louis XII of France. Given Giles's close association with Julius II, it is hard to see how it could be otherwise. He assures his readers that God will never allow His Italy utterly to be submerged, but also reminds them that Italy, by its infidelity to God, made it easy for foreigners to invade and ravage it.[2]

The circles radiating out from their center in the Vatican come to cover the whole territory once held by the Roman empire, and thence to the rest of the world. The Church somehow succeeds to the empire, especially to the empire in its idealized form embracing all mankind.[3] A certain identification of the Church with the empire was by no means original with Giles and, indeed, was part of the patrimony he inherited from the Fathers of the Church and the medieval tradition, and which had found some expression even in canon law.[4] Giles habitually speaks of the Church in terms which, though in some cases mediated through

---

[1] Siena G. X. 26, pp. 60, 197; Vat. Lat. 6325, fol. 191r; Évora CXVI/1-30, fol. 28v; Ang. Lat. 502, fols. 5v, 134r.

[2] Ang. Lat. 502, fols. 69r, 70r, 72r-v, 170(a)r, 222r, 261r, 266r, 321r. But see also *ibid.*, fol. 232r, where Giles intimates that the pope's horizons must extend beyond the Italian peninsula. See Vincent Ilardi, "'Italianità' among some Italian Intellectuals in the Early Sixteenth Century," *Traditio* 12(1956), pp. 339-367.

[3] Évora CXVI/1-30, fols. 50r-v, 54v-54(a)r, 69r; Ang. Lat. 502, fols. 5v, 20r-v, 183v, 189v-190r; *Scechina*, vol. I, pp. 116-121; vol. II, p. 178.

[4] See, e.g., J. B. Sägmüller, "Die Idee von der Kirche als Imperium Romanum in kanonischen Recht," *ThQ* 80(1898), pp. 50-80; Ladner, *Idea of Reform*, pp. 118-125, esp. 118: "Renovation of the empire, accompanied by age-old traditions of ruler worship and of the eternal rejuvenation of Rome, became one aspect of Christian reform ideology." See also Giuseppe Toffanin, "La religione degli umanisti e l'idea di Roma," *La Rinascita* no. 1, 1(1938), pp. 20-39; Wilks, *Problem of Sovereignty*, pp. 254-287, on the concept, "papa est verus imperator;" R. Folz, *L'idée d'Empire en Occident du V au XIV siècle*, Paris 1953, pp. 15-21, 87-101.

Scripture, ultimately were borrowed from politics. The Church is queen, kingdom and empire, and the apostles are princes.[1] The most direct identification occurs when Giles speaks of the senate and people of Rome as synonymous with the Roman and Christian religion.[2] Christ is the emperor of heaven and earth, and He elevates His spouse, the city of Rome, to the rank of empress.[3] The degree to which Giles is prepared to exploit the idea of the Church as the sublimated prolongation or fulfillment of the empire is made clear when he compares the imperial rule of the two great Juliuses—Julius Caesar and Pope Julius II. Whereas the former Julius, thinking himself ruler of the whole word, in fact ruled only half of it, the present Julius, by reason of the discovery of the New World, really does reign supreme over the whole human family.[4]

In spite of these remnants of imperialism in his ecclesiological thought, Giles was keenly aware that there were important differences between the historic Roman Empire and the Church of his own day.[5] As we have seen, he alludes to Virgil's line and concludes that, in contrast with the Romans who ruled by force of arms, the Church finds its strength in piety, i.e., in virtue, prayer and sanctity.[6] Giles severely forbids clerics, and especially the pope, to take up arms, which is alien to their calling, and considers that, as a matter of fact, their real duty is to try to wrest arms out of the hands of those who have resort to them.[7]

Giles was too much a realist, however, to make this prohibition absolute, and he allows the pope, like his illustrious predecessor, Peter, to take to the sword against "Malchus, the slave of the Prince of this World."[8] By Malchus he means the Turk or, it would seem,

---

[1] E.g., Ang. Lat. 502, fols. 16r, 16v, 179v; *Scechina*, vol. I, pp. 135, 158, 207, etc.

[2] Vat. Lat. 6325, fol. 40r.

[3] Naples V. F. 20, fol. 277r, undated letter to Antonio Zocolo and the Augustinians in Rome.

[4] Siena G. X. 26, pp. 204-205, letter to Julius II, August 18, 1508. See also Ang. Lat. 502, fol. 194r; Évora CXVI/1-30, fols. 54(a)v, 58v: "... qui unus [Julius II] senseris te imperare Romanis."

[5] Ang. Lat. 502, fol. 6v: "... prius armis sub Romanis, inde vera pietate sub pontificibus."

[6] Ang. Lat. 502, fols. 6v, 7v, 234r, 241r, 281r-284r, 319v; Mansi, vol. XXXII, col. 674; "Oratio post 3am sessionem," p. 521-522. *Aeneid*, 6.403.

[7] Ang. Lat. 502, fols. 70r, 71r, 143r-v, 185v-188r, 241r, 244r; *Scechina*, vol. I, p. 205.

[8] Ang. Lat. 502, fols. 71v-72r. Giles further identifies Malchus as anyone "qui male audiat, male de fide sentiat." See also Mansi, vol. XXXII, col. 673. Jn. 18.10.

any obstinate heretic. The secular rulers, specifically the emperor, should assume the actual leadership on the battlefield, but Giles has no qualms about the pope actually declaring the war and compelling the princes to join in it, nor, unlike some of his humanist contemporaries, does he find the concept of "*pia bella*" or "*pia arma*" in itself logically or religiously repugnant.[1] Without misgiving he defines the Church's obligations in terms of Virgil's imperial ideology: "*parcere subjectis et debellare superbos.*" Although in general he tends to reserve the "putting down of the proud" to the emperor, he is willing to apply the whole verse to Julius II.[2] This need not be interpreted, of course, as resort to actual arms, but could simply signify any punitive measure, e.g., restrictive legislation against the impious philosophers.

Giles was anything but a warmonger, and he senses that there is some incompatibility between the sword and the Church. He is reluctant to permit the papacy and the clergy to wage war against other Christians, even though he never voices a forthright condemnation of the campaigns of Julius II.[3] He did have to face, nevertheless, the very real threat of the Turks, and this threat forced upon him a searching examination of any pacifist idealism to which he might have been attracted. Since he did not with precision discriminate a secular authority neatly independent from that of the Church, he often appears extremely inconsistent on this subject of the Church and warfare. In general, however, his thought can be reduced to the following

[1] *Scechina*, vol. I, p. 116; vol. II, p. 175: "... quia hucusque pia bella gesserunt ad civitates hosti eripiendas, ... ad pietatem propagandam; et idcirco religio vigebat, piique animi tam bellis quam aliis actionibus a scopo religionis non aberrabant; pro causa divina et certabant et alia peragebant." See also "Oratio post 3am sessionem," pp. 526, 528; Mansi, vol. XXXII, cols. 673, 676; Ang. Lat. 502, fols. 48v, 145r, 146r, 228v, 324v. On the question of humanists and a just war, see Robert P. Adams, "Erasmus' Ideas of his Rôle as a Social Critic ca. 1480-1500," *Renaissance News* 11(1958), pp. 11-16.

[2] *Aeneid* 6.853. Évora CXVI/1-30, fol. 79v; Ang. Lat. 502, fol. 266r. But see also "Oratio post 3am sessionem," p. 526: "Pontificis est religione interna pacare, Caesaris externa subjicere; utrumque certe Romanum et subjectis Christianisque omnibus parcere et superbum insurgentemque Maumetem debellare." See also Ang. Lat. 502, fol. 73v, and *Scechina*, vol. I, p. 110. Giles is surely not the first to apply this verse to the Church. See, e.g., Saint Bernard, Letter 363, *MPL*, vol. CLXXXII, col. 568: "Est autem Christianae pietatis, ut debellare superbos, sic et parcere subjectis; ...." On Augustine's rejection of the verse, see Ladner, "Die mittelalterliche Reform-Idee," pp. 34-35.

[3] There is approval of Julius's activities in restoring obedience among the cities of the Papal States, Évora CXVI/1-30, fols. 57r-60r. See also Siena G. X. 26, pp. 230, 267-268; Mansi, vol. XXXII, cols. 673-674; Martène, *Veterum scriptorum collectio*, vol. III, col. 1259. See also above, note 2, p. 121.

points: (1) War is an evil, especially among Christians, and must be forestalled if at all possible; (2) at times one is forced to fight out of legitimate self-defense or for some higher motive, and on those rare occasions war can be a good thing, "*pia bella*;" (3) the Church, in the person of the pope, is the best judge as to when a justifiable cause for war is verified, and when it is verified the Church must give moral leadership; (4) actual leadership in battle belongs to the emperor, and this is one of the most important duties of his office; (5) *de facto*, the necessary conditions for a pious war against the Turks now obtain.

The Turkish threat absorbed a massive portion of Giles's thought and energies, and there can be no doubt that he was genuinely concerned. Discouraged though he was by the bickering among the Christian princes of his day, he never let escape an opportunity to harp upon the necessity of their joining in the "holy expedition." With good reason he feared the Turks would capture Rome and overrun the rest of Europe, and he reminded Charles V in the *Scechina* that they were already at the gates of Vienna.[1] Giles was, moreover, hard-headedly realistic about what the final result would be of the fall of Constantinople: within a few generations the Orthodox would abandon their faith, with consequent terrible loss to Christianity, and even become allies with the Turks against the West.[2]

Although fear was important in Giles's motivation for a war against the Turks, he did not fail to relate the prospect of a Christian victory over them to his eschatological hope for the religious unity promised mankind. The Turks were the beast of the Apocalypse, and the hour

---

[1] *Scechina*, vol. II, p. 228. See also Martène, *Veterum scriptorum collectio*, vol. III, col. 1247, where Giles enumerates his efforts over the years to persuade Christians to unite against the Turks. See also *ibid.*, col. 1246; Ang. Lat. 502, fols. 43v, 83v-84r, 165r-v, 261v, 268r, 319v, 320r-v; "Oratio post 3am sessionem," pp. 526-527; Siena G. X. 26, pp. 280-282. On the imperative nature of the Turkish question at the Fifth Lateran Council, see E. Guglia, "Die Türkenfrage auf dem Laterankonzil," *MIÖG* 21(1900), pp. 679-691. Guglia also makes the point that this question had to some extent become a rhetorical commonplace, a standard subject for public declamation, *ibid.*, pp. 684-685. For the document issued by the council on the question of peace among Christians and the expedition against the Turks, see *Conciliorum decreta*, pp. 585-590. On the purely defensive aspect which the Turkish question assumed in the late Middle Ages, see Oscar Halecki, "The Defense of Europe in the Renaissance Period," *Didascaliae: Studies in Honor of Anselm M. Albareda*, ed. Sesto Prete, New York 1961, pp. 123-146, esp. 124. For a study of the different attitudes towards the Turkish problem in the fifteenth and early sixteenth centuries, see Robert H. Schwoebel, "Coexistence, Conversion, and the Crusade against the Turks," *Studies in the Renaissance* 12(1965), pp. 164-187.

[2] Évora CXVI/1-30, fol. 64v.

had arrived for its slaying. This duel between the Church and the beast, taken in its full cosmic dimension, would contribute to the reform and rejuvenation of the Church of the tenth age.[1] As a result of the happy issue of this struggle the pope, victor over the impious, would be able to restore to the Church the city of Jerusalem and the sepulchre of its beloved spouse.[2]

As has been mentioned, one of the emperor's principal functions in the Church was to effect the military victories over the Church's enemies for which the pope called. He was to defend with his sword the best interests of the papacy, "*res pontificiae*," and, when summoned, he was to wage for the Church the "war of the Lord." As emperor he had the duty to defend Rome, his capital city, against attack and violence of every kind.[3] This leads us to ask what his other duties were in the Church and what, in a broad way, was his relationship to the pope.

Giles, who saw in Constantine's recognition of the Church the first step in its morally downgrade course through history, did not really question the wisdom of the political alliance of the Church with the emperor which this recognition brought in its wake. He invokes the classic patristic and medieval metaphors and titles to describe this relationship, and the emperor is in turn "*advocatus ecclesiae*," "*defensor ecclesiae*," "*pastor ecclesiae*." His task is explicitly related to that of the apostles.[4] Most striking of all, in his struggle against Islam he takes

[1] Ang. Lat. 502, fol. 305v; Évora CXVI/1-30, fols. 72v-75r. See also Halecki, "Defense of Europe," p. 126: "The Union of Florence [1439] ... made it particularly clear that the problem of religious reunion was inseparable from that of the struggle against Islam, ..."

[2] Évora CXVI/1-30, fols. 61v-63v, 74r-75r; Ang. Lat. 502, fols. 125r, 308r; *Scechina*, vol. II, p. 175. On the centrality of Jerusalem and the holy places as symbols of eschatological yearnings in Crusade preaching, see the index in Alphandéry and Dupront, *L'idée de croisade*, vol. I, p. 237. See also *ibid.*, p. 134: "Jérusalem céleste et Jérusalem terrestre se confondent dans la vision montaniste des peuples marchant vers la cité mysterieuse, ..." Giles, as an Augustinian hermit, felt a spiritual kinship with Peter the Hermit, and this fact may help account for his great sense of responsibility in this matter, since truly successful expeditions to the Holy Land were in his mind works promoted by hermits. See, e.g., Ang. Lat. 502, fols. 143v-144r, and Alphandéry and Dupront, *L'idée de croisade*, vol. I, p. xiii. See also Robert Konrad, "Das himmlische und das irdische Jerusalem im mittelalterlichen Denken," in *Speculum historiale: Festschrift Johannes Spörl*, eds. Clemens Bauer, et al., Munich 1965, pp. 523-540. For the attitude of the Jews of the period, see Silver, *Messianic Speculation*, pp. 110-112.

[3] Ang. Lat. 502, fol. 78v; *Scechina*, vol. I, p. 116; vol. II, pp. 177-178.

[4] *Scechina*, vol. I, pp. 160-161, 217, 219; vol. II, p. 146; Ang. Lat. 502, fol. 54r. On Constantine's being likened to an apostle, see Max Vogelstein, *Kaiseridee-Romidee, und das Verhältnis von Staat und Kirche seit Constantin*, Breslau 1930, p. 75.

on a truly messianic aura, and becomes in fact the "Messiah, or certainly the Messiah's minister."[1]

Beneath this rhetoric and symbolism what Giles envisioned was a close working arrangement between pope and emperor, between the two heads of the Church.[2] Between these two heads there was a diversity of function, which in general can be described as an assignment to the emperor of all military and punitive measures, "*debellare superbos*," and to the pope the function of teaching and sanctifying. Each was supreme in his own order.[3] Giles seems willing, on rare occasions, in a sort of emergency, to permit the emperor to take matters into his own hands to assure the selection of a suitable candidate for the papal throne.[4]

On the other hand, in spite of the generous titles Giles bestows upon the emperor, there is no doubt that he regarded the pope in the final instance as enjoying superior authority in the Church. It was to him that Christ through Peter transmitted "all power," and he was the one who held "all right and all judgment," constituted as he was to preside over things human and divine.[5] In keeping with the already venerable ecclesiastical tradition, Giles earnestly desired to ensure the Church's freedom to manage its own affairs, i.e., the "*libertas ecclesiae*." While it was the emperor's task to promote this freedom of action of the Church, Giles realized full well that the emperors themselves had been some of the greatest offenders against it. What the papacy particularly had to vindicate for the Church was its liberty to elect the pope himself without imperial dictation of the candidate.[6] Great though Giles's respect was for the emperor, and intimate though he believed his relationship to the papacy to be, in the last analysis he felt that a wary eye must regularly be fixed on him, lest he usurp what was not rightfully his.

---

[1] *Scechina*, vol. II, p. 281: "... Messias, ... aut certe Messiae minister et imago...." See also *ibid.*, vol. II, pp. 103, 146. On the emperor-myth in the Crusades, see Alphandéry and Dupront, *L'idée de croisade*, vol. II, pp. 9-15. On the sacred and messianic qualities with which the emperor was invested in the Middle Ages, see Folz, *L'idée d'Empire*, pp. 82-86, 178-184, esp. 183-184 on Charles V.

[2] Ang. Lat. 502, fol. 138v: "... duo religionis capita...." See also *Scechina*, vol. I, p. 219; vol. II, pp. 26 and 281-282: "... futurus es Messias, cum Clemente VII, ... tu [Charles V] cum pastore Clemente...." See Vogelstein, *Kaiseridee*, p. 88.

[3] "Oratio post 3am sessionem," pp. 525-526; Ang. Lat. 502, fols. 45r, 48r.

[4] Ang. Lat. 502, fols. 74r-v, 82v, 88v, 124r-v, 220r. On the canonical "emergency" theory in the early sixteenth century, see Jedin, *Trent*, vol. I, pp. 96-100.

[5] Ang. Lat. 502, fols. 86r, 200v, 259r. See also *Scechina*, vol. II, p. 133.

[6] Mansi, vol. XXXII, col. 672; Ang. Lat. 502, fols. 44v-46v, 54v, 67v, 78r, 143r.

For Giles, then, the Church was in its essence Roman, revolving round the city of Rome as its axis and continuing in a sublimated form various traditions and institutions of the Roman Empire. There was, however, a dark and unsavory aspect to the Roman character of the Church. The Epistle to the Romans described the sins of the city in outspoken terms, and from the First Epistle of Peter was easily inferred an identification of Rome with the unchaste Babylon. During the Middle Ages similar accusations were transferred to Christian Rome and were used to indict it for its crimes, more heinous for being committed in so sacred a spot.[1] Whether Rome merited the rhetoric of reproach which became associated with its name is really beside the point. There were enough scandals and misdeeds, or simple human foibles, to provide grist for the rhetorician's mill, and the generally pessimistic mental filters through which Rome was viewed magnified and even distorted whatever negative element was there. This style of thought represented an intellectual tradition innocent of genuinely historical and sociological procedures of verification, and it fostered a style of expression which relied upon symbol and loose metaphor to articulate truths felt to be obvious and beyond the need of sober vocabulary. Giles inherited these styles and, in particular, their application to the city of Rome. Acutely aware of the holiness which Rome should radiate as the capital city of Christianity, he was struck by the contrast between the ideal new Jerusalem and the shocking phenomena he daily beheld. For him, too, Rome often seemed to be another Babylon, a harlot, and he could hardly imagine it as the see chosen by the apostles.[2]

---

[1] Giles suggests this idea, Ang. Lat. 502, fol. 173(a)r: "Utinam tam ab hominibus probitate, virtute, moribus ornaretur quam a Deo gloria insignita, auctoritate donata, felicitate aucta, diuturnitate servata, viribus, robore, firmitate munita est [Roma]." See Hubert Jedin, "Rom und Romidee im Zeitalter der Reformation und Gegenreformation," in *Kirche des Glaubens: Kirche der Geschichte*, Vienna 1966, pp. 143-152. Rom. 1.18-32. 1 Pet. 5.13.

[2] Naples V. F. 20, fol. 87r, letter dated the vigil of the feast of St. Paul, 1504, to Serafino Ferri: "Salutat te Babylon universa." See also Siena G. X. 26, pp. 190-191, letter dated July 6 (II Nonis Quintilis), 1508, to Antonio Puccio: "... non possum non flere illam [Romam] saepe prospectans quod ab initiorum sanctimonia tantum desciverit, ut vix mihi Roma apostolorum sedes videatur.... Si enim caput est, cur non sanctimoniae, cur non probitatis, cur non virtutum, cur non religionis est caput? ... Sed age gratias immortali Deo, quod te [Antonio Puccio] Babylonis habitatorem Babylonis participem non facit. Oro ego te per caelum, per pietatem, per salutem tuam, studeas eum esse te, qui nec bestiae Apocalypsis signum excipias, ..." See also *Scechina*, vol. II, p. 144: "... urbem Romam, quam Petrus Babylonem appellavit." See also Ang. Lat. 502, fols. 90v, 173(a)r.

What were the specific faults with which he reproached the City? At times in the "Historia" he reproves the populace for its inconstancy, and especially for the ill treatment it meted out so often to the popes. On a more personal level, he disliked preaching there because of the reluctance of the Romans to listen to sermons, and the fact that they did not esteem a preacher unless he first proved to them that he was a man of learning. Their morals were so bad that one did not know where to begin in addressing a sermon to them.[1] His summary judgment of the Rome of Alexander VI is bitter and uncompromising, a city completely under the sway of gold, violence and lust.[2] The most specific indictment, however, was leveled against the priesthood of the city, and Giles sees in Charles V's sack the just release of the pent-up anger and indignation of the Lord, who for so long a time had withheld the torrent of His wrath. The priests were untrained, ignorant, incontinent, avaricious. There were even usurers and panderers among them. The horrors they suffered in the sack were fitting punishment for their unworthy lives—their pride, their wealth and their worldly power.[3]

Giles makes a curious accusation against Rome in the *Scechina*. He tells the emperor that in the sack Rome received the requital she deserved for saying that she was unique among cities.[4] Such a reproach raises the question as to whether Giles thought Rome might have, by

[1] Ang. Lat. 502, fols. 82v, 83r, 212v; Naples V. F. 20, fols. 63v-64r, letter dated January 6, 1503, to Serafino Ferri: "Roma, praeter admodum paucos cum sanctissimis feminis, nec libenter audit, nec quos audit plurimi facit, nisi eruditissimi sint quos audiant [sic]." Also *ibid.*, fol. 105v, letter dated May, 1505, to Antonio Zocolo: "Scribo ad reverendissimum dominum protectorem spe ut numquam me Romam praedicaturum trahat. Nec animus, nec mens, nec cor pati potest ut istuc amplius redeam, functurus praedicandi officio. Adeo enim animus contabuit visis moribus, ut quod istuc dicturus essem nulla omnino ratione invenirem."

[2] Ang. Lat. 502, fol. 260v: "... nihil jus, nihil fas. Aurum, vis et Venus imperabat."

[3] *Scechina*, vol. I, p. 136: "... ut intelligas [Charles V] quanto tua saecula in errore versentur, quibus cogitare non posses, quanto cum stomacho e caelo aspiciamus passim admitti ad excelsum sacerdotii munus vulgus, ignavos, imperitos, incompositos, incontinentes, lusores, adolescentes, mercatores, trapezitas, plerumque milites et gladiatores, ne usurarios dixerim et lenones. Continui, conticui, cohibui me multis annis.... Cum ad summum venisse saecula vidi tua, exercitum immisi non nisi tuum, qui barbaram illuviem trahens omnia diripuit, evertit, incendit.... Sic de eorum superbia, opibus, potentia triumpharunt! Dicunt impii, si curat sacra numen, cur haec patitur? Respondeo, quia curat ideo haec non modo patitur sed etiam facit."

[4] *Scechina*, vol. I, p. 155: "... ob superbiam dicentis, ego sum, non altera." See also *ibid.*, vol. I, p. 158: "... quia contemnis, idcirco et contemneris."

her sins, lost the special prerogatives which were hers. This suspicion seems to be confirmed by what Giles has to say about Rome's most serious crime, her impenitence. After all the city suffered, especially from the sack and the floods which shortly followed, Rome still refused to mend her ways.[1] There is only one activity in which Rome knows no equal, and that is sin.[2] The Lord's patience has had its fill. If the Romans do not repent, there is nothing left but to destroy them utterly.[3]

We could easily infer from these threats that Giles thought it was at least possible, if not probable, that Rome be obliterated and that the capital city of the Church be moved elsewhere. It is difficult altogether to exclude this interpretation, and visionaries like Saint Bridget (ca. 1303-1373) and Saint Frances of Rome (1384-1440) had predicted the destruction of the city because of its sins long before Giles appeared on the scene.[4] It nevertheless seems more in keeping with the total complex of Giles's thought not to attach too literal a sense to these threats. We have already caught some glimpse of the elaborate ecclesiology he constructed on the history and myths of the city. The *Scechina*, in which the most apodictic threats occur, does not as a whole leave one with the impression that Giles felt compelled to throw overboard his Roman ecclesiology because of what might be implied by this menacing posture. Sometimes in the same paragraph in which a threat or a cry of despair is uttered, there is expressed the hope, almost the promise, of a restoration to virtue.[5] Giles may very

---

[1] *Scechina*, vol. I, p. 98: "Non emendat quae debet Roma, non instaurat." Also *ibid.*, vol. I, p. 105, where the Shekinah speaks as the divine agent: "ac nec sic [with punishments] quidem quidquam profeci."

[2] *Scechina*, vol. I, p. 105: "Urbem Romam caput feceram, quae beneficii oblita nulli peccando cedit." Also *ibid.*, "Video actum nihil [by the chastisements], medicinam non modo non sanasse sed ad majorem peccandi licentiam, audendi petulentiam, habendi cupiditatem, famem, rabiem irritasse."

[3] *Scechina*, vol. I, p. 170: "Abradetur quae relicta est pars media. Quod tuis [Charles V] copiis superfuit e medio tolletur. Huc oculos, huc animos, huc voces convertite, Romani, ne funditus pereatis." See also Ang. Lat. 502, fols. 90r-v, 262v, 273r.

[4] See Graf, *Roma nella memoria del medio evo*, pp. 730-731. The *Zohar* speaks of the destruction of Rome, *The Zohar*, trans. Harry Sperling and Maurice Simon, vol. I, New York 1933, pp. 370-371.

[5] *Scechina*, vol. I, pp. 98-99: "Non emendat quae debet Roma, non instaurat.... Cura [Charles V] rugam auferre, impietatem, haeresim, hostem, tollere maculam, ut quae non recte habent tua opera, cura, studio, pietate repurgentur reponanturque et suae integritati restituantur." See also *ibid.*, vol. I, p. 136; vol. II, p. 146; Ang. Lat. 502, fols. 126r, 170(a)r-173(a)v.

well have believed that Rome, because of her stubborn refusal to correct her faults, was to suffer even greater disasters than those already experienced, but it is hard to imagine he thought the city would altogether perish. No matter how great its sins, Rome was the site of the new Jerusalem and the new Temple, the custodian of the tomb of blessed Peter, and the providential capital of the eternal empire of Christian piety.

In the context of Giles's condemnation of the Rome of his day for its sinful and worldly indulgences, a word must be said about his attitude towards the architectural and artistic renaissance which the city was experiencing. We have already discussed his enthusiasm for the new Vatican basilica envisioned by Julius II, and we have suggested that this fitted ill with his longing for a return to the rustic simplicity of the early Church. In actual fact, despite a severe attitude towards wealth insofar as it provided the means for self-indulgence on the part of individual Christians, Giles did not really want the Church, as a corporation, to return to the primitive destitution he loved to hold up as the ideal. This was particularly true as regards the buildings and furnishings used for divine worship. In these he wanted not merely an appropriate decency, but actual magnificence and splendor.[1]

The best evidence we have of what Giles thought in this matter is in a letter of instruction which he sent to one of his fellow Augustinians on the restoration of the Church of the Trinity in Viterbo. Confronted with concrete reality Giles sets down a general principle of his own practical activity, which he obviously feels is worthy of the members of the order and of all Christians. For himself, he says, there are only two alternatives: not to build at all, or else to build in a truly magnificent manner. Only thus is God's honor satisfied and the order saved from ignominy.[2]

---

[1] Ang. Lat. 502, fol. 245r: "... ut Deo, sicut passim testantur oracula, in victu vel paupertas probata sit vel frugalitas, in sacris cultus magnificentia splendorque placuerit, ut tamen commendandi sunt qui his utuntur ad religionis culturam, ita damnandi qui ad appetitus libidinem abutuntur." For his nostalgia for the early simplicity, see *ibid.*, fol. 37r. See Siena G. X. 26, pp. 267-268, on Julius's building program. Also see Mansi, vol. XXXII, cols. 670, 673; Ang. Lat. 502, fol. 267v.

[2] Naples V. F. 20, fol. 90v, letter dated June 12, 1505, to Serafino Ferri: "Ego semper aut nihil agendum aut honorifice magnificeque agendum quidquid agi oporteat existimavi. Quod si magnificentia ac splendor ubique honestus est, in aedificiis ipsis atque imprimis publicis non modo honestus mihi visus est sed necessarius. Da igitur operam ut quod divini honoris gratia fit, nostra cum ignominia non fiat." See also Siena G. X. 26, pp. 157, and esp. 79.

Drawing so much of his historical material from the *Liber pontificalis*, it is not surprising that he came to extol as one of the papacy's principal tasks the building and decorating of churches. In his letter to Leo X upon his accession to the papal throne he inculcates the fostering of the arts and the restoration of churches as among the pontiff's principal duties.[1] But it is to the new Saint Peter's that Giles again and again recurs. He is lavish in his praise of Julius for undertaking the immense project and insistent with Leo that he continue it. It is hard to conceive of any building that, even in its planning stages, was farther from the simplicity of Giles's primitive Church than Julius's basilica. What is most remarkable, therefore, is that Giles praises it for precisely those qualities which we would expect him to find most offensive—its splendor and its soaring height.[2]

The other great artistic monuments of the Rome of Julius and Leo, however, receive little attention and are not the objects of any particularly great enthusiasm. The sheer magnitude of the new Saint Peter's caught Giles's imagination, and the basilica had for him a symbolic value which other Renaissance achievements in the arts lacked. He has not a word, for instance, about the Vatican apartments decorated by Raphael or about the Sistine ceiling of Michelangelo.[3]

---

[1] Martène, *Veterum scriptorum collectio*, vol. III, col. 1259, letter undated. See also Ang. Lat. 502, fols. 155r, 217v; *Scechina*, vol. II, p. 30. In a sermon in Santo Agostino in 1516 he praised Lorenzo de' Medici because he "... fe' fabrichar tante chiesie, tante librarie et tante belle cose," Sanuto, *I diarii*, vol. XXIII, col. 487.

[2] Ang. Lat. 502, fols. 112v-113r, 185r, 193r-194v, 278v, and esp. 267r-v: "Ad templum ... exstruendum animum injecit [Julius II] idque, sicuti est visere, ea mole, ea altitudine, magnificentia, splendore erigere aggressus est, ut cum universa antiquitate contendat, quod utinam tam mature absolvendum quam magnifice incohandum cogitasset." See also Évora CXVI/1-30, fols. 58v-60r; Mansi, vol. XXXII, col. 673. See also "Breve Leonis Papae X quo indulgentiam plenariam concedit eleemosynas praebentibus," *Analecta Augustiniana* 9(1921-1922), pp. 26-28.

[3] Giles describes several of Julius's building projects, including his enlisting Bramante in the task of laying out wide and straight streets in Rome, and he speaks of the pope as a person who "aedificandi studio non parum delectabatur," Ang. Lat. 502, fol. 267v. In 1512 Andrea Sansovino's (1460-1529) statue of Saint Anne, the Virgin and Child was installed in Giles's own church of Sant' Agostino. Giles describes the celebration on this occasion, in the form of a "poets' contest," to honor the donor, Johann Goritz (ca. 1450-1527), the papal protonotary and patron of the arts, Ang. Lat. 502, fol. 197v. Giles fails to name Sansovino and does not mention the fresco of the prophet Isaiah painted by Raphael over the place where the statue stood. See G. Haydn Huntley, *Andrea Sansovino*, Cambridge, Mass. 1935, pp. 65-67; Oskar Fischel, *Raphael*, trans. Bernard Rackham, vol. I, London 1948, pp. 298-299, and Vincenzo Golzio, *Raffaello*, Città del Vaticano 1936, pp. 208, 333-334. Giles mentions Giotto's (1276?-1337) coming to Rome

This relative lack of awareness points up the fact that Giles's interest in Saint Peter's was religious rather than artistic. He surely did not exclude art from religion. As a matter of fact, he promoted the idea of their mutual interaction, but he did this in a rather abstracted manner, without descending to particulars about monuments being constructed before his very eyes. Involved though he was in the literary and rhetorical developments of his day, he gives the impression of being rather detached from the artistic ferment in Rome. He gives us a good insight into his scale of values when he tells us that it is a much better thing to build monuments in men's souls with deeds of true Christian charity than it is to spend money for the construction of churches.[1]

In any case, Giles felt that the erection of churches was in itself a deed of piety and one worthy of the Roman pontiffs, even if it was not their most important duty. For this purpose, and for the alleviation of the needs of the poor, he would allow the Church as a corporation to acquire wealth and property, and he quotes with approval the reason Countess Matilda (ca. 1045-1115) supposedly gave for leaving her alodial properties to the Church: it is not fitting for the Church of God, the spouse of Saint Peter, to have to beg.[2] Giles thought that for ecclesiastical dignitaries a certain measure of pomp was required by their office.[3] He nevertheless saw wealth as one of the principal corrosives of Christian virtue and ecclesiastical probity, and he never tires of repeating his warnings about its dangers. In the abstract he admitted that it was not wealth itself but its abuse which led to corruption. In fact, however, it was extremely difficult not to turn wealth to one's own advantage and use it for sinful self-aggrandizement.[4]

Giles esteemed Martin V (1368-1431) as the pope who laid the first foundations for the Renaissance magnificence which he beheld rising

---

for work in the old Saint Peter's, Ang. Lat. 502, fol. 202r, and Gentile da Fabriano's (1370?-1427) painting in the Lateran basilica, *ibid.*, fol. 221v. He commends Leo X's interest in music, *ibid.*, fol. 14v. See also Siena G. X. 26, p. 157.

[1] Ang. Lat. 502, fol. 41v.

[2] Ang. Lat. 502, fol. 151v: "Non enim fas est, inquit, ... ecclesiam vero Dei optimi maximi ac divi Petri sponsam mendicare, ..."

[3] See Sadoleto, *Opera omnia*, vol. IV, pp. 304-305. See also *Scechina*, vol. I, p. 137.

[4] Ang. Lat. 502, fol. 11v: "... atque inopia pios, copia reddit impios." *Ibid.*, fol. 17v: "Raro coeunt opes atque probitas." See also *ibid.*, fols. 31v, 38v, 39v: "... non accusari divitias sed abusum, non splendorem ad sacrorum ornamenta sed luxum in peccatorum incitamenta damnari oportere."

around him. But he perceived in the ecclesiastical splendor of Renaissance Rome the same ambiguity he noted through the long course of the Church's history: the splendor for the churches was good and praiseworthy in itself, but men in general are too spiritually weak to make good use of it. As regards the accomplishments of Martin V, it had to be admitted that his policy of restoring the city and its churches ended by depriving Rome of virtue and leading to all sorts of abuse.[1]

Europe was emerging into a new economy based on capital, and preoccupation with the problems of wealth and poverty was not unique with Giles. It nagged the late Middle Ages, especially after the writings of the Joachimite tradition and the ideals of the Spiritual Franciscans gained widespread currency, and it was a subject of serious discussion in the Florence of the *Quattrocento*.[2] Giles reflects this concern. He was, after all, a member of a mendicant order, dedicated by his very profession to witnessing to the spiritual values of voluntary poverty. Giles knew that Plato himself confirmed Christ's teaching on the necessity of spurning earthly goods and on the praiseworthy ideal of communal sharing of life's necessities. Aristotle's derision of Plato's position was proof of the Stagirite's impiety and further evidence that his philosophy was irreconcilable with Christianity.[3] In this matter as in so many others, Giles's belief that Rome's riches were directly responsible for its moral decline and for the ecclesiastical abuses of the day was not based on empirical investigation and dispassionate analysis of the data available to him. Wealth's power to undermine virtue was a commonplace of the traditions Giles knew, and to propose it as explanation for the problems of Church and society was as religiously and intellectually respectable as it was scientifically inadequate.

---

[1] Ang. Lat. 502, fol. 223r: "Ecclesia [sic] enim gloria, quae ad divinarum rerum cultum et ad virtutum incitamenta facere deberet, ita abutimur, ut ad nostras illam cupiditates convertamus." See also *ibid.*, fols. 234r, 245r.

[2] See Hans Baron, "Franciscan Poverty and Civic Wealth in Humanistic Thought," *Speculum* 13(1938), esp. pp. 20-21, 25-26, 29-31. See also Cantimori, *Eretici italiani*, pp. 12-13, and Garin, *La cultura filosofica*, pp. 63-66. See also Scholem, *Major Trends*, p. 234, on the stress on poverty as a religious value which the *Zohar* introduced into rabbinical Judaism.

[3] Ang. Lat. 502, fol. 155r: "... nisi quod res humanas opesque contemneret, id quod in Republica fieri jussit Plato, ut meum tuumque auferretur, quo quieta felixque respublica redderetur; risitque Aristoteles, rem numquam ab hominibus receptam, non videns a Dei Filio esse in hac parte recipiendam." Also see *Scechina*, vol. I, p. 200: "Ubi eo ventum, ut is irrideatur qui de sacris agat; qui undique ingentes congerat opes, is unus sapientissimus et dicatur et habeatur."

CHAPTER FIVE

REFORM IN CONCEPT AND PRACTICE

The norm for ecclesiastical renewal which Giles enunciated in his inaugural sermon for the Fifth Lateran Council is well known and has already been referred to very early in the course of our study: "Men must be changed by religion, not religion by men."[1] For Giles this norm did not merely keynote the spirit with which the council was to address itself to its task, and much less was it simply a clever turning of a phrase. When expanded to its full dimensions it can be seen as a remarkably serviceable epitome of Giles's thinking on the problem of reform and as the great abstract ideal against which he tested his particular reform measures. We shall try in the present chapter to illustrate what the implications of this norm were in the thought of Giles of Viterbo, and then proceed to examine the specific reforms he advocated. These reforms give content to his vocabulary and provide a concrete basis for evaluating his more abstract statements of principle.[2] Although the proposals Giles makes for the universal Church are extremely interesting and valuable in this regard, he never had the opportunity actually to try to put them into effect. For this reason his reform measures as prior general of the Augustinian order are all the more significant, and supply us with one of the few instances in the early sixteenth century of an articulated ideal of reform combined with ample opportunity to reduce it to practice in an ambiance of unquestioned orthodoxy.

The fact that Giles's norm has at times been accepted as a clear statement of a general assumption of Catholic reform efforts must not obscure for us the fact that it had for Giles himself certain resonances which it could not have for others.[3] The best indication we have that this is the case are the antecedents which Giles associates with what is

---

[1] Mansi, vol. XXXII, col. 669: "... homines per sacra immutari fas est, non sacra per homines: ...."

[2] Father Martin's biography of Giles studies in detail his activities as a reformer and the specific problems he faced with individual convents, provinces, etc. That aspect of Giles's career, therefore, will be treated very briefly here.

[3] See, e.g., Cantimori, *Eretici italiani*, p. 6; Jedin, *Trent*, vol. I, p. 169. For a summary of leading themes of reform thought of the *Quattrocento*, see Garin, *La cultura filosofica*, pp. 166-182.

almost a paraphrase of it: "We must imitate the divine, not expect the divine to imitate us."[1] One of the many digressions of the "Historia" concerns the sacred origin of numbers and their transcendent meaning. Speaking of the number four, Giles tries to make the point which so often engages him: everything in the created world has its source and prototype in God. Realities in the world are explained, therefore, by reference to the divine prototypes, and these prototypes are in no way dependent upon their earthly counterpart. It is at this juncture that Giles interjects the principle that we must conform ourselves to the divine, and not vice versa.[2]

We see, then, that the norm, "Men must be changed by religion," really has metaphysical ramifications, deriving especially from Giles's Neoplatonism and his cabalism. It is a religious and ethical explication of the same principle which led Giles to believe that the divisions of Christian history correspond to the supereminent ten of the Godhead. For Giles the divine realities tend to burst the relatively modest confines of exemplary and final causality and to impose upon nature and history a course which is determined to a significantly specific degree from above. If Giles's norm has any polemical overtones whatsoever, these relate less to the politico-ecclesiastical conspiracy of Pisa of 1511 than to those philosophers and theologians who would try to invert the divinely established order of reality and who would think to confect from the elements of this world a standard by which to mark the limits of the supernatural. One of the official visitors Giles himself sent to reform several Augustinian convents asked him to be patient and to remember that time and moderation would be required before the reform could be put through in all its vigor. To this Giles curtly replied that he was not employed in a work whose author requires time, quality, place and disposition before he can accomplish

---

[1] Ang. Lat. 502, fol. 100r: "Imitemur enim divina nos oportet, non a divinis imitandi nos sumus, ..."

[2] Ang. Lat. 502, fol. 100r: "Ad numerum [4] redeo, quem quoniam Deus in se habet idcirco est hominibus traditus, non quoniam in nobis ille est idcirco in divinis celebratur. Pudet certe pigetque, quod quidem probi alioqui viri et eruditi contendunt, ideo duodecim non undecim esse tribus, quod totidem in homines perturbationes esse compertum sit. Imitemur enim divina nos oportet, non a divinis imitandi nos sumus, ut illa deceat antecedere, nostra sequi." Also *ibid.*, fol. 107r: "... sed ideo potius septem facta diebus esse omnia, quoniam sacrum Dei numerum secuta sunt, ... atque ea quae proveniunt, iis unde proveniunt quam maxime fieri potest similia esse decet." Also *ibid.*, fol. 252r-v: "... id quod saepe diximus dicique oportet saepius, causas sequi, imitari, effingere necesse est ea quae a causis proficiscuntur."

anything, but in one whose Author's mere word created the universe.[1] The philosopher whose metaphysics most directly conflicted with Giles's was the worldly Aristotle of Padua, and at the time Giles proposed his norm for reform at the Lateran Council the problems raised by Padua were never far from his mind.

Giles's norm reflects, therefore, a metaphysics, and it embodies a whole set of values and assumptions which he will try to bring to bear on every particular question of abuse and reform. This set of values and assumptions rests upon the fundamental belief that the divine causality imposed a sacred and inviolable order upon the world. This order, though not altogether lacking dynamism, is established from all eternity, and it neither can nor should in any way be adjusted to what might be thought of as creature exigencies. Included in this stable order of the universe are the institutional structures and doctrinal formulations of the Church, and any questioning of these realities which might suggest change, modification or reinterpretation of them is particularly impious. In this sense Giles's norm for reform can be considered conservative. It wants to conserve and to preserve intact forms and truths delivered to man from on high at a happier period of his history, and it provides very few criteria for a critical review of these forms and these truths. Like his contemporaries, Giles thought that the authentic traditions of the past were easily recognized and that their authenticity was easily discerned from the corruptions resulting from history's inevitable decline. With sincere good faith Giles introduced all his reforms in the name of the authentic past. The fact that we now know that one or other of them, such as the cabala, would have been in actual fact of revolutionary import for the life of the Church in no way affects the conservatism of Giles's intentions. The misgivings Giovanni Francesco Pico (ca. 1469-1533) felt that Ficino's philosophy might finally result in a desire to "reform religion by men" most surely was not substantiated in Ficino's disciple, Giles of Viterbo.[2]

---

[1] Siena G. X. 26, p. 120, letter undated: "Non respondebimus his quae affers exemplo naturae extremos motus minime patientis, sed tempus et modum in omni actione desiderantis. Cum miremur te [Magister Antonius Astensis], virum alioquin eruditissimum putare ea quae a Deo per gratiam proficiscuntur tarditati et signitiei naturae esse similia. Non enim in illius auctoris opere versamur qui quidquid agit cum tempore, cum qualitate, cum loco, cum accepto aliunde subjecto ac denique non nisi per dispositiones tandem agit, sed ... illius gratiam quaerimus, in illius operibus versamur qui dixit et facta sunt, mandavit et creata sunt."

[2] On G. F. Pico, see Cantimori, *Eretici italiani*, pp. 5-7. In 1530 Giles criticizes his own age thus, *Scechina*, vol. I, p. 104: "... vestra [Charles V] saecula collapsa ... ad humana ... conversa sunt." The reason Giles attributes to Julius II for not

Giles's conservatism permeates his thinking even on disciplinary reform, where we might expect a certain relaxation of principle and a greater willingness to adapt to the needs of the concrete situation. But it is precisely in this area that Giles utters his clearest statement of reform policy: "We are not innovators," "*Non enim nova facimus*."[1] This policy was announced on the occasion of his laying down in a convent undergoing reform certain very minor rubrics to be observed in the celebration of the liturgy and certain particulars of daily discipline, which suggests that no particulars were too minute to escape from the pre-established pattern: "We are not innovators. We are simply trying, in accordance with the will of God, to bring back to life those ancient laws whose observance has lapsed."[2]

In his opening oration at the Lateran Council Giles speaks of the need the created world has of "continual innovation," "*continua innovatione*."[3] This innovation, however, has nothing to do with an abandonment of the past, but requires, rather, a return to it and its pristine forms, as the context makes clear. In terms reminiscent of the humanists' cry for a return to the literary documents of antiquity Giles calls for a return "to the ancient and original purity, light and splendor, a return to the sources."[4] Giles's official letter to the Augustinian order upon the accession of Leo X to the papal throne, just a year after the opening of the council, specifies the negative elements this return implies. The Church will be rejuvenated by the removal of whatever evil habit it has acquired.[5] Even more explicit is his letter in 1517 to

---

allowing Bramante to change the direction in which Saint Peter's basilica faced and to move the apostle's tomb is: "... immota oportere esse sacra," Ang. Lat. 502, fol. 194r. See also *ibid.*, fol. 83r, and Vat. Lat. 6325, fol. 116v: "... sacra enim ... mutare fas non est, ..." See also *ibid.*, fol. 169r: "... ne quis sacra oraculorum mutet, ut quoties de divinis agitur, non prophanorum usus, sed oraculorum consuetudo consulatur."

[1] Siena G. X. 26, p. 261.

[2] Siena G. X. 26, p. 261, letter undated, to Antonio Pulcri: "Non enim nova facimus, sed leges patrum in ista patria extinctas, Deo ita jubente, suscitamus." Giles on one occasion does make some reluctant concession to the instability of the human condition, *ibid.*, p. 263.

[3] Mansi, vol. XXXII, col. 669.

[4] Mansi, vol. XXXII, col. 669: "... in veterem puritatem, in antiquam lucem, in nativum splendorem, atque in suos fontes...." Also *ibid.*, col. 676: "... et in antiquum splendorem munditiamque restitui." For the celebrated principle concerning "innovation" laid down by Pope Stephen I (254-257) which played such an important role in the reform ideologies of the early Church, "Nihil innovetur nisi quod traditum est," see Ladner, *Idea of Reform*, pp. 139, 298, 410-411.

[5] Siena G. X. 26, p. 288, letter undated: "... sponsa juvenescet, depositoque malorum inveterato habito, renovabitur." Giles's words hint at the ancient dis-

Cardinal Giulio de' Medici, the future Clement VII, wherein the cardinal's task is outlined precisely in terms of the removal of accretion and the restoration of lost, but once possessed, prerogatives.[1] The ideas of "*restituere*" and "*instaurare*" occur often in Giles's writings and seem to have no perceptible difference of meaning, both connoting a return to a previous age, truth, practice or condition.[2] Occasionally, especially in the *Scechina*, the process by which this return is accomplished is exclusively described as one of purgation and castigation.[3]

One of the most interesting aspects of Giles's conservative reform ideology is the eremitical ideal which he proposes, or at least suggests, for the Augustinians. This ideal derived ultimately from the origins of the order. In Giles's case the ideal has a bearing not only on his concept of the order and its function, but also on his concept of the Church and the ideal towards which the Church should be reformed.

The Augustinians came into being as a distinct order in the Church in 1256 when Pope Alexander IV (1254-1261) united into one body various congregations of Italian hermits who were following the rule of Saint Augustine. The official title given the order was "Hermits of Saint Augustine," but the purpose which the pope had in mind for it was far removed from anything which conventionally could be called eremitical. Alexander IV wanted another active mendicant order, after the pattern of the Dominicans and Franciscans, to cope with the new religious problems arising out of Europe's changing social and economic conditions. The Augustinians responded to the pope's hopes, and with vigor and distinction threw themselves into the new life assigned to them. The eremitical origins of the order led, however, to a certain confusion in ideals, and the attempt to reconcile the

---

tinction between truth or tradition and custom, "Oratio post 3am sessionem," p. 523: "... inveteratae consuetudinis squalore posito, ..." On this distinction, see Ladner, *Idea of Reform*, pp. 137-138.

[1] "Libellus" (in *Scechina*, vol. I), p. 31: "... [ut] divina instauretis, rebus sacris si quid temere inculcatum sit amputetis, si quid vel temporis vel incuriae detritum restituatis."

[2] E.g., Ang. Lat. 502, fol. 170r; "Libellus" (in *Scechina*, vol. I), p. 31; *Scechina*, vol. I, p. 136; vol. II, p. 146; Naples V. F. 20, fol. 70v; "Oratio post 3am sessionem," p. 520: "Verum enimvero instaurari omnia oportet eisdem ex quibus constat initiis." For "instaurare" as possibly implying a somewhat new condition, see Ang. Lat. 502, fols. 18v, 19r. For the application of the idea of "instauratio" to the individual Christian soul, see "Oratio post 3am sessionem," p. 520. In this connection, see Ladner, *Idea of Reform*, pp. 2, 49.

[3] *Scechina*, vol. I, p. 104: "... catigandae [novae legis], purgandae, renovandae."

eremitical with the mendicant way of life seems to have become in some instances a rather disturbing concern.[1]

This confusion was intensified by the Pseudo-Augustine's *Sermones ad fratres in eremo*, which promoted the idea that a true revival of religion would come with a return to the monastic life as practiced by Augustine and his companions at Tagaste. Among the hermitic groups united by the papal bull of 1256 the Tuscan were dominant, and, as we already mentioned, they believed that after Augustine was baptized at Milan in 387 he lived for some time in Tuscany, there founding the first monastery of Augustinian hermits. Augustine's supposed visit to the hermitage of Lecceto helped persuade the brethren of that house to look upon themselves as the genuine heirs of Augustine's monastic ideals.

Giles was convinced that Augustine had founded the Tuscan hermits, as his short outline history of the hermits and his letter to the friars of Lecceto show, and he suggests that his knowledge of Etruria's providential place in religious history helped incline him to accept this view.[2] Giles was, of course, aware of the "Great Union" effected by the papacy in the thirteenth century, but he does not see in it any significant change in the order's character or any conflict with the eremitical ideal. What the pope did was to bring a certain conformity in dress and customs among the diverse groups and unite them under one name. Giles gives no indication that any intrinsic change in the order's spirit or purpose had occurred.[3]

Giles traces the eremitical ideal back beyond Augustine. He intimates, indeed, that Christ and the apostles were the true initiators of the eremitical life. Christ disdained the cities and market places, and

---

[1] See Martin, "Giles and Lecceto," pp. 234-236, and Arbesmann, "Henry of Freimar's 'Treatise'," pp. 37-145. For an excellent discussion of the methodological problems inherent in trying to reconstruct an authentic "*imago primi saeculi*" of any religious group and the bearing such a reconstruction has on the ideal of reform, see Michel de Certeau, S.J., "L'épreuve du temps," *Christus* 13(1966), pp. 311-331.

[2] Aug. Gen. Archives, Rome, Cc. 37, fol. 112r, and Martin, "Giles and Lecceto," p. 249: "Aurelius Augustinus, quo nihil umquam uberius mundus peperit, sacris vacare non recte posse videbatur, nisi prima divinorum rudimenta mox sacris initiatus in Etruria exercuisset. Extant in Monte Pisano, extant ad Centumcellas vestigia plane insignia, extant in universo Tusco sola loca quae ille et incoluit et monachis incolenda dedit. Vestra [Lecceto] tunc domus coepit, tunc monticulus Ilicum comis opacus umbras obtulit primis illis patribus, ubi divinis commentationibus incumbere quietissime possent." See also Ang. Lat. 502, fol. 39r.

[3] Ang. Lat. 502, fols. 39r, 150r, 171v-172r. Giles gives Innocent IV (1243-1254) credit for beginning the unification of the order, and sees Alexander IV as completing the task.

elected to preach on the obscure shores of the Sea of Galilee. The apostles chose the deserts and forests as the places ideally suited to Christianity, and it was their decision, Giles implies, which Sylvester reversed by returning to the cities and palaces.[1] There is no forthright identification of the apostles as hermits, but the implication that they led a life in some way eremitical is hard to escape. Hence, when Giles writes to his subjects in the Augustinian order and tells them that their rule and way of life is apostolic, we must not conclude that this signifies an abandonment of the eremitical ideal.[2]

The Christian program which Giles proposes is, therefore, often colored with elements proper to a strictly eremitical life. It is in the woods and desert places that true Christian wisdom is acquired, and the bucolic life, free from cares and temptations, is surely the best, modeled as it is after the pattern of life of the young David.[3] In the history of the Church Giles celebrates the virtues and great deeds of those who consecrated themselves to the eremitical ideal, such as Peter the Hermit and Pope Celestine V, and he finds in the "humility of the hermits" the right antidote for the "pride of the philosophers."[4] To the Augustinians themselves he holds up for emulation the virtues of the holy men of the congregation of Lecceto, men who never spoke except under urgent necessity and who were the enemies of all laughter and levity.[5] As prior general he grants to his subjects, on an individual basis, permission to retire to the "desert" for their soul's welfare, convinced that this desire is inspired by the Holy Spirit.[6] He himself yearned for the peaceful mountain retreat of Cimino near Viterbo, where he might read, contemplate and take spiritual pleasure

[1] Aug. Gen. Archives, Rome, Cc. 37, fol. 112r: "Christus post hos [Elijah and John the Baptist], etiam post congregatos apostolos, in desertum se locum saepe transfert, cum ceterum vitam maxima ex parte solitariam exegisset." Ang. Lat. 502, fol. 63r: "... apostoli ... sylvas pro patria, pro domibus antra, feras sibi pro comitibus ascivere." See also *ibid.*, fols. 37r, 169v, on Sylvester.

[2] Ang. Lat. 1170, fol. 22r, letter dated October 3, 1508, to Stefano Zoalio: "Cum enim lex et regula nostra sub sanctis sit apostolis, hoc est, ad eorum vitae imitationem constituta, quae in tribus votis est posita, ubi essentia religionis existit, ..."

[3] Ang. Lat. 502, fols. 62v, 170r; Évora CXVI/1-30, fol. 67r; Vat. Lat. 6325, fol. 169v: "Magnus namque Augustinus meus, ut eremi ac solitudinis studiosior, ita et divinarum rerum disputator acutior, ..."

[4] Ang. Lat. 502, fol. 166v. Also *ibid.*, fols. 39r, 41v, 123r-v, 128v-129r, 143v-144r, 174v.

[5] Martin, "Giles and Lecceto," p. 250.

[6] Siena G. X. 26, p. 297, undated fragment.

in the Gospel.[1] After just a short while in office as head of the Augustinians he wrote to a good friend in the order that the happy person is he who, conscious of how short life is, lives for himself, apart from the tumult of human affairs.[2]

We cannot dismiss this exaltation of the retired life of the hermit as mere unreflective repetition of religious truisms. The tone is too sincere and the repetition too thematic to admit so simple an interpretation. On historical grounds Giles was convinced of the Christian and Augustinian values of the eremitical ideal, and he must have seen in the hermitic style of life a practical program designed to implement Plato's insistence upon the necessity of turning away from the shadows of this world to a truer reality.[3] Giles does not seem to have been much aware of the fact that his thought and practice were often inconsistent with the eremitical ideal he loved to extol. He surely did not shirk the order's responsibility in the active ministry, and he indicates that he was fully aware it had to bear its share of the Church's care of souls.[4] There is evidence to indicate that he himself did find the administration of the order an oppressive burden, even though he was reasonably successful at it. Nevertheless, his own intellectual interests were so alive, so intimately bound up with the contemporary Italian scene, and gave him such deep satisfaction, that it is almost inconceivable that he entirely isolate himself in an uncompromisingly solitary life. What Giles really wanted was the semi-seclusion of the scholar which would provide him leisure for writing and prayer as well as sufficient contact with others to stimulate his thinking. For the order he seemed to admit a hermitic life in which more or less frequent ministerial excursions into the "world" would be allowed, even recommended, and these would consist, for example, in the lenten sermon series and other occasional preaching assignments. For the rest, it seems, Giles felt that one had to make the best of a bad situation, and to accept whatever duties and circumstances were thrust upon one by necessity and ecclesiastical authority.

It is in the context of the supposedly authentic hermitic character of the Augustinian order and the direct link with Saint Augustine himself which the monastery of Lecceto provided that we must locate

---

[1] Naples V. F. 20, fols. 106r-v, 181r. See Pélissier, "Pour la biographie," p. 799. See also Ang. Lat. 502, fol. 299v, and Vat. Lat. 6325, fols. 121r, 172r.

[2] Naples V. F. 20, fol. 158r, to Serafino Ferri, September 30, 1507.

[3] See Russell, *Dissent and Reform*, pp. 188-191.

[4] Ang. Lat. 1170, fol. 18r, letter dated May 23, 1507, to Stefano Zoalio.

the fact of Giles's inscribing himself as a member of Lecceto in 1503 and his concern to spread the observant movement among the houses of the order. His exhortation to the friars of Lecceto in his "De Ilicetana familia," written probably between 1503 and 1506, is rich in its suggestion of the rustic and secluded life which he associates with the congregation affiliated to this observant monastery.[1]

Lecceto as early as 1387 was set aside from the jurisdiction of the Sienese provincial and put directly under the prior general in order that it might, without local interference, become a model for religious observance. Because of the Augustine-legend the hermitic ideal was strong there. The Lecceto reform or "observant" movement spread throughout the Italian provinces of the order, with Naples being the first to follow Lecceto's example. As the movement spread, two separate jurisdictions grew up: the conventuals were under their provincial, as always, and the observants' monasteries, now numerous, were joined into so-called congregations under a vicar who, in theory, ruled in the name of the prior general. This double jurisdiction in time brought many problems in its wake, as is well known from the story of Luther, but in the beginning it seemed to be a humane juridical solution to the problem of divergent interpretations of the rule.[2]

About the time of his joining the congregation of Lecceto Giles undertook to do his part in spreading the observance, even though he then held no official position in the order. Through a series of rather elaborate negotiations he succeeded in having the Augustinian monastery of Viterbo incorporated into the Lecceto congregation and brought under its jurisdiction. The result seems to have justified the labors expended, for in 1505 Giles was able to congratulate the prior on having achieved a complete success in the increased discipline and sanctity of life which was evident in the monastery.[3] Giles's devotion to the observance perdured, and as prior general he boasted of his ties with it and that he had never ceased to labor for its spread.[4]

Before taking up the topic of Giles's particular reform program we ought to recall once again the frame of reference in which it was initi-

[1] This is the text published by Martin, "Giles and Lecceto," pp. 247-253. See also Siena G. X. 26, p. 167.

[2] See Martin, "Giles and Lecceto," pp. 237-241; Böhmer, *Luthers Romfahrt*, pp. 36-75; Weijenborg, "Neuentdeckte Dokumente."

[3] Martin, "Giles and Lecceto," pp. 243-247.

[4] Siena G. X. 26, p. 243, letter dated March 3, 1511, to the congregation of Toledo: "Ego vero quomodo observantiam possum laedere, qui ante hoc munus [prior generalship] in observantia vixi, post hoc munus numquam destiti [sic] pro observantia laborare?"

ated. Giles believed that he was living in an age of general renovation and restoration which was so all-inclusive as to be truly cosmic in its dimensions. The revival of Platonic theology, the revival of the arts and literature, the revival of Scripture studies—these were joined with the discovery of the New World, the conquest of the Turks, and the eschatological hope for the religious unity of mankind to convince Giles that the long awaited reform of the Church was about to take place. In his speculation Giles is much less interested in this general restoration from the viewpoint of the human activity required to bring it about than he is from that of the eternal divine plan which ineluctably is reaching its fulfillment. His reform measures within the Augustinian order, so disciplined and conventional, seem strangely distant from his speculative vision, and there seems to have been relatively little correlation of the two in Giles's own mind. Giles's vision emphasizes the providential character of history's course. Without denying free will or man's responsibility, Giles anticipates a complete renovation, not a more or less imperfect adjustment of the Church to a limited number of particular new situations and new problems, which itself within the space of a few years will have to undergo a further readjustment. His vision taught him only that man and his institutions degenerate and are restored, not that they change in any other way.

The restoration Giles expected is guided to its fulfillment by God's providential plan and galvanized into movement by the divine energies diffused in the created world. Giles has little to say in any explicit way about how this providential determination of human affairs is reconciled with human activity, which he presupposes, and with human freedom, which he surely does not want to deny. Perhaps we catch a glimpse of his thinking on this question in his description of grace as divine fury, "*divinus furor*." This fury, Bacchic in its intensity, snatches the mind from its engagement with earthly realities and translates it to a contemplation of the divine mysteries. It is a "holy insanity," imbuing its recipients with the violence they need in order to win for themselves the kingdom of heaven, as the Gospel prescribes.[1] Descriptions of grace couched in these terms leave us

[1] Vat. Lat. 6325, fol. 5r: "... illuminatio siquidem, vel rapit mentem tantum ad divina, et tunc furor Bacchi, ..." *Ibid.*, fol. 173v: "... ille Platonicus [Menon] ait, mortales non nisi divino furore correptos bonos fieri, quae quidem sententia oraculo consentit, quo pradicatum est, caeli regnum vim pati, atque a violentibus mortalibus rapi [Mt. 11.12]. Ut enim malus furor infra humanam sortem rapit mentem, ita divinus spiritu vehementi supra hominum vires in caelum usque correptam mentem vehit, ..." *Ibid.*, fol. 179v: "Est igitur altera Dei similitudo in

with the impression that its impulses can be rather overpowering and that, though perhaps not robbing man of his freedom, they do deliver the human agents of history into God's directing hands.

In any case, there is nothing phrenetic about Giles's attitude towards his own reforming activities within the Augustinian order. His official correspondence and registers are sober in the extreme, without the slightest suggestion of the furious. To a certain extent these official documents betray such a different mentality from his sermons and long treatises that we would be tempted to question the authenticity of one or the other were this not in each instance so well attested as to be beyond doubt. No matter what inference we draw from the terms in which Giles occasionally describes grace's activities, he himself did not swerve from a program of rather standard measures in the reform he undertook of the order. His reform prescriptions in no way suggest the frantic or the rapturous.

Although Giles's zeal for the reform of the order avoided all fanaticism and excess, there is no denying the fact that it had a character of fierce and driving urgency. We have already seen that even before he was elected to the prior generalship he labored successfully for the spread of the observance. From the moment he assumed office the order's reform became the principal concern of his life, and he allowed it to consume his time and talents with prodigal generosity. After a relatively short period as prior general he reported in several letters to members of the order that day and night he neither did nor thought of anything except reform.[1] What he demanded of himself he expected

---

anima ex natura, altera ex divina et benevolentia et liberalitate, bonos enim viros divino quodam et auxilio et furore Menon fieri vult." Also *ibid.*, fols. 210r, 212r-v, and Naples V. F. 20, fol. 95r, letter dated August 15, 1505, to Serafino Ferri: "O sancta, o felicia, o vere aurea saecula, quae Johannes intuitus, qui in furorem ac sanctam extra corpus insaniam rapiebatur!" On "furor" in the Renaissance, see Chastel, *Art et Humanisme*, pp. 60, 296, and Wind, *Pagan Mysteries*, p. 145. This concept was exploited by Ficino, who derived it from Plato. See, e.g., "Epistolarum libri, I, VI, IX," *Opera*, vol. I, pp. 673, 830, 927; "In Platonis Jovem epitomae," *Opera*, vol. II, pp. 1281-1284. The concept did not die in the sixteenth century. See, e.g., Paul Tillich, *The Interpretation of History*, New York 1936, p. 87.

[1] Ang. Lat. 1170, fol. 21v, letter dated October 3, 1508, to Stefano Zoalio: "Sumus die noctuque in labore reformandi, nihilque aliud agimus, inspicimus, cogitamus nisi ut, jubente et pontifice et protectore, collapsa nostra respublica faciem recuperet antiquae majestatis." The same statement occurs in a letter to a different addressee in Siena G. X. 26, p. 123. See also *ibid.*, pp. 4 and 79, letter undated as to year of composition, to prior at Naples: "... et quamquam dies noctesque non aliud agendo conteramus, quam ut Augustinensem [sic] religionem moribus componendis emendemus, ..."

of others, and in almost the same words he informed the superior of the convent at Amelia that his only concern, too, was to be reform.[1] Quite literally every page which survives of Giles's registers as general of the order contains the word "*reformatio*," and this litany reaches a climax towards the end of his term of office when he reports a letter to the Augustinians of Bologna in which he publicly and solemnly called upon God to witness that there was nothing he desired so much as the reform, and that he was prepared to affirm this truth when he appeared before Christ on the Last Day.[2] Paolo Giovio's (1483-1552) insinuation that Giles's religious interests were insincere could not have been farther from the truth.[3]

Giles felt that he had a God-given vocation to promote with every means at his disposal the reform of the Augustinian order, and at times he strikes a note which suggests a rather ruthless and unbending pursuit of his goal.[4] In describing other reformers in the history of the Church he obviously favors those who proceeded in their task without compromise.[5] As the Fifth Lateran Council drew to a close without an abatement of the attacks on the mendicants, his concern became urgent indeed, and, besides his repeated injunctions and exhortations to superiors and canonical visitors, he now imposed the obligation of accepting the reform measures upon the individual members of the order under the most serious moral and juridical penalties. Disqualification for office in the order and deprivation of voice in its government were the principal sanctions he invoked.[6]

Giles's threats were not idle ones and from the very first he warned he would be severe towards the rebellious.[7] On occasion he actually

[1] Siena G. X. 26, p. 25, letter undated as to year, to prior at Naples: "Tu haec nocte dieque et curabis et cogitabis, ..."

[2] Aug. Gen. Archives, Rome, Dd. 12, fol. 143r: "4 Dec. 1517. Conventui Bononiensi publice scripsimus dolentes quod quidam nos de reformatione non curare dixerint, testantes Deum et angelos nihil post Deum et salutem in terris magis quaerere, confirmaturi idem usque ante Christi tribunal in magni judicii die," as quoted in Martin, "Egidio da Viterbo," p. 387.

[3] *Elogia doctorum virorum*, Antwerp 1557, pp. 187-189.

[4] Siena G. X. 26, p. 194, undated, to the province of Portugal: "Misit enim me Dominus, ut evellam et destruam, atque ut plantem postea et aedificem." Jer. 1.10.

[5] Ang. Lat. 502, fol. 56v: "... non amputat [Pope Gregory IV, 827-844], non resecat, sed eripit radicitus et evellit." See also *ibid.*, fol. 113v.

[6] Martène, *Veterum scriptorum collectio*, vol. III, col. 1263, undated letter to the Paris convent: "Mandamus insuper subditis omnibus cujuscumque conditionis, ut reformationem suscipiant in meritum obedientiae et sub poena privationis vocis activae et passivae: ...."

[7] Siena G. X. 26, p. 18, letter dated July 24, 1506, to the convent at Milan.

spelled out in detail the punishment which was to be given a delinquent: for thirty days he was, for example, not to associate with the other friars; on Fridays his diet was to be coarser than the others'; on Fridays he must prostrate himself before the door of the refectory as the others entered and left; he was to be suspended from the celebration of Mass and from performing other sacred functions; and on the last day he would have the discipline administered to him publicly.[1] If this sort of punishment were unsuccessful the prior could throw the offender into jail, or expel him from the convent and send him to Giles for more effective disciplining.[2] In extreme cases Giles had no scruples in counselling that the secular arm be brought in to carry the punishment into effect.[3]

Giles endeavored to get the superiors and masters of theology in the order committed to reform by exacting from them oaths promising to promote it. This oath was taken under penalty of being deprived of the position one might attain in the order and possible charge of perjury.[4] Giles very deliberately appointed superiors with a view to their potential effectiveness in carrying out the reform, and he did not hesitate to remind them of this fact when occasion required.[5] If he felt it were justified he was not afraid to issue a reproof to a friend whose conduct or attitude seemed contrary to his reform ideal.[6]

Consumed as Giles was by the need he felt to make the reform effective with the greatest possible speed and thoroughness, it would have been easy for him to become a zealot and an unbearable martinet. This never happened. Amidst exasperating provocation he did not lose his sense of fairness or allow his disciplinary duties to outweigh

---

[1] Siena G. X. 26, pp. 27-29, undated letter to the prior of the convent of Saint Paul.

[2] Siena G. X. 26, p. 80, undated letter to the prior at Naples. See also *ibid.*, pp. 38, 164-166; Aug. Gen. Archives, Rome, Dd. 12, fols. 10r, 11r, 88v. See also Ang. Lat. 688, fol. 23r, on the reception back into the order of apostates and fugitives from it.

[3] Siena G. X. 26, p. 270, letter dated September 24, 1511, to Petrus Gervasius: "... et contumaces acerrime punies, etiam si opus sit cum auxilio brachii saecularis."

[4] Ang. Lat. 688, fols. 61v-62r, letter dated July 26, 1517, to Gabriele della Volta. In this letter the form is given for such oaths: "Ego ... publicam juravi reformationem, et communi vitae pro viribus operam dare, quod nisi fecero et gradibus privari et perjurum haberi volo."

[5] Ang. Lat. 688, fol. 32v, letter dated July 7 (Nonis), no year, to the prior at Padua.

[6] Ang. Lat. 1170, fol. 32r, letter dated May 25, 1522, to Stefano Zoalio. The year is a mistake. It should be 1512.

the obligations of charity which he felt his Christian profession imposed upon him. Although he described his mission in prophetic terms of uprooting and destroying, he knew that in actual practice he would try to heal what was bruised and broken.[1] Even when urging punishment of subjects who refused to reform, he prescribed that this be done "not without compassion."[2] He was, moreover, fully aware that within a religious order it was extremely difficult to find sanctions which were truly effective, and that in general a superior was forced to rely upon exhortations and admonitions. Giles adds, not without cynicism, "...and you see how nicely crimes are corrected by words alone."[3]

What must be emphasized is that Giles wanted the reform carried through in a manner which witnessed to the Christian love and charity which inspired it in the first place. His own attitude towards his subjects was clear: "I am incapable of not loving those whom I govern."[4] The ideal which he held up to the superiors of the order was that of the Good Shepherd, and he reminded them that they had the care of all their subjects, the good and the bad.[5] In the reform they were to proceed without haughtiness or offense, in a spirit of charity, patience and humility, so that all would see that the reform was from God and the Holy Spirit.[6]

---

[1] Siena G. X. 26, p. 24, and Naples V. F. 20, fol. 177r, letter dated September 1, 1507 to Antonio Zerra: "Etsi rectoribus dictum esse scimus ac cuicumque publicum gubernandi locum obtinenti, Reges eos in virga ferrea et tamquam vas figuli confringes eos [Ps. 2.9.], nosque a sanctissimo domino nostro et reverendissimo domino protectore idem fere audivimus, eo tamen consilio administrationem suscepimus non ut fratres nostros veluti vasa figuli frangamus, sed ut siquid fractum fuerit consolidemus confirmemusque." His fair procedure in the case of a serious offense which brought the whole order under criticism is seen in Ang. Lat. 1170, fol. 41v.

[2] Siena G. X. 26, p. 105, letter dated November 19, no year, to the prior at Naples. See also *ibid.*, p. 28, and Ang. Lat. 1170, fol. 43v, letter dated February 8, 1518, to Stefano Zoalio: "Non sunt viscera claudenda misericordiae illis qui post plura errata emendationem suscipiunt, et vitam in melius reformare desiderant."

[3] Naples V. F. 20, fol. 158v, letter dated September 30, 1507, to Serafino Ferri: "Vide quam apte corrigi flagitia solis verbis possint."

[4] Ang. Lat. 1170, fol. 33r, letter dated June 30, 1513, to Stefano Zoalio: "Ego quos rego non amare non possum." See also Martin, "Egidio da Viterbo," pp. 215-217.

[5] Siena G. X. 26, p. 93, to an unnamed prior, September 8, 1507.

[6] Siena G.X.26, p.260, letter undated, to Antonio Pulcri: "Cupimus et volumus ut primo ista reformatio fiat non cum impetu, non cum imperio verborum, non cum clamore aut ullo tumultu, sed in caritate, in patientia, in spiritu humilitatis,

Indicative of the manner in which he wished the order governed is the consideration with which he heard requests which on the surface seemed opposed to the very measures he was trying to enforce. Although one of the major planks in his reform platform was insistence upon common life, i.e., that the friars live in the monastery and that they do this without distinction in matters of food, clothing, etc., he was willing to give permission to live outside an Augustinian convent if a good reason seemed to call for it. He fully realized, for instance, that the divine command to care for one's parents took precedence over the merely human traditions of the order, and in case of sickness or other serious need on the part of parents he granted permission to go to care for them.[1] This same permission he sometimes granted for the sake of health.[2] Even inside the houses of the order he was willing to allow a certain amount of preferential treatment if he felt this would be for the good of the subject concerned.[3]

The fact that in every disciplinary case Giles proceeded very strictly according to the norms of the order's and the Church's law is the best indication we have of his balance and fairness. He did not allow impatience, personal annoyance or reforming zeal to upset provisions established for the defense of subjects against excesses stemming from precisely these impulses. He is scrupulously careful that punishment or prosecution not ensue until the offender has been given the three warnings required by canon law.[4] In the case of a friar against whom many complaints had been lodged, he cites him to himself to plead his case, lest he be condemned unheard.[5] He conceded broad delegation to visitors and superiors to carry out reform measures, but he asked that the modesty and charity and humanity with which they

---

ut omnes sentiant hanc rem esse a Deo et Spiritu Sancto." This is advice to the visitor of the Paris convent, one of the most refractory Giles had to deal with. See also his reproof to Pope Boniface VIII, Ang. Lat. 502, fol. 198v: "... non oportere insolenter imperare mortalibus, ..." See also Évora CXVI/1-30, fol. 37r.

[1] Siena G. X. 26, p. 181, entitled "Pro manere volentibus extra ordinem," undated: "... ne tamen mandata Dei propter traditionem hominum nostris institutionibus postponamus, petenti tibi ut parenti tuae et infirmae et inopi suppetias feras, annuendum putavimus." See also *ibid.*, p. 300.

[2] Aug. Gen Archives, Rome, Dd. 12, fols. 99v, 100v.

[3] Ang. Lat. 688, fol. 45v; Ang. Lat. 1170, fol. 46r.

[4] Siena G. X. 26, p. 266, undated letter to the Augustinians in Venice. He reproaches Boniface VIII for his use of "clamosarum legum scientiam," but this does not mean he himself despised legal procedures, Ang. Lat. 502, fol. 198r.

[5] Ang. Lat. 1170, fol. 40v, letter dated May 26, 1516, to an unnamed convent: "Citamus eum ut causam possit suam agere, et ne inauditus condemnetur."

acted be in direct proportion to the generous grants of authority they had received.[1] He did his best to inculcate a sense of justice in the superiors of the order, laid down careful regulations to ensure that in case of any serious accusation the defendant had a just trial, and announced as his ideal that every one of his subjects receive perfectly fair treatment.[2]

The care Giles displayed to adhere to canonical procedures is all the more remarkable when we recall the external pressures being brought to bear upon him to reform the order. We have his own word for it that Julius II's appointment of him as vicar general, which practically assured his subsequent election as prior general, was prompted by the belief that Giles could carry out an effective reform program. As a matter of fact, it is hard to discover what other motive the pope could have had in making this choice, and we know from other sources that Julius, quite contrary to the popular estimate of him, was concerned about the spiritual condition of the religious orders and of the Church in general.[3] Giles often adduces the insistent urgings of Julius in explaining to his brethren the necessity of implementing the reform.[4] Leo X continued this papal prompting, which was intensified by

---

[1] Siena G. X. 26, p. 285, undated, "In calce quarundam litterarum." On delegation, see also *ibid.*, p. 45.

[2] Ang. Lat. 688, fol. 45r, letter dated May 18, 1512, to the Augustinians in Venice: "... ut religio recte, juste ac nullius prorsus injuria, quantum in nobis est, administretur." See also *ibid.*, fol. 44v. An interesting insight into Giles's attitude towards ecclesiastical law is provided by Sadoleto's report of a conversation between Lorenzo Campeggio (1474-1539), Cajetan and Giles on whether or not the laws of fasting bound under pain of serious sin. Giles opposed the more liberal views of the other two, but all three were of the opinion that the pope ought to change the law so as to remove this scruple from the consciences of the faithful. See Sadoleto, *Opera omnia*, vol. IV, pp. 323-324.

[3] Naples V. F. 20, fol. 136v, letter dated July 15, 1506, to the Augustinians at Siena: "Id autem facietis si monasteriorum, si fratrum denique omnium mores emendabitis. Ea enim spe dominus noster papa et reverendissimus dominus protector nos accersivere et ea lege curam nobis ordinis credidere, ut omnia faciamus, omnia tentemus, ... ut antiquae religionis majestas et sancta nostrarum legum facies, quantum fas erit nobis, reparetur cureturque, ut a divi Augustini institutis divi Augustini familia, quam minime fieri poterit, dissentiat." See also *ibid.*, fol. 177r. On Julius II and reform, see "Nonnulla Iulii Papae II brevia Aegidio Viterbiensi directa," *Analecta Augustiniana* 9(1921-1922), pp. 17-20, and Pastor, *History of the Popes*, vol. VI, pp. 443-446, 448-450.

[4] E.g., Ang. Lat. 1170, fol. 23v; Siena G. X. 26, p. 201, and the sources mentioned in the previous note. Giles's respect for Julius's accomplishments is well illustrated in Siena G. X. 26, pp. 266-269, undated letter to unnamed provincial. See also Pélissier, "Pour la biographie," pp. 801, 802-803, and *passim*.

the interest taken in this question by the Fifth Lateran Council.[1]

The attack which the council launched against the mendicants after the death of their defender, Julius II, is well known. It was another outburst of the quarrel between the regulars and the seculars which had dragged on all through the high and late Middle Ages, but never before had the controversy reached such a peak of intensity and seriousness as now.[2] The bishops intended to make an end once and for all of the privileges of the mendicants, especially as regards exemption from episcopal jurisdiction in questions touching the "*cura animarum*" and the friars' temporal holdings. By means of a compromise it was, somewhat paradoxically, concessions from the bishops in these two areas which Leo X secured for the friars in 1515 and 1516, but only on the basis of the friars' promise that they concede in other matters and then set about putting their house in order.[3] Giles and Cajetan, the superior general of the Dominicans, were the most active defenders of the mendicants, and the former actually undertook for Leo X a diplomatic mission to Emperor Maximilian in the winter of 1515-1516 partly in order to use the occasion to help the mendicants' cause.[4]

Giles himself pronounced the opening oration at the council, a ringing call to reform. His correspondence leaves us with the impression that so long as Julius was alive he did not sense the full degree of danger in which the exempt orders were soon to find themselves from that very council. His letter to the order upon the accession of Leo X, for example, does not show signs of any particular anxiety, and he still speaks of his great hopes for the council without any suggestion that he is expecting a frontal attack from it.[5]

---

[1] E.g., Siena G. X. 26, pp. 288-290, undated letter to the whole order. See Pélissier, "Pour la biographie," p. 811, and "Brevia aliquot Leonis X Aegidio Viterbiensi directa," *Analecta Augustiniana* 9(1921-1922), pp. 23-24.

[2] See Jedin, *Trent*, vol. I, pp. 135-138, and Pastor, *History of the Popes*, ed. Francis Ralph Kerr, vol. VIII, pp. 393-397. For Giles's activities in the controversy, see Martin, "Egidio da Viterbo," pp. 380-387.

[3] For the two documents of the Lateran Council on the exempt orders, see *Conciliorum decreta*, pp. 603-608, 621-625.

[4] See Martène, *Veterum scriptorum collectio*, vol. III, col. 1263, undated letter to the Paris convent: "Nos ne ultimum religionis exitium videremus, urbe egressi sumus, Italiam percurrimus, Alpes nivesque transivimus, in Germaniam media hieme per hanc nostram et aetatem et valitudinem summis cum laboribus et vitae periculis mitti toleravimus." Giles praises Cajetan's work for the mendicants, *ibid.*, col. 1265, letter to the whole order dated January 13 (Idibus), 1517: "Multum generalis Praedicatorum reverendissimus profuit, multa doctissime, copiosissime, constantissime adduxit." See also *ibid.*, col. 1264, on Cajetan.

[5] Siena G. X. 26, pp. 288-290, undated. See also *ibid.*, pp. 280-282. By 1517

The storm broke, however, and it was bitter and uncompromising.

Giles describes the full fury of the outburst. In his letters and registers he quite frankly relates that the council had declared war on the mendicants and that it had the intention of utterly destroying them.[1] He writes that a great and horrendous storm had broken over the order and that the bishops' attack in the council raged against the mendicants without relent.[2] The bishops want to rid the Church of all mendicants and delete from memory their very name.[3] He relates in some detail his own desperate and prolonged efforts to save what he could, running from the bishops to the cardinal protector, to the pope, to representatives of the civil powers.[4]

The upshot of the whole exhausting affair was that, besides the urging of his own idealism, Giles now was motivated in his strivings for reform by fear of the complete suppression of the order, or at least of substantial curtailment of the privileges which made possible its independent life. Without mincing words he quite bluntly wrote in a circular letter to the whole order that unless the friars reformed they would be destroyed.[5] It was not a question of pious exhortations

---

Giles was fully aware that, just as the character and temperament of Julius forestalled the bishops' onslaught, Leo's mildness invited it. See Martène, *Veterum scriptorum collectio*, vol. III, col. 1264, letter to the whole order dated January 13 (Idibus), 1517: "Hactenus quadrennio laboravimus. Extincto enim Julio secundo, pontifice maximo, ac creato Leone X, omnium mortalium mitissimo, humanissimo, clementissimo, reverendissimo, reverendos dominos prelatos spes incessit invadendarum religionum et abrogandorum privilegiorum, quod diu totis animis exoptaverunt, et ad id, a quo Julii durities absterruit, Leonis tum mansuetudo tum lenitas invitavit."

[1] Siena G. X. 26, p. 295, letter dated 1517, to the whole order: "Nam Lateranensis synodus ... ita nos angit, ita nobis bellum indixit, ut ... actum de privilegiis, actum de libertate, actum de universa religione jam sit." *Ibid.*, p. 297, letter undated, to the provincial of Paris: "Concilium [nos] ut de medio tollendos aggreditur."

[2] Martène, *Veterum scriptorum collectio*, vol. III, cols. 1262-1263, undated letter to the Paris convent: "Magna enim atque horrida nos invasit tempestas, episcoporum impetus in Lateranensi concilio in nos et mendicantes omnes jam triennio saevit."

[3] Siena G. X. 26, p. 323, letter dated December 6 (VIII Idus), 1516, to Deodatus Senensis: "Concilium episcoporum totis ut aiunt nervis insurgunt [sic], ut nos et mendicantium nomen aut deleant aut insectent." See also Ang. Lat. 1170, fol. 41v; Aug. Gen. Archives, Rome, Dd. 12, fol. 71r: "... instante gravissimo concilii periculo...." Also *ibid.*, fols. 71v, 91r, 93r, 93v, 95r, 96v, 97r, 98r, 99r, etc.

[4] Siena G. X. 26, pp. 324-327, undated letter to the whole order.

[5] Siena G. X. 26, p. 295, letter dated 1517, to the whole order: "... ut nisi reformatione verissima severissimaque nos emendemus et Dei hominumque favorem et auxilium imploremus, ... actum de universa religione jam sit."

on the part of the council, but a serious and unambiguous threat that they would lose their exempt status and pass under direct episcopal jurisdiction.[1] The actual implementation of this threat had so far been averted only by the slightest hairsbreadth. Three courses were now open to the Augustinians. They could either allow themselves to be reformed directly by the papacy, as was *de facto* happening to the Franciscans, or they could hand over the reform to a particular observant congregation within the order, as the Dominicans were doing, or they themselves could undertake a reform which would be under the general and call for the cooperation of the whole body. He chose this last, though he knew it to be difficult.[2] No one had more experience than he of the weight of inertia to be overcome or of the extent of the abuses to be brought under control.

Before proceeding any further perhaps we should try to give some idea of what the particular abuses in the order were which Giles was trying to combat. From his constant harping on the necessity of leading the "common life" we must infer that there was a rather widespread abuse among the friars of obtaining for themselves food, clothing and certain privileges which were not accorded to all on an equal basis. Giles wants to eliminate, for instance, the use of linen instead of wool as the material for the friars' habits. He frequently lays down minute prescriptions for the celebration of the liturgical offices, so that we must assume that here some rubrical inexactitude, more or less serious, had crept in. Silence very often was not properly observed in the dormitories, refectory and choir. In many convents, we infer, the brethren were allowed to go about the city without the companion which the rule required, and the privacy and order of the house were often disturbed by outsiders, so that in some cases cloister itself was not strictly kept.[3]

---

[1] Martène, *Veterum scriptorum collectio*, vol. III, col. 1264, letter to the whole order, January 13 (Idibus), 1517: "... ut ... in jus episcoporum transiremus: ...." See also Aug. Gen. Archives, Rome, Dd. 12, fols. 122r, and 71r: "Scripsimus ad provinciales, priores, rectores, ac fratres omnes provinciae nostrae Pisarum ut, instante gravissimo concilii periculo, totum animum in reformationem conjiciant."

[2] Martène, *Veterum scriptorum collectio*, vol. III, col. 1266, letter to the whole order, January 13 (Idibus), 1517: "... aut, tertio, nos per nos ipsos instituendi, et ad integram formam legis redigendi sumus. Quod summa cum difficultate fieri posse intelligo."

[3] See, e.g., Siena G. X. 26, pp. 19, 30, 34, 45-46, 48-49, 51, 56, 81, 88, 126, 136, 153-155, 183-184, 209-211, 259-263. A fair idea of the nature of the reform measures Giles was concerned with can be gleaned from the "Acta capituli gene-

These were the points which consistently and with monotonous regularity came up for correction and reproof. There were, however, particular instances of more serious, even spectacular, abuses and scandals. In certain convents the unrest and indiscipline had reached such proportions that there was open insubordination towards superiors as well as violent disputes among the subjects themselves and with outsiders, so that Giles actually had to forbid the bringing of arms into these houses. There seem to have been, in fact, a few cases in which loss of life occurred.[1] Some convents were none too exact in financial matters, refusing to pay debts, acquiring property by dubious methods, and even engaging in some practices smacking of simony. In certain houses there was trafficking in the goods of the order and illicit alienation of Church property.[2] There were, moreover, some instances of friars frequenting prostitutes, and, as regards the friars' contact with nuns as chaplains and confessors, there seems to have been a rather general carelessness about observing the conventional reserves expected of them, without necessarily implying any more serious offense.[3] Most shocking of all was the notorious case of the prior who publicly took a wife and then had the effrontery to put her in charge of the affairs of the monastery.[4]

The extreme cases, however, were rare, and restricted to relatively few houses of an order which then numbered about fifteen thousand

---

ralis Venetiis celebrati, anno 1519," *Analecta Augustiniana* 9(1921-1922), pp. 31-39. See also "De capitulis generalibus ordinis tempore Aegidii Viterbiensis celebratis," *Analecta Augustiniana* 9(1921-1922), pp. 171-182.

[1] To the convent in Milan, Siena G. X. 26, pp. 17-19, and esp. 48, letter undated: "Ut diris sceleribus, nephandis scandalis, et crebris jam conventus istius infelicissimi caedibus et homicidiis occurramus, ..." On the same case, see *ibid.*, pp. 8, 13-14, 15-17, and Ang. Lat. 688, fol. 17v. To the provincial of Sicily, Siena G. X. 26, p. 49, letter dated November, 1506: "Si clari viri veniunt circumveniuntur insidiis, si visitatores mittuntur verberantur, et pro dolor interficiuntur." See also *ibid.*, p. 8. The question can be asked whether domestics and boarders in the monastery may not bear some responsibility in these cases. For instances of insubordination, etc., see *ibid.*, pp. 146-151, 235-237; Ang. Lat. 1170, fols. 24r, 39r-v; Aug. Gen. Archives, Rome, Dd. 12, fol. 23v.

[2] See, e.g., Aug. Gen. Archives, Rome, Dd. 12, fols. 27v, 40v, 83r, 98r. On the alienation of property, see Martin, "Egidio da Viterbo," pp. 230-232.

[3] Aug. Gen. Archives, Rome, Dd. 12, fols. 11v, 32v, 76v, 78v, 83v. See also Vat. Lat. 3146, fols. 29v-30r, and Ang. Lat. 1170, fol. 43v. Some letters speak of individual cases of scandal and crime without specifying what is meant, e.g., Siena G. X. 26, pp. 26, 31, 39, 197.

[4] Ang. Lat. 688, fol. 20v, letter dated June 17, 1507, addressed to Gabriele della Volta. On defection from the order, see Siena G. X. 26, p. 88. On blasphemy and indecent conversations, *ibid.*, p. 145. On Irish friars drinking outside the monasteries, Aug. Gen. Archives, Rome, Dd. 12, fol. 101r.

members or so. No large order at any time in its history has been entirely free of such scandals and, in the absence of a statistical study, we are inclined to wonder if the number was really disproportionately larger during this particular period of Augustinian history. There was, of course, the serious jurisdictional problem which we shall discuss later, and it would be misleading to minimize the difficulties Giles had to face. In any case, Martin judges that, though there may have been a certain laxity of observance in some houses, we cannot infer that substantial rot and decay had set in throughout the order.[1]

What is to be said, then, about the almost despairing tone of Giles's letters and his conviction that the religious spirit of the order had been in a state of complete collapse for the past hundred years?[2] There are several factors which must be taken into consideration to understand Giles's feeling. First of all, his judgment must have been influenced by his view of Christian history as a course of more or less steady decline as the Church chronologically distanced itself from the age of Christ and the apostles. Needless to say, such a view tends to make the observer more keenly aware of the vices of his age than its virtues. Giles's hermeneutics, which saw beneath the surface meaning of any sacred word or event a more recondite and sublime meaning, allowed him to fit whatever abuse he discovered into this pessimistic pattern and to confer upon it a symptomatic value beyond what others might discover there. Giles's conviction that his age was extremely wicked found confirmation also in the fact that many of his contemporaries were persuaded of the same thing.[3] Furthermore, Giles proposed for the Augustinians an ideal of observance which was extremely exacting. Gabriele della Volta, who was to succeed him as prior general, described it as impossible.[4] As superior Giles had every serious case of scandal brought to his attention. The contrast between the real and the ideal thus was made especially acute. Platonic withdrawal from

---

[1] Martin, "The Augustinian Order." Giles's suggestion that certain abuses were so bad that they were not even to be written, Ang. Lat. 1170, fol. 29v, almost certainly does not indicate a general policy he imposed upon himself or others.

[2] Ang. Lat. 1170, fol. 23v, letter dated May 20, 1508, to an unnamed convent: "Collapsa est religio per centum ferme annos a sacra et veneranda illa sanctimoniae majestate ...." See also Siena G. X. 26, pp. 219-220.

[3] E.g., Erasmus in the prefatory letter to the 1518, Basel, edition of his *Enchiridion militis Christiani:* "Quis vere pius non videt ac suspirat hoc saeculum longe corruptissimum?" *Opus epistolarum*, vol. III, 1913, p. 366.

[4] Ang. Lat. 688, fols. 18v-19v, letter of Giles to Gabriele della Volta dated September 18, 1508.

the material and eremitical withdrawal from human society tended to set up a conflict of purposes in an active order like the Augustinians which could hardly leave a perfectionist like Giles other than in a state of some perturbation. One is almost tempted to say that a certain unrealistic religious idealism was as much responsible for the crisis in which the order found itself as was any general laxity and real abuse which might have existed. Nor can we fail to mention that in speaking of the degenerate condition of the order Giles availed himself of the rhetoric which his age so generously provided and which has ever been part and parcel of the standard equipment of the reformer. In the early sixteenth century, especially, ecclesiastical scandal was not something which the preacher hid from the eyes of the curious, but something which of its very nature demanded to be decried and exposed to public view.[1]

We can now turn our attention to the broader question of the Church as a whole and to the measures and norms which Giles felt should be adopted in its reform. To some extent we shall have to illustrate this area of reform by examples and principles taken from the more specific instance of the Augustinian order, but this extension is justifiable for several reasons, not the least of which being that the two questions were by no means wholly distinct either in themselves or in Giles's mind.

Before descending to particulars, however, we must note one of the basic assumptions upon which Giles's reform program is based, the need of external discipline to sustain and foster interior renewal. Enough has already been said to indicate that one of the most important results he sought was a further interiorization of the religious life, a greater and more successful emphasis upon prayer, contemplation and recollection. He was not, as should be clear by now, a narrow legalist, eager to multiply rubrics and regulations or convinced he could find salvation in them. On the other hand, almost in spite of his Platonism, Giles realized how intimate was the dependence of spirit upon form. He was by no means ready to dispense with the one in order to save the other. This must be clearly understood in order to make sense out of some of the measures he proposed. He himself enunciated the guide-line of his program when he enjoined that both

---

[1] See *Conciliorum decreta*, p. 613. Giles suggests something of his own attitude, at least within the order itself, in an undated letter to an unnamed Augustinian convent, Siena G. X. 26, p. 62: "Venit enim justitiae tempus, quando oportet curanda vulnera videantur, non dissimulanda."

soul and body fall under the scope of the reform.[1] His reform would be total reform, in which attention would be given to structure in order to penetrate to spirit.

Purification of doctrine was among the principal reforms for which Giles labored. What he meant by this, in the concrete, was a condemnation and rejection of Peripatetic philosophy as practiced at Padua. From his belief in the cabala and in a gradual increase in the understanding of Scripture over the course of the ages we might have expected something more drastic in the question of doctrinal reform than Giles actually presents. But such an expectation would be utterly unfounded, misunderstanding the conservative intent of these beliefs. No matter what their implications might be, Giles surely did not want to propose by them the substitution of some new and different truth for an old one. His concept of a constantly developing understanding of Scripture implies, as a matter of fact, a sense of continuity with the truth of the past. In the case of the cabala, it was its supposed antiquity which particularly attracted him and which, we must assume, blinded him to the fact that in style, method and content it threatened to undermine the foundations of Christian doctrinal formulations. Like the Jewish cabalists themselves in their relationship to orthodoxy, Giles sincerely professed his loyalty to Catholic teaching, and he interpreted the cabala simply as an older and more genuine understanding of it.[2]

In religious truth, especially, it is antiquity and nearness to the source which are the touchstones for authenticity.[3] Giles feared all "*res novae*" in doctrine, and he would find inconceivable any form of revisionism which would touch papal or conciliar teaching.[4] As we have often pointed out, he believed in the inerrancy of the Roman or

---

[1] Siena G. X. 26, p. 281, letter dated April 17 (XV Kalendas Maias), 1512, to the prior at Naples: "Reformatio fiat interna animae et externa corporis." *Scechina*, vol. II, p. 260: "... non pelliculae circumcisione contentus Messias, universum corpus ferro, flagris, mucronibus objectavit, ut mortales non signo cuticulae, sed vera exactaque expiatione intus forisque purgaret—intus mentes, foris affectus."

[2] See Scholem, *Kabbalah Symbolism*, esp. pp. 5-31, 96-97.

[3] Massa, *Fondamenti metafisici e testi inediti*, p. 64: "... at divinis accedendum est oraculis, ut voluit Plato, ac de divinis rebus credendum est majoribus, teste Timaeo, qui, Deo propiores, divina et suspexere et posteris suscipienda tradidere."

[4] Berengar (ca. 999-1088) and Pope John XXII (1316-1334) are criticized for their eagerness for "*res novae*" in doctrine, Ang. Lat. 502, fols. 95r, 201r. See also *ibid.*, fol. 36r; Vat. Lat. 6325, fols. 129r and 169r: "... ne quis sacra oraculorum mutet, ..." On the doctrinal aspects of reform ideologies, see Ladner, *Idea of Reform*, e.g., pp. 136-139, 147-150, 409-413.

Vatican Church, and he seems to have considered that the Church's principal function as regards doctrine was the negative one of defending the deposit of faith from attack and eradicating whatever doctrinal corruption might be taking root.[1] This task was to be performed with vigor, and those who taught false doctrine were peremptorily to be dealt with, "*E medio tollito!*"[2] The Church's prerogative for doctrinal purity was actively exercised through the councils and popes, and Giles assumed that their teaching was conformable to the Gospels and to the message of Christ.[3]

Attention might once again be directed to Giles's belief in the close relationship between doctrine and morals. Wealth and bad morals tend to beget doctrinal corruption. Laxity in matters of doctrine, in turn, sets off a chain reaction of other evils in the Church and looses upon it God's chastising hand.[4] Reform, therefore, is a question which touches all aspects of Christian and ecclesiastical life, and must proceed simultaneously in doctrine and discipline. Giles reminded Leo X that he and the Lateran Council were to correct the Church both in its words and in its deeds.[5]

A large part of the moral reform which Giles looked for in the Church can conveniently be considered under the general headings of the three traditional religious vows. Giles surely did not envision that everybody in the Church be constrained to live under the obligations of these vows. But from the very fact that the vows express, in a sense, a reaction to some of the most obvious moral abuses of which man

---

[1] Ang. Lat. 502, fol. 156v: "... Vaticana ecclesia sola trinitatem exacte cognoverit, sola in illius intelligentia non erraverit." *Ibid.*, fol. 124v: "Habet [Pope Leo IX, 1049-1054] statim Vercellense concilium ubi pontificum munus esse docet fidei partes integras tueri, nulla illam nota labefactari sinere, de ea et statim et semper et quaerere, si quid divariarit emendare." *Ibid.*, fol. 40v: "... quia enim optimi pontificis praecipuum munus est fidem orthodoxam integram, intactam et nulla ex parte suo tempore laesam esse voluit [Pope John I, 523-526], paratus itaque pati extrema omnia quam tangi fidem ecclesiae vel Romanae vel Vaticanae." See also *ibid.*, fol. 93r.

[2] Ang. Lat. 502, fol. 164v. See also *ibid.*, fols. 34r, and 5v: "[God constituted the Vatican His holy mount] ubi praeceptum et caput fidei semper vigeat, et longe lateque philosophis sceptro aeternum stabili imperetur."

[3] Ang. Lat. 502, fol. 164r: "... qui, si vera narrent [Peripatetics], necesse sit evangelia falsa, Dei filium mendacem, sacri vel senatus vel concilii patres esse deceptores, pontificem maximum veteratorem et generi humano illudentium esse caput."

[4] Ang. Lat. 502, fols. 36r, 176v, 218r.

[5] Ang. Lat. 502, fol. 28r: "... tu conciliumque tuum emendandae, castigandae reipublicae tuae tum in his quae fiunt, tum in his quae dicuntur occurras, ..."

is capable it is not surprising that Giles's thought can easily be organized under them. This principle of organization, moreover, is by no means extrinsic to Giles's own categories, for he often returns to the virtues represented by these vows when discussing the general moral reform of the Church, especially of the clergy. It was only natural that he should do so, since the importance he attached to the vows was as obvious from his decision to live under them as from his words of praise for them.[1]

What Giles has to say about chastity concerns almost exclusively the clergy. Although he scolds the laity scarcely at all for sins of fornication or adultery, he on several occasions takes the clergy seriously to task for its failure to live continently. The reason for singling them out is that chastity is the virtue most characteristic of their state of life, and, hence, any sin against it is all the more detestable.[2] His most bitter denunciation is of Pope Innocent VIII (1484-1492) because of the evil example of his unchastity and the general weakening of the Christian fabric which ensued from it, as became clear in the ruinous pontificate of Alexander VI. Giles's great hopes for Leo X are partially based upon the new pope's pure life.[3] The licentiousness of the clergy must be stamped out, either by the good example of the papacy or by some other means, before God's wrath will be lifted and the renovation of the Church and the world can take place.[4]

Poverty was for Giles a serious ideal. The reason he esteems it is that Christ by word and example taught it was a great spiritual good. Plato confirmed what Christ taught, whereas the impious Aristotle laughed at the idea of poverty. To a certain extent Giles tended to identify Christian poverty with the eremitical poverty he believed Christ and the apostles practiced, and which Augustine imitated and prescribed for his hermits.[5]

---

[1] See, e.g., Ang. Lat. 1170, fol. 22r; Siena G. X. 26, p. 24, and Martin, "Giles and Lecceto," p. 249.

[2] Ang. Lat. 502, fol. 251r: "... tamquam nulla peculiarior sacerdoti virtus, nulla accomodatior putanda videatur esse quam castitas, ..." See also *ibid.*, fol. 317r. He recommends chaste thoughts to Charles V, *Scechina*, vol. II, p. 113. For his esteem for virginity, *ibid.*, vol. II, pp. 159, 160.

[3] Ang. Lat. 502, fols. 250v-251r, 260v, 287v, 301v.

[4] *Scechina*, vol. I, p. 136.

[5] Siena G. X. 26, pp. 33-34, letter undated, to the convent at Perugia: "Excitant [nos ad instaurationem monasterii] denique ea ipsa quae Dominus noster coepit, nos erudiens et facere et docere. Si quae fecit videmus, ita se ipsum exinanivit ut ubi caput reclinaret non haberet. Si doctrinam pensemus, nisi quis, inquit, renuntiaverit omnibus quae possidet non potest meus esse discipulus." Lk. 14. 33.

In this question, however, it would be a mistake to see in Giles a continuation of the tradition of the Spiritual Franciscans. Though he extolled poverty in terms of unqualified praise and at times seems almost to identify it with destitution, he never quite steps over into the extreme Franciscan position. As a matter of fact, he explicitly rejects the view that Christ, the apostles and the primitive Church had no possessions whatsoever, and he judges it to be an insane and unholy doctrine, condemned by the Church.[1] He often considers poverty in the context of giving alms to the poor, and thereby he identifies it not with the absence of wealth but with detachment from the goods of this world which one might possess. Disdain for wealth, especially when coupled with generosity towards the poor, constitutes for Giles the true "evangelical piety."[2] Within the Augustinian order the daily practice of poverty came to mean principally the so-called common life, i.e., accepting what was provided by the order and the community, and, though Giles assumes that food and clothing would be simple, he gives no indication that he wants to cut expenses to the bone. He continued, without question, the custom of each master of theology in the order having a servant.[3] We have already seen, furthermore, that in the construction of new houses or churches he insisted upon good quality in design and materials. Very significant in this regard is his inclusion of the building of new monasteries and convents as among his reform tasks.[4]

It is important to observe that when Giles speaks of a "reform of

---

See also Ang. Lat. 502, fol. 39r: "Dominus ait, nunc exsurgam [Ps. 12(11). 5], surgendi ratio in solitudine vitaque solitaria. Hanc unus instituendam excolendamque accepit Augustinus, elegitque non Africam, non Asiam, non alias Europae regiones, sed ut aureae aetatis reliquiae in apostolorum pauperie institutisque perseverarent, Etruriam delegit, oram aetatis aureae, et olim Jani, et nunc Christi pontificumque perpetuo consecratam, atque ibi in Monte Pisano prius, inde ad Centumcellas, et in universa maritima eremitas statuit, Christianae pauperisque simplicitatis aurum observantes." On Christ and Plato agreeing on poverty against Aristotle, see *ibid.*, fol. 155r.

[1] Ang. Lat. 502, fols. 200v, 219v, and 243r. For the condemnation of this position by John XXII (1316-1334) in 1323, see *Denz.*, no. 930(494).

[2] Ang. Lat. 502, fols. 172v, 242r, and *Scechina*, vol. I, p. 98.

[3] Aug. Gen. Archives, Rome, Dd. 12, fol. 22v.

[4] Siena G. X. 26, p. 79, letter undated as to year of composition, to the prior at Naples: "... et quamquam dies noctesque non aliud agendo conteramus quam ut Augustinensem [sic] religionem moribus componendis emendemus, bonis artibus introducendis ornemus, monasteriis, domibus, aedificiis exstruendis augeamus, ..." Giles considers it a bad thing for his monasteries to be too poor, *ibid.*, pp. 200-201. See also *ibid.*, pp. 237-239.

morals" he sometimes had in mind something quite different from clerical or lay unchastity and avarice, and something for the most part much less vicious. For Giles "*mores*" was a broad term which he used to denote the standard discipline of a Christian life, especially as lived within a religious order. For his Augustinians he used the term to mean the common life and all the observances and customs which were prescribed in the rule, constitutions and papal briefs.[1]

To a considerable extent obedience within the order consisted precisely in an exact fulfillment on the part of each friar of the directives of these documents, which were often simply codifications of customs and usages for daily life within the houses and churches of the order: the places and manner in which silence was to be observed, the material and cut of the habit, the procedure in obtaining permissions, practical norms for works of the ministry, the duties and privileges of superiors, the education of the members and of the novices, etc. The reforming superior's task, as a matter of fact, was defined in terms of reducing to daily practice the "holy majesty of the laws."[2] The only initiative which was expected of him was to find means to make the already existing legislation a living force within his monastery, province or congregation. As we have already mentioned, during Giles's prior generalship the rule was printed at Venice, along with the commentary on it by Hugh of Saint Victor, the constitutions, several important papal documents, etc., and an accompanying letter by Giles.[3] This letter commends to the friars the rule and the official documents interpreting it.

The full importance of this publication cannot be grasped until one sees what great stress Giles lays upon the materials contained in it in his reform correspondence within the order. Time and again he insists that in the houses of the order the rule, constitutions and other official

[1] Naples V. F. 20, fol. 205r, letter dated July 6, 1506, to Deodatus Senensis: "Duo sunt quae fieri a te velim, ut studia tua cura ferveant, ut mores emendentur, habitus, incessus, consuetudines aliaque omnia quae ad castigatam spectat vitam." See Jedin, *Seripando*, vol. I, p. 157, on Giles and the problem of the common life.

[2] Siena G. X. 26, pp. 14-15, letter dated July 23, 1506: "Tu [prior at Siena] ... alii alibi studiosi praeficiendi sunt patres, qui in ultro operam spondentes sacram legum majestatem in usum reducant. Hos ego amaturus ornaturusque sum." See also *ibid.*, p. 218. For some of the details Giles insisted upon, see *ibid.*, pp. 45-46. For the important decrees of the general chapter of 1507, which further illustrate Giles's detailed reform prescriptions, see Martin, "Egidio da Viterbo," pp. 191-198.

[3] *Regula beati Augustini una cum expositione Hugonis de Sancto Victore*, ..., Venice 1508. Giles's letter appears on fol. 89r.

documents be read daily, and, what is more, be observed down to the last detail, "*ad amussim*."[1] The order's reform consists in going back to the observance of its original charters, and for this reason Giles instigates a search in the Augustinian houses for all documents, "*quae vetustatem sapere videantur*."[2] A return to the ancient and sanctioned traditions of the order, both in its great ideals and in the minute details of daily procedure, was a hallmark of Giles's reform of the Augustinians and suggests the mentality with which he approached the reform of the Church as a whole.[3] Giles had no doubts that these traditions were univocal and, as such, recoverable in their original form, nor that any particular modification of them in the light of changed economic or social conditions might be called for.

Within the Church Giles assumes the existence of a moral obligation of obedience to ecclesiastical authority and in particular to the pope. He tolerated no customs which clashed with the common ecclesiastical practice, and he ordered that in such matters the Augustinian convents be made to conform with the rest of the Church.[4] Papal documents, even relatively recent ones, are grouped among works representing the order's oldest traditions and placed on a par with them. These documents have an authority deriving from the teaching and ruling function of the Church and of the Roman Pontiff

---

[1] Siena G. X. 26, pp. 24, 26, 38, 198, 218.

[2] Siena G. X. 26, p. 31, entitled "In calce quarundam litterarum," undated: "Ceterum injecimus animum ut religionis antiquitates, si quae existant, investigemus. Quare in omnibus monasteriis provinciae tuae [unnamed] cura si quae sint bullae veteres, si qui libri cum historia nostrarum rerum, si qua denique monumenta sint quae vetustatem sapere videantur. Ea omnia et diligentissime quaeras et ad nos accuratissime scribas." See also Ang. Lat. 688, fol. 23v, and Siena G. X. 26, p. 24, letter undated: "Legantur cottidie leges nostrae.... Vosque [friars of convent in Amelia] ita vitam instituatis ut ab illis legibus quam minime fieri potest discedatis." *Ibid.*, p. 26, letter undated, to the prior at Bologna: "[All that the friars do] ad amussim nostris legibus institutisque patrum conformentur." Ang. Lat. 1170, fol. 23v, letter dated May 20, 1508: "Quodque de sapientia dicitur, idem nos dicere possumus de legum nostrarum severitate atque custodia, quia illa praesente affuere nobis omnia bona pariter cum illa, at contra bona omnia, illa discedente, discesserunt. Vobis [unnamed] igitur mandamus in obedientiae meritum ut ... antiquas leges ametis, Neapolitana decreta [capituli generalis, 1507] suscipiatis, illa ad unguem servetis, ..."

[3] Siena G. X. 26, p. 198, entitled "Litterae praesidentiae," undated: "Cupientes nos nostrorum patrum ritus optimos imitari, neque a religionis instituto divertere, ..." See also *ibid.*, p. 261.

[4] Aug. Gen. Archives, Rome, Dd. 12, fol. 5v: "... etiam jubemus ut quaedam quae contra consuetudinem sanctae Romanae ecclesiae in suis conventibus fiunt ad uniformitatem ecclesiae reducat [superior]."

which gives them a preferential position. The fact that Giles petitioned from the pope new grants of authority for himself and new indulgences for the order shows the importance he attached to them. He demanded the same respect for the precepts of the pope, "*pontificis pastoris*," as he did for those of the order's founder, "*Augustini parentis*."[1]

Failure to obey the pope led to an evil which Giles detested and which had wrought so much havoc and misery in the Church of his own day—schism. The Turkish menace helped make him even more acutely aware of division from the "Greeks" than he otherwise might have been, but the threatened schism of the Council of Pisa in 1512 brought the problem even closer to home. Without hesitation Giles did his best to rally the order around the cause of Julius II and "Church unity," very solemnly intoning a letter on this question with an identification of the pope's cause with Christ's, "He who is not with me is against me" (Mt. 12.30).[2] It is hard to conceive a more emphatic thesis than Giles's on the meaning of obedience to the pope in the Church, "What else is it to obey God than to follow Peter?"[3] Plato's teaching that the greatest possible unity should obtain in the well ordered republic confirmed for Giles what he already knew from the teaching of Christ and the history of the Church, and disclosed another aspect of Aristotle's uncomprehending impiety.[4] The Church should not be torn into parts and segments, but as one body be united by one faith and under one head.[5]

---

[1] *Regula beati Augustini*, p. 89r: "... ut Augustini parentis ac pontificis pastoris praeceptis obtemperaremus." See also Siena G. X. 26, p. 31, and Pélissier, "Pour la biographie," p. 804. On his seeking indulgences for the order from Julius II, see Siena G. X. 26, pp. 51-53, 232.

[2] For this letter, see Siena G. X. 26, pp. 266-269, undated letter to unnamed provincial. His concern for the unity of the Church in the face of the Pisan schism comes out clearly in "Oratio post 3am sessionem," pp. 522-524.

[3] Évora CXVI/1-30, fol. 56v: "Quidnam est aliud obedire Deo nisi Petrum sequi?"

[4] Ang. Lat. 502, fols. 225v-226r: "... curarentque [cardinales] id quod ad optimam rempublicam pertinere Plato arbitrabatur, ut quam maxime fieri posset esset una, rem a Peripatetico temere damnatam, a Dei filio in evangelio, ab eius senatu in actis apostolorum divina ratione receptam,...." He praises Leo X for avoiding favoring factions in his selection of cardinals, *ibid.*, fol. 314r.

[5] Siena G. X. 26, p. 111, letter undated, to the vicar of a Spanish observant congregation: "... sit anima una et cor unum in Deo, cumque una sit et fides et caput." Here he is specifically speaking of unity within the order, but his words bear extension to the Church as a whole. He is proud of the Augustinians' tradition of loyalty to the pope, Ang. Lat. 502, fol. 201r.

We have already spoken of Giles's eschatological hope for the religious unity of mankind. For all men to be gathered into the one flock it was necessary that they be united under the one shepherd. Although on occasion Giles sees the emperor as universal shepherd, it is clear from the general trend of his thought that the pope is properly invested with this high function when there is question of ecclesiastical unity. Reparation of schism and strengthening of unity tended, as reform aims, to put greater, rather than less, emphasis upon the papacy and the Church's central administration.

There must have been some interdependence between Giles's more detached reflections upon the importance and mystical significance of religious unity in the Church and his practical experience as prior general of the Augustinian order. The jurisdictional split between the observants and conventuals led to many problems, and surely did not make Giles's reforming tasks any easier, especially because of the somewhat indistinct character of the authority he enjoyed over the observants.

In 1507 there were spread throughout the Augustinian order ten different observant congregations, interleaved with twenty-six conventual provinces. In order to assure a more literal adherence to the rule the observant congregations for one hundred and fifty years had been favored by the priors general and the Holy See with privileges and exemptions, so that they acquired a considerable, though varying, degree of autonomy. The Lombard Congregation, for instance, operated in almost complete practical independence of the rest of the order. Nationalism and local patriotism often fostered this spirit of independence, and the result was an administrative problem of considerable proportions by the time Giles became prior general.[1]

One of Giles's principal aims was to strengthen the central authority in the order and especially to assure clear jurisdiction of the prior general over the observants. In 1507 he obtained from Julius II a papal brief empowering him to bring the observants more directly under his office, and the general chapter of the order held in the same year approved this aspect of Giles's program. In 1515 Leo X confirmed and amplified what Julius II had earlier granted.[2] Giles did not lose his esteem for the observance as an ideal, but he did discover that the laxity of some observants really belied their name.[3] If the order as a

[1] Martin, "Egidio da Viterbo," pp. 174-184.

[2] Martin, "Egidio da Viterbo," pp. 175, 199-200, 358-363.

[3] Siena G. X. 26, pp. 46-47, letter dated September 29, 1506, to the vicar of an

whole were to be reformed, the prior general had to be able to compel obedience on the part of the observants and especially be able to force them to receive canonical visitors and new superiors who had the authority to restore them to the primitive discipline they professed.

Giles's efforts to unify the Augustinians were surely motivated by the practical consideration that he felt that only thus could the reform of the order be sustained.[1] This practical consideration, however, meshed perfectly with his theory of ecclesiastical unity and his hope for the final religious unity of mankind. Divisions and disobedience within the order, where all should be united as of one heart and one head, in one faith and under one pastor, was equivalent to schism and rent the Christian body.[2] What was desired in the order, as in the Church, was that there be accomplished the perfect harmony of one flock under one shepherd.[3]

Giles hoped for undisturbed peace and unity within the Church and for the gathering of all men into the great Christian reality. He did not feel, however, that either of these aims meant the absorption into one jurisdiction of the various bodies within the Church. Quite the contrary is true. The bitter contest with the bishops at the Lateran Council was fought precisely to assure the order's independence from them, and many of the other privileges which he sought to maintain guaranteed a measure of liberty in routine matters even from the Holy See. Giles laid great emphasis on making certain that the order's privileges remained intact at a moment when certain other reformers felt that they were the major obstacle to effective pastoral work on the part of the secular clergy and to effective administration of the dioceses

---

observant congregation: "... ut cum observatores fratres appellari velint, observent plane nihil, nec quidquid conveniat minus, quod magno cum dolore dicimus, quam observantiae nomen." See also *ibid.*, e.g., pp. 223-225, 239-247.

[1] Martin shows this to be the case in the pages cited above. See also Weijenborg, "Neuentdeckte Dokumente," esp. pp. 171-172, on Giles's desire to effect a "Verstärkung seiner Macht" over the German observants. It would be unfair to interpret these negotiations as a simple case of ecclesiastical power politics.

[2] Siena G. X. 26, pp. 111-112, undated letter to the vicar of a Spanish observant congregation.

[3] Siena G. X. 26, p. 202, letter dated August 21, 1508, to an unnamed provincial: "...unus fiet vivendi modus, una mandatorum observatio, unum denique ovile et unus pastor. Quod uti efficiamus, Domino adjuvante, omnem operam, omne studium, omnem diligentiam posituri sumus." His words concerning the monastery at Viterbo have a broad application, Ang. Lat. 1170, fols. 38v-39r, letter dated May 30, 1514: "... renovationis fundamenta, quorum primum ac maxime necessarium est ut membra absque capite esse non permittantur, sed cuique gregi pastor praesit, ..."

by the bishops, helping to foster the terrible evil of episcopal non-residence.[1] Giles gives no indication that he was ready to make any concessions on this point, nor that he even considered the possibility that a curtailment of privilege could possibly have contributed to the order's or the Church's welfare. As he indicated when he resigned as prior general, the preservation and defence of the indults, privileges, indulgences and favors which the order had received was one of the first duties of his office and, if not identical with the order's reform, it was at least so intimately related to it that the one was unthinkable without the other.[2]

Giles's devotion to the papacy and his conviction that it constituted the focal point for the religious unity of mankind did not blind him to the reprobate aspects of recent pontificates, nor to the abuses which were being carried on in the Roman Curia. We do not have from his pen a concise program for the reform of this branch of the Church such as Tommaso Giustiniani (1476-1528) and Vincenzo Quirini (1479-1514) drew up for their "Libellus ad Leonem X" in 1513.[3] We can, nevertheless, construct from his writings a fairly good picture of what he thought the principal abuses were and, hence, what would have to be extirpated if the Church were to achieve the full renovation he so keenly desired.

Julius II, rather paradoxically, had been concerned to assure the canonical and non-simoniacal election of the pope, and Giles implies that he, too, saw in this provision the basis for a reformed papacy. His support for the council's decree against this abuse would have

[1] See Jedin, *Trent*, vol. I, pp. 135-136, 441-444. In actual practice Giles wanted his friars to cooperate as much as possible with the episcopacy, as is clear in the case of Cardinal Ximénez de Cisneros of Toledo (1436-1517), Siena G. X. 26, p. 225, letter dated May 5, 1510, to Franciscus de la Parra of Toledo.

[2] Ang. Lat. 1170, fols. 44v-45r, letter dated February 27, 1518, to an unnamed convent: "Fecimus non quae debuimus, sed quae potuimus in ordine defendendo, in conventibus quos potuimus reformandis, in studiis moribusque probis excitandis, in exemptionibus, apostolicis indultis, privilegiis, indulgentiis, favoribus impetrandis, et universa libertate in Lateranensi concilio defendenda." He expressed his duty of defending the order, Siena G. X. 26, p. 185, letter dated simply May 20, to a certain Magister Augustinus: "Injuriam enim nobis illatam pati Christiane debemus, a republica tamen nostra arcere ac propulsare par est." For his insistence on the order's privileges, see Martène, *Veterum scriptorum collectio*, vol. III, cols. 1263-1265. See also Ang. Lat. 502, fol. 172r.

[3] These specific suggestions were not included in the final copy of the "Libellus," but Hubert Jedin published them as an appendix to his article, "Vincenzo Quirini und Pietro Bembo," *Miscellanea Giovanni Mercati*, vol. IV, *StT* vol. CXXIV, Città del Vaticano 1946, pp. 423-424.

been whole-hearted. In his eyes even the most just subsequent pontificate could not ratify an illegitimate election.[1] A canonical election, conversely, did not at all mean that the new incumbent was confirmed in good works. Of the possible misuses of the papal office one of the most dangerous for the Church and most execrable in itself was nepotism. This terrible abuse, besides the many evils it brought in its train, violated the mystique of utter and exclusive devotion to the Church which was characteristic of the papacy. For the pope the Church was wife, children and family.[2]

Intimately bound up with the problem of nepotism, of course, was the question of the nomination of members to the Sacred College of Cardinals. Giles was clear on the care and disinterest with which these prelates should be chosen and on the outstanding spiritual and intellectual qualifications they should have. The reasons are obvious: the cardinals play an active role in the highest level of ecclesiastical government and it is from their number that the pope himself ordinarily is chosen.[3]

The efforts of Nicholas V and Paul II to rid the Roman Curia of simony and venality had failed, according to Giles, not least of all because Innocent VIII, imitating Sixtus IV, promoted a curial policy which actually increased the incidence of these abuses. Liturgical and sacramental offices were performed for financial gain, "*non numinis sed nummi gratia,*" and the number of secretaries, abbreviators and other bureaucratic functionaries in the Curia had been increased beyond all real need. With almost prophetic insight Giles observed that it was no wonder if the Curia had a bad name in foreign countries.[4]

---

[1] See Ang. Lat. 502, fols. 54r, 72r, 89v, 149r. For the council's decree on this abuse, see *Conciliorum decreta*, pp. 576-579.

[2] Évora CXVI/1-30, fol. 56v: "Pro uxore, pro liberis, pro universa cognatione ecclesia tibi [Julius II] est. Hanc unam amas, hanc divitem, hanc auctam, hanc propria majestate fulgentem reddere et cogitas et laboras." See also Ang. Lat. 502, fols. 142v, 173r, 202r, 214r-v, 322v.

[3] Ang. Lat. 502, fols. 154v, 155v, 201v, 243v. His qualifications for the pope, *ibid.*, fol. 48r: "... tum moribus probatissimus, tum sacrarum rerum doctrina ac pia eruditione clarissimus."

[4] Ang. Lat. 502, fol. 250r: "Nec mirum si male apud exteras nationes audit curia, ..." See also *ibid.*, fols. 203v-204r, 230v, 240r, 248r-v. See the Fifth Lateran Council's documents on reform, *Conciliorum decreta*, pp. 584-585, 590-601. Giles himself simultaneously held several relatively small benefices. See Signorelli, *Egidio da Viterbo*, pp. 85-86, 102-103, as well as Ang. Lat. 502, fol. 232r, where Giles implicitly commends Pope Calixtus III (1455-1458) for his refusal to accumulate episcopal benefices.

The restoration of sacred studies and learning, an important aspect of Giles's program for the Augustinians, was needed also in the renovation of the Church as a whole. For Giles the pope should be a man not only of irreproachable virtue but also outstanding for his knowledge of theology. Of the two keys given to Peter one was the key of wisdom, which in this case was equivalent to learning.[1] As among his chief duties the pope was to look after scholars and help provide for their support, just as he did for churches and for the poor.[2]

We have already commented on the relationship Giles saw between good studies and good morals. Sacred learning produced, moreover, even more desirable spiritual results than moral uprightness, gently leading to an almost mystical love for the person of the Redeemer.[3] If the Church was to be spiritually renewed, it must dedicate itself to such learning, and especially to the study of Scripture as understood in the cabala. If this study is neglected religion itself will be misunderstood, neglected and even abandoned.[4]

The energy and determination which Giles would have brought to bear on a practical reform of clerical education can be seen from the vigorous measures he adopted within his own order. Martin has described his efforts in some detail, and pointed out that Giles felt that the ultimate success of his total program depended to a great extent on the training and studies of the young men of the order.[5] He did his best to raise the standards of the *studia*, trying to restore to them a truly international flavor and awarding academic honors only on the basis of proved accomplishment. Texts could be multiplied to show the esteem in which he held sacred studies and to prove that he put them on a par with virtue as a restorative force within the order.[6]

---

[1] See Ang. Lat. 502, fol. 48r; Siena G. X. 26, p. 62.

[2] Ang. Lat. 502, fol. 217v.

[3] Paris Lat. 527[2], fol. 148r; *Scechina*, vol. I, p. 199.

[4] *Scechina*, vol. I, pp. 69-70: "Aperturus [ego, Shekinah] itaque, et Deo auctore et te principe [Charles V], clausam portam [secrets of the ancients], et quae nemo hactenus novit, pietatis studiosis allaturus, scribam quae hostes nostri in arcanis premunt, eo consilio ut renovanda ecclesia suscipiat, quae suae religioni, sententiae, judicio probabit convenire, quae secus atque alio sentiet vergere et respuat et confutet." "Libellus" (in *Scechina*, vol. I), pp. 32-33: "... religio in sua lege non comprehenditur, non comprehensa negligitur, neglecta relinquitur, ..."

[5] Martin, "Egidio da Viterbo," pp. 194-196, 245-250, 259-267.

[6] E.g., Siena G. X. 26, p. 7, letter dated July 14, 1506: "... atque ita a te [prior at Naples] agi volumus ut non minus eruditionis quam probitatis, nec minus litterarum quam vitae te rectorem sentiant." See also *ibid.*, pp. 19-23, 26, 36, 79, 85-86, 131, 138-139, 290; Ang. Lat. 3, fol. 769v; Naples V. F. 20, fol. 205r; Pélissier, "Pour la biographie," pp. 803-804.

Like his spiritual father Augustine, the friar was to excel in learning as well as in virtue.[1]

From the evidence which is available it seems that Giles did nothing to initiate during his prior generalship any change in the subject matter of clerical education in the direction of his own Neoplatonism or cabalism. He speaks of the study of "*litterae sacrae*" in his letters, but, lacking any further specification, we must take this simply as a generic term which conventionally would give emphasis to Augustine and Giles of Rome. This is perfectly conformable with what we know of his attitude towards the traditions of his order and, surely, if he had tried to make changes as drastic as a substitution of the cabala or Ficino's Platonic theology there would be unmistakable evidence in his correspondence. Had he held office longer he might have tried to effect some change along this line, for as he grew older his convictions on the value of the cabala grew deeper. While he actually was prior general, however, he made no organized efforts in this regard, although there were certainly individual instances of his encouraging friars in the study of the cabala and "*Caldaeas litteras*."[2]

Having seen the reform ideals and particular reform measures Giles proposed, we might now ask who the agents were by whom the reformation would be effected. In a section of the "Historia" in which he describes the declining morals of the sixth Christian age, he lists three possibilities—the Church itself, the lay powers, and "the bloody sword of impious enemies."[3] The clear implication of all Giles wrote is that it was desirable that the Church, especially in the person of the pope, directly assume the responsibility to carry out the reform. The papacy is undoubtedly for Giles the preferred reform agent, and it is rather moving to see how he turned to each pope in succession, hoping to find in him the sorely needed restorer of ecclesiastical probity.

After the disastrous pontificate of Alexander VI Giles's happiness was great in the election of Francesco Piccolomini as Pius III. For Giles this honest and sincere prelate was destined to be the reformer Christianity required, but men's sins were so great God removed him after a pontificate of only twenty-six days.[4] Giles repeatedly urged

[1] Siena G. X. 26, p. 138, entitled "Pro lectoratu," undated.

[2] Ang. Lat. 1170, fol. 40r, letter dated September 20, 1516, to Stefano Zoalio; Ang. Lat. 3, fol. 769v.

[3] Ang. Lat. 502, fol. 75r: "... quod nisi sacerdos faciat, aut prophana vis domesticorum faciet, aut cruentus gladius impiorum."

[4] Naples V. F. 20, fols. 70r-71r, letter dated October 24, 1503, to Serafino Ferri. See also Ang. Lat. 502, fols. 68r, 127r, 263r-264v.

Julius II to decisive action in the reform of the Church and to extend the scope of the reform measures he had already undertaken. The time had come to restore religion and to extinguish impiety. All that was needed was for Julius to set about the task with his accustomed energy and vigor.[1]

The hopes Giles placed in Leo X were discussed in the last chapter. Time and again Giles reminds Leo of his high responsibilities to reform the Church. He is the "*instaurator*" and the "*propugnator*" from whom the "moribund spouse of Christ" awaits to be recalled to life.[2] His task is to bring peace to his flock, crush the Turks, promote the study of the sacred language, preserve Christian doctrine from the attacks of impious philosophers, and make his people like himself in piety and purity of life.[3] From the second Medici pope, Clement VII, Giles expects similar accomplishments, even though in the description of Clement's reform obligations his cooperation with the emperor receives more emphasis than was ever the case with his cousin, Leo X.[4]

Giles assigns to councils a reforming function, and his expectations for the Fifth Lateran Council were great, as his opening oration shows.[5] The Council of Pisa of 1511 taught him that the episcopacy could be maneuvered into schismatic positions, and the Lateran Council itself, canonical though it was, taught him the bitter lesson that a council could be used as a launching pad for attacks that were neither just nor pious.[6] Nevertheless, Giles did not feel the institution

---

[1] Évora CXVI/1-30, fol. 65v: "Tua esse tempora quibus, si velis, si ea mente sis quam arbitramur, impietatem extinguas, religionem instaures, ..." Naples V. F. 20, fol. 281r, letter undated, to Antonio Zocolo and the Augustinians in Rome: "Putrescentia cures, collapsa instaures, errata castiges, corriges inversa, revoces antiquata, in hostem utrumque [domestic and foreign] quantum potes manu moveas. Id Eliseus, id divus Petrus, id sponsa agendum suadet, id denique Dominus ipse in Matthaeo [Mt. 10.34], Non veni igniens pacem mittere in terram sed gladium."

[2] Ang. Lat. 502, fol. 21r-v.

[3] Ang. Lat. 502, fols. 21r-v, 304r, 316v-318v, 319v-320r, 325r-v; "Libellus" (in *Scechina*, vol. I), p. 31.

[4] *Scechina*, vol. I, pp. 66, 76, 94, 219, 220, 233; vol. II, pp. 26, 223, 281, 282.

[5] Mansi, vol. XXXII, cols. 670-673. See also "Oratio post 3am sessionem," p. 523; Ang. Lat. 502, fols. 122r, 142v, 146r, 158r, 187r, 222r, 321r; Siena G. X. 26, pp. 288, 295. It was in the sixth and seventh centuries that the realization of the necessity of almost constant conciliar reform first dawned, and after that the idea came to the foreground in all great reform periods, Ladner, *Idea of Reform*, p. 303.

[6] Ang. Lat. 502, fol. 246v: "... parum justa ac minus pia."

itself was to be abandoned because of possible abuses of it, and in the *Scechina* of 1530 he approves the idea of the emperor promoting the convocation of a council in order to bring peace to Germany and to help accomplish the renovation of the Church.[1] In the *Scechina*, we recall, he attributes to the councils the function of completing Christ's teaching through clarification of the meaning of Scripture. To the negative doctrinal function of condemning false teaching, so prominent in his statements of what he expected from the Lateran Council, has been added this more positive one.

Mention must be made of the leading role official canonical visitors played in Giles's reform of the Augustinian order. These men, appointed by the prior general himself, were carefully chosen for their piety, prudence and zeal for reform. It was only by employing such men and giving them almost plenipotentiary powers that Giles thought the reform could be made to move from house to house and from province to province. Monasteries caught in the doldrums of religious laxity were incapable of saving themselves, and some force from the outside had to be applied in order to spur them into action. Because of the extensive use he made of this institution in his reform of the order, we can legitimately suppose that he would have employed a similar one in the reform of the Church as a whole.[2] It is in the light of the effective use Giles made of visitors that we can understand his persistence in trying to centralize the administration of the order and also, to some extent, his strong emphasis on the papacy as the key to ecclesiastical unity and reform. One agency was needed, in the Church as well as in the order, which had clear and unchallenged authority to overcome all paralyzing lassitude and to break down local and regional resistance by infusing new energies from the outside.

The second potential agent of reform was the lay powers. Although on occasion Giles sees in Christian princes such as Manuel of Portugal or Ferdinand of Aragon (1474-1516) religious restorers, he really believed that it was only the emperor who commanded the universal allegiance and authority to carry out the all-inclusive reform which

---

[1] *Scechina*, vol. I, p. 76. See also *ibid.*, p. 69, and Pastor, *History of the Popes*, vol. X, p. 149.

[2] On the visitors, see Martin, "Egidio da Viterbo," pp. 277-303, 363-376. Giles's esteem for them and the broad powers he delegated to them is seen in Siena G. X. 26, pp. 15-17, letter dated July 24, 1506, to the visitor of the convent in Milan.

was called for.[1] He assumes that in this great undertaking the emperor collaborates with the pope. Nevertheless, Charles is the recipient of the solemn commission to cleanse the Church of impiety and heresy and to restore it to youthful integrity, and he is to issue the command that the text of Scripture be properly emended and reformed.[2]

What are the specific ways in which the emperor is to implement the renovation of the Church? Giles seems to suggest that some portion of the emperor's reforming functions fall to him by default, either on the part of his predecessors or of the clergy, but he does outline some tasks which are proper to his office.[3] We have already taken note of the emperor's mission to open up the newly discovered lands to Christianity and to promote the study of Scripture. As regards the latter, Charles must use his authority to gather the necessary books and then to apply scholars to the new methods and texts, fulfilling the Gospel injunction to search the Scriptures.[4] Related to the former task is the emperor's role, as the "new Moses" and "the prince of the holy war" to conquer the Turks, and to expedite the religious unity of mankind by forcing the reluctant into the one fold, "*intrare compelleres*" (Lk. 14.23).[5]

The emperor performs, moreover, the much more somber task of the avenger of divine justice and the heavenly appointed scourge of the people of God, who reforms by bloodshed what cannot be reformed any other way, as the sack of Rome so dramatically evidenced.[6]

---

[1] On Ferdinand as an "ampliatorem instauratoremque Christianorum," see Naples V. F. 20, fols. 283v-284r, letter undated, to Antonio Zocolo. He is here specifically referring to Ferdinand's military and political exploits. For further mentions of Ferdinand, see Évora CXVI/1-30, fols. 45v, 50v, 65v. On Manuel, who is called "ad novae legis instaurationem," see Évora CXVI/1-30, e.g., fols. 1r, 55r, 67v.

[2] *Scechina*, vol. I, p. 99: "Cura rugam auferre, impietatem, haeresim, hostem, tollere maculam, ut quae non recte habent tua opera, cura, studio, pietate repurgentur reponanturque et suae integritati restituantur. Jube sacra oracula veritati quadrare, adjecta expurgi, dempta recuperari, inversa ad amussim reformari."

[3] *Scechina*, vol. I, pp. 98-99: "... aliorum negligentia, ut quod omisere tu efficias, quod neglexere cures, quae collabi et ruere passi sunt tu restituenda atque instauranda complectaris." See Jedin, *Trent*, vol. I, pp. 93-100, on the prevalence of the emergency-theory of Church government and the devolution of authority in the late fifteenth and early sixteenth centuries.

[4] *Scechina*, vol. I, pp. 161-162: "Jube sapientes tuos litteras numerare, verba ponderare, ... jube libros quaeri qui Romae sunt; jube eos a studiosis revolvi, arcana requiri, innumerabilia legis prophetarumque loca cognosci ...."

[5] *Scechina*, vol. I, pp. 69, 133-134, 160-161, 233. See also Ang. Lat. 502, fol. 220r.

[6] *Scechina*, vol. II, pp. 144, 150.

The Turks, of course, were the objects of Giles's constant fear and he saw in them the principal instrument God would dispatch to inflict the punishment of His wrath, "*cruentus gladius impiorum*." Terror, calamity and bloodshed, therefore, were also agents of reform. Just as God used Satan as His minister to test the just Job, so He now can use the armies of the Turks to test and purify the Church.[1] His purpose, of course, is not to destroy His beloved spouse, but to restore and beautify her, to lead her back to the path of righteousness and to show her how far she had strayed from Him.[2]

That God might use the Turks as His avenging ministers did not mean that He particularly loved them, nor that Christian leaders were justified for that reason in adopting an indifferent or passive attitude towards them.[3] With unflagging energy Giles persevered to the end of his days in trying to rouse the pope, the emperor and the Christian princes to their solemn duty to take up arms to ward off the Turkish peril. Interpreting the prophecies, he promised Leo X sure victory, for himself or at least for his successors. In the *Scechina* he pitted East against West, as Pompey against Caesar, and he encouraged Charles V with the hope of victory if only he would set out.[4]

The defeat of the Turks was part of the happy culmination to be expected of the tenth age, part of the long delayed manifestation of the harmony of the universe. It would be symptomatic of the opening of the Church to the whole human family. Fulfillment of the eschatological promise of the one flock and the one shepherd could not long be delayed once the great apocalyptic enemy went down in defeat.[5] Giles ardently desired to see these splendid events come to pass, but he became ever more aware that they could not be accomplished without some measure, more or less great, of anguish and bloodshed. The Church and the world reflected the divine realities, and in achieving religious renovation they were set to the pattern of the

---

[1] See, e.g., *Scechina*, vol. II, p. 165; Siena G. X. 26, p. 323. See C. A. Patrides, "'The Bloody and Cruell Turke': The Background of a Renaissance Commonplace," *Studies in the Renaissance* 10(1963), pp. 126-135.

[2] Ang. Lat. 502, fols. 62r, 69r, 152r, 173(a)r-v.

[3] Ang. Lat. 502, fol. 70v.

[4] Ang. Lat. 502, fols. 304v-307v; *Scechina*, vol. II, p. 148; Évora CXVI/1-30, fols. 45v, 60v-61v, 62r.

[5] Ang. Lat. 502, fols. 25v-26v, 268r, 302v-312r, 321v. See Alphandéry and Dupront, *L'idée de croisade*, vol. II, pp. 279-289.

Messiah. Like Him they, too, had first to suffer, and thus to enter into their glory.[1]

---

[1] *Scechina*, vol. II, p. 150: "Nuncque tempus instat quando prius per Elohim furorem demolienda, ac deinde Adonai benignitate instauranda, restituenda, illustranda sint omnia. Sed sicut in orbe condendo praecessit nomen Elohim, Adonai in fine operis decus lucemque rerum hominem adduxit, ita in recreando per Messiam, et nunc, te duce [Charles V], si sapias, audias instaurando, Elohim vim antecedere, sequi Adonai necesse est .... Eadem duo ipse idem exposuit, oportuit pati Messiam atque ita intrare gloriam suam [Lk. 24.26]. Utrumque condidit, utrumque recuperavit per Messiam, utrumque nunc collapsa instaurat tuo saeculo. Evertet Elohim, si ades, hostilia, sin cedis, tua, atque haud ita multo post Adonai orbem in meliorem faciem permutabit." This theme of the Church's recapitulating in its history the suffering and resurrection of Christ is found, e.g., in the Joachimite tradition. See Benz, *Ecclesia spiritualis*, pp. 26-27, 303.

CONCLUSION

THE THOUGHT OF GILES OF VITERBO ON CHURCH AND REFORM

Giles of Viterbo described his writings as tumultuous, and anyone who tries to study them can hardly fail to be aware of the accuracy of that description. The distractions of Giles's administrative duties and the absorption of his remaining time and energy in a relentless pursuit of ever further knowledge, especially of Semitic languages and Jewish literature, dealt heavy blows to his ability to organize his thought. This ability was already reeling from the cumulative impact of his love for rhetoric and mystical theology and from the free rein given his imagination by cabalistic hermeneutics. Giles employed his intellectual gifts much more happily in intuition than in ordered analysis and systematic construction of argument. The genius of his thought did not consist in the easy capacity to disclose and isolate the underlying presuppositions which governed it, nor to reduce these to their essential by excluding all digression and ruthlessly stripping away all embellishment. Moreover, any attempt to try to perform these functions for him inevitably distorts the style and very character of the original.

No good purpose is served, however, by allowing fear of distortion to paralyze our efforts to analyze Giles's thought and to induce order and system into it. Giles's own failure to provide us with a neat *précis* of his purposes and fundamental assumptions does not mean that these were not operative in his thought, nor that some of them were not so pervasive as to be serviceable as organizational principles for the whole. To refuse to expose them and relate them to one another would be as much a distortion as to create the impression that Giles's own writings moved with the same logic and coherence as such an exposition would seem to imply.

Nor can we allow ourselves to be inhibited in such an undertaking by fear that we thus obscure the fact that Giles's thought developed and matured over the course of the years, and that the letters and sermons of the young Augustinian friar are not simply identical in spirit, purpose and insight with the *Scechina* of the aging cardinal. In actual fact Giles moved from editorship of works of Giles of Rome to enthusiasm for Ficino's Plato to a final and unswerving commitment to the cabala. His earlier interest in literature and metaphysics he attempted to integrate with a study of history, and all of these he finally brought to bear on exegesis of the text of Scripture. From Latin and Greek he advanced to Hebrew and Aramaic. These and other developments have been pointed out in the course of the book. Perhaps simply by calling attention to them now we can forestall any slighting of them that the effort to emphasize continuity of principle and persistence of theme might otherwise operate.

There is no better entrance into Giles's thought on Church and reform than the norm he declaimed for the fathers of the Fifth Lateran Council: "Men must be changed by religion, not religion by men." Giles was fully aware that this norm expressed his deepest convictions on the basic orientation which the reform of the Church should take, but it is doubtful if even he realized how extensive were its implications in his thought and how aptly it could be used as a device to explore it more thoroughly. The view can perhaps be sustained that Giles's statement of reform principle contains a religious truth of abstract and perennial value, independent of the specific meaning it had for him and detached from the concrete historical circumstances in which it was uttered. Such a view is certainly not without merit, but it is alien to the task in which we have been engaged. Our purpose has been to discover precisely how narrow, how limited, and how culturally conditioned the norm was—how personal to Giles of Viterbo and how evocative of a particular style of thought which no longer generally obtains.

What Giles's norm almost immediately discloses about his thought on Church and reform is what we have termed its conservative intent. The sacred traditions of religion are constant, and it is to them that man must try to conform his own instability and variability. These traditions are the heritage of belief and usage received from the past, and they will be the given for all reform in the future. They reflect the divine realities and, hence, unless reform is to be an impious inversion of the order of the universe, they must be preserved from all attack and erosion. The human exigencies of the moment are always to be measured against these traditions and they are never so peremptory as to justify a revision of them.

In order to understand this conservative frame of reference we must take a further step into Giles's thought to examine the really key concept of providence. Mention has often been made of its importance in discussing individual problems in the course of the book, but we had to wait until all the ground was covered to see how very dominant it is in Giles's thinking. Although he himself at times explicitly pushes this concept to some very single-minded conclusions, as in his theory of the inviolability of the text of Scripture, it often simply lurks in the background as an only partially visible guide-line for the direction his thought is taking.

This world and its history, as he never tires of telling us, are a reflection of the divine being and activity, "*sicut in caelo et in terra.*" What the created universe particularly reflects is the divine harmony, the perfect distribution of parts to whole and the perfect adjustment of even the minutest particulars to the total reality. It is providence which thus harmoniously disposes the universe. Sacred history, especially, is the "*providentiae imago.*" In the history of God's people Giles sees the earthly fulfillment of a heavenly design. He thus easily attributes a sacral character to events of biblical and ecclesiastical history, and he confers upon religious traditions and institutions which appear in this history a value which derives not so much from the particular historical circumstances which produced them as from the fact that they were called into existence by the divine will. These traditions and institutions thus acquire a character and dignity which are rather independent of concrete conditions of time and place.

What we have just been saying, however, seems to contradict our insistence upon Giles's consciousness of history and his care to relate the Church and its institutions to historical reality. We must, therefore, subject this consciousness to examination and try to illustrate the method which was constituent of it and from which resulted his understanding of the nature and meaning of history. In so doing we shall see how decisive his historical consciousness is for his thought on reform and how little relationship it has to the critical study of history which is cultivated today.

Giles regarded history as a sacred vision of the operations of providence, a continuation of the story of God's people whose narrative began in the Old and New Testaments and whose course was revealed to those who properly searched the Scriptures. This vision was not a subject for detached contemplation, but was a practical and prophetic instrument to spur the pope, the emperor and Giles himself to intensified efforts to promote the renewal of the Church. It accepted the view that the Roman Empire marked man's final and definitive political form. For its understanding of the past it relied heavily upon number symbolism and upon Hesiod's scheme for the steady debasing of history's metals. Giles's vision understood the Church's continual decline in history as practically a metaphysical consequence of the increasing chronological distance between it and the age of Christ. The farther the Church receded in time from the source of its life and holiness the more impure and corrupt it must become. Giles identified all these elements with the dispositions of providence and then fitted them upon the historical data he wanted to render intelligible. What we must underscore is that these myths, principles and procedures did not derive from this data and were not particularly subject to modification by it.

The consequences of Giles's method are many. First of all, in spite of his elaborate divisions of the historical past into twenty distinct ages, he really had very little awareness of differentiation in history, except for an illegitimately introduced measure for quantity of religious virtue. The sense of historical perspective which we know today is found in Giles only in rudimentary form and faint adumbration, suggestive though we may see even this to be for the broader question of Renaissance historiography. Giles was conscious of a distance between his age and the normative excellence of antiquity, but he was not conscious of any difference between them which could not be expressed in terms of better and worse. For him, we might say, the past was homogeneously continuous with the present, culturally undifferentiated from it. He was, at best, only peripherally aware of how the Tuscan hermits differed from the order created by the "Great Union" of 1256, of how the economic situation of Sylvester's times differed from that of the Medici's, and of how the political reality of the age of Julius Caesar differed from that of Pope Julius II. From the time of Adam, or at least from the time of Christ, the only spiritually significant changes which had occurred were, broadly speaking, increases or decreases of realities already present in the world, and of these changes the most predominant was a continual decrease in Christian virtue and piety.

Underlying Giles's conservative reform ideology, therefore, was a view of history. This view derived from sources unrelated to the pertinent historical data. It was, as a result, incapable of seeing the actual differentiation in institutions and patterns of life and thought which have characterized different periods of the historical past. More important still, it was incapable of seeing the bearing such differentiation had on the Church, actually altering its structure, functions, problems and needs. Giles viewed the past as a reality homogeneously identifiable with the present. As such, it was as easily known as was the present, and its intellectual recovery or reconstruction presented no particular methodological difficulties. The present's relationship to the past, moreover, could be understood only as a degeneration from it, or as a felicitous continuation, recovery or perfectioning of it. Giles must insist on the restoration of forms, usages, beliefs and traditions from the past. His view of history will not let him do otherwise.

What Giles failed to do was to relativize the past. Due to the methodological limitations of his age he had no really effective tools to expose, for instance, the human conditioning of God's word in Scripture or to show how dependent upon a particular social and political situation was the early marriage of the Church with the empire. The absolutizing of the Hebrew alphabet and language was perhaps the most telling and extreme instance of what was a general tendency in his historical thought. If a reality in the past is not culturally relative, it is culturally absolute. There is no possibility of a critical review of it which will release the present from its authoritative grasp.

Giles's view of certain elements of the past as sacred and humanly unconditioned helps explain how easily he could reconcile intellectual traditions which today we know to be so different from one another. Giles had noble and worthy motives prompting him to seek this fundamental identification, e.g., of the cabala with Christian doctrine and of scholasticism with Ficinian Neoplatonism, but the endeavor was made honest by a view of history which knew no important differentiation in genuine religious truth except that of more and less, of depth and surface. Some of these traditions may have had more truth, some may have had less truth, but none had a different truth.

The *a priori* application to history of beliefs and principles which in themselves had nothing to do with history produced important hermeneutical repercussions, partially insulating Giles from the very data he was trying to understand. Even events to which he was contemporary were filtered through these pre-established interpretative screens. Giles's decrying the collapsed state of the Church in which he lived, for instance, cannot be taken at its literal value. He had neither the method nor the historical perspective to answer the delicate question of how the present condition of the Church compared with any previous condition. The Church was indescribably corrupt and the need for reform was imperatively urgent because the structure he superimposed upon history told him it had to be so.

From Giles's point of view, therefore, what was needed was not to examine the Church's condition but to proclaim its need. For this proclamation Giles had ready to hand a vocabulary of reproach inherited from the Middle Ages. To a metaphysics, or metahistory, of decline was subjoined a saturnine rhetoric of decline, and these together, perhaps as much as actual abuses in the Church, created in Giles a sense of religious tension and expectation which was messianic in its exigency for fulfillment. The darker and more somber were the colors in which the present was painted the more dazzlingly brilliant must the imminent renovation be.

Furthermore, Giles's analysis of the significance of the events of Church history, both those of the past and those of the present, was formulated under the influence of the belief that beneath the ordinary meaning of any sacred word or event lies another more sublime meaning, a meaning hidden in God but also available to certain select initiates. All being and all history is imprinted with the inexhaustible truth of God. By a study of the sacred books and the sacred disciplines God's providential plan of history is revealed. The events of history are thus shown to have a larger meaning than merely human research and study can uncover, and this meaning is disclosed only in the spiritual sense of Scripture, which is unattainable with the merely human tools of grammar and syntax. This hermeneutics, although it did not preclude on Giles's part all valid insight into the problems of his day, certainly tended to fit such insight into an already concluded argument and an already established scheme of history. It also, in effect, dispensed with the need of empirical investigation. Giles was in this way, as well as through his Augustinian and cabalistic illumination, rather effectively shielded from the empirical and was free to construct his picture of the Church and its needs in accordance with his preconceptions and untested intuitions. These preconceptions and intuitions he will in many instances try to correlate with past and present events, but in very few cases have they originated from these events or been checked and ratified by them. Before he examined the evidence Giles was already in a good position to know how badly reform was needed, what were the causes of the abuses, what remedies should be applied to these abuses, and what the final result of the restoration of the Church and the world would be.

Neither the homogeneity of the past nor its decline in virtue from the perfection of the Golden Age of Christ ruled out all dynamism and positive development in sacred history. As a matter of fact, the provision Giles makes for an ever-increasing understanding of doctrine and Scripture is one of the most arresting aspects of his thought. The idea of development, however, is not limited to this area, but is applied to the totality of sacred history, always implying continuity with the past and homogeneous growth. Under the guidance of providence the Church moves from Jerusalem to Rome, and thence expands to envelop Etruria, Italy, Europe and, with the discovery of America, the whole world, just as time itself reaches a great climax and culmination. The present restoration of the Church and the world does not merely reproduce the original state, but amplifies and completes it, in the fulness of time, in the fulness of peoples, in the fulness of doctrine—*plenitudo temporis, plenitudo gentium, plenitudo doctrinae.*

Since Giles makes allowance for such development and since as a Christian he recognizes the existence of sin and abuse, we must ask what norms he provides for knowing if a particular event, doctrine or institution originates and develops in accordance with the genuine designs of providence. How does he discriminate the authentic from the fraudulent? The first and clearest norm he offers is the acceptance and approval of the Church. Enough examples have been adduced in the course of the book to illustrate what Giles means by this norm and the widely ranging scope he gives it, applying it to doctrines and institutions. In some form or other such a principle was operative in all orthodox medieval theology as an unquestioned tenet of Christian belief, and in this instance it demonstrates the controlling and normative function Giles attributes to principles which were associated in his mind with Christian orthodoxy. The regulative function which the Church performs is also the most effective device of which Giles disposes to liberate himself from history's absolutes. Giles's speculations never deprived him of his humanity and his practical sense; he readily concedes to the Church the faculty to dispense from its own discipline and he made ample use of this faculty in his administration of the Augustinian order.

Giles implicitly provides another norm for deciding if something is authentically providential: does it foster the "Christian values," e.g., contemplation, poverty, withdrawal from things of sense, the expansion of the Church, a deeper understanding of Scripture? In the case of philosophy the acid test of its validity and truth is its ability to confirm religious oracles and, especially, to produce virtue and piety in its adherents. All truth is a reflection of subsistent Truth. The attainment of truth, therefore, should bring into conformity with the living Verity not only the intellect but the whole moral and religious pattern of one's life as well. By employing this norm Giles is able to reject Aristotle and embrace the theology of Plato, anticipating the judgment of the Church.

These norms Giles perhaps found adequate to filter out what he knew to be false and fraudulent, but they failed to subordinate and synthesize all that was left. This failure accounts for a number of unresolved ambiguities in his thought. As we have been indicating, Giles's writings are at times tumultuous in this sense, too, as well as in that of a surface organizational disarray. For the various reasons we are trying to make clear, Giles's style of thought encouraged an assembling of different and disparate traditions, and we should hardly be surprised if these did not always blend themselves into easy concord. Some logical inconsistency, or at least curious juxtaposition, was inevitable.

One of the most striking of these juxtapositions derives from the myths and figures of speech Giles uses in speaking of the Church. At one moment the Church is identified with the empire, is centered in the city of Rome and eagerly would assimilate all that the arts of the past and present can offer. At another moment the Church is likened to a hermitage, withdrawn from human society. The apostles are, quite literally, both princes and hermits, and it is not easy to see how these attributes can be reconciled, even granting that the empire of which they are the princes is essentially spiritual. The new Saint Peter's basilica resembles but little the mountain caves of the Church's first age. What is, in other words, the relationship between the Church and the world, and what bearing does this have on Giles's concept of reform?

The oscillation of the Church between hermitage and empire is never quite resolved and reveals Giles's failure to satisfy himself on the relationship between the active and contemplative life as well as on the larger question of the Church and the world. On this latter question the strong unitary emphasis in Giles's thought tends to break down distinctions between the Church and the world, especially as the end of time draws near. With Giles there is no worry that the Church might ultimately be assimilated unto the world and lose its identity, but rather there is the unwavering certainty that the Church eventually will absorb the world and bring all human reality into its own doctrinal and institutional framework. This eschatological resolution, however, does not solve the problem for other, more normal, periods of the Church's history. Needless to say, the question of whether the Church is to withdraw from ordinary human society in studied unconcern for its material fate, or is to attempt to penetrate it, even to the point of assuming to itself contingent features of its culture, is of primary consideration for the orientation of any reform.

Another seemingly curious juxtaposition in Giles's thought is the insertion of sober, prosaic and practical reform measures into a context of historical culmination. His belief that the tenth age had begun does not seem to have affected his attitude towards his reform tasks except to increase his sense of urgency. The best explanation for this contrast of tone between his speculation and his practice is that his conservatism, in the sense we are describing it, came mightily to his aid. In no matter what age or state the Church found itself the reassertion of the rule and traditions of the Augustinian order was the proper way to proceed in the order's reform. Whatever limitations such a concept of reform might have, it at least has the advantage of saving the reformer from the worst excesses of the theological fashion of the moment. In this case Giles's speculations did not interfere with his efforts to simplify the administration of the order and to restore its discipline. His very belief in the suitability of his reform measures for the needs of his age suggests that there was little communication between the two levels at which his thought moved, the practical and the speculative or visionary. Just as his historical vision does not seem to have affected the nature of the measures he adopted, neither did his belief in the appropriateness of these measures penetrate to his speculation to intimate to him that, as his age was not in need of more drastic reform measures than others, it was not incomparably and essentially more corrupt than them, and therefore not more historically climactic.

Perhaps the most ultimately irreconcilable of all Giles's juxtapositions is that of the cabala alongside his detestation for all novelty in theology and doctrine. The introduction of such a potentially revolutionary element as the cabala under the respectable name of a return to the authentic past demonstrates with dramatic clarity how precarious and equivocal such attempted returns can be. Our imagination staggers at the prospect of what the adoption of the cabala would have meant for the subsequent history of western theology.

Without any doubt Giles's views on the nature of providence predisposed him to accept the cabala's method and doctrine, and these views were in turn confirmed and further specified by what the cabala taught. The world and especially the Scriptures were a reflection of the Godhead, incised with inexhaustible and dynamic depth of meaning. By providential necessity not only each verse or word or letter of Scripture but even the least line or dot was of inviolable integrity and bursting with meaning. Christian truth was thus part of the Old Testament, so that Scripture became the providential instrument for the conversion of the Jews, one of the great signs of the final unity towards which the world was tending.

The very vivid and explicit manner in which Giles saw Scripture and the events of history as pregnant with divine meaning directs our attention to what we might describe as the sacral nature of his thought, viewing all created reality as somehow touched by the divine. Giles's deepest concerns were religious. His thought is sacral, therefore, not simply because by education and profession he had been led to read and assimilate works of theology, but because it mirrors and manifests Giles's own personal search for God and his desire to find Him always and everywhere present. Given Giles's hermeneutics and the few and simple norms he has for judging how something may or may not be identifiable with Christian values and beliefs, he is able to roam through all history and the whole corpus of ancient literature to find Christianity there. Giles's attitude towards Plato, the poets and the other religiously acceptable writers of antiquity was formed under the conviction that God was near to all men and guided them, in accordance with His great harmonious governance of the universe. In striking contrast with what has in the past often been characterized as the paganizing tendency of Renaissance humanists, Giles provides an example of the opposite extreme.

It was Giles's sensitivity to the sacral nature of the universe which rendered him hostile to Aristotle. Aristotle rejected providence, thus divesting created reality of its sacred meaning. In the total complex of Giles's thought we can readily see why he found this aspect of the Paduan Aristotle so detestable and frightening. Unlike the Fifth Lateran Council, which fastened onto other questions raised by Paduan Aristotelianism for its criticism and condemnation, Giles singles out this doctrine for his most pointed denunciations. Aristotle, moreover, espoused an epistemology which consecrated a movement of knowledge upwards, from the senses to the intellect, and, hence, he ruled out the necessity of illumination from above by the Sun of Justice. He weakened the moral fabric by counselling the acquisition of wealth, and his natural philosophy focused attention on the things of sense.

The special providence under which the Church lived, as an essentially inerrant and indefectible body, persuaded Giles to accept its judgments on authors and traditions towards which he might not otherwise have been so favorably disposed because of their known contact with Aristotle. The scholastics are the case in point. The Church had approved them, and their doctrine was confirmed by their holy lives. Giles assumes rather than proves that they therefore had purified Aristotle of all that was pernicious.

The Church's prerogatives, doctrinal and other, can be understood in their fulness and richness only when we realize that the Church is the Mystical Body of Christ. As the institutional prolongation of Christ into history the Church enjoys a wisdom and spiritual power analogous to His. The spiritual life of grace flows down into the Church from Christ, and in achieving its religious renewal the Church is set to His pattern: it first must suffer in order to attain its glorious renovation.

Giles's thinking on reform must be seen in the total context of this complete renovation which is prescribed for sacred history. The reform of the Church is not an isolated event effected by human agents through a more or less conscious manipulation of ideas and institutions, but it is an aspect of the general religious renovation towards which history has been tending. All mankind is moving towards a religious climax.

This total renewal, therefore, embraces much more than we would conventionally consider the Church. But in Giles's mind no very clear distinction between the Church and the world was operative in this question. There were, for instance, three distinct revivals of learning and literature, and these all in some way took place within and for the sake of the Church—the revival of theology with Ficino, the revival of scriptural studies with the cabala, and the revival of poetry with Pontano, Poliziano and Sannazzaro. The renewal should touch all reality and be extended to all mankind. What Giles especially hoped for was that the Church would attain the long-promised fulness of time, doctrine and peoples, as all mankind was united into the one flock under the one shepherd.

The unitary aspect of Giles's thought is especially important as applied to Church and reform. On both the doctrinal and institutional level he was against every form of schism and division, and tried to discover factors which could be employed to bring about some sort of intellectual or institutional communion—within the Church and the order, with Plato and the ancients, with the "Greeks," and even with the Jews. He sought to effect this unity by seeing everything revolving around a single pivot which gave form and stability to widely diverging particularities. This pivot was the Roman or Vatican Church.

The holy mount of the Vatican was the geographical and historical center of the Christian world. At the very time when God constituted Jerusalem the holy city for the temporary kingdom of the old Law He was preparing Rome through the Etruscans as the city for the new and eternal Law. The city was sanctified by the life and death of Peter and Paul, and by the holiness which radiated from the tomb of the Prince of the Apostles. The pope was the successor of Peter and the divinely appointed shepherd around whom mankind had been promised to find its spiritual unity. The Church over which he ruled was to extend its imperial sway to the farthest ends of the earth, defeating the Turks and bringing to pass the universalist predictions of Virgil and the Gospel. The emperor, as papal partner and assistant, assured the Church a certain measure of military and political security so that it might operate in full spiritual liberty. The doctrinal orthodoxy of the Roman or Vatican Church was the inerrant and indefectible norm which ensured mankind its intellectual unity in religious truth. The Church itself could never be tainted with heresy in its official teaching, and it had the duty to stamp out all error in those who gathered around it. There would ultimately take place, therefore, the union of all men in one faith and one body, united under one head and centered in one city. The promise and earnest of the past, so obscured in the present, would be fulfilled in the future.

We thus come back once more to the conservative nature of the reform ideology which Giles of Viterbo represents. Certain events, truths and institutions within the context of sacred history have a character which is immune to any intrinsic process and which partakes of the sacral and providential nature of the history in whose course they came into being. These consecrated realities flow from above. There is no method or perspective in Giles's sense of history for relativizing them, nor is there any empirical basis in his epistemology for testing or modifying them. Giles is forced, thus, to a heavy reliance on custom and tradition, forced to take as his norm for distinguishing the authentic from the corrupt a more or less extraneous factor such as supposed antiquity or some form of ecclesiastical approval.

Giles's reform, then, consisted in a reaffirmation and rejuvenation of authentic values and institutions received from the past. Supernatural realities, whether in the realm of ideas, morals or institutions, were somehow absolute, and the idea that they might be reinterpreted for a particular age could only connote that human weakness was being indulged in a manner which was unjustifiable. Instability and change, indeed, were the hallmark of human frailty, and it would be a betrayal of the reformer's mission to base his program on man's weakness. In particular instances, of course, the Church or the order might dispense from the observance of some purely disciplinary regulation, or even abolish a purely disciplinary law. But this did not touch the principle that man was saved by adhering to the stable and eternal values and by doing his best to conform to them. Giles's reform was not conceived as a set of particular measures suited to the specific needs of the sixteenth century. It enunciated an ideal and a program which would be equally valid at any moment of the Church's history. True reform consisted in a resounding reaffirmation and thorough implementation of the ancient customs, the ancient laws, the ancient practices, the ancient beliefs and the ancient traditions.

Giles's belief that the reform of the Church could be effected only by a return to what was ancient and more genuine is a sentiment which surely was not peculiar to himself. It expressed the conviction of his age and, as a naked and abstract proposition, undoubtedly could be subscribed to by many religious reformers even today. There is perhaps a sense in which every religious reform must be a return to the authentic past. The problem today, however, is that we realize with greater keenness than Giles ever did or ever could how difficult such a return is. We realize how difficult authenticity is to discover, how manifold are its possible expressions in history, and how humanly conditioned and culturally relative was even its original articulation. For Giles authenticity was univocal and recoverable, and he lacked our awareness of how ambiguous and elusive it can be.

BIBLIOGRAPHY

This bibliography contains only those works, manuscript and printed, which were cited or referred to in the book. No attempt has been made to list other works which were consulted but not actually used, and far less has any attempt been made to list all the works which conceivably could relate to specific topics touched upon in the course of the book. Since Father Martin is preparing a complete catalogue of Giles's manuscripts and library, I have not undertaken to do that here. Father Martin kindly let me use a preliminary version of that catalogue as a point of departure for my own research. I have acknowledged below each instance in which I am specifically dependent upon it for information.

I. MANUSCRIPT AND ARCHIVAL SOURCES

Évora, Portugal

Biblioteca Pública:

Cod. CXVI/1-30.

"De ecclesiae incremento," 80 fols., oration delivered by Giles in Saint Peter's basilica, December 21, 1507, and later sent as a "*libellus*" to King Manuel I of Portugal, along with an introductory letter. This manuscript was discovered by Father Martin. Fol. 2v is blank; fol. 3 r-v is missing

Florence

Biblioteca Mediceo-Laurenziana:

Cod. Ashb. 287.

"Vita et epistolae Aegidii Cardinalis Viterbiensis ab Henrico Norisio." Eighteen letters (fols. 37r-44v, 57r-58r), including four from Julius II, excerpts from registers, from the "Historia XX saeculorum," etc. The excerpts from the registers were published by Pélissier, "Pour la biographie." See also Martin, "Registers," pp. 151-153; Kristeller, *Iter italicum*, vol. I, p. 84; and Enrico Rostagno, ed., *I codici Ashburnhamiani della R. Biblioteca Medicea Laurenziana di Firenze*, vol. I.5, Rome 1917, pp. 355-357.

Milan

Biblioteca Ambrosiana:

Cod. D. 100 inf.

Latin translation of the Koran along with the Arabic text, a transcription dating from 1621 of two tomes compiled for Giles in Spain in 1518. See Martin, "Egidio da Viterbo," p. 115*.

Munich

Bayerische Staatsbibliothek:

Cod. Lat. 307.

"Nicolaus de Lira, de differentia translationis nostrae ab Hebraica in toto Veteri Testamento," with marginalia by Giles. See Zumkeller, "Manuskripte," p. 67, and Carolus Halm and Georgius Laubmann, eds., *Catalogus codicum Latinorum Bibliothecae Regiae Monacensis*, vol. I.1, Munich 1868, p. 56.

Naples

Biblioteca Nazionale:

Cod. II. F. 7.

"Orphei et aliorum laniamenta," 227 fols., translations and excerpts made for Giles in 1526-1527 by Scutelli; see, e.g., fols. 1r-3v, 184r, 207r, 227r. See Kristeller, *Iter italicum*, vol. I, pp. 409-410.

Cod. V. F. 14.

Three letters from Giles to Julius II and one to Antonio Zocolo, ca. 1506-1510 (fols. 1r-2v). See Kristeller, *Iter italicum*, vol. I, p. 419.

Cod. V. F. 20.

Collection of 239 letters, from, to and about Giles, 1494-1517, with three eclogues, probably the archetype, incomplete, for Ang. Lat. 1001. See Kristeller, *Iter italicum*, vol. I, pp. 419-420. The codex contains 302 fols., not 283 as given by Kristeller. Twenty-five letters from this collection were published in Martène, *Veterum scriptorum collectio*, vol. III, cols. 1233-1268. In *Iter italicum*, vol. II, 1967, p. 548, Kristeller lists codex XIII. AA. 51 as "Letters of Seripando, and of Egidius Viterbiensis (1510)." The shelf number has been changed to XIII. AA. 50, according to the present system of the Biblioteca Nazionale, and the codex contains only one letter of Giles's, 1510, on fol. 55r (unnumbered).

Cod. IX. B. 14.

Autograph of Giles's "Historia XX saeculorum." See Kristeller, *Iter italicum*, vol. I, p. 405; Pélissier, "Manuscrits de Gilles de Viterbe," pp. 239-240, and *De opere historico*. The text of the "Historia" occupies 250 fols. of this codex, in which there are two different numerations. This work, addressed to Leo X, was not begun until after he became pope (e.g., Ang. Lat. 502, fol. 2r), 1513, and was not completed until Giles left for his legateship in Spain and Portugal in 1518 (Ang. Lat. 502, fols. 323v-324r). On fol. 285r of Ang. Lat. 502 Giles gives the year in which he is writing, 1517. Pélissier's dates, 1509-1516, are to be rejected, *De opere historico*, pp. 41-43. Eugenio Massa is preparing an edition of this work. The library has another copy of it, Cod. IX. B. 12, and Zumkeller lists a further copy in Dresden, "Manuskripte," p. 67.

Paris

Bibliothèque Nationale:

Cod. Hébreu 927.

Hebrew translation of some commentaries of Averroes, corresponds to no. 61 of the Ridolfi list published by Astruc and Monfrin, "Livres du Cardinal Gilles," and was presumably owned by Giles. See H. Zotenberg, ed., *Catalogues des manuscrits hébreux et samaritains de la Bibliothèque Impériale*, Paris 1866, p. 162.

Cods. Lat. 527^{1-2}.

"Traductio et expositio librorum Cabalae et Talmudis," autograph; correspond to nos. 2 and 7 of Ridolfi list. See Secret's comments, *Scechina*, vol. I,

pp. 11-12, 15-17, and Ph. Lauer, ed., *Catalogue général des manuscrits latins' Bibliothèque Nationale*, vol. I, Paris 1939, p. 184.
Cod. Lat. 596.
"Glossarium chaldaicae linguae et Cabalae vocabula," autograph in part; corresponds to no. 4 of Ridolfi list. See *Scechina*, vol. I, pp. 18-19, and Lauer, *Catalogue général*, vol. I, p. 212.
Cod. Lat. 598.
"Interpretatio et annotationes in librum decem Sephirot et in libros Cabalae," autograph; corresponds to no. 9 of Ridolfi list. See *Scechina*, vol. I, pp. 12, 18, and Lauer, *Catalogue général*, vol. I, pp. 212-213.
Cod. Lat. 3363.
Pseudo-Joachimite "In Isaiam" (fols. 79r-149r), probably corresponds to no. 21 of Ridolfi list and probably was owned by Giles; and the autograph of Giles's "Scechina," begun in 1530 at the request of Clement VII (table of themes, fols. 154r-156v; letter to Clement VII and text, fols. 157r-349v), published by Secret. See Marie-Thérèse d'Alverny, et al., eds., *Catalogue général des manuscrits latins, Bibliothèque Nationale*, vol. V, Paris 1966, pp. 291-293.
Cod. Lat. 3395.
"Resolutio Lutheriana super propositione sua XIII de potestate papae" (pp. 1-40), corresponds to no. 28 of Ridolfi list and is a copy of Luther's text, *WA*, vol. II, pp. 183-240; and a memorial for Leo X on the Lutheran question, 1521 (fols. 33r-78v, or pp. 43-134), corresponds to no. 29 of Ridolfi list. See d'Alverny, *Catalogue général*, vol. V, pp. 341-342, where the date for the memorial is erroneously given as 1520. For further specific information on this memorial, see my note, p. 18.
Cod. Lat. 3461.
Aleander's "Opusculum super verbis evangelii" (fols. 1r-19v), corresponds to no. 43 of Ridolfi list; see Massa, "Intorno ad Erasmo;" and some sermon notes attributed to Giles (fols. 20r-56r), corresponds to no. 30 of Ridolfi list. See d'Alverny, *Catalogue général*, vol. V, pp. 445-446, where the attribution of the "Opusculum" must be corrected from Giles to Aleander.
Cod. Lat. 6589.
Index to Aristotle and to his errors, composed by Giles (fol. 581r) before he was created a cardinal in 1517; corresponds to no. 11 of Ridolfi list. See *Catalogus codicum manuscriptorum Bibliothecae Regiae*, vol. IV, Paris 1744, p. 260.
Cod. Lat. 7863.
Anonymous "Oratio ad Carolum Caesarem," corresponds to no. 27 of Ridolfi list. See my note, p. 18, and *Catalogus BibliothecaeRegiae*, vol. IV, p. 407.

Rome

Biblioteca Angelica:
Cod. Grec. 102.
Alexander of Aphrodisias's commentary on Aristotle's *Metaphysics*, probably owned or used by Giles. See Martin, "Egidio da Viterbo," p. 36, and Georgius Muccio and Pius Franchi de' Cavalieri, eds., *Index codicum Graecorum Bibliothecae Angelicae*, Florence-Rome 1896, p. 141.
Cod. Lat. 3.
"Dictionarium sive liber radicum, Aegidio Viterbiensi Cardinali interprete," a Latin translation of David Kimhi's Hebrew dictionary, 785 fols. See Pélissier, "Manuscrits," pp. 231-232, and H. Narducci, ed., *Catalogus codicum manuscriptorum praeter Graecos et Orientales in Bibliotheca Angelica olim coenobii Sancti Augustini de Urbe*, vol. I, Rome 1893, p. 1.

Cod. Lat. 351.
Copy of Giles's "Historia XX saeculorum," 399 fols. See Pélissier, *De opere historico*, and "Manuscrits," pp. 238-239; Narducci, *Catalogus*, p. 177.
Cod. Lat. 502.
Copy of Giles's "Historia XX saeculorum." See Pélissier, *De opere historico*, and "Manuscrits," p. 240; Narducci, *Catalogus*, p. 223. The "Historia" ends on fol. 325v, but due to the fact that the folio numeration from 170-179 is repeated, the text actually runs for 335 fols.
Cod. Lat. 688.
Correspondence, 86 letters, principally from Giles to Gabriele della Volta, 1494-1517 (fols. 1r-65r). See Pélissier, "Manuscrits," pp. 235-236, and Narducci, *Catalogus*, p. 292.
Cod. Lat. 762.
Contains ten letters from Giles to Gio. Francesco Libertà and Sebastiano da Rimini, 1528-1531 (fols. 2r-7v). See Pélissier, "Manuscrits," pp. 236-237, and Narducci, *Catalogus*, p. 316.
Cod. Lat. 1001.
Largest collection of Giles's correspondence, in eight books, 1494-1517, along with three eclogues, 314 fols. See Pélissier, "Manuscrits," pp. 237-238, and Narducci, *Catalogus*, pp. 416-418. There are 409 letters in this codex, instead of 369 as indicated by Pélissier.
Cod. Lat. 1118.
"Annales, seu Chronicon ord. Eremit. S. P. Augustini," 1256-1633, 200 fols., including extracts from Giles's registers as prior general (fols. 140r-146r). See Martin, "Registers," p. 151, and Narducci, *Catalogus*, p. 471.
Cod. Lat. 1156.
"De Ilicetana familia," composed by Giles probably before June of 1506, published by Martin, "Giles and Lecceto," pp. 248-253. The text and the letter of Fra Basilio to Pietro Soderini occupy ten folios. See Pélissier, "Manuscrits," pp. 228-231, and Narducci, *Catalogus*, p. 487. This same work is to be found in Naples V. F. 20, fols. 123r-125v, 127v-131r, and Ang. Lat. 1001, fols. 105v-111v.
Cod. Lat. 1170.
Correspondence, 65 letters, mostly from Giles to Stefano Zoalio, 1507-1517 (fols. 18r-46v, 90v-91r), eight of which were published by Pazzaglia, "Lettere inedite." See Pélissier, "Manuscrits," pp. 234-235, and Narducci, *Catalogus*, pp. 489-490.
Cod. Lat. 1244.
Translations of Origen, etc., made for Giles in 1512, fol. 151r. See Pélissier, "Manuscrits," pp. 233-234, and Narducci, *Catalogus*, pp. 526-527. This codex contains 151 fols., not 280 which Pélissier indicates. See Wind, "Revival," pp. 416-418.
Cod. SS. 11.11(4).
Some notes on Arabic grammar (fols. 26r-41r), composed at Giles's request, fol. 26r. See Martin, "Egidio da Viterbo," p. 115*.

Augustinian General Archives.
Cod. Cc. 37.
"Eremitarum vita" (fols. 112r-116r), Giles's outline history of eremitical life.
Cod. Dd. 12.
Register of Giles's generalship, 1514-1518. See Martin, "Registers," pp. 147-148. On Dd. 11 and Ff. 1, see *ibid.*, pp. 148-155.

Siena

Biblioteca Comunale:

Cod. G. X. 26.

The only surviving collection of Giles's correspondence as prior general, some 245 letters and fragments of letters from Giles, 1506-1517, 331 pp. See Kristeller, *Iter italicum*, vol. II, p. 164. Of the letters published by Signorelli in "Appendice I" of his *Egidio da Viterbo*, thirty-five are from this codex.

Vatican City

Biblioteca Apostolica Vaticana:

Cod. Barb. Grec. 62.

"Iamblichi de mysteriis liber," with marginalia by Giles, e.g., fol. 102v. See Valentinus Capocci, ed., *Codices Barberiniani Graeci*, vol. I, Vatican City 1958, pp. 64-65.

Cod. Barb. Lat. 322.

"Porphyrii ... ansae ad rerum divinarum captum" (fols. 133r-144r), done by Scutelli at Giles's wish in 1526, fol. 144r. See Kristeller, *Iter italicum*, vol. II, p. 458, where the fols. are mistakenly given as 138-149.

Cod. Neofiti 1.

Palestinian Targum to the Pentateuch. See Diez-Macho, "Una copia del Targum," and the other articles referred to in my note, p. 88, of chapter three.

Cod. Ottob. Lat. 1786.

"Omnis Graecorum theologiae tabula et in Iamblichum De mysteriis Aegyptorum," excerpts collected by Scutelli at Giles's wish, 1526-1527, as indicated on fols. 1r-3r. See Kristeller, *Iter italicum*, vol. II, p. 419, and Giovanni Card. Mercati, *Codici latini Pico Grimani Pio*, *StT* vol. LXXV, Vatican City 1938, p. 255n. I am indebted to Father Martin for the reference to Mercati.

Cod. Ross. 412.

Greek text of Aristotle's *Nicomachean Ethics*. This codex belonged to Niccolò Perotti (1429-1480), and then to Giles. See Kristeller, *Iter italicum*, vol. II, p. 465, as well as the two studies by Giovanni Mercati, *Per la chronologia della vita e degli scritti di Niccolò Perotti*, *StT* vol. XLIV, Rome 1925, p. 130, and *Note per la storia di alcune biblioteche Romane nei secoli XVI-XIX*, *StT* vol. CLXIV, Vatican City 1952, p. 31. I am indebted to Father Martin for the references to Mercati.

Cod. Ross. 558.

Greek text of some works of Plato, possibly owned by Giles. See Mercati, *Note per la storia*, pp. 35-36.

Cod. Ross. 962.

Greek text of Proclus's commentary on Plato's *Alcibiades*, possibly owned by Giles. See Mercati, *Note per la storia*, pp. 36-37.

Cod. Vat. Grec. 237.

"Procli Diadochi" (fols. 76r-317r), with marginalia by Giles according to Martin, "Egidio da Viterbo," p. 113*. See Iohannes Mercati and Pius Franchi de' Cavalieri, eds., *Codices Vaticani Graeci*, vol. I, Rome 1923, pp. 303-304.

Cod. Vat. Lat. 3146.

A version, probably preliminary, of Giles's "Libellus de litteris Hebraicis" (fols. 1r-26v) and seventeen letters from Giles (fols. 27r-37v), ca. 1515-1516. See Secret's comment, *Scechina*, vol. I, p. 23n, and Kristeller, *Iter italicum*, vol. II, p. 359. In *Iter italicum*, vol. II, p. 478, Kristeller describes codex R. V. b. of the Fondo Chigi as "Letters by Aegidius Viterbiensis, Lelio Torelli, Donato Giannotti, Nic. Machiavelli and others." The codex in question, however, does not contain these letters, and I was unable to locate the one which presumably does.

Cod. Vat. Lat. 5567.

Petrus Galatinus's "Commentaria in Apocalypsim." See Kristeller, *Iter italicum*, vol. II, p. 334.

Cod. Vat. Lat. 5808.

Copy of the "Libellus de litteris Hebraicis," published by Secret. See Secret's comment, *Scechina*, vol. I, p. 23n, and Kristeller, *Iter italicum*, vol. II, p. 335.

Cod. Vat. Lat. 6325.

Copy of Giles's "Sententiae ad mentem Platonis," 216 fols., commentary on the first seventeen distinctions of the first book of Peter Lombard's *Sentences*. Giles was working on this text at least by 1510, and did not lay it aside, incomplete, until at least 1512 (fols. 122v, 195v, 205r). Eugenio Massa, who is preparing an edition of this work, published an excerpt from it (fols. 49v-79v) in *I fondamenti metafisici e testi inediti*, pp. 54-110. For descriptions of this manuscript and of other copies of this same work, see *ibid.*, pp. 49-53. See also Kristeller, *Iter italicum*, vol.II, p. 380, and Paquier, "Un essai de théologie platonicienne." Massa's excerpt is based on Vat. Lat. 6325, Ang. Lat. 636,, Naples VIII. F. 8 and Naples X VI. H. 71.

II. PRINTED WORKS

"Acta capituli generalis Venetiis celebrati an. 1519," *Analecta Augustiniana* 9(1921-1922), pp. 31-39.

Adams, Robert P., "Erasmus' Ideas of his Rôle as a Social Critic ca. 1480-1500," *Renaissance News* 11(1958), pp. 11-16.

Alciato, Andrea, *Le lettere di Andrea Alciato giureconsulto*, ed. Gian Luigi Barni, Florence 1953.

Aleander, Girolamo, *Lettres familières de Jérome Aléandre (1510-1540)*, ed. Jules Paquier, Paris 1909.

Alphandéry, P., and Dupront, A., *La chrétienté et l'idée de croisade*, 2 vols., Paris 1954 and 1959.

d'Alverny, Marie-Thérèse, "Quelques aspects du symbolisme de la 'Sapientia' chez les humanistes," *Umanesimo e Esoterismo: Archivio di Filosofia* (1960), pp. 321-333.

Anichini, G., *L'Umanesimo e il problema della salvezza in Marsilio Ficino*, Milan 1937.

Annio da Viterbo (Nanni, Giovanni, O. P.), *Berosi sacerdotis Chaldaici antiquitatum libri quinque*, Wittenberg 1659.

— *Glosa [sic] sive expositio super Apocalypsim*, Cologne 1531.

Antoninus of Florence, Saint, *Chronicorum opus*, ed. Petrus Maturus, S. J., 3 vols., Lyons 1586.

Arbesmann, Rudolph, O.S.A., "Henry of Freimar's 'Treatise on the Origin and Development of the Order of the Hermit Friars, and of its True and Real Title,'" *Augustiniana* 6(1956), pp. 37-145.

Aristotelismo padovano e filosofia aristotelica, Atti del XII congresso internazionale di filosofia, vol IX, Florence 1960.

Astruc, Charles, and Monfrin, Jacques, "Livres latins et hébreux du Cardinal Gilles de Viterbe," *Bibliothèque d'Humanisme et Renaissance* 23(1961), pp. 551-554.

Augustine, Saint, *Opera omnia*, 12 vols., *MPL* vols. XXXII-XLVII, Paris 1861-1862.

— *Regula beati Augustini*, Venice 1508.

Balan, P., *Monumenta reformationis Lutheranae*, Ratisbon 1884.

Baron, Hans, "Franciscan Poverty and Civic Wealth in Humanistic Thought," *Speculum* 13(1938), pp. 1-37.
Bataillon, M., *Érasme et l'Espagne*, Paris 1937.
— "Évangélisme et millénarisme au Nouveau Monde," *Courants religieux et Humanisme à la fin du XV et au début du XVI siècle: Colloque de Strasbourg, 1957*, Paris 1959, pp. 25-36.
Battisti, Eugenio, "Il significato simbolico della Cappella Sistina," *Commentari* 8 (1957), pp. 96-104.
Bembo, Pietro, *Epistolarum Leonis decimi pontificis maximi nomine scriptarum libri sexdecim*, Venice 1535.
Benz, Ernst, *Die christliche Kabbala: Ein Stiefkind der Theologie*, Zurich 1958.
— *Ecclesia spiritualis*, Stuttgart 1964 (photo-reprint of the original 1934 edition).
Bernard, Saint, *Opera omnia*, vol. I, *MPL* vol. CLXXXII, Paris 1879.
Bessarion, *In calumniatorem Platonis*, Venice 1503.
Biblia sacra cum glossa interlineari ordinaria et Nicolai Lyrani postilla, vol. III, Venice 1588.
Blau, Joseph, *The Christian Interpretation of the Cabala in the Renaissance*, New York 1944.
Bloch, Renée, "Écriture et tradition dans le Judaïsme," *Cahiers Sioniens* 8(1954), pp. 9-34.
Bloomfield, M. W., "Joachim of Flora: A Critical Survey of His Canon, Teachings, Sources, Biography and Influence," *Traditio* 13(1957), pp. 249-311.
Boas, George, *Essays on Primitivism and Related Ideas in the Middle Ages*, Baltimore 1948.
Boccaccio, Giovanni, *Genealogie deorum gentilium libri*, ed. Vincenzo Romano, 2 vols., Bari 1951.
Böhmer, Heinrich, *Luthers Romfahrt*, Leipzig 1914.
Bouwsma, William J., *Concordia Mundi*, Cambridge, Mass. 1957.
— "Postel and the Significance of Renaissance Cabalism," *Journal of the History of Ideas* 15(1954), pp. 218-232.
Bruni, G., "Egidio Romano antiaverroista," *Sophia* 1(1933), pp. 208-219.
Calcagnini, Celio, *Opera aliquot*, Basel 1544.
Cantimori, Delio, "Anabattismo e Neoplatonismo nel XVI secolo in Italia," *Reale Accademia Nazionale dei Lincei, Rendiconti, Classe di scienze morali, storiche e filologiche*, serie VI, 12(1936), pp. 521-561.
— *Eretici italiani del Cinquecento*, Florence 1939.
Cassirer, Ernst, "Giovanni Pico della Mirandola: A Study in the History of Renaissance Ideas," *Journal of the History of Ideas* 3(1942), pp. 123-144, 319-346.
Cassuto, U., *Gli ebrei a Firenze*, Florence 1918.
Centi, T. M., O.P., "L'attività letteraria di Santi Pagnini (1470-1536) nel campo delle scienze bibliche," *AFP* 15(1945), pp. 5-51.
de Certeau, Michel, S.J., "L'épreuve du temps," *Christus* 13(1966), pp. 311-331.
Chastel, André, "L'Antéchrist à la Renaissance," *Cristianesimo e Ragion di Stato; L'Umanesimo e il Demoniaco nell'arte*, Atti del II congresso internazionale di studi umanistici, ed. Enrico Castelli, Rome 1953, pp. 177-186.
— *Art et Humanisme à Florence au temps de Laurent le Magnifique*, Paris 1961.
Chenu, M.-D., O.P., *La théologie au douzième siècle*, Paris 1957.
Codex iuris canonicis, Città del Vaticano 1963.
Cohn, Norman, *The Pursuit of the Millennium*, London 1962.
Conciliorum oecumenicorum decreta, eds. Joseph Alberigo, et al., Rome 1962.
Congar, Yves M.-J., O.P., *Vraie et fausse réforme dans l'église*, Paris 1950.
Corsano, A., *Il pensiero religioso italiano dall'Umanesimo al Giurisdizionalismo*, Bari 1937.

Crouzel, H., "Pic de la Mirandole et Origène," "*Bulletin de littérature ecclésiastique* 66(1965), pp. 81-106, 272-288.
Dagens, J., "Humanisme et évangélisme chez Lefèvre d'Étaples," *Courants religieux et Humanisme à la fin du XV et au début du XVI siècle: Colloque de Strasbourg, 1957*, Paris 1959, pp. 121-134.
Daniélou, Jean, S.J., "Aux sources de l'ésotérisme judéo-chrétien," *Umanesimo e Esoterismo: Archivio di Filosofia* (1960), pp. 39-46.
Dannenfeldt, Karl H., "Egypt and Egyptian Antiquities in the Renaissance," *Studies in the Renaissance* 6(1959), pp. 7-27.
— "The Pseudo-Zoroastrian Oracles in the Renaissance," *Studies in the Renaissance* 4(1957), pp. 7-30.
— "The Renaissance Humanists and the Knowledge of Arabic," *Studies in the Renaissance* 2(1955), pp. 96-117.
"De capitulis generalibus ordinis tempore Aegidii Viterbiensis celebratis," *Analecta Augustiniana* 9(1921-1922), pp. 171-182.
Deneffe, A., "Die Absicht des V. Laterankonzils," *Schol.* 8(1933), pp. 359-379.
Diez-Macho, Alejandro, "Una copia completa del Targum Palestinense al Pentateuco en la Biblioteca Vaticana," *Sefarad* 17(1957), pp. 119-121.
Douglas, Richard M., *Jacopo Sadoleto (1477-1547): Humanist and Reformer*, Cambridge, Mass. 1959.
Duhem, P., *Le système du monde*, vol. V, Paris 1917.
Dupront, Alphonse, "Croisades et eschatologie," *Umanesimo e Esoterismo: Archivio di Filosofia* (1960), pp. 175-198.
Eliade, Mircea, *The Sacred and the Profane: The Nature of Religion*, New York 1961.
Epstein, Isidore, *Judaism*, Baltimore 1964.
Erasmus, Desiderius, *Opus epistolarum Des. Erasmi Roterodami*, eds. P. S. Allen and H. M. Allen, 12 vols., Oxford 1906-1958.
Erasmus, H. J., *The Origins of Rome in Historiography from Petrarch to Perizonius*, Assen 1962.
Ermini, Giuseppe, ed., *L'attesa dell'età nuova nella spiritualità della fine del medioevo*, Todi 1962.
Eusebius of Caesarea, *De evangelii praeparatione*, *Georgio Trapezuntio interprete*, in *Opera omnia*, Basel 1542.
Faber, Johann, *Opus adversus nova quaedam et a Christiana religione prorsus aliena dogmata Martini Lutheri*, Rome 1522.
Felice da Prato, *Psalterium*, Venice 1515.
Ferguson, Wallace K., *The Renaissance in Historical Thought*, Cambridge, Mass. 1948.
Ficino, Marsilio, *Opera omnia*, 2 vols., Basel 1576.
Filalteo, L. (Maggi, Lucillo), *Philaltei libri tres epistolarum*, Pavia 1564.
Fiorentino, F., "Egidio da Viterbo e i Pontaniani di Napoli," *Archivio storico per le province napoletane* 9(1884), pp. 430-452.
Fischel, Oskar, *Raphael*, trans. Bernard Rackham, 2 vols., London 1948.
Folz, R., *L'idée d'Empire en Occident du V au XIV siècle*, Paris 1953.
Garin, Eugenio, *La cultura filosofica del Rinascimento italiano*, Florence 1961.
— "Cusano e i Platonici italiani del Quattrocento," in *Nicolò da Cusa: Convegno interuniversitario, 1960*, Florence 1962, pp. 75-100.
— "La 'dignitas hominis' e la letteratura patristica," *La Rinascita* no. 4, 1(1938), pp. 102-146.
— *Italian Humanism: Philosophy and Civic Life*, trans. Peter Munz, New York 1965.
Geiger, Ludwig, *Johann Reuchlin: Sein Leben und seine Werke*, Leipzig 1871.
Gesamtkatolog der Wiegendrucke, 7 vols., Leipzig 1925-1938.
Giles of Rome, *De ecclesiastica potestate*, ed. Richard Scholz, Weimar 1929.
— *Egidii Romani comentaria in VIII libros physicorum Aristotelis*, Padua 1493.

— *Egidii Romani eremite de materia celi questio, Egidii Romani de intellectu possibili contra Averoim questio aurea*, Padua 1493.
— *Giles of Rome: Errores philosophorum*, ed. Josef Koch, trans. John O. Riedl, Milwaukee 1944.
— *Primus tomus operum D. Aegidii Romani*, Rome 1555.
— *Primus Sententiarum*, Venice 1521.
Giles of Viterbo, "Lettere inedite del Card. Egidio Canisio [sic] Viterbese," ed. Fiovo Giuseppe Pazzaglia, Rome 1915.
— "Oratio habita post tertiam sacri Lateranensis concilii sessionem," Rome 1512 (?).
— *Scechina e Libellus de litteris Hebraicis*, ed. François Secret, 2 vols., Rome 1959.
Gillet, Robert, O.S.B., "Temps et exemplarisme chez saint Augustin," *Augustinus Magister*, vol. II, Paris 1955, pp. 933-941.
Gilmore, Myron P., *Humanists and Jurists*, Cambridge, Mass. 1963.
Gilson, Étienne, "Autour de Pomponazzi," *AHDL* 28(1961), pp. 163-279.
— "Cajetan et l'Humanisme théologique," *AHDL* 22(1955), pp. 113-136.
— "Marsile Ficin et le *Contra Gentiles*," *AHDL* 24(1957), pp. 101-113.
Giovio, Paolo, *Elogia doctorum virorum*, Antwerp 1557.
Golzio, Vincenzo, *Raffaello*, Città del Vaticano 1936.
Gombrich, E. H., "Renaissance and Golden Age," *Journal of the Warburg and Courtauld Institutes* 24(1961), pp. 306-309.
Graf, Arturo, *Roma nella memoria e nelle immaginazioni del medio evo*, Turin 1915.
Grant, R. M., *Gnosticism and Early Christianity*, New York 1959.
Gregory of Rimini, *Gregorius de Arimino in primo et secundo Sententiarum*, Venice 1503.
Guasti, Cesare, *I manoscritti Torrigiani donati al R. Archivio di Stato di Firenze*, Florence 1878.
Guglia, E., "Studien zur Geschichte des 5. Lateranconcils," *SAW* phil-hist. Cl., no. 10, 140(1899), and no. 3, 152(1906).
— "Die Türkenfrage auf dem Laterankonzil," *MIÖG* 21(1900), pp. 679-691.
Guitton, J., *Le temps et l'éternité chez Plotin et Saint Augustin*, Paris 1933.
Gundersheimer, Werner L., "Erasmus, Humanism, and the Christian Cabala," *Journal of the Warburg and Courtauld Institutes* 26(1963), pp. 38-52.
Gutiérrez, David, O.S.A., "Al margen de libros y artículos acerca de Lutero," *La ciudad de Dios* 169(1956), pp. 609-637.
Halecki, Oscar, "The Defense of Europe in the Renaissance Period," *Didascaliae: Studies in Honor of Anselm M. Albareda*, ed. Sesto Prete, New York 1961, pp. 123-146.
Hay, Denys, "Italy and Barbarian Europe," *Italian Renaissance Studies: A Tribute to the Late Cecilia M. Ady*, ed. E. F. Jacob, London 1960, pp. 48-68.
Headley, John M., *Luther's View of Church History*, New Haven 1963.
Hodius (Hody), Humfredus, *De bibliorum textibus originalibus libri IV*, Oxford 1705.
Hopper, V. F., *Medieval Number Symbolism*, New York 1938.
Huntley, G. Haydn, *Andrea Sansovino*, Cambridge, Mass. 1935.
Ilardi, Vincent, "'Italianità' among Some Italian Intellectuals in the Early Sixteenth Century," *Traditio* 12(1956), pp. 339-367.
Jedin, Hubert, *Girolamo Seripando: Sein Leben und Denken im Geisteskampf des 16 Jahrhunderts*, 2 vols., Würzburg 1937.
— *A History of the Council of Trent*, trans. Ernest Graf, O.S.B., 2 vols., New York 1957 and 1961.
— *Kirche des Glaubens: Kirche der Geschichte*, 2 vols., Vienna 1966.
— "Die römischen Augustinerquellen zu Luthers Frühzeit," *ARG* 25(1928), pp. 256-270.

— "Vincenzo Quirini und Pietro Bembo," *Miscellanea Giovanni Mercati,* vol. IV, *StT* vol. CXXIV, Città del Vaticano 1946, pp. 407-424.

Joachim of Flora, *Expositio magni prophete Abbatis Ioachim in Apocalipsim,* Venice 1527.

Julius II, "Nonnulla Iulii Papae II brevia Aegidio Viterbiensi directa," *Analecta Augustiniana* 9(1921-1922), pp. 17-20.

Jung, Eva-Maria, "On the Nature of Evangelism in Sixteenth-Century Italy," *Journal of the History of Ideas* 14(1953), pp. 511-527.

Justin Martyr, *Iustini philosophi et martyris opera,* ed. J. von Otto, 3rd ed., vol. I.1, Jena 1875.

Kahle, Paul, *The Cairo Geniza,* 2nd ed., Oxford 1959.

— "Zwei durch Humanisten besorgte dem Papst gewidmete Ausgaben der hebräischen Bibel," *Essays Presented to Leo Baeck,* London 1954, pp. 50-74.

Kalkoff, P., *Forschungen zu Luthers römischem Prozess,* Rome 1905.

Kawerau, D. G., "Aus den Actis generalatus Aegidii Viterbiensis," *ZKG* 32(1911), pp. 603-606.

Kleinhans, Arduinus, O.F.M., "De vita et operibus P. Galatini, O.F.M., scientiarum biblicarum cultoris," *Antonianum* 1(1926), pp. 145-179, 327-356.

Kolde, T., "Luther und sein Ordensgeneral in Rom in den Jahren 1518 und 1520," *ZKG* 2(1878), pp. 472-480.

Konrad, Robert, "Das himmlische und das irdische Jerusalem im mittelalterlichen Denken," *Speculum historiale: Festschrift Johannes Spörl,* eds. Clemens Bauer, et al., Munich 1965, pp. 523-540.

Kristeller, Paul Oskar, "Francesco da Diacceto and Florentine Platonism in the Sixteenth Century," *Miscellanea Giovanni Mercati,* vol. IV, *StT* vol. CXXIV, Città del Vaticano 1946, pp. 260-304.

— *Iter italicum,* 2 vols., Leiden 1963 and 1967.

— "Paduan Averroism and Alexandrism in the Light of Recent Studies," *Aristotelismo padovano e filosofia aristotelica,* Florence 1960, pp. 147-156.

— *Il pensiero filosofico di Marsilio Ficino,* Florence 1953.

— "The Platonic Academy of Florence," *Renaissance News* 14(1961), pp. 147-159.

— "The Scholastic Background of Marsilio Ficino," *Traditio* 2(1944), pp. 257-318.

— "Sebastiano Salvini, a Florentine Humanist and Theologian, and a Member of Marsilio Ficino's Platonic Academy," *Didascaliae: Studies in Honor of Anselm M. Albareda,* ed. Sesto Prete, New York 1961, pp. 207-243.

— *Supplementum Ficinianum,* 2 vols., Florence 1937.

— *Le Thomisme et la pensée italienne de la Renaissance,* Montreal 1967.

— "Two Unpublished Questions on the Soul of Pietro Pomponazzi," *Medievalia et Humanistica* 8(1955), pp. 76-101.

Kuiters, R., O.S.A., "The Development of the Theological School of Aegidius Romanus in the Order of Saint Augustine," *Augustiniana* 4(1954), pp. 157-177.

Lactantius, *De ira Dei,* ed. Samuel Brandt, *CSEL* vol. XXVII, Vienna 1893.

Ladner, Gerhart B., *The Idea of Reform: Its Impact on Christian Thought and Action in the Age of the Fathers,* Cambridge, Mass. 1959.

— "Die mittelalterliche Reform-Idee und ihr Verhältnis zur Idee der Renaissance," *MIÖG* 60(1952), pp. 31-59.

— "Two Gregorian Letters: On the Sources and Nature of Gregory VII's Reform Ideology," *Studi Gregoriani* 5(1956), pp. 221-242.

— "Vegetation Symbolism and the Concept of Renaissance," *De artibus opuscula XL: Essays in Honor of Erwin Panofsky,* ed. Millard Meiss, vol. I, New York 1961, pp. 303-322.

Landgraf, Artur Michael, *Dogmengeschichte der Frühscholastik*, 4 vols. (8 parts), Regensburg 1952-1956.

Leo X, "Breve Leonis Papae X quo indulgentiam plenariam concedit eleemosynas praebentibus," *Analecta Augustiniana* 9(1921-1922), pp. 26-28.

— "Brevia aliquot Leonis X Aegidio Viterbiensi directa," *Analecta Augustiniana* 9(1921-1922), pp. 21-26.

Letters and Papers, Foreign and Domestic, of the Reign of Henry VIII, ed. J. S. Brewer, vol. III. 2, London 1867.

Levi, Anthony, S.J., *French Moralists: The Theory of the Passions (1585-1649)*, Oxford 1964.

Levita, Elijah, *Massoreth Ha-Massoreth*, ed. and trans. C. D. Ginsburg, London 1867.

von Leyden, W., "Antiquity and Authority: A Paradox in the Renaissance Theory of History," *Journal of the History of Ideas* 19(1958), pp. 473-492.

Lombard, Peter, *Libri IV sententiarum*, eds. Patres collegii S. Bonaventurae, 2 vols., Quaracchi 1916.

Lonergan, Bernard J. F., S.J., "Existenz and Aggiornamento," *Focus* 2(1965), pp. 5-14.

Lovejoy, Arthur O., and Boas, George, *Primitivism and Related Ideas in Antiquity*, Baltimore 1935.

de Lubac, Henri, S.J., "A propos de la formule: Diversi, sed non adversi," *RechSR* 40(1951-1952), pp. 27-40.

— *Exégèse médiévale*, 2 vols. (4 parts), Paris 1959-1964.

— "Les humanistes chrétiens du XV-XVI siècle et l'herméneutique traditionelle," *Ermeneutica e Tradizione: Archivio di Filosofia* (1963), pp. 173-182.

Luther, Martin, *D. Martin Luthers Werke: Kritische Gesamtausgabe*, vols. I, II, III, VII, Weimar 1883, 1884, 1885, 1897.

— *D. Martin Luthers Werke: Kritische Gesamtausgabe: Tischreden*, vols. II and III, Weimar 1913 and 1914.

McNamara, Martin, M.S.C., "Targumic Studies," *CBQ* 28(1966), pp. 1-19.

Mansi, Joannes Dominicus, ed., *Sacrorum conciliorum nova et amplissima collectio*, vol. XXXII, Paris 1902.

Marrou, Henri-Irénée, *Saint Augustin et la fin de la culture antique*, 4th ed., Paris 1958.

Martène, E., and Durand, U., *Veterum scriptorum et monumentorum historicorum, dogmaticorum, moralium amplissima collectio*, vol. III, Paris 1724.

Martin, Francis X., O.S.A., "The Augustinian Order on the Eve of the Reformation," *Miscellanea historiae ecclesiasticae*, vol. II (Bibliothèque de la Revue d'histoire ecclésiastique, Fascicule 44), Louvain 1967, pp. 71-104.

— "Egidio da Viterbo, 1469-1518: A Study in Renaissance and Reform History," unpublished doctoral dissertation, Cambridge University 1958.

— "Giles of Viterbo and the Monastery of Lecceto: The Making of a Reformer," *Analecta Augustiniana* 25(1962), pp. 225-253.

— "The Problem of Giles of Viterbo: A Historiographical Survey," *Augustiniana* 9(1959), pp. 357-379; 10(1960), pp. 43-60.

— "The Registers of Giles of Viterbo," *Augustiniana* 12(1962), pp. 142-160.

Martin, M. FitzMaurice, "The Palaeographical Character of Codex Neofiti 1," *Textus* 3(1963), pp. 1-35.

Massa, Eugenio, "Egidio da Viterbo e la metodologia del sapere nel Cinquecento," *Pensée humaniste et tradition chrétienne aux XV et XVI siècles*, ed. H. Bédarida, Paris 1950, pp. 185-239.

— "Egidio da Viterbo, Machiavelli, Lutero e il pessimismo cristiano," *Umanesimo e Machiavellismo: Archivio di Filosofia* (1949), pp. 75-123.

— *I fondamenti metafisici della 'dignitas hominis' e testi inediti di Egidio da Viterbo*, Turin 1954.
— "Intorno ad Erasmo: Una polemica che si credeva perduta," *Classical, Medieval and Renaissance Studies in Honor of Berthold Louis Ullman*, ed. Charles Henderson, Jr., vol. II, Rome 1964, pp. 435-454.
Merzbacher, F., "Wandlungen des Kirchenbegriffs im Spätmittelalter," *ZSavRG*, kan. Abt. 39(1953), pp. 274-361.
Momigliano, Arnaldo, "Time in Ancient Historiography," *History and Theory* 5(1966, Beiheft 6), pp. 1-23.
Mommsen, T., "Saint Augustine and the Christian Idea of Progress," *Journal of the History of Ideas* 12(1951), pp. 346-374.
Monnerjahn, E., *Giovanni Pico della Mirandola*, Wiesbaden 1960.
di Napoli, Giovanni, *Giovanni Pico della Mirandola e la problematica dottrinale del suo tempo*, Rome 1965.
— *L'immortalità dell'anima nel Rinascimento*, Turin 1963.
Nardi, Bruno, *Saggi sull'Aristotelismo padovano dal secolo XIV al XVI*, Florence 1958.
— *Studi su Pietro Pomponazzi*, Florence 1965.
Nicholas of Cusa, *De pace fidei*, eds. Raymond Klibansky and Hildebrand Bascour, O.S.B., *Opera omnia*, vol. VII (Heidelberg), Hamburg 1959.
Oberman, Heiko A., "'Facientibus Quod in Se est Deus Non Denegat Gratiam,' Robert Holcot, O.P., and the Beginnings of Luther's Theology," *HThR* 55(1962), pp. 317-342.
— *The Harvest of Medieval Theology*, Cambridge, Mass. 1963.
Offelli, Siro, "Il pensiero del concilio Lateranense V sulla dimostrabilità razionale dell'immortalità dell'anima umana," *Studia patavina* 2(1955), pp. 3-17.
O'Malley, John W., S.J., "Giles of Viterbo: A Reformer's Thought on Renaissance Rome," *Renaissance Quarterly* (formerly *Renaissance News*) 20(1967), pp. 1-11.
— "Giles of Viterbo: A Sixteenth-Century Text on Doctrinal Development," *Traditio* 22(1966), pp. 445-450.
— "Historical Thought and the Reform Crisis of the Early Sixteenth Century," *ThSt* 28(1967), pp. 531-548.
— "A Note on Gregory of Rimini: Church, Scripture, Tradition," *Augustinianum* 5(1965), pp. 365-378.
Ossinger, J. F., *Bibliotheca Augustiniana*, Ingolstadt 1768.
Paquier, Jules, "Un essai de théologie platonicienne à la Renaissance: le commentaire de Gilles de Viterbe sur le premier livre des Sentences," *RechSR* 13 (1923), pp. 293-312, 419-436.
Pastor, Ludwig, *The History of the Popes*, eds. F. I. Antrobus and Francis Ralph Kerr, 14 vols., London 1923.
Patrides, C. A., "'The Bloody and Cruell Turke': The Background of a Renaissance Commonplace," *Studies in the Renaissance* 10(1963), pp. 126-135.
Pélissier, L.-G., *De opere historico Aegidii Cardinalis Viterbiensis*, Montpellier 1896.
— "Manuscrits de Gilles de Viterbe à la Bibliothèque Angélique," *Revue des bibliothèques* 2(1892), pp. 228-240.
— "Pour la biographie du Cardinal Gilles de Viterbe," *Miscellanea di studi critici edita in onore di Arturo Graf*, Bergamo 1903, pp. 789-815.
Percopo, Erasmo, *Vita di Giovanni Pontano*, Naples 1938.
Perez de Valencia, Jacobus, *Centum ac quinquaginta psalmi Davidici*, Lyons 1517.
Pico della Mirandola, Giovanni, *De hominis dignitate, Heptaplus, De ente et uno*, ed. and trans. Eugenio Garin, Florence 1942.
— *Opera omnia*, Venice 1557.
Pieper, Josef, "The Concept of Tradition," *The Review of Politics* 20(1958), pp. 465-491.

Pontano, Giovanni, *I dialoghi*, ed. Carmelo Previtera, Florence 1943.
— *Lettere di Giovanni Pontano a principi ed amici*, ed. Erasmo Percopo, Naples 1907.
Pratt, Kenneth J., "Rome as Eternal," *Journal of the History of Ideas* 26(1965), pp. 25-44.
Preuss, Hans, *Die Vorstellungen vom Antichrist im späteren Mittelalter, bei Luther und in der konfessionellen Polemik*, Leipzig 1906.
Proclus, *The Elements of Theology: A Revised Text with Translation, Introduction and Commentary*, ed. and trans. E. R. Dodds, 2nd ed., Oxford 1963.
Rahner, Hugo, S.J., *Greek Myths and Christian Mystery*, trans. Brian Battershaw, London 1963.
Randall, John Herman, Jr., *The School of Padua and the Emergence of Modern Science*, Padua 1961.
Raynaldi, O. (Rinaldi, Odorico), *Annales ecclesiastici*, vol. XI, Lucca 1754.
Reeves, Marjorie, "The Abbot Joachim and the Society of Jesus," *Medieval and Renaissance Studies* 5(1961), pp. 163-181.
— "Joachimist Expectations in the Order of Augustinian Hermits," *RThAM* 25(1958), pp. 111-141.
Renaudet, Augustin, ed., *Le concile gallican de Pise-Milan*, Paris 1922.
— *Préréforme et Humanisme à Paris pendant les premières guerres d'Italie (1494-1517)*, Paris 1916.
Reuchlin, Johannes, *De arte cabalistica*, Hagenau 1517.
— *Reuchlins Briefwechsel*, ed. Ludwig Geiger, Tübingen 1875.
Rice, Eugene F., Jr., "The Humanist Idea of Christian Antiquity: Lefèvre d'Étaples and his Circle," *Studies in the Renaissance* 9(1962), pp. 126-160.
Ridolfi, Roberto, "*La biblioteca del Cardinale Niccolò Ridolfi (1501-1550)*," *La Bibliofilia* 31(1929), pp. 173-193.
Roth, Cecil, *The Jews in the Renaissance*, New York 1965.
Russell, Jeffrey Burton, *Dissent and Reform in the Early Middle Ages*, Los Angeles 1965.
Sackur, Ernst, *Sibyllinische Texte und Forschungen*, Halle 1898.
Sadoleto, Jacopo, *Opera quae exstant omnia*, 4 vols., Verona 1737-1738.
Sägmüller, J. B., "Die Idee von der Kirche als Imperium Romanum im kanonischen Recht," *ThQ* 80(1898), pp. 50-80.
Sanuto, Marino, *I diarii*, vol. XXIII, Venice 1888.
Savonarola, Girolamo, *Triumphus crucis*, ed. Mario Ferrara, Rome 1961.
Schmidt, Roderich, "Aetates mundi: Die Weltalter als Gliederungsprinzip der Geschichte," *ZKG* 67(1955-1956), pp. 288-317.
Scholem, Gershom G., *Major Trends in Jewish Mysticism*, 3rd ed., New York 1961.
— *On the Kabbalah and Its Symbolism*, trans. Ralph Manheim, London 1965.
— "La signification de la Loi dans la mystique juive," *Diogène* no. 14(1956), pp. 45-60; no. 15(1956), pp. 76-114.
— *Ursprung und Anfänge der Kabbala*, Berlin 1962.
— "Zur Entwicklungsgeschichte der kabbalistischen Konzeption der Schechinah," *Eranos Jahrbuch* 21(1952), pp. 45-107.
— "Zur Geschichte der Anfänge der christlichen Kabbala," *Essays Presented to Leo Baeck*, London 1954, pp. 158-193.
Schwoebel, Robert H., "Coexistence, Conversion, and the Crusade against the Turks," *Studies in the Renaissance* 12(1965), pp. 164-187.
Secret, François, "Aegidiana Hebraica," *REJ* 121(1962, 4 série, vol. I), pp. 409-416.
— "L'astrologie et les kabbalistes chrétiens à la Renaissance," *La Tour Saint-Jacques* no. 4(1956), pp. 45-56.
— "Les Dominicains et la Kabbale chrétienne à la Renaissance," *AFP* 27(1957), pp. 319-336.

— "Egidio da Viterbo et quelques-uns de ses contemporains," *Augustiniana* 16 (1966), pp. 371-385.
— "Un éloge oublié d'Egidio da Viterbo par Antonio Telesio," *Augustiniana* 13(1963), pp. 511-514.
— "Girolamo Seripando et la Kabbale," *Rinascimento*, seconda serie 3(1963), pp. 251-268.
— "L'interpretazione della Kabbala nel Rinascimento," *Convivium*, anno 24, nuova serie (1956), pp. 541-552.
— "Les Jésuites et le Kabbalisme chrétien à la Renaissance," *Bibliothèque d'Humanisme et Renaissance* 20(1958), pp. 542-555.
— *Les kabbalistes chrétiens de la Renaissance*, Paris 1964.
— "Notes sur Egidio da Viterbo," *Augustiniana* 15(1965), pp. 68-72.
— "Notes sur Egidio da Viterbo," *Augustiniana* 15(1965), pp. 414-418.
— "Notes sur les hébraïsants chrétiens de la Renaissance," *Sefarad* 22(1962), pp. 107-127.
— "Notes sur Paulus Ricius et la Kabbale chrétienne en Italie," *Rinascimento* 11 (1960), pp. 169-192.
— "Pico della Mirandola e gli inizi della Cabala cristiana," *Convivium*, anno 25, nuova serie (1957), pp. 31-47.
— "Le symbolisme de la Kabbale chrétienne dans la 'Scechina' de Egidio da Viterbo," *Umanesimo e Simbolismo: Archivio di Filosofia* (1958), pp. 131-154.
— *Le Zôhar chez les kabbalistes chrétiens de la Renaissance*, Paris 1958.
Seidlmayer, Michael, "'Una religio in rituum varietate': Zur Religionsauffassung des Nicolaus von Cues, *AKultG* 36(1954), pp. 145-207.
Seznec, Jean, *The Survival of the Pagan Gods*, trans. Barbara F. Sessions, New York 1953.
Signorelli, Giuseppe, *Il Cardinale Egidio da Viterbo: Agostiniano, umanista e riformatore (1469-1532)*, Florence 1929.
Silver, A. H., *A History of Messianic Speculation in Israel from the First through the Seventeenth Centuries*, New York 1927.
Stern-Taeubler, Selma, "Die Vorstellung vom Juden und vom Judentum in der Ideologie der Reformationszeit," *Essays Presented to Leo Baeck*, London 1954, pp. 194-211.
Tateo, Francesco, *Astrologia e moralità in Giovanni Pontano*, Bari 1960.
Thomas Aquinas, Saint, *Commentum in quatuor libros Sententiarum*, 2 vols. (3 parts), *Opera omnia*, vols. VI and VII, Parma 1856-1858.
— *De veritate*, ed. R. Spiazzi, O.P., Turin 1949.
— *Summa theologiae*, eds. Petrus Caramello, et al., 4 vols., Turin 1948.
Tigerstedt, E. N., "Ioannes Annius and *Graecia Mendax*," *Classical, Medieval and Renaissance Studies in Honor of Berthold Louis Ullman*, ed. Charles Henderson, Jr., vol. II, Rome 1964, pp. 293-310.
Tillich, Paul, *The Interpretation of History*, New York 1936.
Toffanin, Giuseppe, *Giovanni Pontano: Fra l'uomo e la natura*, 2nd ed., Bologna 1938.
— "La religione degli umanisti e l'idea di Roma," *La Rinascita* no. 1, 1(1938), pp. 20-39.
— "Umanesimo e teologia," *Bibliothèque d'Humanisme et Renaissance* 11(1949), pp. 205-214.
Torelli, Luigi, *Secoli Agostiniani*, vol. VII, Bologna 1682.
Trucchi, Francesco, *Poesie italiane inedite di dugento autori*, vol. III, Prato 1847.
Turner, Ralph V., "*Descendit ad inferos:* Medieval Views on Christ's Descent into Hell and the Salvation of the Ancient Just," *Journal of the History of Ideas* 27 (1966), pp. 173-194.

Ullman, B. L., "Renaissance—The Word and the Underlying Concept," *Studies in Philology* 49(1952), pp. 105-118.
Vajda, Georges, *Introduction à la pensée juive du moyen âge*, Paris 1947.
— *Recherches sur la philosophie et la Kabbale dans la pensée juive du moyen âge*, Paris 1962.
Valla, Lorenzo, "Laurentii Vallae opuscula tria," ed. M. J. Vahlen, *SAW* phil-hist. Cl. 61(1869), pp. 7-66, 357-444; 62(1869), pp. 93-149.
Vasoli, Cesare, "La profezia di Francesco da Meleto," *Umanesimo e Ermeneutica: Archivio di Filosofia* (1963), pp. 27-80.
— "Temi e fonti della tradizione ermetica in uno scritto di Symphorien Champier," *Umanesimo e Esoterismo: Archivio di Filosofia* (1960), pp. 235-289.
Vignaux, Paul, *Philosophy in the Middle Ages*, trans. E. C. Hall, New York 1959.
Vogelstein, Max, *Kaiseridee-Romidee, und das Verhältnis von Staat und Kirche seit Constantin*, Breslau 1930.
Walker, D. P., "Origène en France au début du XVI siècle," *Courants religieux et Humanisme à la fin du XV et au début du XVI siècle: Colloque de Strasbourg, 1957*, Paris 1959, pp. 101-120.
— "Orpheus the Theologian and Renaissance Platonists," *Journal of the Warburg and Courtauld Institutes* 16(1953), pp. 100-120.
— "The *Prisca Theologia* in France," *Journal of the Warburg and Courtauld Institutes* 17(1954), pp. 204-259.
Weil, Gérard E., "Le Codex Neophiti I: A propos de l'article de M. FitzMaurice Martin," *Textus* 4(1964), pp. 225-229.
— *Élie Lévita: Humaniste et Massorète (1469-1549)*, Leiden 1963.
Weijenborg, Reinhold, O.F.M., "Neuentdeckte Dokumente im Zusammenhang mit Luthers Romreise," *Antonianum* 32(1957), pp. 147-202.
Weinstein, Donald, "Savonarola, Florence, and the Millenarian Tradition," *ChH* 27(1958), pp. 291-305.
Weisinger, H., "Renaissance Accounts of the Revival of Learning," *Studies in Philology* 45(1948), pp. 105-118.
Weiss, R., "Traccia per una biografia di Annio da Viterbo," *Italia medioevale e umanistica* 5(1962), pp. 425-441.
— "An Unknown Epigraphic Tract by Annius of Viterbo," *Italian Studies Presented to E. R. Vincent*, Cambridge 1962, pp. 101-120.
Widmanstetter, J. A., ed., *Liber sacrosancti evangelii de Jesu Christo*, Vienna 1562.
Williams, George H., *The Radical Reformation*, Philadelphia 1962.
Wilks, Michael, *The Problem of Sovereignty in the Later Middle Ages: The Papal Monarchy with Augustinus Triumphus and the Publicists*, Cambridge 1964.
Wind, Edgar, *Pagan Mysteries in the Renaissance*, New Haven 1958.
— "The Revival of Origen," *Studies in Art and Literature for Belle da Costa Greene*, ed. D. Miner, Princeton 1954, pp. 412-424.
— "Typology in the Sistine Ceiling: A Critical Statement," *ArtB* 33(1951), pp. 41-47.
Yates, Frances A., *Giordano Bruno and the Hermetic Tradition*, London 1964.
Zumkeller, Adolar, O.S.A., "Joachim von Fiore und sein angeblicher Einfluss auf den Augustiner-Eremitenorden," *Augustinianum* 3(1963), pp. 382-388.
— "Manuskripte von Werken der Autoren des Augustiner-Eremitenordens in mittel-europäischen Bibliotheken," *Augustiniana* 11(1961), pp. 27-86, 261-319, 478-532.
— "Martin Luther und sein Orden," *Analecta Augustiniana* 25(1962), pp. 254-290.
The Zohar, trans. Harry Sperling and Maurice Simon, 5 vols., New York 1933-1934.

INDEX OF PERSONS

INDEX OF SUBJECTS